TAMING THE
INFORMATION
TSUNAMI

D1807278

BILL BRUCK

PUBLISHED BY
Microsoft Press
A Division of Microsoft Corporation
One Microsoft Way
Redmond, Washington 98052-6399

Copyright © 2002 by Bill Bruck

Library of Congress Cataloging-in-Publication Data pending.

Printed and bound in the United States of America.

1 2 3 4 5 6 7 8 9   QWT   7 6 5 4 3 2

Distributed in Canada by Penguin Books Canada Limited.

A CIP catalogue record for this book is available from the British Library.

Microsoft Press books are available through booksellers and distributors worldwide. For further information about international editions, contact your local Microsoft Corporation office or contact Microsoft Press International directly at fax (425) 936-7329. Visit our Web site at www.microsoft.com/mspress. Send comments to *mspinput@microsoft.com*.

Acquisitions Editor: Alex Blanton
Project Editor: Kristen Weatherby

Body Part No. X08-24248

To Abby

Contents at a Glance

Table of Contents

Acknowledgments

I would like to extend my gratitude to the Microsoft Press staff, especially Kristen Weatherby and Alex Blanton. I'd also like to thank my agent at Waterside Productions, Margo Maley, for her continued support over the years.

I would especially like to thank my wife, Anita Bruck, and my mother, Lucy Bruck, for their support, encouragement, and patience during the course of this project.

Introduction

For years, I've felt that there was something missing in books about using technology effectively—both those I read and those I've written. From books and workshops on management and personal development, I learned a great deal about principles and practices, but not *how* to implement them using the technology tools that I love. From computer books and classes, I learned how to use a host of different applications, but not *what* to do or *why*. It always seemed to me that the effective knowledge worker needed to start with basic principles and practices and then use technology to systematize and automate them.

In this book, I've made an attempt to integrate these two pieces of the jigsaw puzzle that together allow us to accomplish work productively and efficiently. For instance, in the section on organizing your day, you'll find a discussion of the "big rocks" principle, practical suggestions for how to do a weekly prioritization, and specific techniques for how to put this into practice using Microsoft Outlook.

Who This Book Is For

This book is written for knowledge workers who use computers in their daily work, and who want to become more effective at using technology to increase their efficiency and productivity.

Knowledge workers, for our purposes, are broadly defined as people who spend a significant part of their daily routine working with data and information. Many of them add value to their organizations by creating new knowledge or intellectual capital; others are consumers of knowledge products and use that knowledge to increase sales or create client deliverables. If this sounds pretty universal, it is, and that's a reflection of how today, we are in an information economy, and our workforce is increasingly technology enabled.

This book is for average folks who use their computers for a number of varied tasks. In my experience, most people use their computers habitually: They find one way to do a task that works, and then they repeat it until it's a habit. It may not have been the most efficient way when they came upon it, and new techniques may be incorporated in new software versions, but they "sing loudest the words they know." As a result, you'll find a range of techniques in this book—from some that are new to you to others that seem extremely simple. They are all chosen because, in my experience as a trainer and consultant, they represent techniques that many people could benefit by starting to use.

In addition, this book is not for specialists. If you spend your days doing financial forecasts and industry trend analyses using complex Microsoft Excel workbooks with formulas that take five minutes to calculate, the chapter on forecasting trends isn't for you! However, this book does provide the basic information that non-specialists need to get their work done, as well as pointers to resources you can use for further information.

This book was written using Microsoft Windows 2000, Microsoft Office XP, and Microsoft Internet Explorer 6.0. Users of other versions of the software may find differences in the details of the procedures, but the central concepts will prove valuable nonetheless. In addition, other applications, Web sites, Web services, and companies referred to in this book will change over time, so I ask your indulgence in advance if a listed resource is no longer available. To partially account for this, you will find search terms that you can use to find the latest resources in particular areas throughout the book.

About This Book

This book is divided into four sections. Each one addresses one of the main activities of knowledge workers:

- Finding Information

- Organizing Information

- Creating Knowledge

- Sharing Knowledge

Within each section, you'll find chapters organized by the types of tasks people need to do. So, for example, in the section on organizing information, you'll find chapters on organizing your day, your files, your e-mail, and your mobile tools. Each chapter may concentrate on one application or may have information on many, as knowledge workers are increasingly task- rather than tool-centric.

As today's workers are increasingly connected to the Internet with persistent, broadband connections, and because they often must be able to work from anywhere, at any time, an emphasis has been placed on Web-based tools. While there is certainly a Microsoft focus to the book (check out the publisher!), I have had the liberty of discussing best-of-class tools and Web services in my writing, and I have taken advantage of it throughout the book.

Conventions Used in This Book

The formatting of this book is designed to help you identify practices and learn techniques quickly and easily.

Procedures are specified using the simplest or easiest-to-understand command sequences, and are not meant to cover all the alternative ways to invoke commands. The names of dialog boxes and commands are in initial caps (whether or not they appear this way on the screen), and text you type is in **bold**.

Screen shots are provided throughout the book to give you a sense of what you will see when you use various features of the software and Web sites discussed. However, you should realize that in this digital world, nothing (including screens) stays the same! The ability to update your software with a few mouse clicks, the changing nature of Web sites, and the ability to configure the appearance of applications on your desktop virtually guarantees that sometimes the screen you see will differ from the screens in the book.

Several elements are used in this book to help you quickly scan through its pages and get the content you need.

- Tips provide shortcuts or recommendations for how best to use an application.
- Cautions provide warnings about common mistakes to avoid, or limitations in the application you should be aware of.
- Notes provide short additional items of information that amplify material presented in the text.
- Sidebars provide more in-depth information that may be of interest to particular readers.
- Each chapter ends with a practical checklist of skills that will help you assess where you might want to go for further information.

Each time you pick up this book, I hope you'll take note of one or two techniques you can try today. I believe that you'll soon find that your investment of time is well repaid by your improvement in productivity, efficiency, and the quality of work you do.

Gathering Information

To add value to your organization by producing and disseminating knowledge, it's important that you start with the basics—by gathering the information that serves as your basic building blocks. Today, the source that people go to most frequently is the Web. Knowledge workers in the twenty-first century need to be as facile with searching for information on the Web as their twentieth-century counterparts were with library card catalogs and journal indexes. To gain that facility, three things are required.

- **Infrastructure.** Master carpenters always have their toolboxes right next to them. They don't have to go back constantly to the look for the right drill bit or chisel; they know what's needed for each job and have it ready at hand. So, too, efficient researchers have spent the front-end time to customize the right toolkits for finding information on the Web.

- **Wired thinking.** To gather information efficiently and effectively, you have to create new habits of thinking and working. You need to not only have the right infrastructure, but also instinctively turn to it whenever you have a question, until using it is as instinctive as a farsighted person picking up reading glasses to see the newspaper.

- **Latest tools.** The tools that are available to gather information change daily, and not only are new tools often available, but also new classes of tools are created with astonishing rapidity. Having created the right infrastructure, and having the right habits, master information gatherers always have their "radar" on, scanning the environment for tools that can make them more effective.

The first three chapters of this book show you exactly how to achieve each of these competencies. In Chapter 1, "Creating Your Infrastructure," you find out how to optimize Microsoft Internet Explorer by modifying toolbars, maximizing your screen "real estate," and personalizing Internet Explorer for your use. You're guided through the process of selecting your default search tool, and learn how to save search results where they'll be available for your use. You even learn how to perform periodic maintenance to keep your tools in top shape.

Chapter 2, "Making People Your Best Resource," shows you how to find the people on the Web who can provide the expertise to make published data come alive. You learn all about e-mail lists—what they are, how to find them, and how to use them. You also find out about newsgroups, how to use Microsoft Outlook Express to participate in them, and how to search Web-based sites that contain newsgroup archives. You even learn about newer Web-based forums and ask-the-expert systems, as well as the online etiquette involved in soliciting information from others.

Chapter 3, "Making the Most of Your Web Searches," adds to your skills by teaching you about advanced techniques and tools. You learn how to use the advanced search functions of different search engines and construct Boolean searches. You find out about advanced tools that can help you with your searches, like search bots and tools that find associated sites for you. You see how to work where and when you want by synchronizing Web sites for offline viewing, and you find out how to use the Invisible Web—the part of the Web that isn't found by the search engines.

Creating Your Infrastructure

Elizabeth is a fact checker for a leading magazine about the digital economy. Her job is to check the facts that are presented in stories to ensure their accuracy, and often to perform original research for stories ranging from the new trends in e-commerce to what effect the new third-generation, high-speed wireless protocols might have on the world economy.

Elizabeth spends her time at her computer—and the application she has open every second is Microsoft Internet Explorer. She can't waste time, so it's vital that she is able to have her tools ready to go and optimized for her use.

Over time, Elizabeth has built a solid infrastructure that has dramatically improved her productivity at doing research on the Web. By ensuring that the tools and sites she uses frequently are easily accessible through toolbars and by personalizing her Internet Explorer options, she has created a system that is extremely efficient. By linking her favorite search tool—in her case, a metasearch engine—to the Search button, she can quickly find the sites she needs. And by using a sophisticated system of saving and organizing the links and files she finds, she has all the information she needs at her fingertips.

For you to be productive as a knowledge worker, you have to create as solid an infrastructure as Elizabeth has done. You need to select your tools and modify them until they fit your requirements and working style. It might seem natural to jump in and get started on the task at hand. However, you'll waste time if you skip this first step. The Pareto time principle (otherwise known as the 80/20 rule) applies here: By investing a little time at the beginning of a project, you can get benefits throughout the time you spend working on the project—and in every succeeding project as well.

There are three things that contribute to creating a solid infrastructure for gathering information.

- Optimizing your search tool (Internet Explorer)
- Finding the right search engine
- Creating methods to efficiently save your search results

This chapter shows you exactly how you can do each one.

Optimizing Internet Explorer

As time goes on and more services are available over the Web, the browser is increasingly becoming a central tool—sometimes *the* central tool—for knowledge workers. And there are a number of things you can do to customize that tool for your use. Take a few minutes to look over these ways to optimize Internet Explorer, and the next time you're at your computer, take 15 minutes to change your Internet Explorer settings. You'll be amazed at how much time you will save.

Modifying Your Toolbars

Many people never think to modify their Internet Explorer toolbars. That's sort of like buying a new car and never programming the radio buttons. You can drive just fine, but you haven't optimized the vehicle for your particular preferences.

There are two ways to modify your Internet Explorer toolbars—by customizing your Standard Buttons toolbar and your Links bar. After you read this section, Internet Explorer should feel like a well-adjusted car seat—the tools and links that you use most often should be on the toolbars—within easy reach.

Customize Your Standard Buttons Toolbar

Your Standard Buttons toolbar is the main toolbar in Internet Explorer—the one with the Back and Forward buttons on it. Customizing this toolbar not only has a functional advantage—it makes the tools you use most more available—but it also has a psychological benefit—it allows you to take control of your tools as you personalize and optimize them for your use. Ideally, your Standard Buttons toolbar should contain only the tools you use most often.

Note   Customizing your Standard Buttons toolbar is especially important if you're using a laptop or have a low-er resolution (800x600) monitor. If your toolbar contains too many buttons, you may have to click the >> to see any hidden buttons.

To customize your toolbar, you'll want to add tools that aren't currently there, remove tools you don't need, and move tools to convenient places. Fortunately, all these operations are very simple. To do so, follow these steps.

1. Right-click anywhere in the Standard Buttons toolbar, and choose Customize.

2. In the Customize Toolbar dialog box, do any of the following.

   - To add a new button, select an available button in the Available Toolbar Buttons list and click the Add button.

   - To remove a button, select a button in the Current Toolbar Buttons list and click the Remove button.

   - To move a button, select it in the Current Toolbar Buttons list and click the Move Up or Move Down button (for example, if you want to change the order of the Print and Home buttons as discussed earlier).

3. Click the Close button in the Customize Toolbar dialog box when you are done.

As you customize your Internet Explorer Standard Buttons toolbar, you will begin to create new work habits. You'll start to have thoughts like, "What changes could I make in my other Microsoft Office toolbars?" When you're doing a task repetitively in an Office application, you'll wonder, "Can I work smarter by adding a button to my toolbar?" This is the true benefit of customizing your tools—creating new thought patterns that help you work smarter every day.

Tip   Consider removing the Edit and Discuss buttons from the Standard Buttons toolbar if you don't use them. Also, you may want to swap the location of the Print and Home buttons on the toolbar so that if you can't see all the tools, the Print button will still be visible (depending on whether you use the Print or Home button more).

Leverage the Links Bar

Just as the Standard Buttons toolbar should hold the tools you use every day, the Links bar should contain the sites you visit every day. This is especially true if you have sites you use to collaborate with others, such as online communities or virtual team environments, such as Microsoft SharePoint sites.

See Also   For more information about SharePoint and other virtual team tools, see Chapter 16, "Sharing Knowledge with Remote Workers."

To quickly add a site to your Links bar, follow these steps.

1. Browse to the Web page.

2. Choose Add To Favorites from the Favorites menu.

3. In the Add Favorite dialog box, edit the default title for the site, if needed. It's often a good practice to use a very short abbreviation or acronym for often-visited sites, so that you can fit more of them on your Links bar.

4. Select the Links folder in the Create In list, and click OK.

You can also remove items and reorder them on the Links bar just as you can with the Standard Buttons toolbar, although the procedures for doing so are slightly different from the procedures for modifying the Standard Buttons toolbar. For more information about modifying the Links bar, see "Saving Results in Your Favorites Folder" on page 14.

Maximizing Screen Real Estate

When searching for information on the Web, you want to be able to see as as many as of your results as you can without scrolling back and forth. If you're working on a laptop or on a screen smaller than 800x600, you may find it helpful to change your Internet Explorer settings to maximize your screen's real estate, as shown in Figure 1-1. The following sections discuss three things you can do to maximize your screen space.

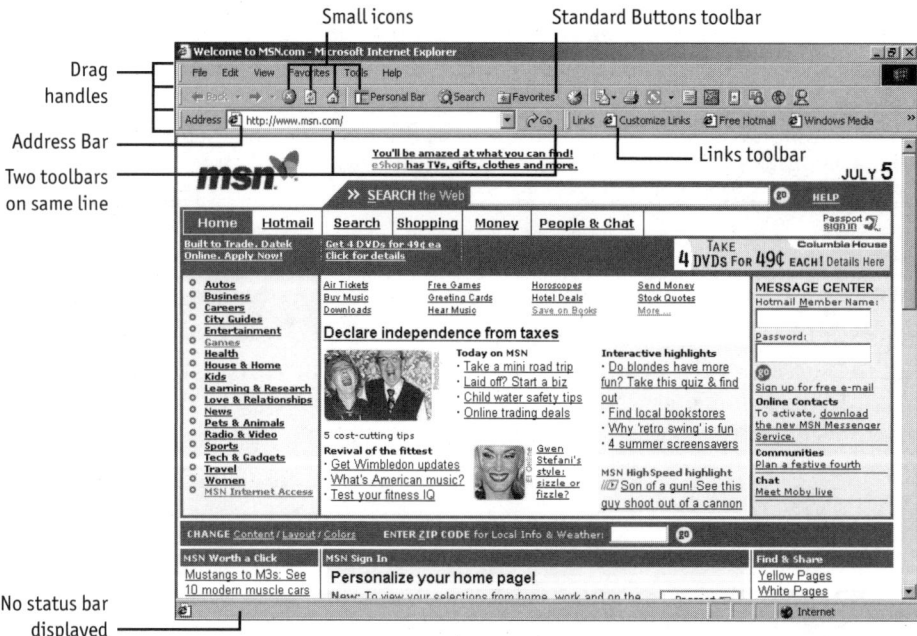

Figure 1-1   *The Internet Explorer screen can be optimized for notebook computers by using smaller toolbar icons, hiding the status bar, and putting toolbars on the same line.*

Use Small Icons on Your Toolbar

By changing the icons on your toolbars to a smaller size, you save wasted screen space. To change the icon size, do the following.

1. Right-click any visible toolbar, and choose Customize from the shortcut menu.

2. In the Customize Toolbar dialog box, choose Small Icons from the Icon Options drop-down list, then click Close to return to Internet Explorer.

Toggle the Status Bar Display

The status bar provides valuable information, such as the address of links you are hovering over, so you need to weigh the information it provides versus the additional screen real estate you gain by turning it off. Fortunately, you can toggle the display easily by choosing Status Bar from the View menu—so you can turn it on and off whenever you like.

Combine Your Toolbars

There are four standard toolbars that ship with Internet Explorer. Usually, you will want to display at least the Standard Buttons toolbar, the Address Bar, and the Links bar. You can save space by putting the Address Bar on the same row with the Standard Buttons or the Links toolbar, if one of these has buttons that you don't use very often. Put them on the same row by dragging the drag handle of the Address bar until it is on the right side of the same row as the Standard Buttons or Links toolbar. (The drag handle is the vertical line on the left of the toolbar, as shown earlier in Figure 1-1.)

Tip   If your screen isn't maximized, a way to increase your screen real estate after you browse to a site is to press the Maximize key—F11.

Personalizing Internet Explorer

You can finish optimizing Internet Explorer by making a few adjustments to personalize it further. These include the following.

- Setting your home page
- Turning on AutoComplete
- Updating your Personal Profile
- Checking your security settings

Set Your Home Page

When you open Internet Explorer, you're connecting from your desktop to the rest of the world. It's a great opportunity for you to get an initial scan on what's happening in your areas of interest. For that reason, it can be very useful to set your home page to a portal site that provides news and information that keeps you informed and up-to-date.

A number of portals are designed for this exact purpose—to provide updates, news, and information for workers in specific industries. For instance, people interested in knowledge management might want to set their home page to brint.com (*http://www.@brint.com*—a site devoted to research and communities focused on knowledge management) while those interested in e-business might use *The Industry Standard* (*http://www.thestandard.com*—the Web version of the business magazine that covers the information economy), and CEOs of start-ups can gravitate to CEOExpress (*http://www.ceoexpress.com*—providing a host of news sources geared toward chief executives). Alternatively, you may want to create your own home page and put all the links that are important for you to see each day on it.

See Also   For more information about creating and saving Web pages, see Chapter 15, "Sharing Knowledge Using the Web."

After you find a site that gives you a bird's eye view of your industry each day, you can set your home page by navigating to that site and following these steps.

1. Choose Internet Options from the Tools menu.

2. On the General tab, find the Home page section at the top of the tab, and then click the Use Current button to set the currently displayed page as your Home page.

Turn On AutoComplete

For those of you who do a lot of research on the Web, any time you can save a few keystrokes, it's wonderful. It's especially great when you don't have to type the same information over and over again. Internet Explorer provides an easy way to do just that—the AutoComplete feature. With AutoComplete, after you type the first few characters of a URL, Internet Explorer attempts to finish the URL based on sites you have visited recently. To turn on AutoComplete, do the following.

1. Choose Internet Options from the Tools menu.

2. Click the Content tab and then click the AutoComplete button.

3. In the AutoComplete dialog box, shown in Figure 1-2, select the check boxes you want to use. Select all options to maximize your benefits from this feature.

Figure 1-2   *AutoComplete makes typing Web addresses quicker, stores information you reuse like your address for forms, and remembers your passwords for you.*

4. Click OK. If you are finished adjusting your Internet Options, click OK again to close the dialog box.

Tip   Another time saver is to enter just the name of the Web site without *http://www.* in front of it. For example, you can enter *msn.com* to get to MSN without entering all of the preliminary information. While this works in most sites, it may not work in the specific site you're looking for. But if it works 90 percent of the time, it's worth it!

Caution   If you share a machine with others or if your machine is in an open space such as a cubicle, you may want to leave User Names And Passwords unchecked for security purposes.

Update Your Personal Profile

While you are changing your preferences, it's a great time to update your profile with the Microsoft Profile Assistant. Your profile securely stores personal information such as your name, address, phone, e-mail address, and the like. Whenever you are at a new Web site that requests this information, you can share it without having to type it again. To change your profile information, follow these steps.

1. Choose Internet Options from the Tools menu.

2. In the Internet Options dialog box, click the Content tab, and click the My Profile button in the Personal Information section. If you already have a profile, the properties dialog box for your profile appears. If no profile has been created, The Address Book – Choose Profile dialog box appears.

3. If your profile exists in the address book already, select an existing entry from your address book to represent your profile and then locate the profile in the address list and click it to select it; otherwise, choose Create A New Entry In The Address Book To Represent Your Profile and click OK.

4. In the Main Identity Properties dialog box shown in Figure 1-3, add the information you want to share in the various tabs, leaving ones you do not want to share blank.

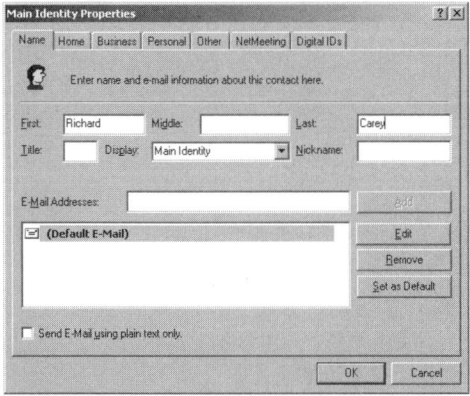

Figure 1-3   *When you set your personal profile, information that you specify can automatically be shared with Web sites that support profiles, so that you don't need to type personal information in Web site after Web site.*

Setting Security

The more often you are gathering information on the Internet, the more often others will want to gather information about you. The reason so much information is freely available on the Web is that the information owners want to form a relationship with you—and often part of that relationship is finding out more about you. Unfortunately, the more open your system is, the more vulnerable it is to malicious intrusion. So it's important that knowledge workers who are active on the Internet, be careful about setting their Internet Explorer security levels.

You set security levels from the Security tab in the Internet Options dialog box, shown next. As you see, there are four content zones that are provided by default.

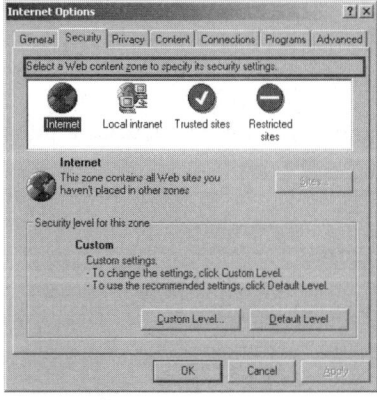

(continued)

(continued)

- Internet is for general Web sites you might visit.

- Local Intranet is for your local Web pages that (hopefully) require little or no security.

- Trusted Sites include major vendors or others with whom you do business or believe to have systems in place that prevent them from infecting your system with harmful viruses, Active X controls, or other mini-programs that can control your machine or gather personal information about you.

- Restricted Sites are ones that, for whatever reason, you want to be especially careful of.

You can leave default settings for each zone, or you can set the options yourself by selecting a zone and clicking the Custom Level button at the bottom of the tab. You see a Security Settings dialog box from which you can choose to enable or disable individual options.

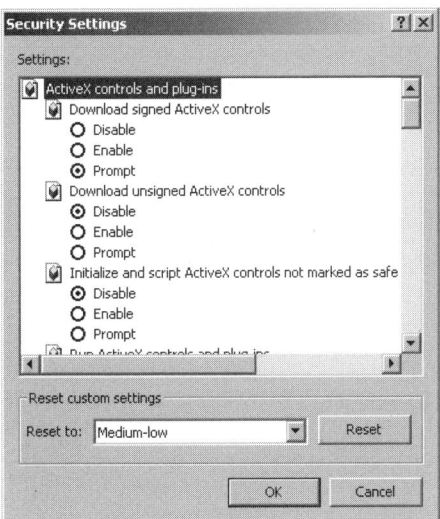

You can add a Web site to any zone except for the Internet zone by highlighting the zone and clicking the Sites button. The Trusted Sites dialog box opens where you can add sites you wish to include in the given security zone. (The Internet zone is the default zone for all sites not listed elsewhere, so you cannot manually add sites to this zone.)

Understanding Search Tools

The Web contains hundreds of millions of pages. The information you need is out there—the question is how to find it. Fortunately there are a myriad of search tools to help you. Although Chapter 3 discusses specialty search tools in detail, part of building your infrastructure is understanding search basics. What are the available tools, and how do they differ? What should your default search tool be?

There are two types of search tools that Internet Explorer provides for you to select as your default search tool.

- **Search engines.** These tools search through the Web using automated programs called *spiders*, and categorize the pages they find. The Internet is so huge that none of them find all the Web pages, and each of them uses a different, proprietary system for classifying the relevance of pages they find. As a result, you have the familiar phenomenon that identical searches on different search engines produce somewhat different results. Two examples are Google (*http://www.google.com*) and All the Web (*http://www.alltheweb.com*)

- **Subject (or Web) directories.** These tools are created by humans, rather than by automated spiders. Web sites are examined and classified for relevance by editors. In addition, a taxonomy is provided so you can start at the top and navigate through a tree-like structure to the sites of interest to you. Two of the most popular are Yahoo (*http://www.yahoo.com*) and Looksmart (*http://www.looksmart.com*).

Many engines today are a combination of the two. They often spider the Web automatically, and then have real people go through and look at the results, weigh them, and create directories from the spidered information.

Tip   Some search engines, such as GoTo.com (*http://www.goto.com*) , allow people to buy top listings rather than have listings reflect popularity or relevance. These ratings-for-hire results are showing up in more and more search engines as time goes on.

Customizing Your Search Settings

After you determine the search tools you prefer, you can set Internet Explorer to use them by default for your searches. You can specify that one search engine be used, or use the Search Assistant that allows you to set different combinations of search tools for finding a Web page, a person's address, or his or her e-mail address. Set your search options by following these steps.

1. In Internet Explorer, click the Search button on the Standard Buttons toolbar.

2. In the Search pane on the left, click the Customize button.

3. In the Customize Search Settings dialog box, choose Use One Search Service For All Searches if you want to use just one service for all of your searches, or choose Use The Search Assistant For Smart Searching if you want to use multiple tools.

4. If you choose one search service, select the desired one from the list box.

5. If you choose the Search Assistant, select the search tools you want to include for each of the three categories. Set the priority for the chosen tools with the up and down arrows at the bottom of each list box.

6. From now on, whenever you click the Search button, you will see your selected search tool by default.

Supercharging Your Searches Using Metasearch Engines

A useful tool for power users is the right metasearch engine. A metasearch engine takes the search text, searches on several search engines, and then displays a list of top ranking results from each of the search engines it covers.

As of this writing, one of the best such metasearch engines is Copernic (*http://www.copernic.com*). Unlike some simpler metasearch engines, Copernic is an application you download onto your computer. You can run it independently, or it will put a button your Internet Explorer toolbar, and set itself as your default search engine so it's invoked whenever you click the Search button in Internet Explorer.

As you can see in Figure 1-4, Copernic displays the search results from a selected list of search engines in one list, ranked by relevance. It also allows you to choose from many pre-configured combinations of search engines and other Web resources that are customized for the type of information you're looking for, and it saves your previous searches so you can easily go back to them. But this is merely the beginning. Copernic allows you to refine your search by adding additional criteria and searching through only the previously found Web pages, validate your search by removing nonexistent Web pages, and set up tracking schedules so you can easily find new references to a search term of interest (for example, your company or you yourself). You can even tag documents of interest and download them for offline browsing—and strip them of associated images for quicker downloading.

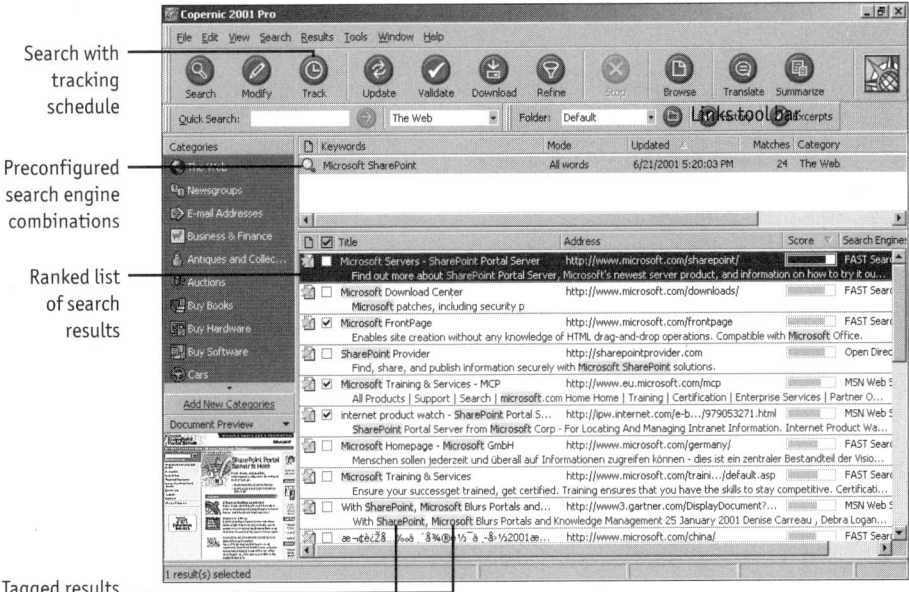

Figure 1-4 *Metasearch engines such as Copernic provide advanced features such as combining the results of all search engines, saving your searches, and scheduling periodic searches.*

Another option is to use a metasearch engine with fewer features, but which doesn't require downloading an application to your computer. Dogpile (*http://www.dogpile.com*) is one such engine. It does not group results, but rather displays them by search engine. It doesn't allow you to save, refine, or schedule your searches. But for a one-time search through several of the most popular search engines, it can be very valuable.

Other Metasearch Engines

Other metasearch engines you might want to investigate include

- *http://www.ixquick.com*
- *http://www.metacrawler.com*
- *http://www.webferret.com*

Saving Search Results

After you find the information you want, you'll often need to save the results for future retreival. One way of saving your results is by saving (and organizing) your links; another way is by saving the Web pages themselves. Saving the links is usually easier and quicker, and ensures that you have the freshest data available. On the other hand, sometimes content is removed from Web sites (such as magazine articles) and you are left with a broken link. This section discusses three ways you can save your results.

- As links in your favorites folder
- As links on Web sites devoted to this purpose
- As files on your computer

Saving Results in Your Favorites Folder

Saving results as links is easy in Internet Explorer. To do so, follow these steps.

1. Browse to the Web page.
2. Choose Add To Favorites from the Favorites menu.
3. In the Add Favorite dialog box, click OK.

Note   You can also check Make Available Offline in the Add Favorite dialog box. This saves a copy of the Web page, as well as linked pages if you so specify, on your computer. You can also synchronize your computer's version with the online version of the Web pages at intervals you specify to update the information on the saved Web page automatically.

However, saving links or offline files in your Favorites folder isn't a terribly effective way to save your search results. All of them are in one folder (the Favorites folder), they all appear whenever you click the Favorites button in the My Places bar of Office applications, and they have the default title of the Web page, which might not be helpful when you want to find that page again. A better strategy is to organize your Favorites folder just as you do your other filing systems, and to rename the Web pages when you save them if the default name is not descriptive of the page's content.

Look at the system shown in Figure 1-5 as an example. There are three major categories —clients, professional development, and tools—in addition to the default menu entries added by Internet Explorer: Links, Media, MSN.com, and Radio Station Guide. Under clients, there's a folder for research on each client. Under professional development, there's a folder for each area of interest, and under tools, there are folders for writing tools and Web development tools.

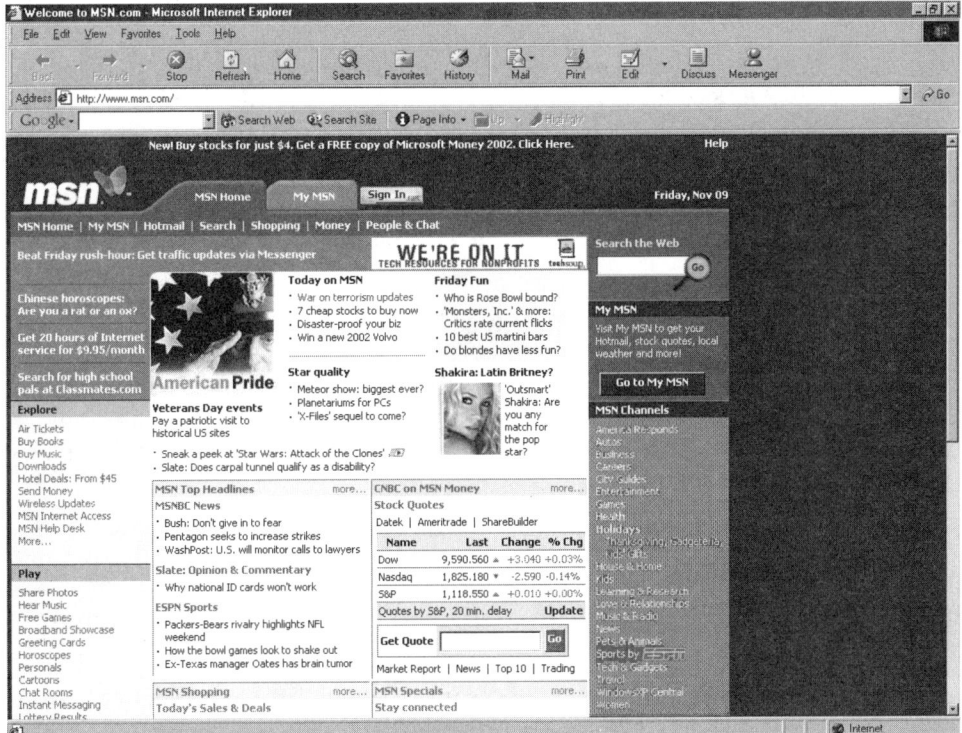

Figure 1-5 *Organize your Favorites with a similar system that you use for your electronic or paper-based filing systems.*

When you decide on your filing structure, you can quickly create the appropriate folder as follows:

1. Choose Organize Favorites from the Favorites menu.

2. In the Organize Favorites dialog box shown in Figure 1-6, you can create new folders, create subfolders, move links into different folders, rename folders and links, and delete folders and links.

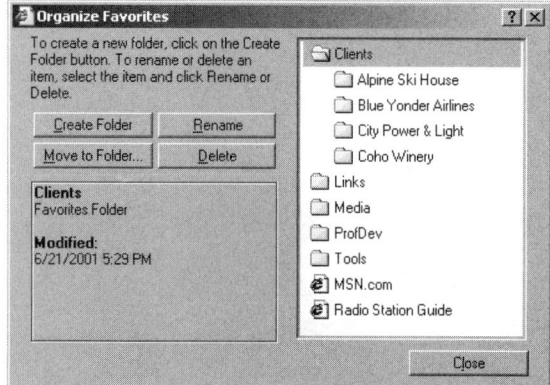

Figure 1-6   *Your Organize Favorites dialog box allows you to create a favorites file structure that organizes all the links you create to information resources.*

Saving Links in Web-Based Bookmark Sites

If you do a lot of research on the Web, you might want to investigate a Web-based bookmark system. These systems offer the following benefits.

- You can write a sentence or two about why you're saving this particular link in a description field.

- You are able to easily read categories in drop-down lists.

- You can quickly create a new category.

- You can access your "bookmarks" (that is, favorites) from any browser and from any computer—at home, work, or on the road.

- You can share selected categories of bookmarks with specific other people, or make them public for anyone to see (a real tool for knowledge workers).

- Some systems such as BLINK (*http://www.blink.com*) also allow you to access your bookmarks from wireless devices, and will analyze sites on your bookmark list for wireless compatibility.

Other Web-Based Bookmark Sites

Web-based bookmark services you might want to check out include

- Clickmarks (*http://www.clickmarks.com*)
- BestBookMarks (*http://www.bestbookmarks.com*)
- TrailMarks (*http://www.trailmarks.com*)
- itList (*http://www.itlist.com*)
- iKeepBookmarks (*http://www.ikeepbookmarks.com*)

Saving Web Pages on Your Computer

If you're concerned that the information might not be on the Web forever, or want to have access to it even when you're not online, you can save the Web page on your computer. One great way to do this is by creating a folder—perhaps called Knowledge Base—and saving all your Web pages in it. You can then use the Fast Searching feature of Microsoft Office XP to do full text searches in this folder to quickly access information you saved.

See Also   For more information about the Fast Searching feature of Office XP, see Chapter 5, "Organizing Your Files."

Caution   Material on the Web might be easy to access and save, but that doesn't mean it's legal to do so. Be sure you understand the copyright restrictions and fair use exemptions before saving copyrighted material on your computer. To find out more about this issue, search for Copyright Web Content.

To save a Web page on your computer, follow these steps.

1. Browse to the page you want to save and then choose File, Save As.
2. Navigate to the folder you want to save the file in.
3. Change the folder name to a more descriptive one if needed, and then click Save.

Note   Saving a file in the default Hypertext Markup Language (HTML) format creates a subdirectory containing all the graphics linked to the file. Instead, you can also choose Web Archive, Single File from the Save as Type drop-down box. The advantage is that you have a single file with all graphics contained in it. The disadvantages is that some browsers such as certain versions of Netscape cannot read these files.

Maintaining Your Infrastructure

There's one last thing you need to do to maintain your solid infrastructure: It's important to perform periodic maintenance, just as all artisans do with their tools. One maintenance item you should consider doing is periodically updating Internet Explorer.

When you update Windows you automatically update Internet Explorer, so this is a great way to get two maintenance items done at once! You can update Windows from the Start menu or from Internet Explorer, whichever is more convenient.

- To update Windows from the Start menu, click Start, Windows Update.
- To update Windows from Internet Explorer, choose Tools, Windows Update.

In either case, you're taken to the Windows Update site. When you choose Product Updates, your software configuration is automatically checked and you see a list of updates you can choose to install. Critical updates are always noted, so you can be sure you install them. (Critical updates sometimes fix security problems that might allow malicious hackers entry into your computer, so it's especially important to install them.)

Summary

It all comes down to your philosophy of work and being productive. In more than 20 years of training and consulting with thousands of folks on how to be more efficient and productive with their computers, I've realized that it really boils down to attitudes. And there are two winning attitudes that can catapult your effectiveness as a knowledge worker: You'll see both of them over and over throughout this book.

The first is the "front-end" attitude. You must be willing to spend a little front-end time to build a solid infrastructure.

The second is the "curiousity" attitude. You must be curious to find out how you can do things faster and better. You have to notice when you're doing a task repetitively, be aware when a routine task is taking many keystrokes, and be willing to spend a few minutes building a tool (or putting it on your toolbar) to allow you to do it more efficiently.

Checklist for Creating Your Infrastructure

Check off the following points as you build your infrastructure to effectively find the information you need to do your job.

[ ]   Modify Internet Explorer toolbars by customizing the Standard Buttons toolbar and putting frequently visited sites on the Links bar.

[ ]   Maximize screen real estate by using small icons on the toolbar, hiding the status bar, and combining toolbars on the same row (if necessary).

[ ]   Personalize Internet Explorer by setting a home page, turning on AutoComplete, and updating My Personal Profile.

[ ]   Set appropriate security levels for the sites you visit.

[ ]   Customize search settings to use the search tools you find most useful.

[ ]   Identify metasearch engines that can provide additional search functionality.

[ ]   Save search results to a Favorites folder or to your computer.

[ ]   Regularly install updates to Internet Explorer.

Making People Your Best Resource

Kendall Keil is an analyst for a nonprofit institute that provides educational services to third-world countries. His manager recently asked him to research Lyme disease treatments used in the United States, to support a presentation he was giving to a professional conference on the treatment of mosquito-borne illnesses. Kendall went to the Web to read as much as he could about the disease, but he found his real information by talking with people.

By searching Lyme-related sites, he found out about two e-mail lists that were used by researchers who shared information with one another about possible treatments. Although he didn't understand much of it initially, by doing a search on unfamiliar terms he quickly developed an understanding. As he became a lay expert, he began to see repeatedly the names of several National Institutes of Health (NIH) scientists whose research he respected. When he sent e-mails to some of them, he was surprised to find that they were more than willing to talk to him about promising new treatment protocols. By creating a free account at WebMD (*http://www.webmd.com*), he found an online community of people who had been undergoing the various treatments, and was able to discuss firsthand how they affected the quality of life of actual afflicted people. This added a personal dimension to the information that his manager used in her presentation.

In short, Kendall built a *social network* of experts and of ordinary people afflicted with Lyme disease. In doing so, he was able to build on information he found on the Web and gain a much richer understanding of the disease.

Kendall's story illustrates the way knowledge workers are increasingly using their computers—not only as tools to connect them to data, but also as gateways that connect them to people-with expertise or personal experience in virtually any subject matter.

In this chapter, you learn about four ways people share knowledge with each other on the Web: e-mail lists, newsgroups, discussion forums, and knowledge-sharing systems.

Joining E-mail Lists

An electronic mailing list is a server-based application that automates e-mail distribution to participants who subscribe to the list. In its simplest terms, when an authorized person sends an e-mail to that list, everyone on the list gets the e-mail. From a user's perspective, you see periodic e-mails in your Inbox that are addressed to the mailing list.

Note   E-mail lists go by many names. Mailing Lists, Lists, Internet Mailing Lists, and Mailing List Servers are some of the names for e-mail lists, while MajorDomo and LISTSERV are the trade names of two of the more popular e-mail list applications. For purposes of consistency in this book, I'll refer to them as simple e-mail lists.

E-mail lists were one of the earliest group discussion tools to be widely adopted on the Internet. They are still preferred by many people because mail comes to your Inbox and you don't need to use any special application or to visit a Web site. The downside of simple e-mail lists is that, unless they are integrated with a Web interface, you have to be careful to address your postings correctly, and it's hard to keep track of multiple threads of discussion. In addition, you might be overwhelmed by the number of e-mails you get in your Inbox daily, unless you learn the special commands to manage it.

See Also   For more information about managing your Inbox, see Chapter 7, "Organizing Your E-mail."

There are many professional groups—especially in academia—that exchange information through e-mail lists. Depending on the content area you are interested in, you might find that you can get a lot of information by reading these exchanges or, if you're sufficiently knowledgeable, by participating more actively in them. Subscribing to the right set of e-mail lists can be one of the best ways to stay abreast of what's happening in your field, because they often contain the most current information on a particular subject (rather than articles or books, whose content was created months or even years ago).

Note   Just being published doesn't make something true. It's wise to adopt the policy used by newspaper reporters and check all your facts with two trusted sources.

E-mail lists are also used for publishing periodic newsletters. In your search to keep on top of the latest information in your field, you may find it valuable to subscribe to e-mail newsletters such as the Microsoft Office News Service, an insider's guide to the Microsoft Office family of products. Subscribe or unsubscribe at *http://www.microsoft.com/info/ unsubscribe.htm*. Subscribing to the right newsletters can be a great way to stay abreast of information in your field, though they are not interactive.

Note Today, many e-mail lists are integrated with Web interfaces that allow you to see the discussion threads on a Web site or receive them through e-mail. An example of this is YahooGroups (*http://www.yahoogroups.com*). YahooGroups even provides a calendar so that you can see the messages that were posted on any given day. These sites make using e-mail lists extremely easy. However, many of the professional mailing lists that contain the latest information that knowledge workers need do not use these Web interfaces, so it's important to understand how the simple mailing list programs work as well.

Understanding E-mail Lists

As you start to use e-mail lists, there are a few distinctions that it will help you to know.

- **Public vs. private lists.** A *public* list is one that anyone can join by sending the proper command to the list server (the program that operates the list). A *private* list forwards a subscription request to the list owner, who decides whether you can join the list.

- **Moderated vs. unmoderated lists.** In a *moderated* list, any request to send information to the list is forwarded to the list owner, who may then filter, format, or abridge the e-mail before sending it to the list members. In an *unmoderated* list, whatever you send to the list is automatically distributed to all subscribers.

- **Opt-in vs. opt-out lists.** An *opt-in* list is one you must send a request to the mail server to join. An *opt-out* list is one to which you can be subscribed by someone else, and you receive until you opt out of it by unsubscribing from the list. Because e-mail lists are an easy way to send an e-mail to thousands of people, they are often used by Web marketers to send spam to people who don't want to receive it. It's considered good form these days to run an opt-in list, where list owners do not subscribe people without their knowledge. Double opt-in lists offer even more privacy. When a subscription request is received by the server, it sends a confirmation e-mail to the subscriber. Unless the confirmation e-mail is returned, the subscription is not completed. That way one person can't subscribe other people to the list without their knowing about it.

Finding E-mail Lists

There are three ways to find mailing lists that are pertinent to your interest: asking some-one, searching on relevant Web sites for lists, or looking at directories of e-mail lists.

Ask Someone

The best way is also the simplest—ask knowledgeable people. It sounds silly, but when you ask someone, you're getting a personal recommendation from a trusted source. Often the person will forward you one of the e-mails he or she got from the list, so it will be easy to subscribe. At the bottom of many of these e-mails is information on how to join the group.

Search the Web

You can frequently find e-mail lists on Web sites that are focused on your topic of interest, Electronic newsletters are usually identified as such, and links to them are often promi-nently displayed on the Web site's home page. E-mail discussions are often found on a "links" page that contains hyperlinks to related resources. Alternatively, there might be a button or link to "discussions" or "communities." There, you'll often find a link to a mail-ing list, newsgroup, or Web forum (discussed in the next sections).

See Also   For more information about the basics of searching for Web sites focused on a particular area, see Chapter 1, "Creating Your Infrastructure." For more information about advanced searching techniques, see Chapter 3, "Making the Most of Your Web Searches."

Use Directories

You can also go to Web sites that contain catalogs of mailing lists. These are often catego-rized, and offer a search feature that looks through the list description for your keywords. Some sites that contain such catalogs include the following.

- **Liszt** (*http://www.liszt.com*).   This is one of the better known catalogs, and is main-tained by topica.com, which offers many associated commercial services. The topica site offers categories and a search command.

- **Tile.net** (*http://www.tile.net*).   This is another long-standing catalog. It does not offer categories, but does provide a search command.

- **List Tool** (*http://www.listtool.com*).   This site offers both a catalog and a search function. It also automates the process of subscribing to the chosen list, by asking you to type relevant information in a simple form.

- **CataList** (*http://www.lsoft.com/lists/LIST_Q.html*).   This is a catalog maintained by L-Soft, the owners of LISTSERV. Naturally, it catalogs only LISTSERV lists.

You can find other sites that list catalogs of search engines by searching for "e-mail lists" in your favorite search or metasearch engine.

Participating in an E-mail List

To reiterate, a simple e-mail list is a server application that allows authorized people to send an e-mail to an address that distributes it to others on the list. To participate in an e-mail list, there are three things you must be able to do.

- You must know how to subscribe to the list (unless someone else subscribed you to an opt-out list).

- If the list is a discussion list, rather than a newsletter, you want to know how to reply to others and start your own topics.

- To control the flow of e-mails to your Inbox, you'll want to know how to manage list options.

Managing Your Subscriptions

Subscribing is the process of putting your name on the e-mail list, after which you will receive all e-mail sent to that list, and (if the list is two-way) you'll be able to send mail to the list as well. Many electronic newsletters provide a simple form on a Web page that enables you to subscribe to the list by just typing your e-mail address. However, if you're using e-mail lists for research purposes, you might want to join a two-way list, and there's often no Web form to do this easily. Instead, you'll need to subscribe to a list by sending a special e-mail.

The subscription e-mail is special in two respects: It must go to a particular address, and it must contain a specific command. You send commands to a different e-mail address from the one you use to send e-mail to everyone on the list. This can get confusing, and many of us have had the experience of receiving "unsubscribe" commands that inadvertently were sent to all list members by mistake. One way to help remember the address is the following rule: Send commands to the server; send responses to the list. Figure 2-1 on the next page illustrates this.

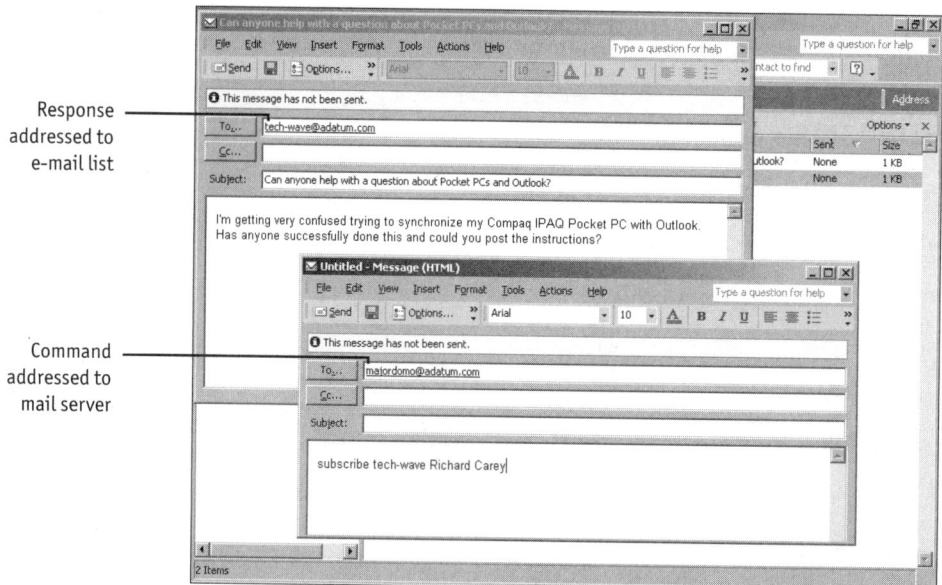

Response
addressed to
e-mail list

Command
addressed to
mail server

Figure 2-1   *You address e-mail differently to send mail to the list rather than to send commands to the mail server.*

Note   The commands used to manage your e-mail list subscription are different depending on the software that is used on the mail server. Two of the most common e-mail list server applications are Majordomo and LISTSERV. Instructions for both appear next.

The address you will use for commands has the format *[list_program]@[domain]*. So, if A. Datum Corporation has a mailing list running on the Majordomo program, commands might be sent to *majordomo@adatum.com*. If you located the mailing list from a Web site, you may find subscription instructions there. Otherwise, to subscribe to a mailing list, do the following.

- **LISTSERV lists.**   Put the following in the body of the e-mail: subscribe *[listname] [firstname lastname]*. You can leave the subject line blank.

- **Majordomo lists.**   Put the following in the text of the e-mail: subscribe *[listname] [e-mail-address]*. You can leave the subject line blank.

Unsubscribing works the same way, except that you use the "unsubscribe" command rather than the "subscribe" command.

When you first subscribe to a newsgroup, you usually get an informational e-mail with instructions on how to send commands to the list, and how to unsubscribe. As you start using lists more, it is worthwhile to save these e-mails—possibly in a special Microsoft Outlook folder in which you save all e-mails with user names, passwords, and e-mail list subscription information—so you can find the unsubscribe command when you need it.

See Also   For more information about creating Outlook folders, see Chapter 8, "Organizing Your Mobile Tools."

Taking Part in Discussions

After you get your first informational e-mail from the list, you will soon start to see e-mail appearing in your Inbox. When you get an e-mail from the list, responding is as simple as clicking the Reply button and writing your response. Here are a few tips for participating.

- It's often valuable to lurk for a while (read without responding) until you get a sense of the social norms that operate in the list. Are long responses tolerated? Do they use quote-backs? Are requests for personal assistance (e-mails directed back to the person individually versus the list as a whole) common?

Note   A *quote-back* is the technique of copying the original person's posting and then putting your reply under it, rather than just replying and assuming that people know who and what you're replying to.

- Be careful not to change the address in the To: box. By default it may go to the list as a whole.
- Understand the group norms and consider whether your information would be valuable to everyone before replying back to one specific person.
- Put the address of the list in your Outlook contacts so you can initiate a message to the group more easily.
- Be sure not to send a command (like unsubscribe) to the members of the list—they should go to the server instead.

Managing Your E-mail List Options

Each e-mail list program has different options, and many of these options may be turned on or off by individual list owners. E-mail list options are invoked by sending commands to the list server. Some of the more common commands that work in both Majordomo or LISTSERV are listed in Table 2-1.

Table 2-1   Common E-mail List Commands

Function	Instructions
Help	Type **Help** in the body of the message. The list server sends back a message containing information about the commands you can use with the mailing list.
List Information	Type **Info [Listname]** (where [Listname] is the name of your mailing list) in the body of the message. This list server sends back a message with introductory information about the list, provided by the list owner (such as where to send list commands, the purpose of the list, and other valuable information).
Archives	Type **Index [Listname]** in the body of the message. The list server sends back a list of files associated with the list. These might include archives of the postings to the list, or other files that have been associated with the list. These files might not have descriptive names, so although they can be a rich source of information, they might not be easy to use. You can then use the Get [Listname] [Filename] command to have a copy of that file sent to you through e-mail.
Digest	Type **Digest [Listname]** in the body of the message (addressed to the list server). You receive one e-mail per day with all the list postings, rather than a separate e-mail each time someone posts to the list. (This command is supported by all versions of LISTSERV, but only in later versions of Majordomo, so don't be surprised if it does not work for a specific list you're subscribing to.)

In active lists, you might receive 30 or more e-mails a day. In this case, you might want to use the Digest command, or consider creating an Outlook folder for e-mails from the list, and using a Rule to automatically move e-mails into this folder as they arrive. This way, you separate them from your other Inbox messages.

See Also   For more information about creating Outlook folders and rules, see Chapter 8, "Organizing Your Mobile Tools."

Reading Newsgroups

A newsgroup is a hierarchically ordered collection of messages that are posted on a computer called a news server. News servers can host thousands of public newsgroups or a selection of private ones. You can use a news reader such as Microsoft Outlook Express to subscribe to newsgroups of interest to you.

Note   Newsgroup messages are carried over Usenet—a network of news servers that predated the World Wide Web. Now, all public news servers are connected to the Internet, but you'll still hear people talk about Usenet Newsgroups, because originally newsgroups were on a different network!

Newsgroups have several more features than e-mail lists. First and foremost, newsgroups present messages in *threads*, ordering messages so related messages follow each other. Second, you can see a certain number of past messages that have been posted prior to your subscribing to a newsgroup. Third, you can create rules for managing your newsgroups.

The downside of newsgroups is that the messages do not come to you in your Inbox; rather, you need to use a second application (Outlook Express—your news reader) to look at them. This makes reading newsgroups somewhat less convenient than reading e-mail lists, because you must take an additional action each day by opening your news reader.

Newsgroups can be used in ways similar to e-mail lists—to share knowledge with online groups that are discussing topics of interest. E-mail lists used by professionals to discuss leading-edge information are often favored by academic groups, while certain types of corporations, such as software manufacturers, as well as unaffiliated interest groups, often host newsgroups to discuss topics of interest.

Understanding Newsgroups

As with e-mail lists, there are a few basic facts that will help you start using newsgroups effectively.

- **Public vs. private newsgroups.** A *public* newsgroup is one that anyone can subscribe to. Usually it is hosted with tens of thousands of other newsgroups on the news server provided by your Internet service provider (ISP). (Each ISP may have a slightly different set of public newsgroups, and might not support all newsgroups—especially adult-oriented ones.) On occasion, there are public newsgroups that are hosted on a corporate news server, but usually you'll find the ones you want on the list of newsgroups provided by your ISP's news server. *Private* newsgroups are used for such purposes as communicating with beta test groups or invitation-only groups for people in a certain industry or thought leaders in a specific subject. While they are not available to the average researcher, it can be very valuable to know people in them and be invited to join one.

- **Moderated vs. unmoderated lists.** Most newsgroups are *unmoderated*—anyone can post to the group. A few groups are *moderated*, meaning a group moderator reviews posts before they are publically seen, and can remove or edit inappropriate posts (like advertisements, personal attacks, or adult-oriented posts).

- **Expired messages.** The newsgroup server stores only a limited number of messages for each newsgroup. In addition, the news reader downloads only approximately 300 of the messages stored on the news server, unless you give it a specific command to download more.

Note The public nature of newsgroups also makes them a favorite target of spammers who can send a posting to thousands of newsgroups at once. Some newsgroups contain more spam than content, so if you're lucky, you might find a moderated newsgroup in your area of interest.

You subscribe to and participate in newsgroups through a news reader such as Outlook Express. When you're using Outlook Express as a news reader, you see three panes, as shown in Figure 2-2. The left pane shows newsgroups you have subscribed to, the top pane shows summary information about messages in the selected newsgroup, and the bottom pane shows the text of the selected message.

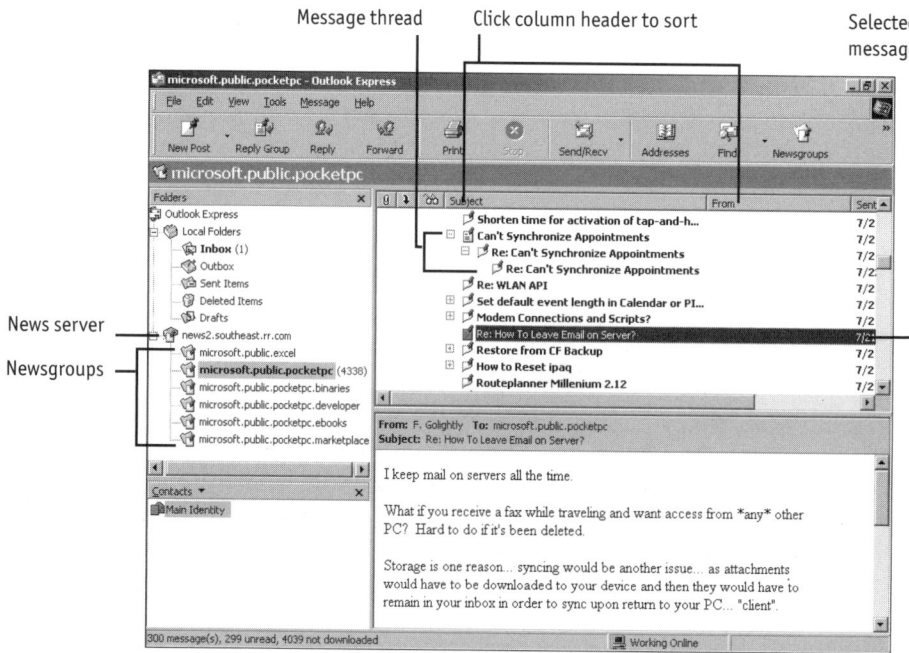

Figure 2-2   *Your news reader organizes newsgroups in folders and puts related messages together in threads, making it easier to organize and follow discussions of interest.*

Finding Newsgroups

There are several ways to find a newsgroup that might provide information you seek. As with e-mail lists, you can asking colleagues for recommendations, or use catalogs like *http://www.tile.net* (which allows you to search for both newsgroups and e-mail lists using keywords). You can also search through Web sites containing archives of newsgroups. For more information about newsgroup archives, see "Finding Archived Information" on page 32. The easiest way, however, is often to search for a keyword that might appear in the title of a newsgroup. You can do so quickly by following these steps.

1. Open Outlook Express and click the desired news server in the left pane.

2. Click the Newsgroups button in the right pane.

3. In the Newsgroup Subscriptions dialog box, type the keyword you want to search for in the Display Newsgroups Which Contain text box.

4. Select newsgroups that might be of interest to you, and click the Subscribe button.

5. When you are finished, click OK. The selected newsgroups appear in the newsgroup folders in the left pane of Outlook Express.

Participating in Newsgroups

After you find a newsgroup that might contain information of interest to you, you'll want to be able to download new messages, find ones of interest, and read and respond to them.

To download and read messages, do the following.

1. In Outlook Express, select the newsgroup in the left frame that you want to participate in.

2. Wait while headers are retrieved from the server and when you see them in the top right pane, click the word Subject in the header row to sort the messages by subject, or click From or Sent to sort them by the author or the date.

Tip   You can click a second time in a column heading to reverse the sort order. This can be helpful if you want to see larger or later messages first.

---

3. Scroll through the message headers until you find a message pertinent to your interests, and then

   - Click it to open it in the the lower pane.
   - Double-click it to open it in its own window.
   - Click a plus sign to the left of the message header to see all the related message headers.

4. To see more messages, choose Get Next 300 Headers from the tools menu. (By default, the news reader retrieves only the latest messages from the newsgroup.)

When you want to post a message to the newsgroup, click the Reply Group button. You see a familiar send e-mail window that is preaddressed to the newsgroup, and has copied the message you are replying to. You can retain or delete the copied message, and type your response. Clicking Send posts the reply to the newsgroup, although you might not see your posting in the message header list immediately.

You can also reply to an individual—perhaps to ask for clarification or more information—by clicking the Reply button rather than the Reply Group button. Similarly, you can start a new thread—perhaps to ask a question about a subject of interest—by clicking the New Post button. In general, however, it is considered good etiquette to look for any Frequently Asked Questions (FAQ) file that is posted in the newsgroup and to read current postings before asking questions that might already have been answered (sometimes many times).

Finding Archived Information

Although news servers do not generally keep all newsgroup messages indefinitely, there are sites that do keep this information and which can be a rich source of material for "information hunters."

The easiest sites to search are Web-based sites, often provided by major portals. One such site is Google (*http://groups.google.com*), which acquired the dejanews archives that provide access to more than a year's postings and to more than 25,000 newsgroups.

In addition, some newsgroups maintain their own archives of postings at sites from which the archive files can be downloaded. You can find a list of public newsgroup archives at *http://www.pbs.org/uti/guide/usenet.html*, or by performing a search in your favorite search or metasearch engine for "newsgroup archives."

As you can see in Figure 2-3, the Google Advanced Groups Search permits you to search by newsgroup, author, subject, date, specific text, and a number of other features. Because of its power and the number of postings it contains, it is the most frequently used newsgroup search tool.

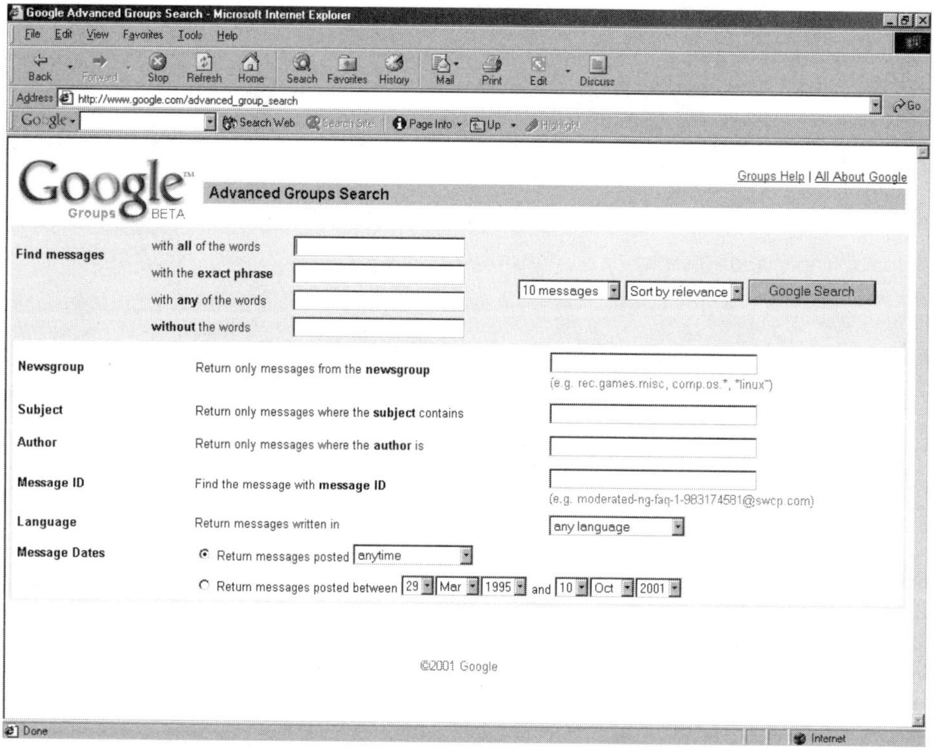

Figure 2-3   *Google allows you to search through the full text of more than 35,000 newsgroups using a number of search variables.*

Using Web-Based Resources

Both e-mail lists and newsgroups predated the Web. As a result, you often participate in them with Outlook and Outlook Express rather than your browser. Since the advent of the Web, however, other types of Web-based applications have evolved that allow people to come together to collaborate, share knowledge, and form communities. Two such applications are discussion boards and knowledge-sharing systems. Being Web-based, these systems are accessed through your browser, and require virtually no instructions to use.

Asking Questions in Forums

In the pre-Internet era, people formed interest groups and talked back and forth using bulletin board systems (BBSs), forums on private, for-fee networks like CompuServ, and through computer conferencing systems that created communities like The Well and The Meta Network. With the advent of the Web, some of these services basically disappeared (like the community bulletin boards), and others evolved through tools such as Web-based discussion forums (also called *discussion boards*) that still allow people to post comments to a structured discussion at any time, but that build in many more community features.

Today, these discussion boards (and their more sophisticated cousins—Web conferencing applications) are starting to replace mailing lists and newsgroups as places where online discussions occur over time and professional communities evolve. Their popularity stems from the fact that they are directly accessible in one's browser (unlike newsgroups), and do not require learning unique commands (unlike mailing lists).

Note   Web conferencing applications are designed to support virtual communities on the Web. They provide additional functionality to Web forum software, such as the ability to see who has read which item; commands that allow you to read only the postings that are new to you since you last logged in; and the ability for administrators to move and copy discussions into different "forums" or areas. While discussion boards are optimized for high volume and short exchanges, Web conferencing applications typically support hundreds rather than thousands of users who hold extended discussions about specific topics.

You typically will find three types of Web forums on the Internet.

- **Support forums.**   These are open discussion forums that are run by companies who want their customers to be able to ask public questions about using their products and services. Questions may be answered by peers or by corporate support staff. Some support forums such as the Microsoft one at *http://communities.microsoft.com/ newsgroups* combine Web forums with newsgroups, allowing you to access the same forums from your browser or newsreader.

- **Public forums.**   These forums are often sponsored by portals and other public Web sites that want to increase "stickiness" (the amount of time users spend on-site) by adding an interactive component to their site. For instance, Yahoo!

(*http://clubs.yahoo.com*) offers a range of "clubs" to the public on areas from business and finance to science. @Brint.com (*http://forums.brint.com*), an e-business and technology portal, provides forums on knowledge management, e-business and electronic commerce, and new economy issues.

- **Virtual communities.**   These provide a space where people can have extended conversations over weeks or months about topics of interest, and in so doing, form communities of practice. Examples of virtual communities include the Well (*http://www.well.com*), Smith Weaver Smith (*http://www.smithweaversmith.com*, shown in Figure 2-4) and the Meta Network (*http://www.tmn.com*).

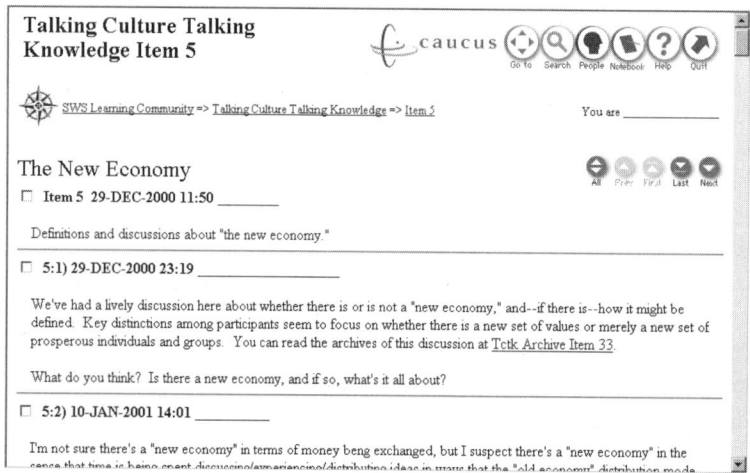

Figure 2-4   *Virtual communities provide the opportunity for more extended discussions with a community of practice.*

There are no specific catalogs of Web-based online communities like there are for mailing lists and newsgroups. That's not bad news, however. Because Web-based discussions are more easily found by the spiders that are used by the popular search engines, there is less of a need for specific tools and catalogs for Web-based discussions. When you do a keyword search in your search engine, you are searching through many of the Web-based discussions as well as other types of Web pages.

The right forum for you depends on the topic you're seeking information on. If it's a technical question about software, you'll probably find what you're looking for in a support forum; if it's general, you'll most likely find your answer in a discussion board attached to a portal; and if you want to have an extended conversation about a topic, you might want to join a virtual community. The best way to locate the right support forums and virtual communities is by looking for links on Web sites that contain the most content on your subject matter.

Because Web-based discussion software is Web-based, it is extremely easy to use. Although software applications have somewhat different features, they do not require any special commands. You generally just read the discussion and either click a respond button or type text in a response box that is at the bottom of the discussion thread. Some Web-based discussion applications even allow you to include Hypertext Markup Language (HTML) commands or upload files right into your message, where they appear as links.

Asking Questions of Experts

A new class of applications has emerged that allows you to ask questions in natural language, and then connects you to common answers or people who can respond in more detail. These products allow you to ask natural language questions, and then they provide links to experts who you can e-mail for further information, as well as for answers to similar previous questions, as you can see in Figure 2-5. Some even allow you to connect to experts in real-time through chat or voice (through your computer). Products of this genre include askme (*http://www.askme.com*), Ask Jeeves (*http://www.ask.com*), abuzz (*http://www.abuzz.com*), expert central (*http://www.expertcentral.com*), and ragingknowledge (*http://www.ragingknowledge.com*).

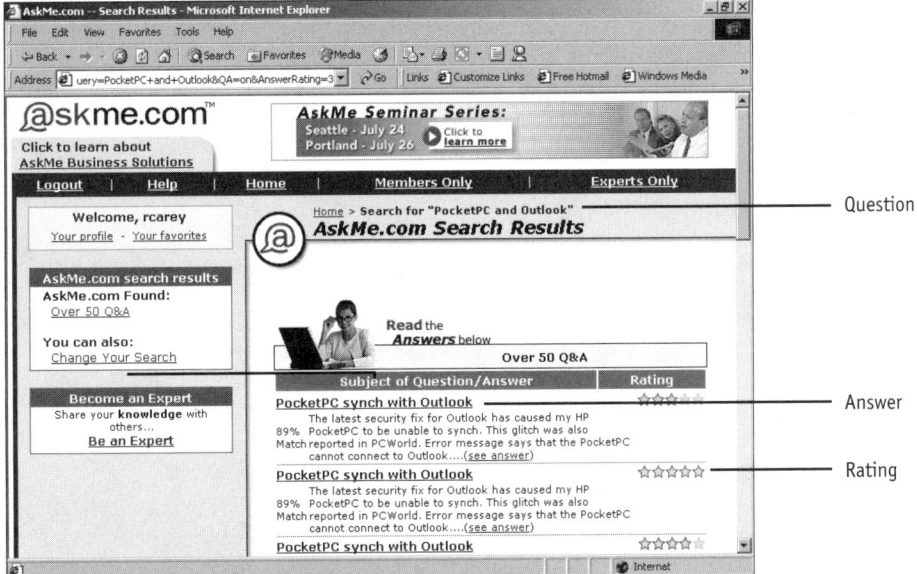

Figure 2-5   *Knowledge-sharing services connect you to experts and allow you to rate how helpful their responses are.*

These knowledge-sharing systems have several components (not all of which are contained in each application), including

- **Taxonomies.**   Many of these systems allow the designers to create categories and subcategories that constitute the domain of information people will ask questions about. For computer support, the categories might start with hardware/software, and then subcategories might include the type of hardware or the specific applications that are being supported. A human resources department might have categories for recruitment, compensation and benefits, and career development, with subcategories of such things as health insurance, retirement, and the like. If taxonomies are implemented, people can choose to use the system by clicking the headings and subheadings until they find the information they want—typically either stored documents or e-mail links to experts in that category.

- **Profiles.**   Some of these systems maintain structured profiles on all the people who will serve as experts. Information might include which categories they are knowledgeable about, as well as when they are available and the maximum number of queries they want to handle per week. Depending on the system, experts might also be asked to upload files that are relevant to particular categories of knowledge.

- **Queries.**   All of these systems provide the ability for users to ask their questions in natural language inquiries; for example, "What's the chief export from the United States?" They use proprietary algorithms to match the inquiry with the available resources.

- **Resources.**   In response to inquiries, the systems might display FAQ files or uploaded data files that are pertinent to the question asked. They might also display relevant questions and answers from a discussion board, or permit you to upload your question into a discussion board. In addition, they might provide you with the e-mail addresses of experts who you can contact privately to answer your question. Some systems allow these experts to upload their private responses into the system so the answer can be accessed by others. Others allow you to start a chat or voice session with the expert—although you might need to pay for this functionality.

- **Ratings.**   Certain services ask users to rate the responses they received or the experts they contacted. These ratings are then factored into the priority given that response or expert when others ask similar questions.

Increasingly, technical support Web sites use services such as this. For instance, Act! (*http://www.act.com*) uses Ask Jeeves for this purpose. You can ask questions in plain English, and Ask Jeeves presents a series of articles. If none of them answer your question, you can use the link to the Act! support forum to ask your question there.

You can also find a number of public Web sites that are staffed by volunteers and powered by a knowledge-sharing system such as these. Responses may include FAQ files and information on the Web site, or an e-mail link to experts who will respond personally. Some of these Web sites include

- **abuzz.**   *New York Times* readers respond to your question online and by e-mail.

- **All Experts** (*http://www.allexperts.com*).   Advertised as the oldest and largest free Q&A service on the Internet, volunteers respond to questions by e-mail.

- **Ask Jeeves.**   Responses to questions include relevant Web-based documents, and an invitation to post the question in a public forum.

In addition to being on public Web sites, these services can also be configured as enterprise knowledge-management applications, available only to those within a corporation.

Check with your Information Technology department to ascertain the availability of any such services within your organization.

To find public knowledge-sharing sites, navigate to one of the sites described earlier and choose Show Related Links from the Tools menu. Go to each site and use the Show Related Links feature of Microsoft Internet Explorer to find additional sites. (This can be easier than doing a direct search because there is no simple term that is used to describe this class of software yet.)

Being Nice on the Internet

As someone who is trying to obtain information, you need to attend to the social dynamics of the situation. You are asking other people to share their knowledge with you. There is often not a reciprocal relationship where you're giving as much as taking. In addition, many of the places you're going are comprised of people who have been interacting for a while, and have formed norms and expectations. They are a community into which you come as an outsider.

As a result, there are a few guidelines you must consider following when soliciting information from other people online.

- **Look for posted guidelines.**   Often e-mail lists post guidelines in their introductory message, newsgroups periodically post a FAQ file for new users, and Web-based communities have a link for new users. Read any information that's available for newcomers, and look for participation guidelines, in addition to technical instructions.

- **Be considerate.**   Look for answers first. It's easier for you to just pop in and ask your question, but that question might have been asked by 20 other people in the last month. If so, you're likely to get an irritated response. Look through old postings to see whether your question has been addressed before asking it.

- **Be focused.**   Be short and specific in your questions, and address them to the people and groups that are likely to be able and willing to help. If possible, try and provide reciprocal information or resources to the people you are requesting help from.

- **Follow general rules of netiquette.**   You can find a number of good ones by searching for netiquette in your search engine, or go to *http://www.albion.com/netiquette* for an excellent summary of netiquette rules.

Summary

People can be your greatest research resource, as long as you remember that they are people, and not "tools" for your use. In this chapter, you learned about four ways you can connect to other people on the Internet—from mailing lists, newsgroups, discussion forums, and knowledge-sharing services.

Your ability to effectively use these resources is partially a matter of knowledge, but mainly a matter of attitude. To truly leverage the power of the Web, you need to think of it as a giant network that connects people to people—not just computers to computers. When you remember this, you'll think about what people and resources are available the next time you need to research information using the Web.

Checklist for Using People-Related Web Resources

Check off the following points as you learn to use different people-related Web resources.

[ ]   Subscribe and unsubscribe to e-mail lists.

[ ]   Use directories to find appropriate e-mail lists.

[ ]   Understand the difference between messages sent to the list and commands sent to the list server.

[ ]   Manage the way information comes to you through e-mail lists.

[ ]   Subscribe to newsgroups using Outlook Express.

[ ]   Participate in newsgroups by sending public messages to the group.

[ ]   Find archived newsgroup information in Web-based sites.

[ ]   Find Web-based communities and discussion boards that pertain to your interests.

[ ]   Use knowledge-sharing systems to ask questions of experts and peers.

[ ]   Understand the basic social guidelines for asking people for information online.

Making the Most of Your Web Searches

Jeff Henshaw had a lot of work to do, and not much time to do it. His dot.com company was desperately looking for a way out of their financial difficulties, and was considering a new direction. A central element in the business plan to be presented to the Board was a competitive analysis of three similar companies. Jeff was assigned to work on one—Fabrikam, Inc.—and its universal Inbox tools. He needed to find out everything he could about such things as Fabrikam's current products, product development strategy, standards, messaging strategy, business model, financial solvency, industry position, management, partners, and distribution model. He had to have the completed report on Fabrikam by close of business.

Fortunately, Jeff had a strategy and a suite of tools that enabled him to get the work done quickly, and get it done right, by using a six-step process.

1. Jeff started by going to Fabrikam's Web site, and reading every word on every page. Where appropriate, he copied paragraphs into a competitive analysis he was building in Microsoft Word.

2. He then did a broad search for the company name, the product names, and the product type using his favorite metasearch engine—Copernic (*http://www.copernic.com*). The quantity of information he found showed him that his search terms were too broad, so he experimented with Boolean searches (ones that use *AND* and *OR*) until he was able to focus on the sites he needed. He went to each one, copying relevant information into his competitive analysis.

3. At each site that had solid information, he used the Show Related Links command to browse quickly to relevant sites, and was able to find a few that described the industry in general that the search engine had not originally found.

4. To get a more qualitative sense of how experts in the field regarded Fabrikam, he posted a message in an online community he was a member of. This community consisted of consultants worldwide who helped organizations with their communications strategies, and within two hours he had several substantive responses. He also did a search on newsgroups and mailing lists to see whether there were further discussions of Fabrikam, and found a few exchanges in one academic LISTSERV when he explored its archive.

5. Next, Jeff decided to further analyze the company's financial information, management team, and industry position. He had several sites bookmarked that provide financial information on corporations, and went to Hoover's and Dun & Bradstreet to get the basic financial figures. A special "people" search in Copernic on the names of the management team provided full biographies, and even two white papers that had been authored by their Chief Technology Officer (CTO). This gave Jeff some insight into the future vision of the company. Finally, Jeff used a catalog of specialty databases to look for articles that had been published in newspapers and trade magazines about Fabrikam, and found that although initially the company had gotten a lot of good press, its technology seemed to be somewhat out of synch with current trends. (This verified what he had heard from others in the online community.)

6. Finishing the report was a snap. With all the information pasted into his Word document, completing his assignment was merely a matter of reading the raw material, summarizing it, and spicing it with a few chosen quotes that were already in the text. Six hours later, he e-mailed it to his Chief Executive Officer (CEO).

Jeff's project contains many of the tasks that knowledge workers face when gathering information. A variety of facts are needed—from financial data to information about people, products, and trends. In addition, to give these facts meaning, a more qualitative approach is often important, where the opinions of experts can serve as the basis for your own conclusions—all supported with accurate and current information.

This chapter outlines the toolset you need to complete projects like the one Jeff was faced with. In this chapter, you learn about

- Advanced search techniques
- Search assistants
- Working offline
- Intelligent agents (bots)

Finally, you see how these tools can all be put together in a search strategy.

Conducting Advanced Searches

After you do an initial search using your favorite search or metasearch engine, you might find that you have too much information. You can then narrow your search using two techniques. Generally, in most search engines you can use operators like AND and OR to narrow your results (a *Boolean search*). Alternatively, you can use specific advanced search capabilities that the various major search engines support, which make it easier to conduct Boolean searches.

Creating a Boolean Search

A Boolean search is one that uses operators, such as AND, OR, and NOT, to create a query that is more exact than the general searches. Boolean searches can be extremely powerful when you understand the purpose of each operator and how to properly combine each one. Table 3-1 lists and describes these operators.

Caution   Although Boolean searches provide the most exact way of constructing a search statement, they are not supported by all search engines. See the next section for more information.

Table 3-1   Boolean Search Operators

Operator	Example
x AND y	Both terms must be present for condition to be true. For example, *candy AND apple* finds a page only if both the words "candy" and "apple" are present.
x OR y	Condition is true if either term is found. For instance, candy OR apple finds the page if either "candy" or "apple" is on the page.
x NOT y	Condition is true if the term is not found. For instance, apple *NOT candy* finds every page that contains the word "apple," but not if the word "candy" is present.
x NEAR y	Condition is true if term x is within a specified number of words of term y. The number of words varies by search engine—it is usually between 3 and 10. For example, *John NEAR Smith* finds every page where "John" is within the specified number of words "Smith." Finds pages containing "John Smith," "John S. Smith," "John Jacob Guggenheimer Smith."
"x y z"	Quotations denote a phrase—a set of words that must be found next to each other in the exact order specified. For example, *"John Smith"* finds pages containing "John Smith" but not ones containing "John A. Smith."
(term)	Parentheses are used to group search terms, and can be nested—one set of parentheses can be placed inside another. For instance, wine *AND (French OR Italian)* Finds pages containing both French wine or Italian wine.
*	An asterisk, in most search engines, serves as a wildcard. Depending on the search engine, it might be placed at the end, middle, or beginning of a word. For instance, *rec*ve* finds both receive and recieve; **cover* finds cover, uncover, and recover; and *man** finds man, manual, and manhole.

You start to experience the power of Boolean searches when you combine techniques. For instance, you might want to find information about a piece of software named Caucus that you believe was written by someone named either Chuck or Charles Roth or Rath. When you do a search on the word Caucus, you get a lot of hits on "congressional caucus" and "black caucus." By combining the search operators, you can refine the search like this:

Caucus AND NOT (black OR congressional) AND ((Chuck OR Charles) NEAR R*th)

Let's pick this apart to understand it. You have two major components here—the name of the software and its author. The name of the software is Caucus—that's simple, but you don't want results containing the black caucus or the congressional caucus, so you use the NOT operator, and because you don't want either term, you say NOT (black OR congressional).

The author's name is a little more complicated, because you have nested parentheses. The easiest way to understand it is from the inside out. Looking at the inner parentheses, you see that the first name is either Chuck or Charles. That's easy. Then you see that one of these two names has to be near R*th. The asterisk is there to catch both Roth and Rath. You use the NEAR operator in case the person has a middle initial or name.

Caution   Although in theory this complex search statement should give you exactly the results you want, in practice search engines interpret parentheses differently, and some don't support them at all. Worse, search engines change their rules periodically. If you want to use complex search statements, the best advice is to experiment.

Using Advanced Search Options

Each of the major search engines supports a different set of advanced search options. For instance, until October 2000, Google supported only the AND operator, not OR. The following is a summary of the options supported by some of the major search engines. It is current as of this writing, but you must regularly check the advanced search page of the engines you are considering using, as they often do change in functionality.

Advanced options are easy to use—they are all available from pull-down menus or text boxes. Look for links such as "Advanced Search" or "Advanced Options" on the main search engine page. Most sites also have some sort of Help on Advanced Search techniques. You may want to check this for each site to learn about the techniques specific to that site.

Google

Google (*http://www.google.com*) does not support Boolean operators, but its advanced search permits you to specify one AND condition, one OR condition, one exact phrase, or one NOT condition. You can also specify the language and include or exclude a specific domain name in your search, as well as where on the page (text, title, URL) the text must occur. You can do successive searches to further narrow your results, and you can search for pages similar to the one found, or sites that link to the page found.

Alta Vista

Alta Vista (*http://www.altavista.com*) supports advanced searching, including all the Boolean operators described in Table 3-1. In addition, you can specify where on a page to look for words by using a colon; for example, title:text looks for the word "text" in the title of the page. You can also specify the language, the page dates, and the sort order for results. It also provides a Search Assistant that helps you create complex searches.

Excite

Excite (*http://www.excite.com*) does not support Boolean operators but its Advanced Search feature at the bottom of the home page does allow you to input any number of search terms, and each one allows you to specify the importance of the term. You can also choose the language and domain type, for example, United States (.com) or a specific domain, and specify display options.

Northern Light

Northern Light (*http://www.northernlight.com*) searches the Web as other search engines do, but it also searches several thousand full-text journals and news resources. Its Power Search choice permits the full range of Boolean operators as well as the country, language, date, and category of the search. Results can be sorted by relevance or date. It even supports putting a plus sign (+) next to required terms.

Using Search Assistants

As the Web has matured, search tools have become more intelligent. Knowing how to conduct advanced searches is still a key skill, but there are a now wide range of "search assistants" that can help you in your hunt for the right information for your project. Search assistants automate the search process, either by conducting searches on your behalf at scheduled times, or by operating in the background while you do other things. There are two common types of search engines that can be particularly helpful for people who are gathering data from the Web, and which help you do the following.

- Find sites related to the one you're visiting
- Perform automated searches on a regular basis

Finding Associated Sites

When you finally find a site that provides information you want, using a search engine, for example, you often still need more information to finish your project. Internet Explorer contains a helpful tool that can quickly direct you to Web sites similar to the one you just found. This can be a great way to ensure you're not missing critical information, or provide an alternative point of view on the topic.

To find similar Web sites, choose Show Related Links from the Tools menu in Internet Explorer. The Search Companion pane (shown in Figure 3-1) appears, showing you a list of sites that are related to the site you're on. In addition, you see a rating of how popular the original site is and contact information about the company or individual who "owns" the site.

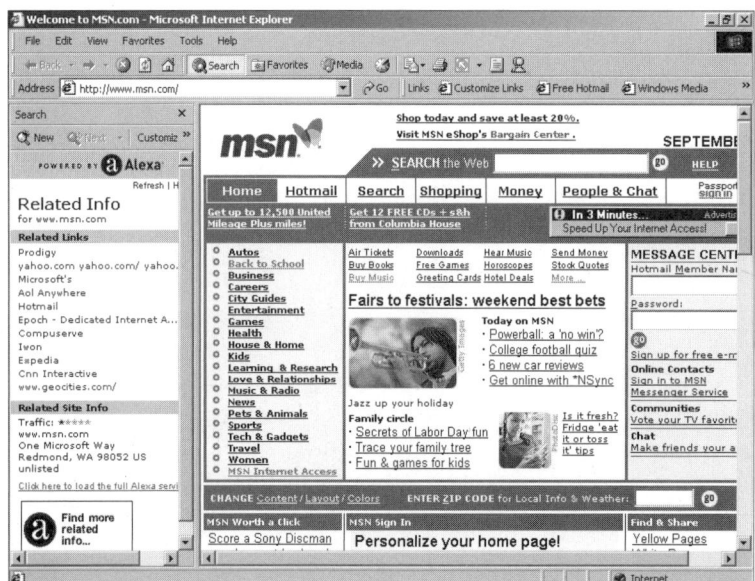

Figure 3-1   *The Show Related Links command lists sites that are similar to the one you've browsed to in Internet Explorer.*

This information is provided by Alexa (*http://www.alexa.com*), a service that tracks site popularity, site interrelationships, and users' browsing and buying activities. You can also install the full Alexa software package, which runs in the background whenever Internet Explorer is open and provides an additional toolbar that adds functionality such as

- Site reviews by Alexa users
- News and finance information related to the site you're viewing
- Product reviews and price comparisons
- Product and comparison searches

Privacy on the Web

Using the full Alexa add-in has pros and cons. The price you pay for the additional information you receive is that Alexa is capturing this information about you as a consumer, and selling it to corporations for their marketing purposes, which some Alexa users might not know. Many users are concerned about personal information being readily available to others, and prefer not to use software like Alexa.

The term "spyware" has emerged for applications that track your browsing behavior. Although Alexa must be consciously downloaded and installed, some spyware might be contained in free programs that are downloaded from the Web. In fact, some Web sites contain software that tracks your browsing behavior, and correlates it with your browsing behavior in *other* Web sites without your downloading anything—by your just visiting the site.

If you are concerned about privacy issues, you might want to visit Spyware Watch (*http://www.spyware.co.uk*) and read its privacy discussions and download its antispyware application, or search for "spyware" in your favorite search engine. Antispyware software lets you know whether there is any spyware operating in your computer, and gives you the option of uninstalling it.

Using Bots

A *bot* is a utility that automatically searches the Web for information of interest to you and reports it back to you—often on a schedule. The word bot is short for "robot," and is now used instead of the older term "agent" (that is, "secret agent"—someone with a mission to gather information), but you might sometimes hear bots referred to as *intelligent agents*. Most bots are free and can be installed on your own computer. They run automatically as long as you have a connection to the Internet.

There are many types of bots that do a variety of automatic search tasks for you. Botspot (*http://www.botspot.com*)—one of the leading sites for information about bots—classifies bots into the types listed in Table 3-2.

Table 3-2 Different Types of Bots

Bot Type	Description
Academic bots	Bots related to the academic community
Design bots	Bots that help design other bots
Chatter bots	Bots that talk to you
Commerce bots	Bots involved with e-commerce such as auction bots that watch auction prices for you
Fun bots	Bots related to virtual reality, predictions, etc.
Game bots	Bots that help you with games
Government bots	Bots related to government sites

(continued)

Table 3-2   Different Types of Bots   *(continued)*

Bot Type	Description
Knowledge bots	Bots that do things such as make graphical representations of taxonomies found on sites, model user preferences, and utilize artificial intelligence to automate a variety of tasks
News bots	Bots that monitor newsgroups, newspapers, and other news sources for information of interest
Search bots	Bots that automate the search process
Shopping bots	Intelligent agents to shop for you
Stock bots	Bots that keep track of selected stocks
Update bots	Bots that let you know when selected Web sites are updated

Stock bots, academic bots, and government bots are focused on people with specific needs, but the news bots, search bots, and update bots are for a wide variety of knowledge workers, so are worth a more detailed description.

News Bots

News bots search newspapers, magazines, and journals to bring you news on topics you specify. You can choose to have information in many ways: through e-mail, on your Web page, or through a customized portal page.

- **E-mail.**   You can receive news stories through e-mail from such sources as InfoBeat, Inc. (*http://www.infobeat.com*), among others. To receive daily news from InfoBeat, for example, you fill in a short form on its Web site with your e-mail address and select the topics you want to receive information on. Different vendors have different numbers and levels of categories from which to select.

- **Web page.**   Moreover (*http://www.moreover.com*) is an excellent bot that searches thousands of news sites, newsgroups, and industry sources for keywords you specify. Headlines from these sources are displayed on your Web page and are updated hourly. Although Moreover requires you to have your own Web site to which you publish your page, it has the greatest ability to focus on stories of interest because not only can you specify categories, but you can also specify keywords to search for. To use Moreover, you go to its Web site and click the link to put a newsfeed on your own Web site. You are taken through a wizard that allows you to format the newsfeed and specify its formatting. It then provides Hypertext Markup Language (HTML) code you can insert in your own Web page that will display the newsfeed.

- **Portal page.**   You can also see news stories from categories you specify on an increasing number of major portal sites such as MSN (*http://www.msn.com*), MSNBC (*http://www.msnbc.com*), or Yahoo (*http://www.yahoo.com*). These sites allow you to customize your own version of the portal by specifying stories and headlines you want to see. MSN, for example, offers more than 100 news, information, and stock resources to choose articles and stories from. However, these portals do not offer the level of keyword specificity provided by a service such as Moreover.

New ways of receiving news emerge almost monthly. MSNBC, for example, offers a downloadable utility that shows an icon in your taskbar when there's a news story on a topic of interest. Next generation news bots, currently in development, will use your navigation habits to learn what topics you are interested in, and then deliver that information to you based on your work patterns.

Search Bots

While news bots focus on news sources, search bots automate the search of Web pages. In fact, the Pro version of the metasearch engine Copernic provides internal search bot capability. After creating a search, you can click the Track button and specify a schedule on which Copernic should perform the search. If the scheduled search returns additional sites, the results are e-mailed to you.

See Also   For more information about Copernic, see "Supercharging Your Searches Using Metasearch Engines" on page 13.

Spyonit (*http://www.spyonit.com*) is a search bot that provides e-mailed updates on targeted searches you perform. It has a number of predesigned "spies," including a FedEx package tracking spy, Stock Spy, or the Competitive Intelligence Spy. You can add a Spyonit button to your toolbar and then click the button to add a site to your spies list each time you come to a site of interest.

Major search engines are also beginning to provide search bots for users. For instance, Northern Light has a Search Alert Service that periodically repeats any search you do using Northern Light and e-mails you the results if new sites are found.

Note   Search engines are also starting to provide value-added services for knowledge management and competitive intelligence. For instance, Northern Light also offers Single-Point—a service that creates a custom information portal for your corporation, categorizing and prioritizing the content sources that are pertinent to your business. Its fee-based RivalEye service monitors your competitors and the competitive landscape, creating a minisite that provides continuously updated information relevant to your company and your industry.

Update Bots

An update bot provides information about when a Web site changes. This might be a competitor's Web site, or a Web site containing resources that are updated periodically. Sometimes the bot can reside on the site itself—for instance, Mind-it (*http://mindit. netmind.com*) allows Webmasters to put a link to Mind-it on selected pages of their own Web sites. Visitors to the Web site can use the Mind-it link to subscribe to that page and receive an e-mail notification if the page changes.

Alternatively, you can load update bots on your own computer and they will perform this same function. C4U (*http://www.c-4-u.com*) is one such bot. After you download it, you can scan any site at intervals you specify. You will be informed of new images, linked files, and new text that appear on the site. You can even create a filter to search for specific terms, for example, looking for the appearance of "XP" on an analyst's Web site.

Tip   To find bots, you can either go to a central site that catalogs bots, such as *http://www.botspot.com*, or you can do a search for "Bots Intelligent Agents" in your favorite search or metasearch engine.

Working Offline

Research done by Gartner, Inc. and other leading analysts indicates that today's knowledge workers want to be able to work when they want, where they want. That means being able to work even when you're on a long airplane trip and aren't connected to the Internet. This can be difficult if your job is to find out information about a product, company, or concept. Fortunately, the Make Pages Available Offline feature in Internet Explorer can provide you with offline data so you can look at Web pages that have automatically been saved to your local hard drive.

Of course, it's possible to *save* a Web page on your local disk, but this feature goes far beyond that. Make Pages Available Offline enables you to specify a Web page as one that should be saved on your local drive, and refreshed according to a schedule you set, so you always have the latest version. What's better, you can specify that subpages under that Web page should also be saved periodically, so you can save a page and also all its supporting pages (that often contain more detailed information).

See Also   For more information about saving Web pages on your local drive, see "Saving Web Pages on Your Computer" on page 17.

You can update a selected Web page according to the preferences you have set and make it available for offline viewing by following these steps.

1. Browse to the desired page in Internet Explorer.

2. Choose Add To Favorites from the Favorites menu.

3. In the Add Favorites dialog box, select the Make Available Offline check box, then click the Customize button.

4. Go through the steps of the Offline Favorite Wizard. Choose whether to make linked pages available offline and the level of links to synchronize. (Remember, however, that the number of links can grow exponentially. Synchronizing more than one or two levels can create a large number of files, taking both time and disk space.)

5. Choose whether to synchronize on a schedule or only when you choose Synchronize from the Tools menu.

6. Click Finish.

Peering into the Invisible Web

Spiders are the intelligent agents that are used by search engines to index pages on the Web. When you see a list of Web pages on your favorite search engine, it's because that engine's spider has indexed that site.

What many people don't know, however, is that spiders cannot index databases. For instance, if you look up an author's name in a search engine, you might well find listings from Amazon.com. However, if you go to the Library of Congress catalog (*http://www.loc.gov*), and look for that author's name, you find additional pages that will never be found by a search engine. Often, the only way to find these pages is by querying the database on that site, because the pages are dynamically generated when you create the database query. They don't exist as static pages on the Web that the spider can find as it searches through the site. When a spider gets to a site containing a database, all it can see is the "front door"—the database form. It can't get to the data inside. That data is invisible to the search engines—hence the term, "Invisible Web."

The Invisible Web can prove to be a rich source of research material for the knowledge worker. This is especially true because, according to some sources, it's growing faster than the visible Web because the trend is away from putting information in static Web pages and toward putting information in databases that generate dynamic pages as requested by the user. Because the chances are great that you'll need to use the Invisible Web as you narrow your search and get into more detailed information, you have to know how to access it.

Accessing the Invisible Web is not like using a regular search engine or browsing Web sites. You start by accessing a catalog of publicly accessible databases, and then using the top-level categories provided to get to the subcategory that might contain databases of interest. You then need to access each of these databases in turn and search for the information you are looking for. What you do next depends on the individual site. Usually, there's a search form you can fill out, and sometimes these forms support Boolean logic, such as the Library of Congress's Boolean keyword search form in Figure 3-2.

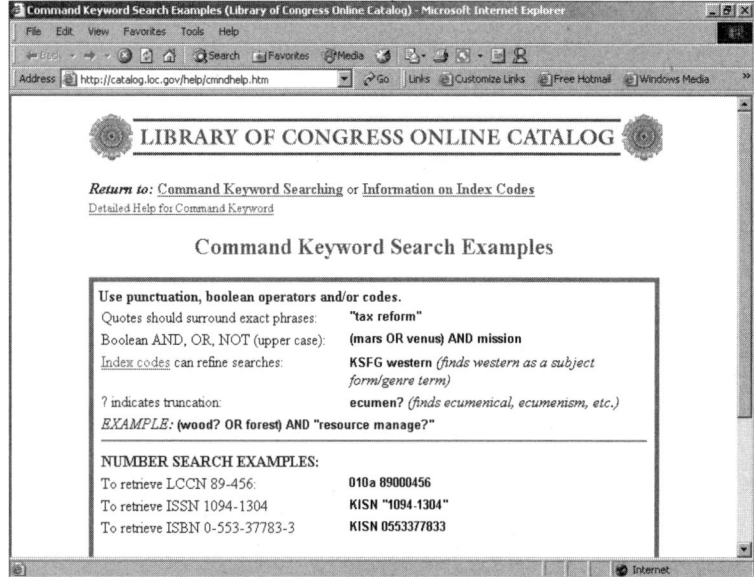

Figure 3-2 *Information in databases such as the Library of Congress's catalog are not displayed in search engine results, but can be searched using Boolean operators.*

Tip   George Washington University reference librarian Gary Price is one of the most recognized authorities on searching the Invisible Web. His site (*http://gwis2.circ.gwu.edu/ ~gprice/direct.htm*) offers excellent articles and tools for searching the Invisible Web, as well as what he calls the Opaque/Almost Invisible Web—sites that contain thousands of pages that are often missed by the general search engines. He provides suggestions for search engines called *crawlers* that are focused on specific topic areas and might reveal more information than you will find using a general search or metasearch engine. Examples include Lawcrawler (*http://www.lawcrawler.com*), Psychcrawler (*http://www. psychcrawler.com*), and ERIC (education resources at *http://www.eric.ed.gov/*).

Some sites that provide catalogs of specialty databases include the following.

- **Lycos** (*http://dir.lycos.com/reference/searchable+databases/*) has a catalog of searchable databases.

- **InvisibleWeb** (*http://www.invisibleweb.com*) has an excellent set of categories that allow you to quickly find the subject you need.

- **WebData** (*http://www.webdata.com*) provides several search tools, among which is a catalog of online databases.

Bookmarking Databases

As you use specialized databases more and more, you'll find it valuable to create subfolders in your Favorites folder for the types of databases you use most often. Some of the ones you might find useful include the following.

Financial/Business

- Hoover's Online (*http://www.hoovers.com*)
- Dun & Bradstreet (*http://www.dnb.com*)
- Bloomberg.com (*http://www.bloomberg.com*)
- CEOExpress (*http://www.ceoexpress.com*)
- Edgar (*http://www.sec.gov*)

People

- Yahoo! People Search (*http://people.yahoo.com*)
- InfoSpace (*http://www.infospace.com*)
- SwitchBoard (*http://www.switchboard.com*)
- Hotbot (*http://www.hotbot.com*)

Technology/e-business

- Business 2.0 (*http://www.business2.com*)
- BizReport (*http:b//www.bizreport.com*)

Putting It All Together

This chapter has given you a lot of information about a wide variety of tools you can use to gather information for your knowledge work. One way you can put all these tools together is by following a search strategy like the following six-step process.

1. **Define your question.**   The first thing you need to do in searching for information is to spend a little front-end time figuring out exactly what information you're looking for. In Jeff Henshaw's case (at the beginning of this chapter), he categorized his competitive analysis task into several topics—financial information, product strategy, and the like. He knew the structure of the deliverable before he started working. And he got this from his manager—not a bad way to define your question! As you define your question, you might consider

   - What type of information will the deliverable provide—numbers, tables, charts, text, qualitative judgments, conclusions, expert opinions, references?

   - Can you make a template of the deliverable that you can copy information you find into, so it's already structured in the right way as you gather it?

   - What is your starting point—a company name, a concept, a trend, a set of facts?

   - What are the concepts related to this starting point, and how would you research it if there were no Internet?

2. **Start with known resources.**   If you have an initial Web site or person's name, start with this. Read every word in these initial Web sites to get a feel for your topic. When possible, copy information into your template but don't worry too much at this point—you're mainly getting a flavor for your topic.

3. **Perform your initial search.**   This step allows you to gather all the information that's available on the visible Web, and then start to refine it.

   - Use your favorite search or metaseach engine, keeping terms fairly broad.

   - Use advanced search features and Boolean logic to refine your search terms and focus on sites of interest.

   - Scan these sites, and bookmark those of interest.

   - Go back to the bookmarked sites and read them more thoroughly, copying information into your template if appropriate.

   - Use the Show Related Sites tool to search for additional sites that your search engines might have missed.

4. **Reevaluate.** Read all the information you gathered and ask two questions.

- Is this information credible? If you're uncertain, how can you verify it?
- What additional information do you need?

5. **Analyze.** As you look at the information you need to obtain or verify, use the following sources to further research the topic.

- Now's the time to use the specialized databases in the Invisible Web to find additional facts, news, or industry reports.
- Now that you're becoming knowledgeable about the subject, you can talk intelligently with experts about it. Use the strategies in Chapter 2 to access other people on the Web who know about your topic.
- Use focused Boolean searches to check facts you're uncertain of and track down their sources.

6. **Prepare your answer.** You have the information you've been seeking; now you can proceed to summarize it, analyze it, or make your own conclusions about it and present it up the line!

Tip Every year new types of search assistants emerge, and every month new entrants in existing categories make their appearance. It's always smart to have a couple of sites that discuss search strategies in your Favorites list and visit them occasionally. You can do a search for "searching strategies," visit a useful site hosted by the University of California at Berkeley (*http://www.lib.berkeley.edu/TeachingLib/Guides/Internet/*), or go to Search Engine Watch (*http://www.searchenginewatch.com*).

Summary

Finding comprehensive information on the Web is no longer a matter of typing a term into a search engine. There are a number of advanced techniques, combined with a variety of new search tools, that can enhance your ability to get to the information you need. By combining the techniques and tools in this chapter with a systematic strategy for conducting your searches, you'll be amazed at the variety of questions you're able to answer and the amount of detail you discover.

Checklist for Becoming a Search Maestro

Check off the following points as you learn the following advanced search techniques.

[ ] Formulate Boolean queries.

[ ] Use advanced search options of common search engines.

[ ] Find sites that are associated with the Web site you're viewing.

[ ] Conduct background searches on keywords from any Microsoft Office application.

[ ] Find bots that automate your search process.

[ ] Synchronize your Web pages with your local hard drive.

[ ] Find databases on the Invisible Web.

[ ] Use a systematic strategy to search the Web.

Organizing Information

If a book is misfiled in a library, it might as well not be there at all. Information that cannot be retrieved cannot be used to create knowledge, and for you to be able to retrieve information effectively it must be *organized*.

Organizing information not only allows you to retrieve it, but it also permits you to make new connections among data. Organized information acts as a catalyst for creative thought, and provides the basic structure that enables knowledge workers to transform it into knowledge that can be used by the organization.

To organize information, you need three things.

- **Tools.** You need to know what tools are available to help you organize your information and how to use the relevant features of those tools.

- **Principles.** Tools alone, however, don't do the trick. You also need to understand fundamental organizational principles that guide your use of those tools.

- **Habits.** Knowing the principles and having the right skills is useless unless you put them into practice consistently. Filing *some* of the library books properly isn't enough.

Part II shows you how to achieve these competencies for the different types of information you need to organize. Chapter 4, "Organizing Your Day," teaches you how to organize your tasks using folders and views, and how to link them to the contacts they are associated with and the files you are working on. You learn how to organize your appointments with your calendar, share that calendar with others, and schedule face-to-face and online meetings. You also learn how to adopt new work habits using principles such as "making time for the big rocks."

In Chapter 5, "Organizing Your Files," you learn how to set up your electronic filing system by choosing appropriate storage media, and creating folder and file naming conventions. You also learn how to find data in your system by using document properties and Microsoft Office XP advanced search features.

Chapter 6, "Organizing Your Data," teaches you how to create databases. You see how to do a simple requirements analysis, and then pick the right tool for your database. You also learn how to create a database in both Microsoft Excel and Microsoft Access, as well as how to convert data from your legacy applications.

If you are constantly overwhelmed by your Inbox, Chapter 7, "Organizing Your E-mail" is for you. In it you see how to create e-mail folders to save your e-mails in, as well as a simple method for quickly processing e-mail as it arrives. You also learn automated techniques for processing e-mail, including creating rules for junk e-mail and how to automatically respond to other specific types of e-mail. You even learn how to find those little nuggets of gold that are hidden in your e-mail archives.

For those people who work away from the office, Chapter 8, "Organizing Your Mobile Tools," teaches you what you need to know. You learn techniques for synchronizing your desktop and notebook Microsoft Outlook data files, as well as techniques for synchronizing Outlook with your handheld device. Seven methods for handling e-mail on the road are presented, along with criteria to help you choose which ones fit your situation the best. You also learn how to make sure the files you need are with you, even when you're not at the office.

Organizing Your Day

Ty Loren Carlson is extremely proud of the new company he started two months ago—Adventure Works. He's been surprised, however, at how many things there have been to do! He thought he would be spending his time taking clients on river adventures in Wyoming, exploring the national park to create new itineraries, and talking on the phone with potential clients. He's doing all that, but seemingly thousands of other duties too. If he's not dealing with the insurance company, he's meeting with his bookkeeper. If he's not getting a business license, he's giving talks to the local Rotary Club. It seems as though with all the appointments he has, he's always late in returning calls and his To Do list has gotten completely out of control.

This crushing experience isn't unique to entrepreneurs. One of the major challenges facing today's knowledge worker is trying to deal with an overabundance of information and an overwhelming number of things to do.

One of the first steps you must take if you are to tame the information tsunami is to organize your day, and the two elements you need to organize are your tasks and your appointments. Microsoft Outlook provides helpful tools for organizing your tasks and appointments, but tools alone are not enough. Many people who use Outlook have not changed their work habits to take advantage of these new tools. Thus, this chapter not only shows you how Outlook can help organize your day but also starts by sharing some best practices to take advantage of it.

See Also   This chapter focuses on organizing your personal work. For techniques on organizing the work you do with other team members, see Chapter 12, "Creating Knowledge with People."

Adopting New Habits

Organizing your day is fundamentally a matter of adopting new habits—of changing the way you approach your job. Even if you haven't seen your desktop in weeks, have been known to be regularly late for appointments, and have no idea what your top priority tasks are, you'll find that by following a few simple guidelines you can get your work back on track. Fortunately, the functions in Outlook make getting organized even easier. They work well with the best time-management practices to enable you to easily make sure you know what your top priorities are, and organize your work to ensure you can focus your attention on them each day and week.

Identifying Your "Big Rocks"

In his book *First Things First*, Stephen Covey (and coauthors A. Roger Merrill and Rebecca R. Merrill) tell a wonderful story about using your time effectively that teaches a central principle of time management.

> I attended a seminar once where the instructor was lecturing on time. At one point, he said, "Okay, it's time for a quiz." He reached under the table and pulled out a wide-mouth gallon jar. He set it on the table next to a platter with some fist-sized rocks in it. "How many of these rocks do you think we can get in the jar?" he asked.
>
> After we made our guess, he said, "Okay, let's find out." He set one rock in the jar ... then another ... then another. I don't remember how many he got in, but he got the jar full. Then he asked, "Is that jar full?"
>
> Everybody looked at the rocks and said, "Yes."
>
> Then he said, "Ahhh." He reached under the table and pulled out a bucket of gravel. Then he dumped some gravel in and shook the jar and the gravel went in all the little spaces left by the big rocks. Then he grinned and said once more, "Is the jar full?"
>
> By this time we were on to him. "Probably not," we said.
>
> "Good!" he replied. And he reached under the table and brought out a bucket of sand. He started dumping the sand in and it went in all the little spaces left by the rocks and the gravel. Once more he looked at us and said, "Is the jar full?"
>
> "No!" we all roared.
>
> He said, "Good!" and he grabbed a pitcher of water and began to pour it in. He got something like a quart of water in that jar. Then he said, "Well, what's the point?"
>
> Somebody said, "Well, there are gaps, and if we really work at it, you can always fit more into your life."
>
> "No," he said, "that's not the point. The point is this: if you hadn't put these big rocks in first, would you ever have gotten any of them in?"

The metaphor of "big rocks" can help you keep your life organized, and *get things done* more than almost anything else I can think of. It's especially helpful if, like so many knowledge workers, you're one of those people who works like mad all day, yet at the end of the day wonders why so many important tasks were left undone.

Often it's because there are so many pebbles and so much sand that fill up your time that you don't ever get around to the big rocks. You might think it's because you don't have time. Actually it's because you didn't make time for the big rocks first.

What are the "big rocks" you should put into your jars first? They are usually a combination of personal and professional responsibilities, such as spending time with your spouse or children, planning a new marketing effort, exercising, or eliminating your administrative backlog. Covey et al. describe these as "high importance, low urgency" tasks because they are valuable to do, yet don't have the sense of immediacy that forces you to deal with them right away.

To make sure you have enough time for your big rocks, use the following four simple steps.

1. Each week identify the big rocks you want to remember.

2. Assign an amount of time you want to spend on each of these tasks.

3. Block out those times on your calendar, and commit yourself to *fitting your other activities around those blocks of time.*

4. If a big rock slips because of another pressing priority, reschedule it immediately.

Why not try this right now? What's one "big rock" you want to attend to today? Schedule a time for it, and then fit the "pebbles" around it.

Spending Time to Save Time

Here's a helpful strategy for getting rid of those piles of paper and getting yourself on track. All it requires is for you to invest a little time to save a lot of time.

The Weekly Organization

The weekly organization takes 10 to 15 minutes first thing Monday morning. After you're finished, you'll know exactly what you need to do for the week and stacks of extra papers and lists of other chores you won't be doing this week anyway won't overwhelm you. Before you do this the first time, set aside a desk drawer for all the papers you're going to defer acting on until next week, and then create a task folder in Outlook called Deferred in which you'll put deferred Outlook tasks. (For information about how to create a task folder, see "Placing Tasks into Folders" on page 62.) Then follow these steps.

1. In your calendar, enter any new appointments for the week. Count up how much time is taken up by appointments. This is time you can't use for other tasks because you have to be somewhere else.

2. Block out time for those high priority but low urgency "big rocks" that help your business or make your life worthwhile.

3. Look at your calendar again. The remaining time is that which is available for phone calls and items on your task list.

4. Move any items that you put in your Deferred folder the previous week back into your main task folder.

5. Now look at the items on your Outlook task list. Based on your available time, move the tasks you know you realistically won't do this week to the Deferred folder.

6. Next, take out any papers from your Deferred drawer, a desk or file drawer set aside to hold lower priority documents or those you don't expect to act on during the week. Combine them in a big stack with the other papers on your desk. (For your electronic documents, create an electronic Deferred drawer in a separate folder.)

7. Go through each piece of paper and sort them into two piles: The first pile contains every paper you must work on or realistically might work on this week. The second pile contains the rest. *Put the second pile in a Deferred drawer out of sight. You can safely ignore it until next week.*

Do this weekly organization first thing on Monday morning or last thing on Friday afternoon, but take 20 minutes when you won't be disturbed to get it done. If you can get to work early on Mondays, you can do it before the phone starts ringing and you'll have your week all set. The results?

- You have a realistic amount of work to do for the week.

- You know what your major goals and big rocks are for the week.

- You aren't faced with a daunting pile or task list of things you'll never get to this week.

The Daily Organization

After you get your week under control, organizing your day becomes a snap. At the beginning of each day, take five to ten minutes and do the following.

1. Review your calendar. Total up your appointments, calculate how much time you have left over, and subtract a factor for unplanned tasks. (That factor can be between 25 percent and 50 percent of your remaining time—don't underestimate the time you spend on spur-of-the-moment crises, short personal phone calls, or even socializing with your coworkers.) The remaining time is what you have available for making phone calls and doing tasks on your To Do list.

2. Next, take your weekly pile of papers. (Remember, you don't need to look at the Deferred pile at all.) Leaf through it and pull out all the papers you must work on or you realistically might work on today.

3. Put the remaining papers in the Deferred drawer. You don't need to look at them again today. There won't be that many papers left.

4. For each one, make an entry in your Outlook task list. Add any phone calls you need to make or other tasks you have to do.

5. Prioritize the tasks using a system like this.

- High = must do today

- Medium = want to do today

- Low = won't do today

This is your day's To Do list. It, along with your appointment calendar, will keep you on track for the day.

Focusing on High Priorities

After you have a system that you're following to organize your day and week, you can use Outlook to help you put those procedures into place. Maintaining your tasks in Outlook will enable you to organize yourself in ways that will leverage your time.

Creating a task in Outlook is as simple as creating an e-mail. To do so, follow these steps.

1. Open Outlook.

2. Point to New on the File menu, and choose Task.

3. In the Task dialog box fill out the fields you need which often include at a minimum: Subject, Due Date, and Priority.

4. Click the Save And Close button.

Caution   Don't mark tasks complete until they're done. Sounds obvious, doesn't it? It's actually a mistake that many people make. Sometimes your task involves others' actions, like requesting a quotation from a vendor. After you send the request, it's easy to think you completed the task but if the vendor doesn't respond, you're left without essential information.

After you start putting your tasks into Outlook, you can organize and manage your task list in several ways.

- Order and reorder your list at any time to view tasks by date, subject, or priority.

- Organize your tasks in folders to track progress on specific projects.

- Track activities associated with people you work with.

- Attach files to tasks so you can go directly to your work by clicking a link in the task.

Placing Tasks into Folders

It might help to put related tasks into a folder for that set of tasks. This is especially useful if you have a large task list and can't get to all of them in one week, as discussed in the preceding section. Try creating folders by time period (Current/Deferred), by subject (Project1/Project2), or even by differentiating personal and professional tasks (Weekday/Weekend or Personal/Professional).

Note   You can also separate tasks into groups using categories, and then sort or filter your list as described later in this chapter. Some people prefer to use folders, however, because it's so easy to drag tasks from one folder to another and by simply clicking a folder you can quickly see all related tasks.

To use folders effectively, you need to know how to create, delete, and move a folder and how to move tasks from one folder to another. Fortunately, all these tasks are simple in Outlook. Refer to Table 4-1 for instructions on completing these tasks.

Table 4-1   Outlook Folder Tasks

Task	Steps
Create a folder	Right-click the Tasks folder, and choose New Folder. In the Create New Folder dialog box, give the folder a name and then click OK. Outlook prompts you, asking whether you want to add a shortcut to the folder in the Outlook Bar. Click Yes to add the shortcut or No if you'd rather not.
Delete a folder	Right-click the folder you wish to delete, and choose the Delete command that applies to your folder. Outlook prompts you to be sure you want to delete the folder. Click Yes if you are sure you wish to delete it or No if you change your mind. If you click Yes, the folder and its contents are deleted.
Move a folder	Drag the folder to another folder. The folder list is refreshed to show the new location of the moved folder.
Move tasks into a folder	Highlight the items you wish to move, and then drag them to the new folder in the Folder List pane.

Changing Views to Organize Information

Each Outlook folder—including task folders—has a variety of views. You can switch between views of the Tasks list by clicking the Current View button on the Outlook Standard toolbar. You can change how you see your task lists (like the sort order, fields, subgroupings, and filters), or you can create custom views that combine all these elements to customize how you see your tasks. But first, let's review how to modify each of these elements individually.

Sort, Group, and Categorize Tasks

One way to organize all the tasks in a folder is to sort them. You can do this by subject, priority, date due, or other parameters. Some users prefer special naming conventions for their tasks. Then when they sort their task list, they can see all their calls, errands, and other tasks together. An example of this is shown here.

- Call: Tom Getzinger
- Personal: Feed dogs
- Errand: Get office supplies
- Alpine Ski House: Draft proposal

You can easily sort the tasks in your task list by clicking the column header for your task list. When you click the column header once, the task list is sorted in ascending order by that field. Clicking the column head a second time re-sorts that field in descending order. A small up or down arrow next to the column name indicates whether the field is sorted in ascending or descending order. See Figure 4-1 for an example.

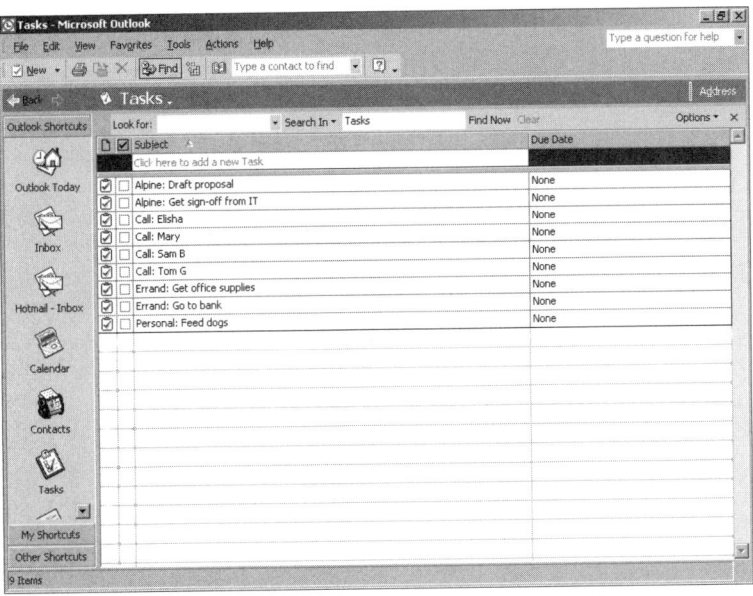

Figure 4-1 *If you think ahead when you name your tasks, you can easily organize them as you sort them by clicking the column name. In this case, the subjects are organized alphabetically in ascending order.*

A slightly more sophisticated way to see related tasks together is to assign each task a category, and then display the tasks grouped by those categories. You can categorize your tasks by creating or editing them in the Task dialog box when adding or editing a task, and then entering a category in the Category field.

You can use predefined categories, and edit the category list by typing a category name. If you want to do a major overhaul on the Category list, click the Categories button in the Task dialog box. You'll see the Categories dialog box, shown in Figure 4-2.

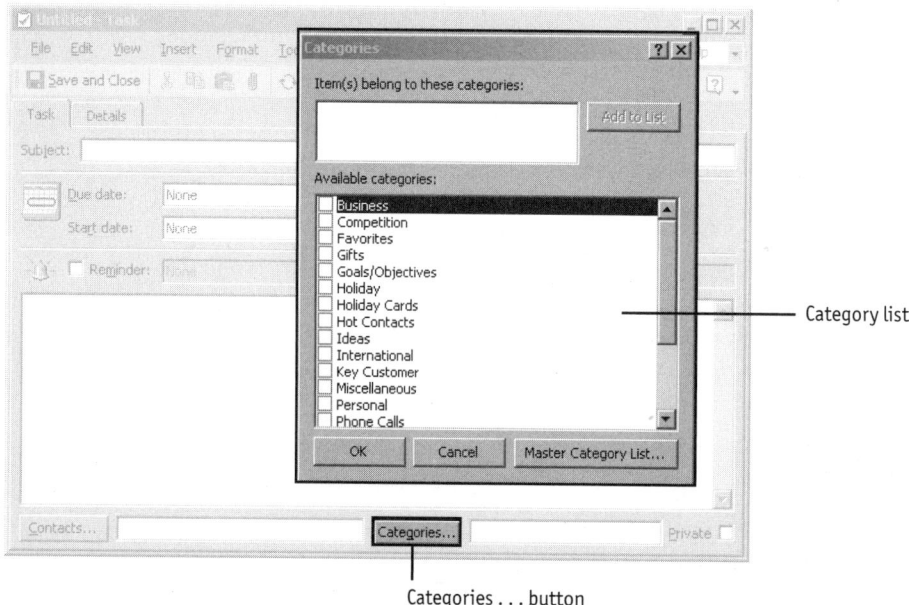

Figure 4-2   *You can view and edit your category list from the Categories dialog box.*

By default, the category field does not appear in the Tasks list so if you are used to entering tasks in the Click Here To Add A New Task box above the Tasks list, you need to add the Category field to the Tasks list, as described in the next section.

After you categorize your tasks, group them by category by clicking the Current View button on the Standard toolbar and then choosing By Category.

Show and Hide Fields

If you are using Task fields that are not part of the default Outlook display, such as Category or % Complete, you can customize the Tasks list so the fields you want appear. It's handy to have commonly used fields appear in the Tasks list because it makes them easy to edit—you don't have to open the individual Task dialog box for each item but instead can modify the information directly in the list.

To change the fields that display in a Tasks list, do the following.

1. Right-click any heading in the current Tasks list, and choose Field Chooser.

2. If you do not see the field you want to insert in the Field Chooser dialog box (shown in Figure 4-3), click the Frequently-Used Fields drop-down list and select a category to display a different set of fields.

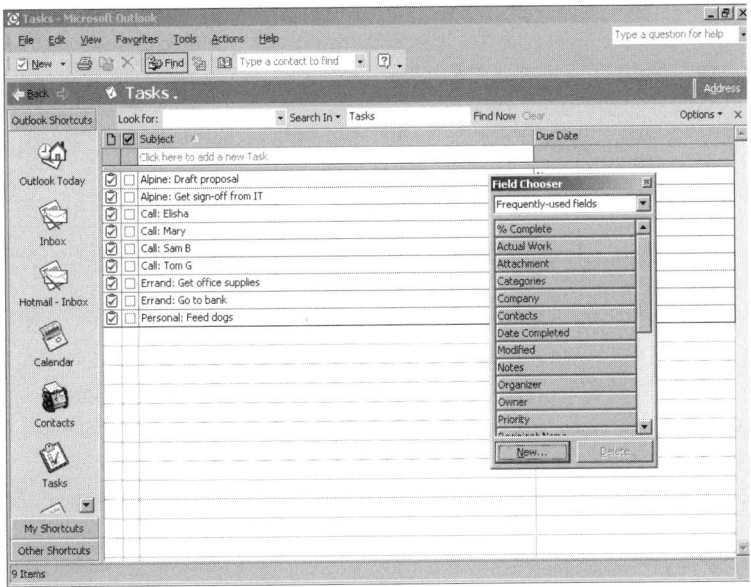

Figure 4-3 *You can display fields that are normally hidden in a Tasks list by dragging them from the Field Chooser dialog box.*

3. Drag the field you want to insert from the Field Chooser dialog box to the spot on the column-heading row where you want it to appear. As you drag, notice that a red double arrow appears indicating the placement of the new column header.

4. Drag other column headings from one spot to another on the column-heading row to rearrange fields as required. Drag a column heading off the column-heading row into the task list itself to no longer display it.

5. Drag the border between two column headings to resize a column, or double-click it to automatically size it.

6. Close the Field Chooser dialog box when you are finished.

Note You can also move, resize, and remove fields from the column-heading row when the Field Chooser dialog box is not open.

Filter Tasks to See a Subset

Sometimes it's useful to filter your tasks so you see only a subset of your Tasks list. Filters can be helpful if you have a number of tasks to work on that are not in the same categories or part of the same project. You can filter the Tasks list to see only high priority tasks or tasks that have been deferred. In Outlook, filters are associated with views so when you create or change a filter, that filter is applied whenever you use a Tasks view. Outlook includes several filters as part of the default Current Views (accessed by clicking View and then Current View), including the Next Seven Days, Overdue Tasks, and Completed Tasks views.

To set a filter, follow these steps.

1. Select the view to which you want to apply a filter.

2. Point to Current View on the View menu, and choose Customize Current View.

3. In the View Summary dialog box, click Filter.

4. In the Filter dialog box, choose options in the Tasks, More Choices, or Advanced tabs or click the SQL tab and create a SQL query.

5. Click OK twice to apply the filter to the current Tasks view.

Note   You can customize an existing view or create a new one to allow you to see your Tasks list exactly as you like it. To do so, choose View, Current View, and then Customize Current Views. From the View Summary dialog box, you can choose options that allow you to customize the fields to display how you want to group them in this view, how the list is sorted, if a filter should be applied, or the formatting of the task list.

Associating Tasks with Your Contacts

In many businesses, it's important to track the activities associated with people on your contact list. This is especially true if the person is a sales prospect or customer and you want to be able to see the e-mails, tasks, and appointments you had with him or her in the past. E-mails are automatically tracked, but you can also track tasks associated with a contact.

Type the person's name in the Contacts box at the bottom of the Task dialog box (that appears when you add or edit a task). If the person is already in your Contacts list, Outlook automatically completes the person's name for you (or click the Contacts button and make a selection from the Contacts list). To see all the tasks associated with that contact, click Contacts in the Folders List pane. Double-click the contact name and click the Activities tab in the Contact dialog box. You will see all activities (for example, e-mails, notes, tasks) for the given contact. Click the Show drop-down list above the list of activities and choose Upcoming Tasks/Appointments to filter the list so that you see only a current list of tasks for this contact.

Note   You can also associate appointments with contacts by filling out the Contacts field in an Appointment dialog box. That way, you track all the meetings or phone calls you have with a contact. For more information about setting appointments in Outlook, see "Scheduling an Appointment" on page 69.

Attaching Files to Tasks

You probably have scores of tasks, many of which require that you work on documents. Consider making your Outlook Tasks list the center of your daily work by linking documents to the tasks they support.

Imagine looking at your Tasks list, and seeing that the top priority is finishing a report you've been working on. You right-click the Attached File icon (which looks like a paper clip) and select View Attachments then the attachment name. The report then opens in Microsoft Word. It's that simple. You don't have to switch from Outlook to Word, and then fish through your file system to find the report file. It's all there, linked to the first task you need to work on today.

This is a "task-centered" rather than "program-centered" way of thinking about your computer, and probably a different way of working. It might seem to take longer in the beginning than your old method, but after you get used to working this way you'll be amazed at how much time you save and how easy it is!

To attach a file to tasks, do the following.

1. Switch to Tasks view by clicking Tasks In The Folders List pane.
2. Select a Tasks list, then double-click a task to edit it.
3. Click the Insert File button (which looks like a paper clip) on the Task dialog box toolbar.
4. In the Insert File dialog box, navigate to the desired file.
5. Click the down arrow to the right of the Insert button, and choose Insert As Shortcut.
6. Click Save And Close. When you return to the Tasks list, notice that there is now a small paper clip icon in the attachment column (also denoted by a paper clip). If you don't see this column, point to Current View on the View menu, and click Detailed List (or add the attachment field to your current view as described earlier in "Show and Hide Fields" on page 64).

Note You can choose Insert rather than Insert As Shortcut in Step 5. However, doing so makes a copy of the desired file in a special Outlook subfolder and you might be confused because the original file is in your regular electronic filing system.

After you attach shortcuts to files for your tasks, you can quickly switch from viewing your To Do list to working on a file to complete a high priority task. Just open the desired task, and double-click the file icon in the Task dialog box. The file opens in its source application (for example, Microsoft Word, Microsoft Excel, Microsoft PowerPoint). After you work on the file, click the Save button to save it back into your electronic filing system.

Keeping an Electronic Calendar

Do you still keep your calendar on paper? Nervous about giving up that appointment book you guard with your life? Maybe it's time to think about switching to an electronic calendar. Look at the following list of benefits, and then decide whether these benefits outweigh the pain of changing how you work. The Outlook electronic calendar allows you to do the following.

- Link appointments to entries in your address book so you have a record of all your contacts with a specific person.

- Search for names, dates, topics, or other information.

- Link notes and files to your appointments, so you remember things you need to review for your meeting.

- Automatically set up an appointment to recur over any period of time you specify.

- Synchronize with your handheld computer or Personal Data Assistant (PDA) such as a Pocket PC.

- Coordinate free meeting times with other Outlook users.

- Share your calendar with others by publishing it or giving them a "copy" of your calendar to store in their own Outlook folders.

- Set audio or visual reminders so you never miss another meeting.

Tip   If you're used to using a Day-Timer or other paper-based calendar, you can print your Outlook calendar in the same format as a Day-Timer page. Put the printed calendar in your Day-Timer and take it with you. To see the available styles, choose File, Page Setup, and then look at the options for Page Size in the Paper tab of the Page Setup dialog box for the print style you prefer. You can even buy special paper for printing Outlook calendars that is the right size, is prepunched, and has the lines drawn in.

In short, maintaining your calendar electronically in Outlook is a great way to keep your day organized—especially if you work with others who also maintain their calendars in Outlook. When your calendar is organized you know, at a glance, what appointments you have for the day and week. In Outlook terms, *appointments* include events you must attend at a certain time: meetings, luncheons, conferences, and the like. They also include tasks you must do at a specific time, like making a phone call or participating in a conference call. They are appointments because they happen at a particular time. A *meeting* is an appointment you schedule with additional Outlook users. With Outlook, not only can you keep track of your appointments, but you can also schedule meetings with others and even publish your calendar as a Web page so that even non-Outlook users know when you are busy.

Scheduling an Appointment

If you decide that keeping your calendar on your computer is for you, it's easy to get started. Grab your paper calendar, close your door for half an hour, and transfer the appointments into Outlook. By the end of the exercise, you'll be familiar with the process and more likely to remember to add new appointments in your electronic appointment book. To schedule an appointment in Outlook, follow these steps.

1. Click Calendar in the Folders List pane. Click the down arrow to the right of the New button on the Standard toolbar, and choose Appointment.

2. In the Appointment dialog box, shown in Figure 4-4, fill out the subject, start time, and end time of the appointment. Fill in other fields as needed.

   - The Importance, Show Time As, Label, and Category fields allow you to organize your appointments and color-code their display.

   - The Reminder field is useful to see an alarm prior to the appointment. Click the Reminder check box and then, from the drop-down list, select the number of minutes prior to the meeting that you want your reminder to be sent.

   - Attaching a file can be useful if you need to review an agenda or a working document prior to an appointment. This works in the same fashion as described in "Attaching Files to Tasks" on page 67, except you are attaching a file to a calendar entry rather than a task.

   - The Notes field is a handy place to record a quick agenda or directions to the appointment. Simply place your cursor in the Notes area and begin typing.

   - You can click the Recurrence button in the Appointment toolbar to schedule multiple instances of a recurring appointment.

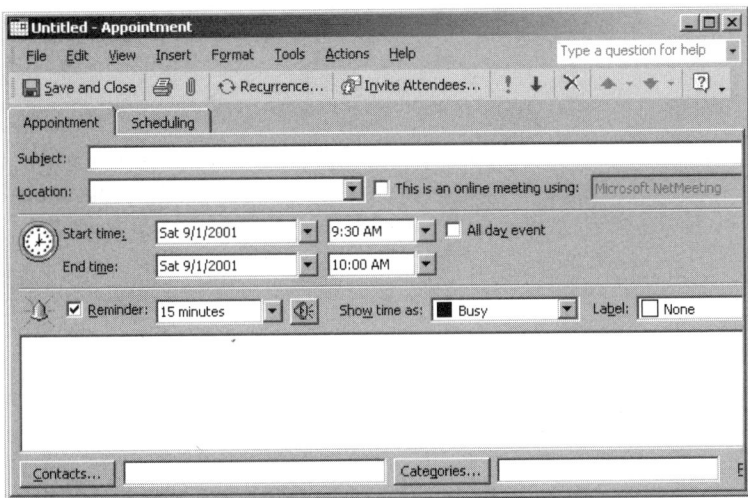

Figure 4-4 *Entering an appointment is easy because appointments, tasks, and e-mails all share very similar dialog boxes.*

After you create an appointment, you view it by clicking the Calendar button in the Outlook Bar. As with tasks, there are several views you can use to see your calendar by clicking the Current View button on the Standard toolbar. If you want to see your appointments in a calendar format, choose Day/Week/Month or Day/Week/Month View With Auto Preview. You can then click the Day, Week, Work Week, or Month button in the Calendar toolbar to see the appropriate timeframe. Other views display your appointments in a list format.

Best Practices for Using Your Electronic Calendar

The following list suggests some habits you might want to adopt to use Outlook most effectively for organizing your day.

- Record *every* appointment in your electronic calendar because it will now be your "official" version of your appointment book.

- Have your calendar with you when you're away from your computer—either by taking a printout with you or using a handheld computer or PDA.

- Enter appointments that you make when you're away from your computer into Outlook as soon as you get back to your desk.

- Enter weekly staff meetings or other meetings that you have regularly using the Recurrence button.

- When you're at a professional association or other type of annual meeting, immediately record the dates for next year's meeting on your printout or in your PDA and get it into Outlook as soon as possible. Outlook can even schedule meetings that occur beyond this calendar year.

- Set an Outlook alarm to remind you 15 minutes or so before important meetings. You'll get a reminder dialog box and an audible alert that will remind you it's time to go.

- Use your calendar to reserve time for administrative or project work. Your calendar can help you ensure you make the time you need to do high priority tasks.

- If you have to be available on the phone for your customers but other work prevents you from being available all the time, schedule a telephone period each day. If people know you generally take and return calls between 3 P.M. and 5 P.M. and you keep this consistent week to week, they will fall into your pattern.

Sharing Your Calendar

Wouldn't it be convenient if you called a client, needing to meet with three folks on their team, and the person you talk to says, "Just a minute, I can tell you when everybody's free." That's exactly what can happen if they are all sharing an Outlook calendar. In fact, if you're using Outlook too, *you* can find out when everyone's free if you all choose to share calendar information on the Web.

Outlook provides several ways to share your calendar. These include the following.

- Sharing calendars with others using Microsoft Exchange Server
- Publishing your free/busy information to a Web server or to another Outlook user
- Publishing your calendar on a Web site
- Exporting Outlook to a Web-based calendar you share with others

Share Calendars with Exchange Server

If your organization is running Exchange Server, you have several choices for sharing your calendar. Usually, there will be standard procedures outlining which of these methods you should use. See your network administrator for instructions for your specific implementation of Microsoft Exchange. Here are several common methods used for sharing calendars with Exchange.

- **Give others permissions to your private folders.** Assuming the system administrator has set policies appropriately, this can be an easy solution because others can see your Outlook folders in the Folder pane as easily as they see theirs.

- **Give others "delegate" permission.** You can also give another person permission to act on your behalf. For instance, you might want to delegate permissions to accept appointments to an administrative assistant or a colleague when you're on vacation. This differs from giving them other permissions because the delegate permission allows them to take actions in your name—others won't even know that someone acted for you.

- **Use a public folder.** You can use public folders (folders that are shared by Exchange users) to share files, a contact list, a task list, or a calendar. A calendar in a public folder is different from your personal calendar, and is usually used to track group activities. Your system administrator usually creates public folders and assigns permissions. Depending on your permission level, you might be able to create and edit events, or merely view them.

- **Access Outlook from the Web.** Your Exchange and Web administrators can also set up Outlook Web Access, a service that allows you to access your Outlook calendar (as well as your contact list, though not tasks) from the Web. This enables organizations to support kiosks (central workstations) or roving workers by allowing them access to Outlook from the Web.

Publish Your Free/Busy Information to a Web Server

If you are using Microsoft Outlook 2002, you can publish your free/busy information on a Web server and share it with others using Outlook 2002. This removes the need for Exchange Server, and still allows you to schedule meetings with others and see when they are free.

You can publish your free/busy information to either the Microsoft Office Internet Free/Busy Service, or to your own Web site if your Web site has the Microsoft Office XP or Microsoft FrontPage XP extensions installed.

The Microsoft Office Internet Free/Busy Service is a Web-based service that periodically sends your free/busy information to a special server maintained by Microsoft and allows you to specify who has access to this information. People who have appropriate access can schedule meetings with you and see when you are free or busy. The service shows only when you are free or busy; it does not show all your appointment details.

Note   To use this free service, you need a Microsoft Passport account. This account, part of the Microsoft .NET initiative, provides a single point of identification to Microsoft for an increasing number of services. The account is free, and you're prompted to sign up for a passport if you don't already have one the first time you use the Free/Busy service.

To enable the Free/Busy feature in Outlook 2002, do the following.

1. Click Options on the Tools menu, and choose Calendar Options.

2. In the Calendar dialog box, click Free/Busy Options.

3. In the Free/Busy Options dialog box, select the Publish And Search Using Microsoft Office Internet Free/Busy Service check box and then click the Manage button.

4. In the browser window that appears, use your Microsoft Passport account to log on to the Microsoft Office Internet Free/Busy Web site, shown in Figure 4-5.

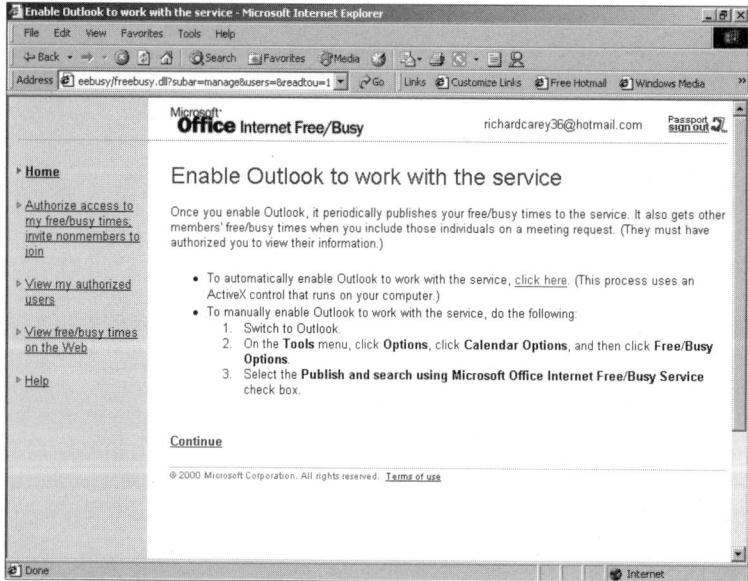

Figure 4-5   *You can share your free/busy information with other Outlook users world-wide by publishing it on the Microsoft Office Internet Free/Busy Web site.*

5. Type the e-mail addresses of people who you authorize to see your free/busy times. You can send e-mails to nonmembers of the service, inviting them to join and telling them they are authorized to see your free/busy times.

6. When you're finished, close Internet Explorer.

7. In Free/Busy Options dialog box of Outlook, choose options for how many months of your free/busy information to publish, how often to publish it, and whether to connect to the Internet and use the free/busy service when creating meeting invitations.

8. Click OK twice. If this is the first time you're using the service, wait while Office installs additional files needed to use the service.

9. From the Calendar Options dialog box, click OK again to return to the main Outlook window.

Note   The Free/Busy service only works for Outlook 2002 or later. Users of Outlook 2000 can install the Team features, and e-mail their calendars to other Outlook 2000 users on a scheduled basis. The calendar will appear as a folder in the folder list; however, it will not show free/busy information when scheduling meetings.

Publish Your Calendar as a Web Page

Another way to share your calendar is to publish it as a Web page. The advantage of this approach is that others can see a professional-looking calendar containing the details of your activities. The disadvantage is that the calendar is just a picture of your schedule: It does not have the same search free/busy times functionality of Outlook, and it cannot be edited. Moreover every time your Outlook calendar changes, you must republish the Web version. However, it's possible to just do this every day or week and have a simple solution for making your calendar public.

To publish your calendar as a Web page, take the following steps.

1. Open your calendar in Outlook.

2. Choose Save As Web Page from the File menu.

3. In the Save As Web Page dialog box, choose a start and end date and whether to save appointment details.

4. Type the URL of the site to which you will publish the data.

The Web calendar allows you to navigate between dates and see details of your appointments, as shown in Figure 4-6 on the next page. You can share your calendar by giving its URL to those you want to have it.

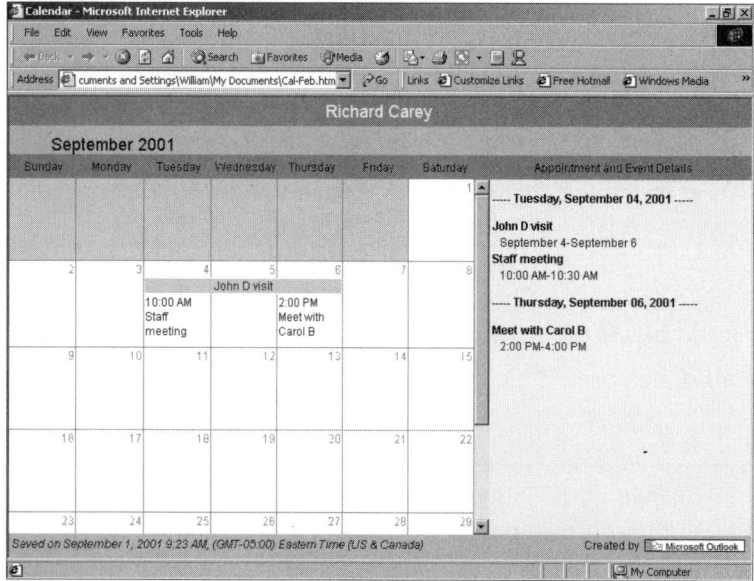

Figure 4-6   *Outlook can create an attractively formatted calendar that you can publish to your Web site.*

Use a Web-Based Calendar

Another alternative is to use Web-based calendars that can interact with Outlook. Such systems are often free, and are offered by major portal sites as well as companies that provide personal and team calendar functionality in return for showing you banner ads. They offer basic calendar features, such as the ability to make and store appointments and display them in a variety of views. Depending on the system, they might also offer the ability to

- Import and/or synchronize data from Outlook, other Personal Information Managers, PDAs, or Pocket PCs
- Maintain task lists or contact lists
- Create recurring appointments
- Maintain group calendars or combine individual calendars
- Schedule meetings with others
- E-mail you calendar reminders or send them to your mobile device

On the other hand, using a Web-based calendar does not provide the other functionality of Outlook (that is, its tight integration with other Office applications). They are often slower to respond, especially because they are maintained on public servers and you have to see advertising to use them. They also may not be as secure as calendars maintained in Outlook.

Two Web-based calendars you might want to investigate if you are interested in this alternative are

- **MSN Calendar** (*http://calendar.msn.com*). This service maintains not only your calendar, but also a task list and contact list. It can import your Outlook calendar and contacts (though not your tasks), and sends you a notification by Pocket PC or wireless phone when you have a reminder. However, it does not automatically synchronize your data with Outlook nor even export to it, and as of this writing, you must have a Hotmail account to use it.

- **MyPalm Portal** (*http://my.palm.com*). This service maintains your address book, calendar, and task list, and also adds other types of items such as birthdays, trips, anniversaries, and reminders. It sends reminders by e-mail to your mobile device but not to your wireless phone. It provides full two-way synchronization with Outlook calendar, tasks, and notes.

Scheduling Meetings with Others

If everyone on your work team uses an Outlook calendar, you can schedule meetings easily. At first, this requirement can be difficult for the more "spontaneous" team members but over the course of a few months, everyone is usually participating. The resulting gains in efficiency more than make up for having to keep individual calendars in a common way.

Tip   When you create a meeting or appointment, make the subject as short as possible so you don't fill up your calendar display with a lot of extraneous words.

When you schedule a meeting, you see blocks of time where each person is free (shown in Figure 4-7, on the next page). Then, you can either pick an appropriate time or allow Outlook to automatically find a time when everyone is free for the specified length of time needed for the meeting.

You can also attach files to a meeting request. This is an effective way to ensure that everyone has the agenda, and that they have copies of all documents that will be discussed at the meeting.

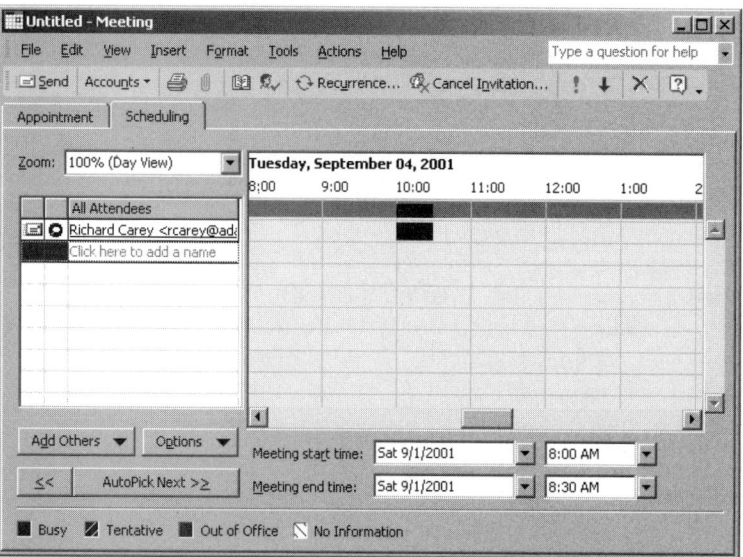

Figure 4-7   *If you know who should come to the meeting and how long it will take, Outlook will find the right time for you.*

Tip   If you are working on a network, an intranet, or an Exchange Server environment, it is better to link to the file on the shared drive or Public Folder than to send a full copy to every person by attaching it to the meeting request. This reduces congestion in the e-mail system. Of course, if some recipients are working on the road and aren't connected to a shared drive, they won't be able to open the link.

To schedule a meeting, follow these steps.

1. Click Calendar in the Folders List pane to access the Calendar.

2. Click the down arrow to the right of the New button on the Standard toolbar, and choose Meeting Request.

3. In the Meeting dialog box, fill out To (click the To button to access your address book to make it easier to send the meeting request to several people at once), Subject, Location, and any other fields for the meeting.

4. To see others' free and busy times, click the Scheduling tab.

See Also   You can also use Outlook to schedule online meetings using Microsoft NetMeeting. This is covered in "Discussing Your Work," on page 234.

Managing Meeting Requests

One of the nice features of Outlook is that not only can you *send* meeting requests, but you can also easily track who has responded and whether they have accepted or declined, and if needed, you can quickly update the meeting time. Here are some hints for effectively managing meeting requests you send.

- Track the responses to your meeting request by opening the meeting request in your Sent Items folder, and then selecting the Tracking tab. You see all invitees' names and whether they have accepted, declined, or not responded to the request.

- Update the meeting request by opening the meeting request in your Sent Items folder, editing the time (or other fields), and then clicking Send Update. An update message is sent to all invitees. Avoid sending a second meeting invitation because this might confuse people.

- You can send meeting invitations to non-Outlook users as well. If their e-mail system is compatible with Outlook, they can accept or decline the meeting and it appears on their calendar if accepted. Otherwise, they see the meeting request as an e-mail and they can respond to it as they do any other e-mail. To set up your Outlook to send meeting requests to other types of e-mail systems, choose Tools, Options, Calendar Options, and check When Sending Meeting Requests Over The Internet, Use iCalendar Format.

Best Practices for Scheduling and Recording Meetings

Here are a few hints for effectively scheduling meetings electronically and ensuring that actionable decisions are made.

- Schedule the resources you need, such as conference rooms and A/V equipment, at the same time you schedule the meeting. (See "Resources" in the Outlook Help system for creating and scheduling resources.)

- Set a reminder the day before your meeting by selecting the Reminder option when you create the e-mail and setting the appropriate lead time from the drop-down box.

- Create an "actionable agenda." Rather than having an agenda item that merely specifies the topic (for example, Adventure Works Proposal), be sure you also specify the desired action (for example, Make Final Decision on Adventure Works Proposal, or Brainstorm Responses to Adventure Works Proposal).

- At the meeting, take minutes with a notebook computer. There's no transcribing, and the minutes are completed, in final format, immediately after the meeting is concluded. Be sure minutes reflect actionable decisions that are made, who is to take the action, what action they are to take, and the timeframe to complete the action. E-mail minutes to participants immediately. This way everyone knows what actions they are to take.

- Consider sending a task request to each person who is assigned a deliverable in the meeting. This way, you can see when each action is completed to ensure the team can move forward.

Seeing the Big Picture

You used your weekly and your daily organization. You created and organized your tasks and appointments. Now, like a general looking over the field of battle, you need to see the big picture before you get down to work. Being able to see an overview of what's in front of you—your tasks, your appointments, and your e-mails—can help keep you focused during the day.

An easy way to do this is with Microsoft Outlook Today, as shown in Figure 4-8. When you click Outlook Today on the Outlook bar, you see your calendar and tasks. You can open individual calendar or task items by clicking them, or complete a task by clicking the check box to the left of it. You can also see how many messages are in your e-mail folders, and click any of them to open the appropriate folder.

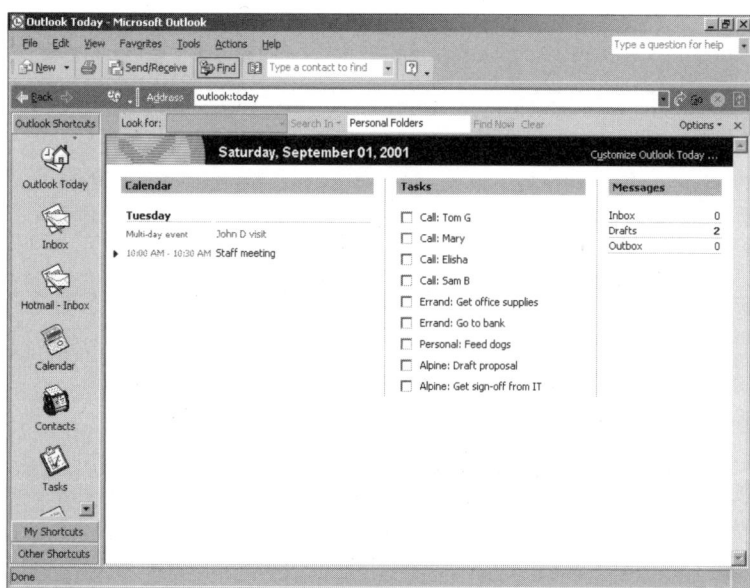

Figure 4-8 *Outlook Today gives you a quick overview of everything you need to do, allowing you to stay focused on your top priorities while keeping your other obligations in mind.*

You can also customize Outlook Today by clicking the Customize Outlook Today link in the Outlook Today pane. You can then make modifications to

- **Startup Options.** Choose to display the Outlook Today pane when starting Outlook for the first time.

- **Messages.** Choose which folders to display message indicators for. This is normally your Inbox, but you can specify others if you use folders to organize your e-mail.

- **Calendar.** Choose the number of days of calendar events to display.

- **Tasks.** Choose whether to show all tasks, or just today's tasks, and how to sort the task list.
- **Styles.** Choose from a variety of predefined styles for displaying Outlook Today information.

Summary

One of the major challenges facing knowledge workers today is needing to do more and more—if not less and less—with at least the same number of hours each day that they used to have. The way to face this challenge successfully is with organization.

As you have seen in this chapter, the proper use of Outlook and basic time-management principles enables you to organize your time so you know what your top priorities are and schedule your time to complete them.

Checklist for Organizing Your Day

The following points will help you develop principles and tools for effectively organizing your day.

[ ] Know what "big rocks" are and how to identify them.

[ ] Organize your week's priorities and tasks in 15 minutes.

[ ] Use Outlook folders to categorize your tasks.

[ ] Organize your tasks by sorting, grouping, categorizing, and filtering them.

[ ] Schedule appointments for yourself and meetings with others using Outlook.

[ ] Share your calendar with others through the Internet or Microsoft Exchange.

[ ] Use a Web-based calendar service.

[ ] Use Outlook Today to see the big picture of your daily activities.

Organizing Your Files

To earn money while going to college, Phil Spencer started working part-time as an Administrative Assistant for Contoso, Ltd.—an 11-person company that resells security services for Webmasters. What Phil is finding is that the electronic filing system is a mess. Everyone has filed everything exactly the way they want to, without any coordination. Some people put their files on their local drives, some on the network. Some put all files in My Documents, some put them in various places throughout drive C. From looking at the filenames, Phil can only identify the purpose of less than 10 percent of the files. In fact, most of the time he can't tell which documents are drafts and which are final copies. As people left the company, their files remained so the result is the filing "systems" of 20 people or more!

Phil is facing a morass of files, some of them valuable, many of them worthless, and people are unable to find the information they need. The CEO knows she has a lot of valuable IP (intellectual property) stored in Contoso's files, but there is no way to capture that data, and new hires have to reinvent the wheel rather than building on past knowledge. Phil realizes that although creating a systematic filing system isn't much fun, it will add more value to the company than virtually anything else he can do. He realizes he has a big job in front of him. Fortunately he also knows that with Microsoft Windows 2000 and Microsoft Office XP, he has the tools to do the job efficiently and well.

Like Contoso, most organizations have a wealth of IP stored—and often hidden—in their electronic filing systems. This chapter teaches you ways you can create a system that will allow you to store and find the information you need, and in so doing, create a basis for knowledge management in your organization. There are two main components to organizing your files—setting up your electronic filing system in the most appropriate way and learning techniques for finding information when you don't know exactly where it is stored.

Setting Up Your Filing System

If you ever worked with a group of people who use a shared filing system, you know you already have a vast storehouse of data in your computer. Unorganized, however, this information is useless. If you can't retrieve it, you can't use it.

The first step in knowledge management is thus organizing the data you already have so it becomes information you can use. There are several tactics that can help you in this regard.

- Save your files in the right place.
- Name your files systematically.
- Organize your electronic folders.

Choosing Where to Save Your Data

If you work in a well-organized corporation, you might have well-thought-out policies and written procedures for how and where to save your data. Many knowledge workers, however, do not. If you're in that situation, first think through where you should save your data. This is true whether you work alone or are part of a team.

Considering Filing Requirements

When setting up a filing system, you might want to start by asking a few questions to determine your requirements.

- Are there frequent situations where individuals work on deliverables that require a number of draft and supporting documents?
- Do teams have similar requirements?
- Do people need to access finished documents from remote locations?
- Do people working from remote locations generally have high-speed Internet connections?
- Does everyone have Office XP and Windows 2000? If not, what's the lowest common denominator?
- Are backups regularly done to all network drives? Are these tested regularly?
- How are backups handled for local drives?

There are several places you can save your work including on removable media, your local hard disk, a network drive, a Web folder or FTP site on the Internet or your corporate intranet, or a SharePoint server. Each has advantages, and each is appropriate in specific circumstances.

See Also SharePoint sites are Web sites that are optimized for collaboration and file sharing. For more information on SharePoint, see "Collaborating Using Microsoft SharePoint" on page 319.

Removable Media

Removable media include floppy disks, Zip disks, and CD-ROMs. Their strong points are security and transportability. If you have sensitive information, consider saving it on removable media so you can determine who sees it. You might also find yourself using removable media if you work on multiple computers that are not connected to each other, and Web-based filing isn't an option because of connectivity.

Although removable media are excellent in certain cases, there are critical problems with using them for your primary data storage.

- All disks fail eventually. Files stored on your hard disk can be easily backed up. Files on removable media are very seldom backed up.

- You gain the tremendous advantage of being able to create a knowledge base when you store your files on a local or network drive.

- If files are on your hard disk, you can index your files to find lost files quickly—even if you know only a few words that are in your document and you forgot what you named it or where you put it.

- You can find old files faster because you don't have to rummage around looking for disks in drawers!

Local Drive

There are several advantages to storing data on your local drive. Some people consider it more secure than storing it on the server because you can set additional passwords to access your computer or even lock your office. Your data is always available when you're at your computer, even if you lose connectivity to the network. There are fewer external constraints on how much data you can store and where you can store it.

On the other hand, in most organizations, data stored on local drives is the users' responsibility to back up and few users actually do regular backups. In addition, although using the local drive is convenient from an individual's perspective, it makes the files unavailable to the rest of the team. It's like files you keep locked up in filing cabinets in your office, rather than putting them in the office filing system.

One practice you might consider is using your local drive for working documents that only you need to edit, and then storing completed deliverables in a group filing system on the network.

Preventing Disaster

I know, I know, you've heard it a million times. Be sure to back up your data. But let me ask you a question—is your data in fact backed up? If you are backing up your data, how recently was it done? Do you have an off-site backup in case of fire or other problems? If your files are on a network or Web storage system provided by an Internet service provider (ISP), when was the last time you tested the system by requesting that a deleted file be restored?

Backing up your data doesn't need to be difficult. Make a recurring task in Outlook to remind you to do an incremental backup every week and a full backup each quarter. You don't need to back up your entire hard disk—it's usually sufficient to back up your My Documents folder and your Outlook folder. If you're on a network at work, remember that although the files saved on the network might be backed up by the system administrator, files on your local drives usually aren't. You might be able to back up your files on another network drive—especially if you have a network at home—but there can be procedural limitations on network disk space and access rights in office environments. Alternatively, consider a high-capacity removable device. The Windows backup utility can back up to any of these destinations easily, and its wizard walks you through the process step by step. To access it, click Start, point to Programs, Accessories, and System Tools, and then select Backup.

Network Drive

If you use a network drive, your documents are available to your entire work team when they are connected to the network. A common practice is to have two areas—a group work area and a private work area. These can be mapped to different drive letters. The group area usually contains a folder structure that parallels the group's projects or teams, while the private area can be user defined.

The advantage of storing information on a network drive is that your documents are usually backed up for you, and you have the possibility of setting up a common filing system to enable anyone in the work group to find all relevant files. Unfortunately, IT policies might create limitations on disk space or what types of files you can save on network drives.

In general, as a technology-enabled work team matures, the network drive becomes the storage medium of choice unless many of its members are working remotely. Network drives allow standardized filing, better visibility of others' work products, and more security for corporate data.

Web Folder

Another choice you can make is to save your data to Web folders. These might be located on your intranet or on an FTP site on the Internet. With newer versions of Microsoft Office, saving files to Web folders is almost as easy as saving them to a local or network drive (see Figure 5-1) and you can provide access to remote workers, partners, key clients, or the public. Web folders are also offering new functionality. For instance, folders in

SharePoint Web sites can contain default templates so new documents created in these folders are all based on the same, Web-based template.

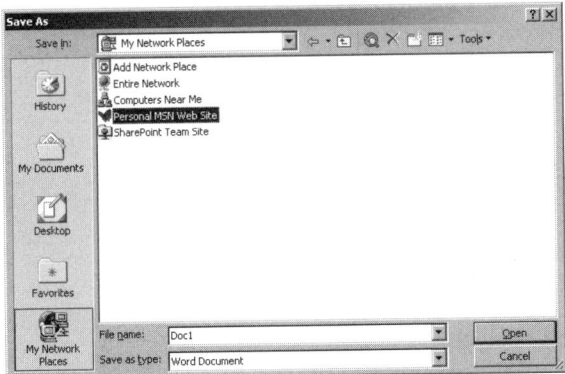

Figure 5-1   *Web folders appear just like any other folder in familiar Office file management dialog boxes.*

Microsoft SharePoint Services allow you to set up sites for your work teams that contain basic tools for online collaboration. In addition to shared files, you can create discussion forums, task lists, announcements, event notices, and more and be notified by e-mail when there are any changes.

For more information about SharePoint Services, see "Collaborating Using Microsoft SharePoint" on page 319.

The disadvantage of using Web folders for data storage is that although they make files more available to remote workers, they make them correspondingly unavailable if you're not connected to the Web. In addition, because access speeds might vary among team members and locations, you might experience distinctly slower times in saving and opening your documents.

This is an area where you will probably see significant change over the next two years. As of this writing, Web folders are used most extensively to publish finished documents, whether for the public (for example, product sheets) or for your team (for example, completed proposals). As broadband access becomes more common and corporations more used to Web-based filing, Web folders as primary storage media will most likely become more common.

Saving Files to Web Folders

The new features of Office 2000 and Office XP are another factor making Web folders attractive alternatives to more common, mapped network drives. It is now easy to do common file management tasks such as saving and opening files from Office, dragging and dropping files from one location to another, and viewing file lists on Web-based sites—if all users have Office 2000 or later. For organizations in which users have earlier versions, they will continue to use network drives for group file storage for some time.

For most people whose computers are connected to a network, saving data on the network is as simple as saving it to a local drive. The network drives you have access to are usually assigned drive letters (that is, mapped) by the administrator, and you can save data to the network just as you do to any local drive. It might be a good idea, however, to contact your network administrator to see how much disk space you have, and what guidelines there are for using the network drive. Also contact your administrator if there are no mapped drives. You might need to follow special procedures (such as typing UNC addresses like \\server\driveletter) to access the storage media.

If you want to save your documents to a Web folder—on the Internet, your intranet, or a SharePoint server—you can add a shortcut to that location so accessing the Web location is as simple as accessing drive C. To do so, take the following steps.

1. Ensure that you know the URL or address to the Web site you will be accessing, and that you have the appropriate UserID and password.

2. Access the Add Network Place Wizard.

   - From the New Document, New Worksheet, or New Presentation task pane, click Add Network Place.

   - From an Open or Save dialog box in Office, click My Network Places in the My Places bar and then choose Add Network Place.

3. Follow the steps of the wizard shown in Figure 5-2 to create a shortcut to an existing network place, typing the location as a fully qualified domain name (that is, including *http://*) when requested, along with a name for the shortcut, your UserID, and password. Your new shortcut appears on the list of My Network Places in Open and Save dialog boxes, and you can save documents to the Web folder as you do to your local drive.

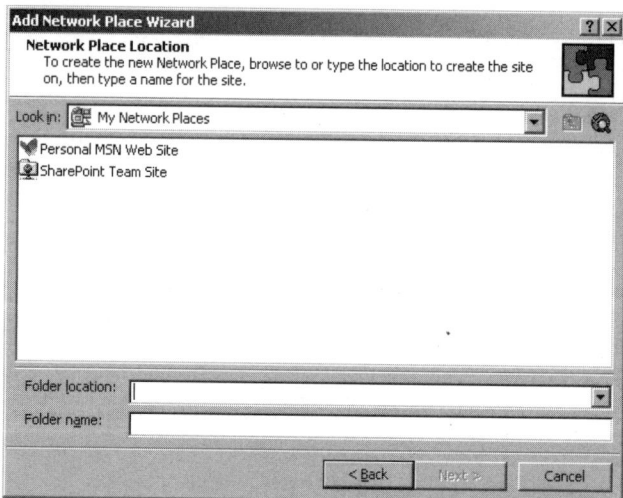

Figure 5-2   *Microsoft Office provides a wizard so you can create a shortcut to your Web folder in My Network Places.*

You can use a similar procedure for creating a shortcut to an FTP site by taking the following steps.

1. Note the address of your FTP site, as well as your UserID and password.

2. From an Office Open or Save dialog box, click the Look In drop-down list and choose Add/Modify FTP Locations.

3. In the Add/Modify FTP Locations dialog box shown in Figure 5-3, type a descriptive name for your FTP site, specify your UserID and password, and click Add. Click OK to return to the Open or Save dialog box.

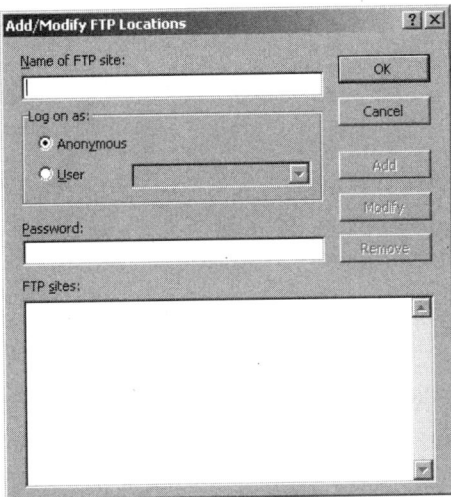

Figure 5-3   *If your server only supports FTP for uploading files, you can still create a shortcut to it with Microsoft Office.*

Your folders and filenames create a classification system by which you—and anyone else in your office—should be able to find information quickly and consistently. In fact, one rule is that you should be able to locate any file in your filing system within 30 seconds; anyone else in your work team should be able to locate any of your files in one minute.

Creating a hierarchy for your folders and naming your files work together. In a well-organized electronic filing system, the way you name your files might depend on how you organize your folders. To create a well-managed filing system, start by organizing your folders and then move to the files within them.

Classify Your Folders

Your folders are the skeleton of your file management system. They create a hierarchy that knowledge management experts refer to as an *ontology* for information that it is crucial for you to maintain.

In knowledge management, the word ontology means a hierarchical categorization, such as a taxonomy, that defines how you think about the "world" of your information. It recognizes that the way you classify your knowledge governs how you think about it, and to some extent, even what exists in your "universe" of knowledge. For instance, naming a folder "learning resources" rather than "training resources" has implications for how you think about the knowledge/skill acquisition process, as the terms "learning" and "training" have quite different meanings to experts in this field.

How you set up the hierarchy of your filing system is a serious matter. Here are some principles that I've used over the years in training thousands of people in personal productivity techniques with their PCs. They aren't cast in stone, but can serve as a starting point for thinking through some of the important issues you need to consider when deciding how to organize your folders.

- **Balance the number of folders and the number of files in them.**   As a rule, it's a lot easier to visually locate files when there are fewer than 50 files in a folder. When your folder has more than 100 files, think about archiving some files or creating a couple of subfolders. On the other hand, if you have 50 folders that each have 5 documents in them consider using fewer folders and organizing your system by the file-names you use, rather than folders you put files into.

- **Stick with two or three levels of subfolders.**   If you have more than this, navigating through the folder structure might start to become inefficient.

- **Coordinate your electronic filing system with your work flow.**   If all your work is client-related, the top-level folders might be client names. If several teams share a network drive, the top-level folders might be team names.

If you use account numbers rather than client names to identify clients, as is sometimes done in law offices, consider naming your folder with the account number and then the client name so people who aren't intimately familiar with all the account numbers will still have a fighting chance of finding the right folder.

- **Remember your paper filing system.**   It isn't the worst idea in the world to have the same system for your electronic and paper filing systems. If you have a well-organized paper filing system, consider using it as a model for your electronic one. If you don't, you might consider revamping them both at once.

- **Think about the future—of your document.**   Consider grouping documents by type, depending on their useful lifespan. For instance, some companies keep proposals indefinitely because they can mine them for material for future proposals. Memos and correspondence are purged after a year. If a separate directory is used for memos and correspondence, it makes purging them easier because these documents are not mixed up with others like proposals that should be retained longer.

- **Strive for consistency.**   Depending on the type of documents you keep, you might want to break the rule against having too many empty folders for the sake of consistency. For instance, if you determine that all client files fall into one of four categories—external correspondence, internal memos, working papers, and background readings—consider having a procedure whereby whenever a new client is retained, you create a client folder and four subfolders: memos, letters, documents, and readings. Each of these folders is a placeholder—some of which might never be used.

However, the consistency of the system permits others to file documents and find them quickly.

- **Deal with drafts.** Most knowledge workers have lots of draft documents lying around, and a corollary says that most people don't have a good system for dealing with these drafts. You should have such a system. In addition to naming the files appropriately, consider where they will be stored. One way to do this is to create a subfolder called Archive where drafts of the finalized document can be placed. Another way is to compress the drafts into an archive file with WinZip (*http:// www.winzip.com*) or a similar program, and keep the archive Zip file in the same folder as the final copy.

One of the handy features of electronic filing systems is how easily you can reorganize them. Here's a simple process you can use.

1. Use Microsoft Word to outline the folder taxonomy. Switch to Outline view, and use Heading 1, 2, and 3 for the levels of your folders. Remember that in Outline view, you can select families (for instance, all the folder names under a second level folder formatted in the Heading 2 style), and use the Promote, Demote, Move Up, and Move Down buttons to reorganize them. This will help you see it as a whole. (See Figure 5-4 for an example.)

See Also   For more information about the Outlining feature in Word, see "Organizing Your Thoughts" on page 272.

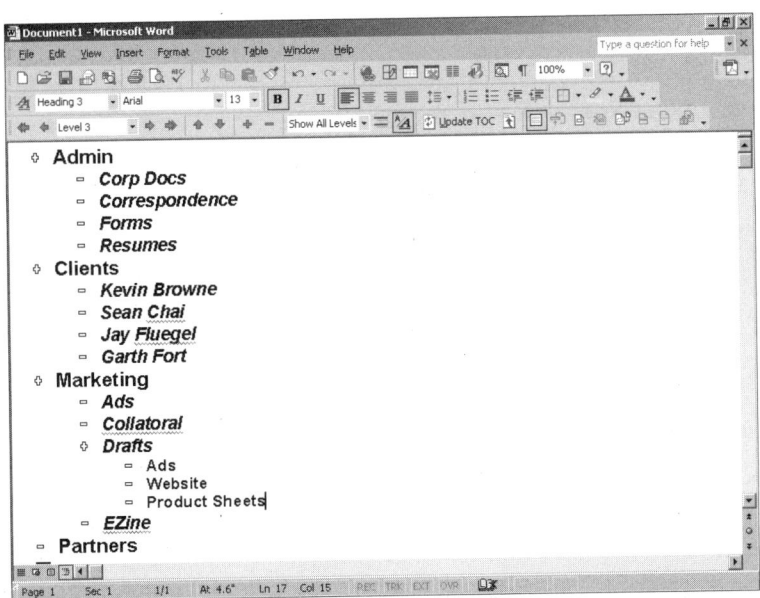

Figure 5-4 *It can be helpful to create an outline of your new electronic filing system using Word's Outline feature so you can see the whole system before you reorganize your file system.*

2. Determine which existing folders remain unchanged, which need to be renamed, which need to be moved, and what new folders are needed.

3. Use Windows Explorer to reorganize your folders.

   - Add new folders by highlighting the parent folder and choosing File, New, Folder.

   - Rename folders by right-clicking them and choosing Rename.

   - Move folders by dragging them to their new positions. Remember you can select contiguous folders by clicking the first one and then shift-clicking the last, and you can select noncontiguous folders by clicking the first one and then control-clicking additional ones.

   - Use these same techniques to drag groups of files into the new folders in which they belong. Remember you can sort files by name or date by clicking the appropriate column heading, which might help you select related ones.

   - If file names are so cryptic that you need to open them to determine which folder they belong in, be sure when you are moving them to rename them according to standardized rules as discussed next.

Some programs like Microsoft Outlook save their data in a special folder hidden several layers deep in your filing system. Others like Quicken save it by default in a subfolder of its program files. Consider relocating the location where these programs save data to a sub-folder of the My Documents folder. This ensures that all your data is in one place, and makes it easier to be certain that backing up My Documents backs up all your data.

Name Files Systematically

In addition to organizing your folders, consider creating a systematic way of naming your files if you are sharing your file storage with other people. It's a good idea even if you work alone because it helps keep you organized as your system grows to hundreds or thousands of files. Here are a few tips to consider when thinking about file-naming conventions.

- **Coordinate your filenames with your folder structure.**   Your filenames should build on your folder names, not repeat them. If you have client folders, you probably do not need the client name in the filename. If the file is in a folder called "memos," it's important to describe whom the memo is to but not important to put the word "memo" in the name.

- **Facilitate file retrieval.**   It's a good idea to put information in the filename that will enable someone to recognize what the file is about by looking at the name in an Open dialog box. While some filing systems use case IDs and file numbers, the file name 2001AA3 13993.doc doesn't tell anyone who's not working with that document on a day-to-day basis anything. Neither do the names "Thoughts On Today's Meeting.doc" or "New Ideas.doc."

- **Think of how you want your files to be grouped and alphabetized.**   For instance, in a correspondence folder, you might want to see files grouped by full name of recipient and then by date. In that case, you can use a name such as "Denise Smith 021030 cvr ltr for proposal.doc" This way, all of Denise Smith's correspondence is grouped together, sorted by date, with a description at the end.

  When putting dates in a filename, put the year, then the month, then the date, to ensure that the files sort correctly. Thus, 021030 reflects a file saved on October 30, 2002.

Unfortunately, there aren't any quick ways to rename hundreds of existing files. In working with your legacy data, start by moving files into the new folder system as described previously. You can usually identify the parts of your filing system that people are likely to need to refer to (such as old contracts, proposals, or manuals), and ignore others (such as memos and correspondence folders). Then you can concentrate on updating the names of legacy files in the most important parts of your filing system.

Avoiding Information Overload

If you don't purge files that are no longer useful, you eventually wind up with a completely unusable filing system. The more outdated files that are in the system, the harder it is to find current information. Two of the most common types of outdated files are ones that are no longer useful because they are so old, and working papers such as drafts that have been superseded by final versions. There are two habits you can adopt to keep your electronic filing system neat and tidy.

- **Create folders with archiving in mind.**   For instance, if you know you want to keep old proposals for three years, correspondence for six months, and work products forever, don't put them in the same folder. If the only thing that's in your correspondence folder is correspondence, you can easily purge the system every six months knowing that all files in that folder can go.

- **Create working folders for specific projects.**   Keep all drafts, correspondence, and copies of files containing supporting data in the working folder. Then at the termination of the project, move the final work product to the appropriate folder for permanent storage and purge the working folder.

When you purge outdated files, you do not have to delete them. You can archive them instead. This is often a much better practice, because when you archive the files, they are still available for future data mining or as a historical record of how a final document was developed.

Given the low price of disk storage, archiving files can be as simple as moving them to a different hard drive on your network—ensuring that you keep the same folder structure on that drive so you can still find files quickly when you need to. If you are archiving files at home or on a laptop where disk space is more limited, consider using a compression program such as WinZip that can reduce the size of your files by 10 percent to 80 percent. You can zip an entire folder at a time, being sure to name it with the original folder name for organizing purposes. You can even store these compressed files on a removable storage medium such as a Zip disk, high-capacity floppy disk, or CD-ROM. The only problem is that you can't use simple search procedures to mine these files for information later—you need to reinsert the media to search through it.

Putting It All Together

If you're working in an organization or a work team, systematizing folder and file naming is a group process. Someone needs to manage the process as they do any other procedural change. Here's what you can do to facilitate the process.

1. Start by getting a clear charter from management for the task, and ensure that the manager communicates this to the work group along with the reason for it. One important point that employees need to recognize is that documents produced by the organization are the organization's intellectual property, not just an individual's work, and it's crucial that the organization be able to inventory and track its property.

2. Obtain input from interested parties as you develop your system—it's easier to negotiate up front than deal with noncompliance later.

3. Write down your system for file naming and make a job aid out of it. It doesn't have to be long—just one side of a sheet of paper or a laminated 5 x 8 card. It should identify file-naming guidelines for different types of files, which files should be saved in which folders, and how often files in different folders are to be archived or deleted.

4. Obtain agreement that for the first few weeks of using the new system, someone will help the team by looking over the files that are saved and moving and renaming them as needed.

5. Ensure that someone is charged with taking a few minutes with new hires to explain the system to them.

6. Get feedback on how the system is working for people, and modify it as needed.

Accessing Your Information

Psychologists tell us that there's much more information in our brain than we usually recognize—many memory problems are retrieval problems, not storage problems. It's essential that you're able to retrieve any information you store in your company's filing system. You need to avoid retrieval problems by being able to find any information that you've stored in the system. Two tools for retrieving information effectively are metadata and the powerful new search feature of Office XP.

Leveraging Metadata

Metadata is literally data about data, and it can be the best friend of those folks whose data is overwhelming them. You can find examples of metadata everywhere, from the cards in a card catalog to the index in a book. Web pages have metadata tags like "keywords" that enable search engine spiders to easily classify the page. In recent years, metadata has become a key concept in the field of knowledge management because it can be such a powerful tool to organize information.

In Office applications, metadata is kept in file properties which provide a rich source of information that enables you to create a detailed document management system. Office provides several tools to help you leverage file properties, including the ability to

- Prompt you for document properties when you save Word documents
- Search for documents with specific properties
- List documents with their properties, and sort by those properties
- Create custom properties for your particular industry

Understand Document Properties

Windows maintains basic information about files you save such as the filename, date saved, and size. Office XP provides additional details about its files. Some of the information is maintained automatically, and some is available for your use. To see the properties of a document, choose Properties from the File menu. You see a Properties dialog box with five tabs, showing you the types of properties Office can save for each file. (See Table 5-1.)

Table 5-1   Document Properties Tabs

Type	Description
General	Provides basic information maintained by Windows: type, location, size, MS-DOS name, created, modified, accessed, and attributes.
Summary	Provides user-definable basic information for a document management system such as title, subject, author, category, and keywords.
Statistics	Provides basic information about the file such as number of words or slides in the document, number of revisions, and total editing time.
Contents	The structure of the file—the Outline for Word documents, slide titles for Microsoft PowerPoint slideshows, and worksheet titles for Microsoft Excel workbooks.
Custom	Built-in fields you can use such as checked by, client, and date completed, along with the ability to enter your own fields. Fields can be text, number, date, or yes/no.

As you start to use document properties regularly, here are a few valuable tips.

- Certain document properties such as the document title are created when the file is first saved. For instance, Author and Company are filled in automatically based on information in the User Information tab of the Options dialog box (Tools, Options). In Word and PowerPoint, the title field is saved based on the first line of the Word document or title of the PowerPoint presentation when the file was first saved, and is not automatically updated thereafter.

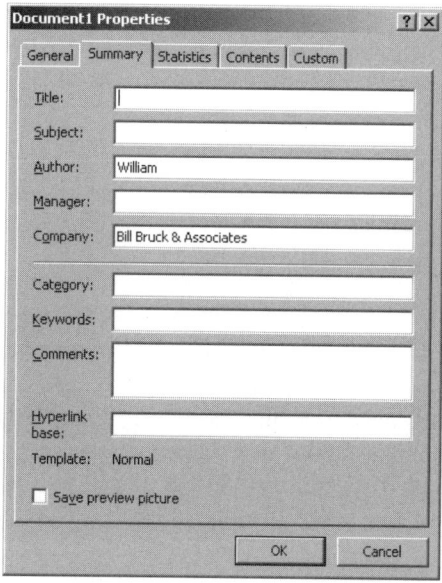

- To display the outline of a Word document in the Contents tab, select the Save Preview Picture in the summary tab of the Properties dialog box. This causes the document headings to appear in the Contents tab.

- To see the properties of a file, use the Properties view of an Open or Save dialog box in Microsoft Office.

- To remove a document's personal properties such as author when the document is saved, choose Tools, Options, Security, and check the privacy options.

Prompt for Information

If you want to use the features provided by document properties, you probably don't want to rely on your memory to set the properties each time you create a document. Instead, you can set the Prompt for Document Properties option. When you save a document for the first time, you will see the Document Properties dialog box and you can fill out the properties you need. To specify this default setting, choose Options from the Tools menu. In Word and PowerPoint, it is on the Save tab; in Excel it is on the General tab.

Create Custom Properties

In many offices, it can be extremely helpful to use document properties other than those available by default. Say that your company resells residential alarm services. Within each of your proposals, it might be helpful to note whether they're a previous customer, who provides their present alarm system (if any), which security analyst did the site visit, and the date of that visit.

The flexibility of custom properties enables you to track all this information. Properties can save text, number, date, or yes/no information. Even better, it can be automatically populated from information that's already in your document—bookmarked text in Word for example. Then you can search for or list documents with these properties. To create a custom property, do the following.

1. Open the file in Word, Excel, or PowerPoint.

2. Choose Properties from the File menu to display the Properties dialog box, and then select the Custom tab.

3. Choose a default property from the list box, or type your name for the custom property in the Name box.

4. Select text, number, date, or yes/no in the Type drop-down box.

5. Type the value for your property in the Value box.

6. Click Add. In the Properties box, as shown in Figure 5-5, click OK to return to your file.

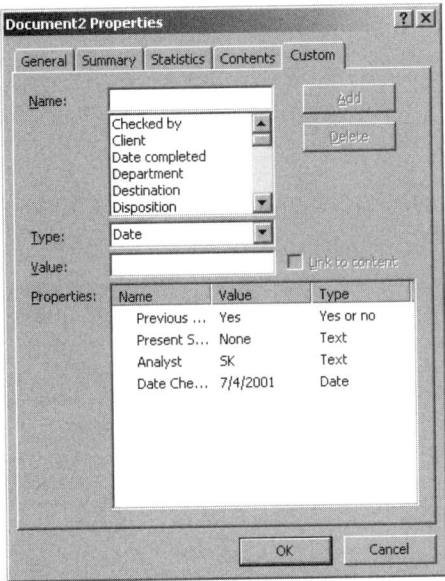

Figure 5-5 *Custom properties—like the ones shown here for proposals—enable you to create a document management system that's tailored to your needs.*

If you want to automatically populate your custom property with information that's in your document, do the following.

1. Depending on the application you are creating a custom property in, do the following.

    - In Word, select the text and then choose Insert, Bookmark. Give the bookmark a name (possibly the same name as the property) and choose Add.

    - In Excel, click the desired cell and type the name of the cell in the Name Box at the left of the Formula Bar.

    - In PowerPoint, select the content you want to link the custom property to.

2. Follow the procedure for creating a custom property, but do not type anything in the Value box.

3. Select the Link To Content check box.

4. Choose the appropriate bookmark (Word), named cell (Excel), or link (PowerPoint) from the Source drop-down box.

5. Click Add. In the Properties box, click OK to return to your file.

Select Files with Specific Metadata

Wouldn't it be nice to be able to list all the documents by a certain author, or sort them by the date created, or group them by category? Office XP allows you to see your files in any of these ways. The secret is using Outlook to view your files because you can't do all these things using other Office applications or Windows Explorer. Set up Outlook to use metadata as follows.

1. In Outlook, click Other Shortcuts in the Outlook Bar and then click My Documents. You see a folder list pane and a pane showing all the documents in the selected folder. Fields that are not normally visible in a detail view of the file list, such as Author and Keywords, are displayed.

2. To display additional fields, right-click a column heading and choose Field Chooser.

3. In the Field Chooser dialog box, click the down arrow to the right of Frequently Used Fields and select All File Fields. You see all the fields that are not currently displayed such as Application, Category, and Characters.

4. Drag the fields you want to display to the column header of the file list pane. You now see the contents of that field for the displayed files. Close the Field Chooser dialog box.

5. To sort by a field, click the field name in the column headings. To sort in descending order, click it a second time.

6. To group by a field, right-click the name of the field in the column headings and choose Group By This Field. You see a Group By box above the column headers, and the files are grouped by the desired field as shown in Figure 5-6.

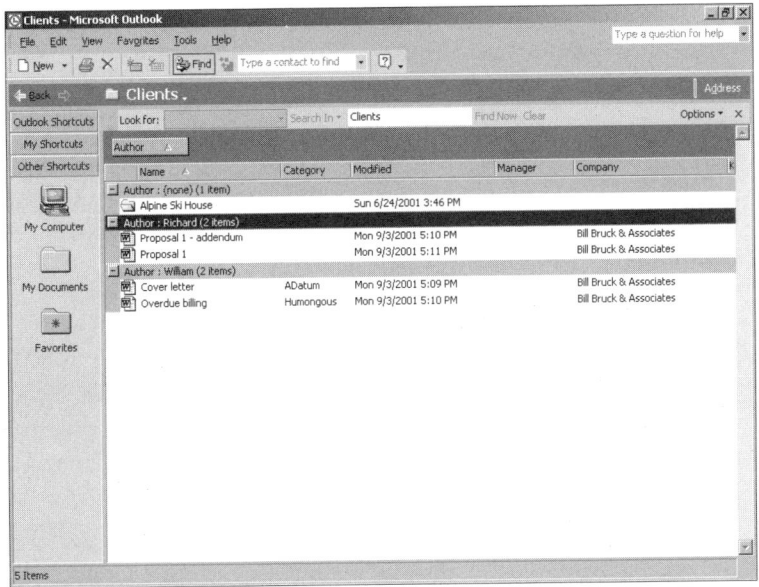

Figure 5-6   *Using Outlook, you can group or sort files by their properties, enabling you to quickly see all files of a particular type. In this example, the documents are grouped by author name.*

7. To remove the grouping, drag the field from the Group By box back to the column header row. To close the Group By box, right-click in the column header row and choose Group By Box.

Viewing Metadata in Windows Explorer

In Windows 2000, you can select additional fields to view and sort by those fields when you are using Windows Explorer, but you cannot group by fields. In addition, you cannot select all the fields available through Outlook. To view additional fields in Windows Explorer, do the following.

1. Open Windows Explorer and click View, Details, if the detail view is not already displayed.

2. Right-click a column header and choose a field from the drop-down list.

3. If the desired field is not on the drop-down list, click More, select the desired fields in the Column Settings dialog box, and click OK.

4. Sort by any displayed property by clicking its name in the column heading. Sort in descending order by clicking its name a second time.

Searching Your Data

Office XP has added a new Search feature that supplements the Find feature found in previous versions of Office, and is even more powerful than the Windows Find feature. When you use metadata that provides specific information about each document and the search function, you can create a true knowledge base from your file storage system.

While a *database* contains data that is systematically organized in fields and records, a *knowledge base* is a repository of information that might not be structured but can be searched. FAQ files and information-sharing systems such as askme.com (*http://www.askme.com*) are examples of knowledge bases which are becoming an increasingly popular way of storing information among knowledge workers in fields as diverse as information technology and the insurance industry.

With the Office XP Search feature, you can do the following.

- Search through My Documents, Outlook, your Web Folders, selected folders in any of these locations, or all locations. (For more information about, see "Choosing Where to Save Your Data" on page 82.)

- Restrict your search to Web pages, specific types of Office files, or specific types of Outlook items.

- Search for text that occurs anywhere in the document or its properties.

- Specify whether to search everywhere (document and properties) or just in a specific property of the document.

- Specify conditions for the type of property chosen. For instance, for numeric properties like size, you can specify that the size should be equal to, not equal to, greater than, lesser than, at least, or at most the value you set.

- Specify multiple search conditions using AND and OR.

- Search Outlook folders using natural language queries; for example, show me all the items in my Inbox from Denise Smith.

- Enable Fast Searching so your searches return results in a matter of seconds. (For more information about Fast Searching, see "Enhance Your Performance with Fast Searching" on page 100.)

Create a Search

You can create a search from within any Office application, and it will look for text in documents of any type you specify, limiting it to any locations you choose. The default basic search looks for *text* within files in specific areas you choose, while an advanced search also allows you to look through *file properties*. To create a search, do the following.

1. In Word, Excel, or PowerPoint, choose File, Search.

2. In the Basic Search task pane shown in Figure 5-7, type the text in the Search text box, specify where to search (My Computer, My Network Places, Outlook) in the

Search in box, and the type of files to search (Word documents, e-mail messages, Excel) in the Results should be box.

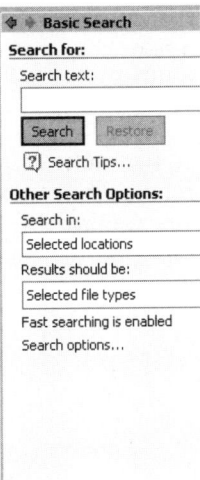

Figure 5-7   *The Basic Search pane allows you to search through the entire text of documents in any location you specify.*

3. Click Search. Your results appear in the Search Results task pane, which replaces the Basic Search task pane. You can click Stop at any time to halt the search, or Modify when the search is done to return to the Basic Search task pane.

4. Alternatively, to access additional search features, click Advanced Search. In the Advanced Search pane, set options as follows.

   - To search only in a specific document property, pick the document property from the Property drop-down list or type the name for a custom property.

   - Set conditions depending on the type of field chosen. For example, for text fields the only condition that is available is Includes. When a numeric field is selected, conditions include equals, not equal to, less than, more than, at least, and at most. Date and yes/no fields display options appropriate to the data types.

   - Type the value to search for in the Value box.

   - You can build more complex queries by entering a value, clicking the Add button, entering a second search value, clicking the And radio button or the Or radio button, and then clicking Add. You can continue to string together complex queries in this fashion.

   - Type values in the Search in and Results should be boxes as you do for a basic search.

5. Click Search.

Enhance Your Performance with Fast Searching

Fast Searching is a new feature in Office XP, replacing the Find Fast feature that was available in previous versions of Office. The advantage of Fast Searching is that it makes the search function more usable by returning results more quickly. On large searches, it can reduce the search time by 95 percent or more. You can also set Fast Searching to index your disk at specific intervals or only when your computer is not in use.

When you first use Fast Searching, Office builds an *index file*. This is a file that contains all the keywords of all the documents you have identified to be fast searched. The index file is approximately 15 percent to 30 percent of the size of the documents you are indexing, and can take an hour or more to create initially. To set Fast Search options, do the following.

The disadvantage of Fast Search is that it might slow your computer operations if you have 64 MB RAM or less or a slow CPU (266 MHz or less), and might leave you short of disk space if you have a small disk. However, this is not a concern for most of today's business computers.

1. From the Basic Search task pane, choose Search Options.

2. In the Indexing Service Settings dialog box, select Yes, Enable Indexing Service to enable the Fast Search feature.

3. Click OK to return to the Basic Search task pane.

Summary

Your electronic filing system can be one of your corporation's biggest knowledge assets. Created and maintained correctly, it allows people to access the relevant documents created by others within seconds and leverage their work in preparing new deliverables.

After reading this chapter, you should have a good sense of how to create a filing system that allows you to keep your data organized and accessible to yourself and to others. You should also know how to effectively use metadata to classify and further organize your documents, and quickly find any document in your system that contains specific text or metadata.

All it requires is planning using some basic principles and a few new skills.

Checklist for Organizing Electronic Files

The following skills will help you create and maintain an organized electronic filing system, and access the data it contains.

[ ] Ascertain the filing requirements of the group you're creating the system for.

[ ] Identify the appropriate storage media for your files.

[ ] Create a folder system that categorizes your data effectively.

[ ] Use file-naming conventions that allow anyone to identify files at a glance.

[ ] Restructure your existing folders and filenames as needed.

[ ] Create custom properties to save important metadata.

[ ] Set Office applications to request that the user fill out properties when files are saved.

[ ] List, sort, and group files by property in Outlook.

[ ] Use the File Search feature to find files that contain text or properties you specify.

[ ] Use the Fast Search feature to speed up the display of search results.

Organizing Your Data

Kaarin Dolliver is a Human Resource specialist at Litware, Inc.—a nationwide outplacement firm that specializes in providing services to corporations who are downsizing. Litware has offices in 30 major metropolitan areas that are minimally staffed with three to ten employees each. When Litware gets a contract, it creates a temporary Outplacement Center in the client's offices in the appropriate city. The center is headed by a Litware specialist, and staffed using part-time contractors.

Each Litware office maintains its own list of contractors. Some lists are in Microsoft Excel, some in Macintosh databases, and some on paper rolodexes. They contain different information about the contractors, and there is no ability to coordinate efforts in employing these contractors. Kaarin has been asked to create a centralized database of contractors who can be accessed through the Web from any Litware office. Contractors must be able to update information about their schedule, expertise, and travel availability, and Litware managers must be able to easily see a list of top candidates to staff new Outplacement Centers as they are needed.

The type of project Kaarin has been asked to undertake contains several challenges that anyone trying to organize corporate data faces.

- Before beginning, Kaarin must get clarity about the specific criteria the local managers use to select contractors. In other words, she must understand the required outputs of the database very specifically.

- She must understand what data is needed to produce the desired results. She needs to know exactly what information must be maintained about each contractor, who has that information, and how and when it will be updated.

- She must then determine how the data is interrelated, decide how complex her database solution must be, choose the appropriate tool, and establish whether she's the right person to create it or whether the project should be outsourced.

- Finally, she needs to ensure that the database is created and existing data is converted from the various forms it's currently in.

This chapter teaches you how to do these same tasks when you're faced with organizing your data into a database. In this chapter, you learn how to

- Perform a simple requirements analysis

- Identify the appropriate tool for your database

- Create a database using Excel or Microsoft Access

- Convert data from other applications

See Also   This chapter focuses on *organizing* your data. For more information about how to analyze data, see Chapter 9, "Creating Knowledge Using Numbers."

Planning Your Database

The worst thing you can do when asked to create a database is to immediately go into Excel or Access, and start defining fields and entering data. For most business applications, this path almost always leads to disaster. Before you start creating anything, you need to have a clear understanding of the functional requirements for the database—what questions the database is supposed to answer. Then you have to identify the information you need to maintain to answer those questions. This determines the most appropriate tool to meet those requirements. Only then should you start to create the database solution.

Analyzing Your Requirements

A requirements analysis is a process that helps you understand how the database should function from the customer's perspective, and allows you to turn those requirements into a set of specifications for the database developer. Your requirements analysis answers the questions "What?" and "Who?" It does not address the question "How?" meaning how the database solution will be built to address these objectives. That comes next.

Tip Think of the person you are constructing the database for as your customer, whether that person is a paying client, an internal customer, or you yourself. This approach can help you save time and money by solving problems before they happen. For example, if you're told you need to store clothing sizes (such as S, M, L, and XL) it might be simpler to "hard code" these values into the database. From the customers' point of view, however, they probably don't want to have to come to you again if another size is added so you have to build this functionality in—even if they forgot to request it.

Ask the following questions when creating and performing your requirements analysis.

- What are the functional requirements for your database?
- Who are the stakeholders involved?
- How is the data presently stored?
- What type of structure (tables, fields, or relationships) is required to implement the database?
- Which tool (Excel, Access, or another) should be used to build the database?
- Should it be built in-house or outsourced to experts?

Assess Functional Requirements

Many times customers come to you with a proposed solution, rather than a problem statement. They might ask you to build a database with certain specifications. This is good information and you should note it, but you need to ensure that initial conversations focus on the business problem to be solved. Questions you must answer include the following.

- What's the general context of this problem?
- What business benefit will result from solving it?
- What specific questions must the database be able to answer?
- What specific information do they need to answer their questions?
- What format do they want to see answers in: Summary tables? Charts? Lists of people who meet certain criteria?

You know you're finished when you have enough information to write a document that has these questions as headings, and can provide a clear answer to each. Be especially detailed in your answers to the last three questions: the questions the database must answer, the specific information needed, and how the customer wants to see the results.

Identify the Players Involved

Customers might be clear on what they want the database to do, but often haven't completely thought through who will do it. Another part of creating a specification for your database is determining the players involved. Make sure you know the answers to these types of questions.

- Who will be entering and editing data? Is it one person or many? Might several people be entering data simultaneously from different locations? Are data entry people familiar with the data, or will validation rules be required to prevent the entering of information in different ways?

- Who will be accessing the data? Do all the people who will be accessing the data know how to construct queries, or do they need simple menus that allow them to pick predefined data summaries? Do these people have unrestricted access to the data, or should different people be able to access only parts of the database?

- Who will be managing the database? Are there different levels of management required, or will one person do database maintenance and control user access?

- Who will be using the results? Do they require different levels of access or to see different sets of results? Do results need to be displayed differently for different people (charts v. tables; paper v. computer)?

- Who is the ultimate customer? The ultimate customer is the person or people responsible for the database request, and who has ultimate sign-off authority. If you don't want to create it twice, you need to get a sign-off from the ultimate customer on the database specifications before creating the application!

Determine Conversion Requirements

Another important question to ask is where the data is presently stored. Is it already in an Excel table, the corporate mainframe, or on note cards? Will there be a conversion involved from the present data into the new database? Similarly, you need to understand whether there is any requirement for other database applications to be able to share the data that you're asked to store.

Determine Your Database Structure

Having analyzed what the customer wants in terms of functional requirements, you can now determine how to fulfill them. To do this, you have to identify what fields you need to maintain about each record and determine how they are related.

An Overview of Databases, Tables, and Relationships

A database is a structured way of saving data. Your Microsoft Outlook contact list is a simple example of a database. All the information about each person is called a *record*. The individual elements of information that are stored, such as contact name, city, and telephone number, are called *fields*. A database is always structured with record and fields, which provides its essential organization. The combination of records and fields makes a database *table*, and by convention, each row in a database table contains a record and each column contains a field. For the purposes of this book, we're going to use these terms to describe our databases, regardless of the software application in which they were created.

A simple database may contain only one table. These databases are often called *flat file* databases. However, as your requirements grow more complex, you might need to create a database with multiple tables of data that are related to each other (called a *relational* database). For instance, if you are creating a learning management system, you have to track all the courses that employees take. There's certain information you maintain about each employee (their ID, name, department, and phone number), and certain information about each course (its name, instructor, and description). Each employee can take any number of courses. If you have a flat file database, you need to enter duplicate information in each record to capture everything you need. For instance, if a person took two courses, you have to enter all their personal information in both records.

A better way to solve this common problem is to create a relational database, in which records in one table are related to the records in the other. In this case, you might have a database containing three tables—Employees (including all employees), Curriculum (including all course offerings), and Courses (containing the employees in each course).

There are other cases like a contact list, in which each employee might have multiple phone numbers. In this case, you can choose to create a relational database so each employee can have as many phone numbers as possible. Alternatively, as is done in Outlook, you may choose to limit how many phone numbers will be maintained for each person, in which case you can have a separate field for each of the limited number of values the field can have (for example, home, work, mobile, and pager). The strategy you pick is governed by the customer's requirements.

First, you need to identify the fields that will organize the information you store about each record in your database. After you have the potential field candidates, you group them together or narrow them down into your final field list. To start, make a list of all the possible fields and then examine it and ask the following questions.

- **Do the fields have the right level of detail?**   For instance, should address information be one field or should it be broken down into Street1, Street2, City, State, Zip, and Country? Will Name suffice, or do you need Prefix, First, Middle, Last, and Suffix? The answers to these questions are governed by how you will use the information in the fields. If you need to sort the list by last name or select only people from a specific state, you have to be more specific.

- **Are the names of your fields consistent?**   It's much easier to import and export data if you use the same names for fields. For instance, is the first name field FirstName, First, or FName? Look at how the fields are named in other databases that your organization uses and, where possible, try and use the same names.

- **What is the specification of each field?**   Identify whether the information in each field is text, numbers, or dates. For each type, determine its properties and format. For text fields, this includes the maximum length and capitalization. For numbers, it includes the type (integer or decimal) and format (currency, percentage, or fixed decimal). For dates, it's the display format (1/1/01 or January 1, 2001).

After you do this, you have the basic building blocks for your database.

Tip   Think through the requirements from the customer's point of view, and ask "Is that the only possibility?" For instance, if the customer says he or she wants to maintain four phone numbers for each contact, ask if there's ever a case in which you need more—for example, the main number, fax, mobile, direct line, and home number. The more time you spend discovering exceptions at the front end, the better your end result will be.

Determining the Right Tool

Having defined the requirements, you have to select the right tool for the job. You could use Excel, Access, or another product.

When your database requirements are simple, use Excel. Because you can create a database so easily with it, there's no point using the more complicated Access when Excel will suffice. If you do not need multiple, related data tables in your database, if a simple data entry form—or no data entry form—is required, and if you'll be the only person entering data, Excel is usually the tool of choice.

If your requirements are complex, such as creating a sales tracking system or a financial system, first check to see whether an off-the-shelf product is available such as Goldmine for sales tracking or Microsoft Money for financial management. These products are usually much more robust than an application you can create from scratch, and cost less than building a new program. Although the data might not integrate as well with other applications as an Access application and you might have to work in different ways from what you're used to, it's often easier to change your processes and procedures than to build a robust application that matches them exactly.

Use Access when you need to construct a complex database, and there's no off-the-shelf product to solve the problem. Access is the choice when you need to create a relational database: one that combines data from different tables. With Access, you can create custom data entry forms and have multiple levels of security for entering, editing, and viewing data. It supports multiple simultaneous users, and (unlike Excel) allows you to store pictures and multimedia files with records, not just text and numbers.

Do You Need Relational Databases?

After you know what fields of information you'll be maintaining, you need to determine whether they will all be in one data table or in multiple tables that are related to each other. This is one of the fundamental pieces of information that will help you decide whether you can build the database in Excel, or whether it needs to be created in Access because Excel doesn't support relational databases.

Start by asking whether any fields might have multiple values. For instance, each person should have only one Social Security Number, so that should be a single-valued field. However, each person might have more than one certification, which should be listed in multivalued fields. (You don't want to list all certifications in a single long field; this would make it very difficult to edit the field, find the people with a particular certification, and so forth.)

If you find that your multivalued fields contain a limited number of values, such as an applicant's last two job titles, you can usually store this information in one data table by creating one field for each of the two job titles. In this case, you don't need a relational database. If, however, you want to store *all* the applicant's previous job titles or any number of phone numbers, a relational database such as Access is more appropriate.

Deciding Who Should Build It

After you complete the requirements analysis and decide what type of tool is needed, you need to make another important decision: Assuming there's no off-the-shelf solution available, should you construct the database yourself or outsource it to an expert? Here are a few guidelines to consider.

- If the requirement is for a simple, flat file database that can be built in Excel, you should probably do it yourself.

- Consider building the Access database yourself if what's needed is a fairly simple relational database, one person will be doing the data entry, there are no complex security considerations, and the structure of the database is similar to the ones Access can help you create using wizards.

- Consider outsourcing the creation of the Access database if the required tables, relationships, data entry forms, and reports don't match what can be created with Wizards; if multiple people will be entering data and validation rules are required; if there are complex security requirements; or if there are sophisticated query and reporting requirements.

You might find that when a simple requirements analysis is done, the problem is more complex than originally anticipated. In this case, it is often extremely unwise to try and save a few dollars by having an inexperienced employee create the database rather than having an expert do it. The time wasted in entering wrong or incomplete data that cannot produce the required business results will often cost far more than what would have been spent to get it done right the first time.

If you do choose to outsource the database creation, the work you did is not lost. In fact, the requirements analysis is exactly the information you need to intelligently scope the project for a vendor and to be sure you're both in alignment about what the desired results must be.

The remainder of this chapter focuses on teaching you the skills you're most likely to need if you choose to create the database yourself—how to create a database with Excel, understand the components of an Access database, and build a simple database in Access using wizards.

Note   In my experience, the average knowledge worker might not be able to create Access databases him- or herself. Simple databases can be created in Excel, but when the complexity of Access is needed, it's almost always better to have a professional create the database, since it will probably need customized tables, fields, relationships, and reports. However, it is worthwhile understanding how an Access database is constructed, because it helps you to understand the underpinnings of your database applications that others have created.

Organizing Data Using Excel

If you determine that the right tool for your database is Excel, you have an easy job ahead of you. Creating an Excel database is a snap, and putting data in it can be as easy as typing it into the worksheet—though Excel also has a few tools like forms and data validation if you want to use a slightly more sophisticated approach.

In this section you learn the basic skills you need to organize your data with Excel, including how to

- Create an Excel database
- Enter data into your Excel database—either directly, or by using forms
- Use validation rules during data entry to prevent mistakes
- Name your database to make it easier to import into other applications
- Link data on Web pages into your Excel database

Creating an Excel Database

Creating an Excel database is as simple as creating an Excel worksheet. To do so, take the following steps.

1. Create a new workbook in Excel.
2. Type your field names in row 1.

Tip A few common formatting options you might want to program include setting a number format for numeric data, setting the alignment to Center and bolding the first row containing field names, and, if you have a long text field, using Wrap Text so you can see the entire contents without it taking up your entire screen. These options are in the Format Cells dialog box, which you access by choosing Cells from the Format menu.

3. Add records to your new database, one per line.

Here are guidelines you should follow to make an effective database.

- Each worksheet should contain only one database, and nothing else. If you have charts, PivotTables, or other information, store it in another worksheet within your workbook.

- Each column represents one field in your database, and each row represents one record, as you can see in Figure 6-1.

	Contact	Company	Website
1	Contact	Company	Website
2	Abbar, Anas	A. Datum Corporation	http://www.adatum.com/
3	Abercrombie, Kim	Adventure Works	http://www.adventure-works.com/
4	Ackerman, Pilar	Alpine Ski House	http://www.alpineskihouse.com/
5	Adell, Jeff	Baldwin Museum of Science	http://www.baldwinmuseumofscience.com/
6	Akers, Kim	Blue Yonder Airlines	http://www.blueyonderairlines.com/
7	Akhtar, Sarah	City Power & Light	http://www.cpandl.com/
8	Alboucq, Steve	Coho Vineyard	http://www.cohovineyard.com/
9	Alexander, Sean P.	Coho Winery	http://www.cohowinery.com/
10	Anderson, Amy	Coho Vineyard & Winery	http://www.cohovineyardandwinery.com/
11	Anderson, Charlie (Charlton)	Contoso, Ltd	http://www.contoso.com/
12	Atkinson, Teresa	Contoso Pharmaceuticals	http://www.contoso.com/
13	Bacon Jr., Dan K.	Consolidated Messenger	http://www.consolidatedmessenger.com/
14	Baldwin, Amie	Fabrikam, Inc.	http://www.fabrikam.com/
15	Barbariol, Angela	Fourth Coffee	http://www.fourthcoffee.com/
16	Barnhill, Josh	Graphic Design Institute	http://www.graphicdesigninstitute.com/
17	Barr, Adam	Humongous Insurance	http://www.humongousinsurance.com/
18	Barrett, Holly E.	Litware, Inc.	http://www.litwareinc.com/
19	Beck, Bradley	Lucerne Publishing	http://www.lucernepublishing.com/
20	Ben-Sachar, Ido	Margie's Travel	http://www.margiestravel.com/
21	Benson, Max	Northwind Traders	http://www.northwindtraders.com/
22	Berge, Karen	Proseware, Inc.	http://www.proseware.com/

Figure 6-1 *An Excel database is a simple worksheet where each column is a field and each row is a record.*

- Put the field names in the first row of the database. Do not duplicate field names—Excel allows it, but it makes it more difficult when you are analyzing or exporting your data.

- Do not allow any blank rows because Excel sees a blank row as the end of the database. You can have blank cells, however, as long as the entire row is not blank.

- Be consistent in how you enter your data. You must use the same values you're using for your data entry if you want to be able to sort, group, or filter your database. For instance, the University of Pennsylvania can be entered as Univ Pennsylvania, U Pennsylvania, U. Penn., or just Penn. Pick one method and use it consistently.

Shortcuts for Entering Data into Excel

You can enter data into your Excel database by typing it directly into the worksheet. Auto-Complete and AutoFill are two shortcuts that save you time when you do so.

The AutoComplete feature examines text entries you make and, as you type, compares them with entries in cells above it. (AutoComplete ignores numeric entries.) If it finds a match, it suggests the previous entry by displaying it in black. If you press Enter, the Tab key, or an arrow key, the entry is completed using the previous text.

If you want to copy values from one cell to another, or if you have a series (perhaps of sequential employee ID numbers) that you want to create automatically, the AutoFill feature can save you a tremendous amount of time. The secret to AutoFill is the *fill handle*. That's the black dot at the bottom right of the active cell(s) (that is, the cell or cells that are selected). When you move your mouse over the fill handle, the mouse pointer becomes a black cross. Drag the fill handle in any direction to copy the contents of the active cell(s), or create sequences. Here are a few guidelines for using AutoFill.

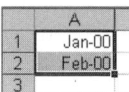

- If the active cell(s) contain text, the contents of that cell or cells will be copied throughout the range of destination cells (the cells you dragged over).

- If a single cell is active and contains a number, that number will be copied throughout the destination cells.

- If more than one cell is active and they both contain numbers (for example, 1 and 2), and you select both cells, a sequence will be created (for example, 3, 4, 5) throughout the destination cells.

- If a single cell is active and contains a date (for example, 2/1/02), day (for example, Mon or Monday), month (for example, Jan or January), quarter (for example, Q1), a sequence of dates is created throughout the destination cells (for example, Mon results in the sequence Mon, Tue, Wed).

- When you use AutoFill, you see a SmartTag (so long as you are using Excel 2002) at the end of the fill series. Clicking the SmartTag provides fill options, such as only filling in weekdays when the active cell contains a day, or filling in formatting rather than values.

Using AutoFill is a handy way to initially populate your database. Often you find that many records in a row have a field that repeats, such as Department, or that there is a numerical sequence, such as employee ID, or date sequence, such as days of the year, from one record to another.

Using Forms for Data Entry

You can also use a form that Excel creates automatically for data entry. The form is a simple yet functional one, and will probably serve your needs for most situations. To enter data with a form, follow this procedure.

1. Open your Excel database.
2. Select your data entry fields in the first row.
3. Choose Form from the Data menu.
4. To enter a new record in the form that appears (see Figure 6-2), type the information in the form and press Enter.

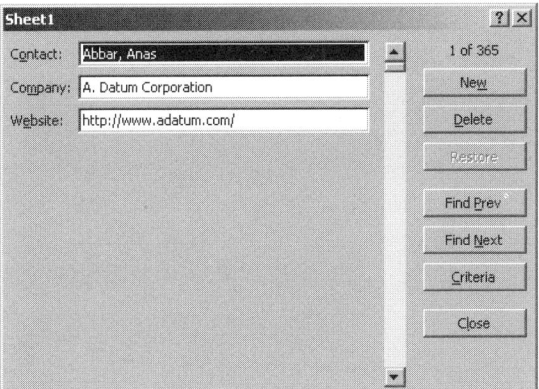

Figure 6-2   *Excel makes data entry easy by automatically creating a form based on the field names in your database.*

5. You can also edit a record by scrolling to it with the scrollbar or clicking Find Prev and Find Next until the record is displayed, and then editing the information in the form.
6. Click Close when you're finished with data entry.

Validating Your Data

Having your data entered the same way in each record is vital, as mentioned earlier, for later analyses. To assist you, Excel provides a data validation feature that can catch many of the mistakes before they happen. With data validation, you can ensure that your entry contains text, dates, or numeric data within specific ranges. It can also provide a prompt that helps you remember what is required when entering data directly, and a custom error message if you make a mistake. To use data validation, do the following.

1. Open your Excel database.
2. Click the column header of the field you want to validate.

3. Choose Validation from the Data menu.

4. In the Data Validation dialog box, choose the type of permitted data (for example, whole number or date).

5. Choose the appropriate options that appear depending on the data type. For instance, if you select date, you can choose an operator (for example, between or greater than) and a start date and end date, as shown in Figure 6-3.

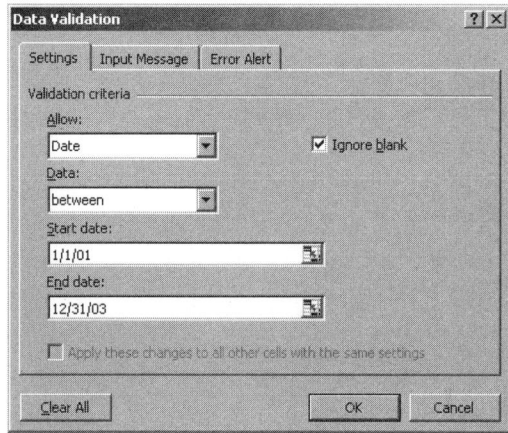

Figure 6-3   *Excel allows you to validate data as it's entered, making it easier to share entry tasks without losing data integrity.*

6. In the Input Message tab, type a title and a message that will be displayed when the user tabs to the cell. If you put constraints on the allowable data, it's a good practice to put this in the input message, for example, enter a date between 1/1/02 and 1/30/02.

7. In the Error Alert tab, choose the style of dialog box (Stop, Warning, or Information), the title, and the message to be displayed when the user enters invalid data. A Stop alert does not allow invalid data entry, while a Warning and Information box does allow it after a user confirmation.

Naming Your Database

When you import an Excel database into certain non-Microsoft programs such as ACT!, the other application does not perform the import unless the database is a named range, which is a simple process. To do so, take the following steps.

1. Open your Excel database.

2. Select the entire database.

Tip An easy way to select the entire database is to click anywhere inside it and press Ctrl+*.

3. Type the name of your database ("database" will do) in the Name Box, as shown in Figure 6-4.

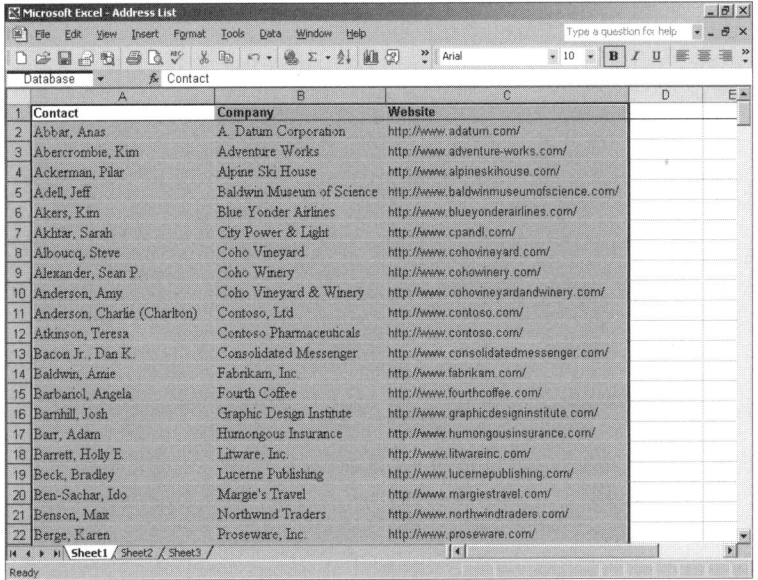

Figure 6-4 *You can easily name a range of cells by selecting them and then typing the name in the Name box.*

Caution If you add records to your database directly by typing them into blank lines at the end of your database after you name your database, the named range will not be accurate. You'll need to reselect the database and name it again. If, however, you use a data entry form to add records to your database, the named range expands to include the newly added records.

Integrating Other Data into Excel

Often when you create a new database to organize your data, you find that the data already exists in electronic form and doesn't have to be manually reentered. It might be on a mainframe computer, in an Oracle database, in a proprietary finance and accounting system, or in an older, PC-based database such as dBase or rBase. The trick is getting the old data into the new system as effortlessly and as accurately as possible.

If your database needs are complex enough that you are using an Access solution, you will probably have the database designer import the data when the application is created. More frequently, however, you will need to import a simple data table such as an employee list and will usually import it into Excel so you can analyze it further.

When your data has been imported, you often find that it is "dirty"—it may contain duplicates, or be in a format (for example, all caps) that makes it hard to use. To utilize your data, you need to know how to import it and then do any data cleanup that is required.

Importing Data into Excel

The easiest way to import data it is to import it into Excel rather than Access. This way you do not need to customize Access forms, reports, or other components in order to immediately use the data. When you open a database file after you import data into Excel, it will often be converted immediately into an Excel worksheet if it was created in a format that Excel supports. In the Open dialog box, you select from a number of data types that Excel can read directly. These include

- Access files
- Query files
- Lotus 1-2-3 files
- XML and HTML files
- Quattro Pro files
- Microsoft Works database files
- dBase files
- SYLK files

If you have files of one of these types, you can import it by opening the file and then saving it as an Excel workbook.

If you have a file that is not one of these file types, the secret is finding a common language that both the legacy database application and Excel understand. That common language is often a *text delimited file*. This is an ASCII text file where each record is on one line, and each field is separated from the next by a delimiter such as a comma (called *comma delimited*) or a tab (called *tab delimited*). In fact, the two most common types of delimited files are comma delimited files and tab delimited files. Virtually every database application—from mainframes through UNIX to PCs—can export a data table as a text delimited file. Ask the database administrator to provide you with a file that is Excel compatible—the administrator will know what you mean.

Note Occasionally, mainframes export their files in another type of format called "fixed field" or "fixed width." Records in these files still take up exactly one line, but they are separated by the number of characters each record takes rather than a delimiter like a tab. Thus, if you have three text fields in the database that each can be 10 characters long, the first 15 characters in the fixed width file read as Field 1, the second 10 as Field 2, and the third 10 as Field 3. If the first field actually contains only 4 characters, the file has spaces to fill out the other 6. Fortunately, Excel can handle these files as easily as delimited ones.

To import a text-delimited file into Excel, do the following.

1. In the Excel Open dialog box, navigate to the folder where the file to be imported has been saved.

2. Choose All Files in the Files of Type box, and then double-click the file to be imported. If the database file is a supported type, you see the data in your worksheet immediately. In this case, you're finished. If Excel cannot import the data in its current form, the Text Import Wizard opens.

3. In the first step of the Text Import Wizard, ensure that Delimited is checked (or Fixed Width, if it's a fixed width file) and then click Next.

4. Choose the delimiter(s) that separate fields in your file. You know you have the right delimiter when the data appears as separate fields, as in Figure 6-5. Set the text qualifier if needed.

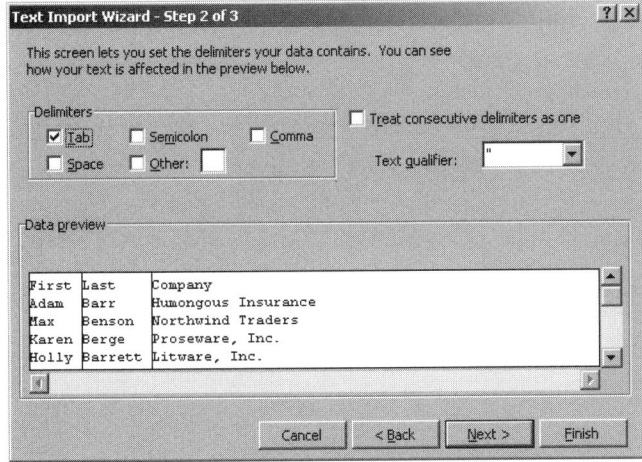

Figure 6-5 *Excel makes it easy to import text files from legacy mainframe or UNIX applications by providing the Text Import Wizard. On this screen, you select the appropriate delimiter for the data you are importing.*

Note The text qualifier is for situations where the delimiter (such as a comma) may appear inside a field (such as Richard Carey, Jr.). To ensure that the field is not truncated (in this case, at Richard Carey), the entire field may be surrounded by a text qualifier such as "Richard Carey, Jr." Quotation marks are the most common text qualifier.

---

5. In the third step of the wizard, set the formatting for each column by clicking the column header and then choosing General, Text, Date, or Do Not Import Column (Skip). (Alternatively, you can format the columns after you finish the import.) If you select Date, you need to choose a date format from the drop-down list adjacent to Date selection.

6. Click Finish to complete the import process.

When you finish working with the file, remember to save it as an Excel workbook; by default it may be saved in the original format from which it was imported.

Cleaning Up Data

After you import your data from your database, you might need to go through a cleanup process. Often you have to check for duplicates—especially if you are combining the results of a data import with existing data. Another common problem is that data from mainframe databases is sometimes comes through the import process in all caps. This can be problematic, for instance, if it contains a mailing list that will eventually be used in a mail-merged letter. Fortunately, Excel provides simple ways to correct both problems.

To remove duplicates from your Excel database, copy only unique records to a new location such as an empty worksheet. This copy is your "clean" database. To copy the records, follow these steps.

1. Click in a cell within the database, and then choose Filter, Advanced Filter from the Data menu.

2. In the Advanced Filter dialog box, ensure that the List Range matches the range of your database.

3. Choose Copy to another location, and specify the location in the Copy to box.

4. Check Unique Records Only, and then click OK. The unique records are copied to the new location.

If you have legacy data that is all uppercase, you can change it to upper, lower, or proper (initial caps) case using appropriate Excel functions. This adds immeasurably to the readability of your database. To change the case of a field in your database, assuming that the labels start in row 1 and the data starts in row 2, do the following.

1. Add a new column to the database, and in the first row type the name of the field to be changed.

2. To convert the text to proper case, note the column letter of the original field (for example, column A) and type the following in the row 2 of the new column: =PROPER(A2), substituting the appropriate letter for "A" in "A2."

Tip Use UPPER(A2) to convert text to upper case, or LOWER(A2) to convert it to lower case. Substitute the appropriate letter for the "A" in "A2."

---

3. Click the cell with your new formula, then drag the fill handle down until the formula appears in every row in the database.

4. Select all the cells in the new column from row 1 to the final row, and choose Copy from the Edit menu.

5. With the range of cells that you copied still highlighted, choose Paste Special from the Edit menu.

6. In the Paste Special dialog box, click the Values check box and click OK.

7. Delete the column in your database containing the original field values (the one with all capital letters), and you're done.

Getting Data from the Web

Increasingly, you might find that there's information on the Web that you want to include in your Excel worksheets. For example, you might want to know the current stock price of a mutual fund or the prime rate as you build a financial worksheet. You can import data from a Web page into your Excel worksheet using a Web Query.

A Web Query is a link to data contained on a Web page to an Excel workbook. Web Queries allow you to link to entire Web pages, tables or individual cells, or areas that have been preformatted with the HTML <pre> tag. What this means to you is that when you browse to a Web page when creating a Web Query, you see areas within the page that you can link to your Excel worksheet. After you include the Web site information in your worksheet, you're able to refresh it from the Web page any time you want.

Here's how to do it.

1. Point to Import External Data on the Data menu, and then choose New Web Query.

2. In the New Web Query dialog box, type the URL of the target Web page.

3. When you see one or more black arrows in small yellow boxes on the source Web page, click the arrows next to the sections you want to import. The arrows change to green checkmarks to let you know which sections you selected, as shown in Figure 6-6.

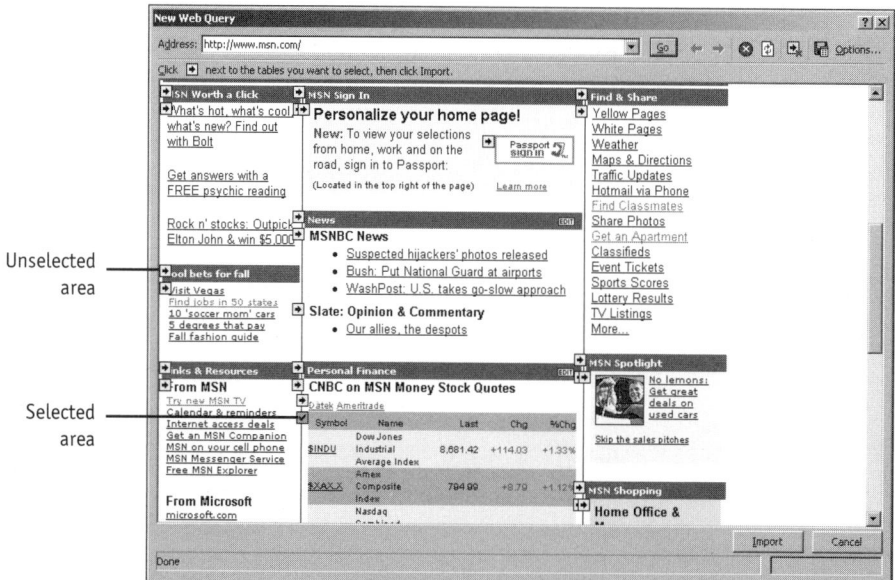

Figure 6-6   *You can create links to areas on Web pages and import them into your Excel worksheets.*

4. Click Import.

5. In the Import Data dialog box, specify the worksheet your data should be imported to and then click Properties.

6. In the External Data Range Properties dialog box, choose when you want the data refreshed from the Web page and specify any formatting options you want.

7. Click OK to return to the Import Data dialog box, and then click OK again to import the data into your worksheet.

That's all there is to it! The selected contents of the Web page are displayed in the worksheet of your choice, as shown in Figure 6-7. You can edit the Web Query at any time by right-clicking the imported data and choosing Edit Query.

Tip   To immediately refresh your Web Query, right-click the imported data and choose Refresh or click the Refresh Data button (!) in the External Data toolbar.

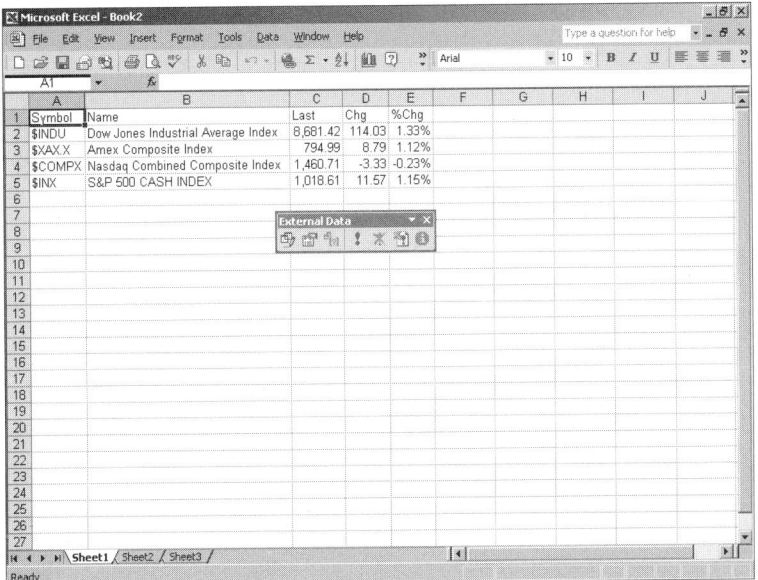

Figure 6-7   *Exported information from Web pages appears in your Excel worksheets.*

Organizing Data Using Access

Creating an Access database is a little more complicated than setting one up in an Excel workbook. Fortunately, Access provides wizards that help you through the basics. The databases you can create using Access wizards are samples that can occasionally be used "as is," but often require extensive customization to meet specific functional requirements.

Although many knowledge workers create Excel databases by themselves, when the database requirements indicate that the power of Access is needed, frequently the application will be created by the IT department or outsourced to a database specialist. It's worth being familiar with the process of creating and doing simple modifications to Access databases, however, because this basic understanding is fundamental to querying *existing* Access databases and creating/modifying reports—a function that is more common for nondatabase specialists.

Before creating a database in Access, however, it's worth spending a few minutes to understand the components that make up an Access database.

Understanding Access Components

There are several types of *objects* that make up an Access database. The ones that, as a nonprogrammer, you're likely to want to create or modify include *tables, forms, queries*, and *reports*.

- **Table.**   The matrix of rows and columns that contains the data in your database, as well as the information about data properties, formatting, and validation rules for fields. It is very much like an Excel database, and in fact, you can use a link to an Excel worksheet in lieu of a table in an Access database and easily convert one to the other.

- **Form.**   Used to enter and edit information in your Access database. Forms can be extensively customized to facilitate the data entry process, and can also contain data validation rules and formatting information for entry fields.

- **Query.**   Extracts selected data from one or more database tables, and presents it in a table format. The query, however, doesn't actually contain data (as a table does); it is dynamically generated each time it is run. Queries can also display summary information or grouped information.

- **Report.**   Presents data from one or more tables or queries, and is generally used for printed output. Access provides tools for formatting reports.

Other database objects you might see include data access pages (used to publish Access data on Web pages), macros (to automate database use), and modules (more sophisticated automated procedures built with Visual Basic). In addition, a *switchboard* is a special type of form used to present menus for using Access applications. Switchboards are created automatically when you create an Access database using a wizard.

Creating an Access Database

If you're not familiar with the process of creating Access databases, the best way to build one is by using one of the database wizards provided by Microsoft. Ten templates are provided with Microsoft Office XP, and more are available on the Microsoft Web site. To create an Access database, do the following.

1. Open Access, and choose General Templates from the task pane.

2. In the Databases tab of the Templates dialog box, choose the template that most resembles the database you need to create and click OK.

3. As you go through the steps of the wizard, note the following.

   - The tables of the database are preset and cannot be changed during the database creation process.

   - In the second step of the wizard, you see a list of database tables along with the available fields for each table. Checked fields are required, while optional additional fields are not checked and appear in italic. Adding additional fields is a convenient way to customize the database to your specifications.

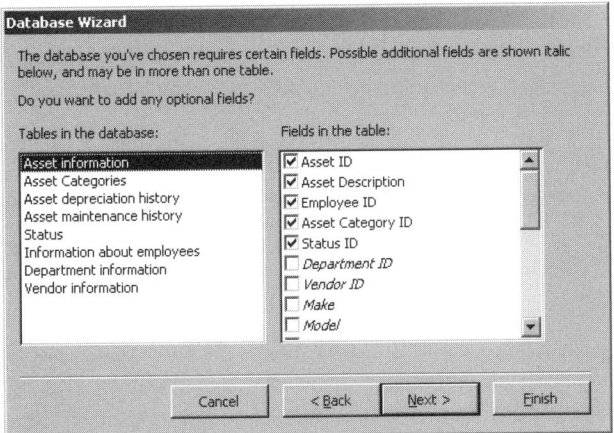

- You can change a number of attributes that govern the database's look and feel.

Looking at the Structure of an Access Database

One of the best ways to get an understanding of how Access works (and how complex a simple Contact Management database can be) is to create a database using the wizard, and then look at the structure of some of its components. To do so, try the following.

1. Create an Access database as described in the previous procedure, using the Contact Management template.

2. Choose Contact Management 1 from the Window menu to open the Database window, and note the following.

   - This window shows you all the components used in this database.

   - Click Tables, Queries, Forms, and Reports in the Objects pane to see the different objects, such as the list of tables shown in Figure 6-8.

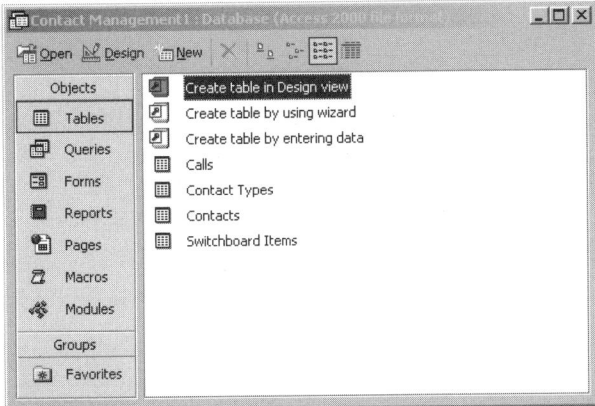

Figure 6-8   *The Database window allows you to add or edit the components that are used to create your application.*

- Options at the top of the Object pane allow you to create tables, queries, forms, and reports using the Design view or using a wizard.

3. Select the Contact table, and click the Design button in the Database window to display its properties. Note the following.

   - All the fields are listed in the top part of the screen with their data type (AutoNumber, Text, or Date/Time).

   - Clicking any field shows its field properties in the bottom part of the screen. Field properties you might commonly set include field size, format, input mask, validation rule, and required.

   - Clicking the Input Mask property displays an ellipsis button. Clicking this button takes you to an Input Mask Wizard that helps you create templates that define how data such as phone numbers and Social Security numbers are formatted, as shown in Figure 6-9.

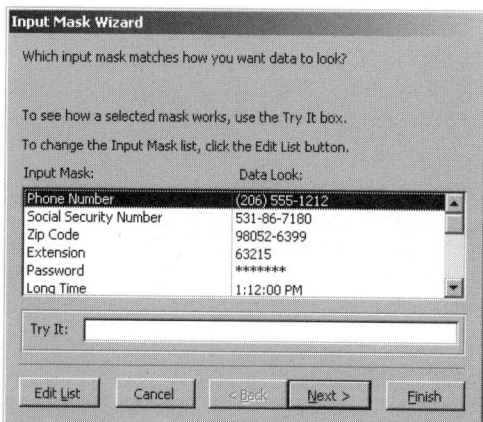

Figure 6-9   *Input masks allow you to format the user's data as it's entered, making it easy to require area codes for phone numbers or the right number of digits for Social Security numbers.*

   - Clicking the Validation Rule property displays an ellipsis button. Clicking this button takes you to an Expression Builder that helps you create rules for data entry.

4. Close the Properties window for the Contact table, highlight the Contacts form in the Database window, and click the Design button to display the properties for the Contacts form. Note the following.

   - You see a grid with all the fields that are to be entered or edited. Click these fields to select them, and then drag them to another area on the form.

   - A floating Toolbox provides tools for adding other fields and design elements to the form.

5. Close the Contacts Properties window, and then click the Relationships button on the Access standard Toolbar to display the Relationships window. Note that

- You can drag the bottom border of the Contacts list to display all the fields in the Contacts table.

- There is a one-to-many relationship between the Contacts table and the Calls table, indicating that any one contact can have many calls associated with him or her, as shown in Figure 6-10.

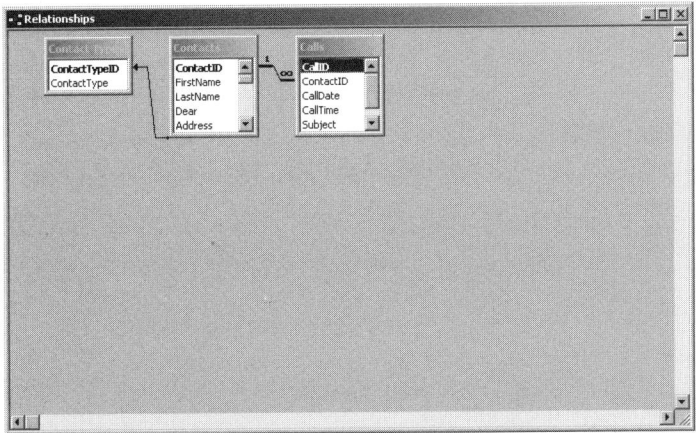

Figure 6-10   *Relationships are displayed visually in Access, allowing you to see which fields are linked.*

6. Close the Relationships window when you're done.

Viewing the properties of a database in this way gives you a good idea of what's involved in creating an Access database or modifying its structure. If you want to create some of your own, you can find further information in *Microsoft Office XP Inside Out* by Michael Halvorson and Michael J. Young, also published by Microsoft Press.

Summary

From a business perspective the most important skills you can take from this chapter are not the techniques for creating an Excel database or using an Access wizard, but rather the ability to rationally define the business problem and determine whether you should build the solution yourself or whether the scope of the problem demands an outsourced solution.

When the requirements are simple, however, you've seen how easy it is to create a database in Excel, add data entry forms and validation rules, and even get information from the Web. You also understand how database applications are built in Access so you can hold meaningful conversations with your Access database designer.

Checklist for Organizing Your Data

Check off the following points as you learn how to effectively organize your data using databases.

[ ] Understand the questions to ask to complete a requirements analysis.

[ ] Specify the fields required for your database, and determine whether a relational database is required.

[ ] Know the criteria for determining what application to use for your database, and whether to build it yourself.

[ ] Create a database using Excel.

[ ] Create a data entry form for your Excel database.

[ ] Make data validation rules for your Excel database.

[ ] Import information from Web pages into Excel.

[ ] Import text files into Excel.

[ ] Change capitalization of imported data and remove duplicates.

[ ] Understand the components of an Access database.

[ ] Use the Database window to examine the structure of an Access database.

Organizing Your E-mail

Jeff Adell's new job is Vice President for eLearning for a major insurance company. He is charged with implementing a series of new initiatives aimed at providing training throughout the organization using various eLearning applications. As such, he is a member of several planning committees, and leads three cross-functional project teams. Every day, Jeff gets more than 100 e-mails (not including junk mail and spam).

Jeff didn't come from an e-mail culture. At his last position, most communications were through voice mail. For the last three days, Jeff hasn't been able to read more than half of his e-mails and feels as though his e-mail is preventing him from doing his job—but he also realizes that responding to e-mail *is* his job.

For many knowledge workers, e-mail is the biggest information tsunami. It can take an hour or more each day to wade through your Inbox, and you still have a pile of items that have not been responded to that keeps growing day after day. And yet, communication is the lifeblood of knowledge workers and e-mail is a primary communications modality. So although effectively managing e-mail can be a challenge, it is one that cannot safely be ignored.

In this chapter, you find several techniques to help you tame this particular tsunami. You learn how to

- Organize your e-mail with an e-mail filing system

- Quickly and effectively process incoming e-mail

- Automate many aspects of keeping your e-mail organized

- Find information in your saved e-mails

Managing Your E-mail

As e-mail has become one of the most common communication modes for many knowledge workers, it follows that e-mail has become one of the toughest information tsunamis to manage. E-mail messages can pile up in your Inbox so quickly that important messages you haven't responded—or can't even find—are scattered among hundreds of unimportant e-mails.

An especially effective way to manage a deluge of e-mail is to use the TRAF system developed by Stephanie Winston for managing paperwork. Winston says that there are four and a half things you can do with a piece of paper that arrives on your desk.

- Throw it away.

- Refer it to someone else.

- Act on it.

- File it.

- Read it. (This is the "half" she refers to, because after you read e-mail, you still need to do one of the other four things with it.)

A variation of this system can be the secret to effectively managing your e-mail. Think of your Inbox as your "action box" that will contain only two types of e-mail messages—messages that you haven't read, and messages that you've read but haven't acted on (called *active* e-mails). Remove all the others from your Inbox, either by deleting them or moving them to your e-mail filing system after you've forwarded them to someone else or acted on them by responding. The result will be a clean Inbox containing only the e-mail you've just received, and the remaining e-mails that you have not yet responded to.

Creating an Outlook E-mail Filing System

Creating an e-mail filing system will allow you to quickly identify the e-mails you need to act on and find old e-mails quickly.

Simply letting e-mail pile up in your Inbox after you've acted on it will not fulfill either of these goals.

The approach you take to creating an effective e-mail filing system depends on the volume of e-mail you generally receive. A good rule to follow is that if you have more than 500 e-mail messages in any one folder, you need to reorganize that folder, either by creating subfolders within that folder or by archiving old items. If a folder contains more than 500 messages, it becomes harder to find what you're looking for.

If your folders don't contain more than 500 e-mails at any given time, you can simply create an e-mail folder named Read Mail. Put all the e-mails you want to save in this folder. To find e-mail you want to retrieve, sort the folder by name or date, or use Outlook's Find feature.

For more information about archiving, see "Archiving Old E-mail" on page 136.

> **Tip**   Before you move your e-mail from your Inbox to a folder, consider whether you really need to retain it at all. Many people automatically save e-mails, even ones that are merely confirming an appointment or transmission. Saving these e-mails takes up unnecessary storage space.

A more comprehensive approach to organizing your e-mail is to create an e-mail filing system. Depending on the type of work you do, you may want to create an e-mail folder for each of the senders that you correspond with regularly, or each of the major projects you are working on. When you've finished acting on an e-mail you want to save, you can then move it to the appropriate e-mail folder and keep your Inbox clear of inactive items. You'll probably also want to create a Read Items folder for the e-mail that isn't associated with one of your primary correspondents or projects.

> **Tip**   To use an e-mail filing system most effectively, display the Folder List pane so that you can see all your e-mail folders, by choosing Folder List from Outlook's View menu.

When you've created your e-mail folder system, it may look like the one shown in Figure 7-1.

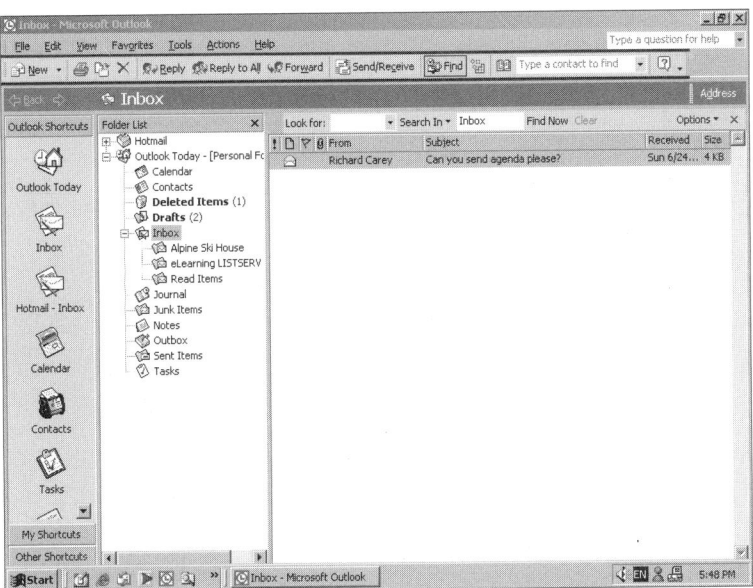

Figure 7-1   *To keep your Inbox "clean," be sure to create folders for each of your projects, teams, or mailing lists, as well as a general folder for other e-mail you've finished processing.*

To create an e-mail folder in Outlook, do the following.

1. Point to Folder on the File menu, and click New Folder.

2. In the Create New Folder dialog box shown in Figure 7-1, type a name for the folder in the Name box. Leave the default of Mail and Post Items in the Folder Contains drop-down list.

3. Select the folder in which you want the new folder to be located.

4. Click OK to create the new folder.

Tip   You might want to select the Inbox as the parent folder for all new folders you create, so that all your e-mail folders are grouped together. This creates a hierarchical folder organization that many people find easy to navigate through.

Once you have your filing system set up, follow these steps to move e-mails from one folder to another.

1. If the folder list is not displayed, choose Folder List from the View menu.

2. In the Folder List pane, click the e-mail folder containing the e-mail you'd like to move.

3. In the list of e-mails, highlight one or more e-mails to be moved, then drag them to the destination folder.

Processing Incoming E-mail

Once you've created an e-mail filing system that supports the type of work you do, it's worth reviewing the way you process the e-mail that comes into your Inbox. Processing your e-mail includes a number of related activities:

- Deciding when to look at your Inbox

- Choosing whether to read individual e-mails

- Reading selected e-mails, then responding to or forwarding them

- Deleting the e-mail, leaving it in your Inbox, or moving it to another folder

Everyone has procedures for processing e-mail, although you probably don't think about what you're doing, when you're doing it. By reviewing and streamlining you e-mail procedures, you can see whether or not you're processing our e-mail as efficiently as you might.

Schedule E-mail Time

For many of us, the Inbox is a seductive siren. It calls us to drop whatever else we're doing, and rush to Outlook and open the mail. If you are a person who multitasks well, reading e-mail when it arrives might be no problem. For others, reading e-mail in the midst of another project creates reconsideration time—some amount of time that must be spent to recapture the mindset you had when you interrupted yourself to read your e-mail.

In reviewing how you process your e-mail you should first decide when is the best time to look at your Inbox. If your work is response-driven and time sensitive, or if you are a good multi-tasker, it might be best for you to read e-mail as it arrives in you Inbox. If this is the case, you can set Outlook to grab new e-mail from your mail server every few minutes by setting Automatic Send/Receive options.

If the previous paragraph does not describe you, you might be better off reading new e-mail once every hour, or only once or twice a day. To avoid temptation, you can set Outlook to grab e-mail from the mail server less frequently, or turn off the notification when new e-mail arrives. This way you won't see the pop-up window or hear sounds when new e-mail arrives from the server to your Inbox and you can better regulate when you review your new e-mail.

To set automatic Send/Receive options, follow these steps.

1. Choose Options from the Tools menu.

2. Click the Mail Setup tab, and then click the Send/Receive button.

3. In the Send/Receive Groups dialog box, you can select options to schedule automatic send/receives when you're online and when you're offline using a dial-up Internet connection. Click Close when you're done.

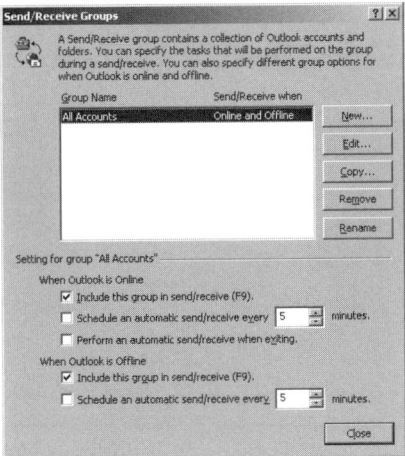

4. In the Options dialog box, click the Preferences tab, and then click E-mail Options.

5. In the E-mail Options dialog box, click Advanced E-mail Options.

6. In the Advanced E-mail Options dialog box, choose notification options in the When New Items Arrive group.

Note In Microsoft Outlook 2002, you can set up multiple e-mail accounts and assign them to different Send/Receive groups using the Send/Receive Groups dialog box. These groups can each have different rules for how often Outlook checks for mail. For example, if you have one work and two personal e-mail accounts and you are setting options for your office computer, you might set up a work group (containing the work account) that checks e-mail automatically every five minutes and a personal group (containing your two personal accounts) that checks e-mail only when you choose Tools, Send/Receive, and specify the personal accounts.

Scan Your E-mail

You can save time in processing your e-mail by taking an additional step prior to reading them: By scanning through your e-mail subjects in the list of e-mails in your Inbox, you can quickly delete the obvious junk mail. If you *preview* the first few lines of messages in addition to displaying the headers, you can also identify messages that can be immediately filed or deleted without further reading. This scanning process can winnow your e-mails down to the ones you really need to attend to.

You can preview your e-mail before opening it in one of two ways:

- Choose AutoPreview from the View menu to display the first few lines of each e-mail underneath its subject in the list of e-mails.

- Choose Preview Pane from the View menu to open a pane that allows you to see the full text of each e-mail without scrolling.

You can see both of these preview options in Figure 7-2.

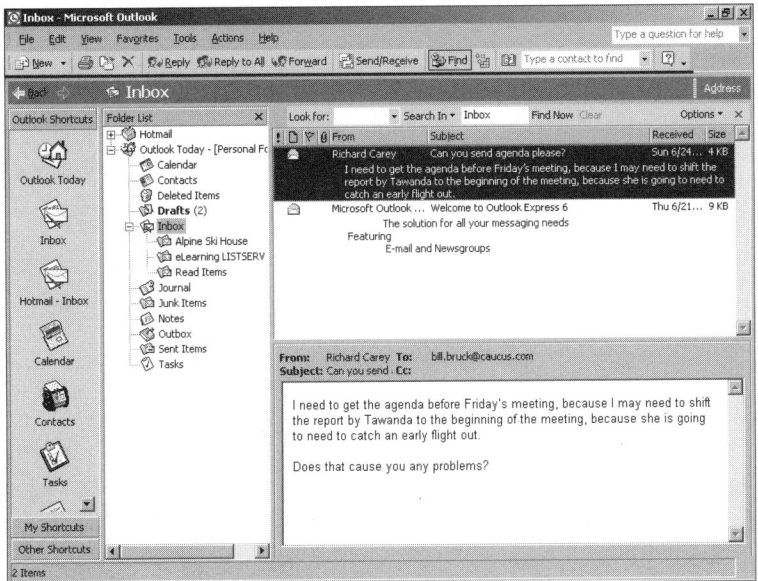

Figure 7-2 *You can quickly identify junk e-mails that can be deleted by using AutoPreview and the Preview Pane.*

Act on Your E-mail

After you've completed your initial scan, you can open each of your remaining new e-mails and read them. Act immediately on the ones you can, by responding to them forwarding them, or taking the action requested of you. Then either file the e-mail or delete it to remove it from your Inbox.

If you're not going to act immediately, you can create a task based on the e-mail. This is a great technique to use when you won't be able to act on the e-mail that day, and you want to make sure it's on your task list so that you can prioritize it with other tasks. The new task you create contains the text and any attachments from the e-mail for your reference. To create a task based on the e-mail, do the following:

1. Drag the e-mail from the Inbox to the Tasks folder.

2. In the new Task window, fill out the form as needed. This includes changing the subject of the task to one that's more descriptive. Click Save And Close when you're done.

3. In your Inbox, file or delete the original e-mail.

Keyboard Shortcuts for Processing E-mail

You can increase the speed at which you process your new e-mail once you remember that it's much more efficient to keep your hands on the keyboard if they're already on the keyboard. Since replying to e-mail is keyboard intensive anyway, learning a few shortcut keys can really make you a speed demon, as you can use shortcuts for deleting and filing e-mails, as well as moving from one e-mail to the next. The keyboard shortcuts shown in Table 7-1 work whether you are reading an individual e-mail in the e-mail window, or you've highlighted an e-mail in the Inbox.

Table 7-1   Shortcut Keys Can Speed Up Your E-mail Processing

Shortcut Key	Function
Shift+Ctrl+V	Move e-mail to another folder
Ctrl+D	Delete e-mail
Ctrl+R	Reply to e-mail
Ctrl+>; Ctrl+<	Move to next or previous item
Ctrl+S	Send e-mail (from e-mail window)

Marking Your E-mail

As your e-mail folders start growing, it's often hard to find important e-mails. It can often be helpful to mark your important e-mail messages to provide a visual indicator to yourself when you look in an e-mail folder. Outlook provides two ways to do this: You can *flag* e-mails, or you can display certain messages in different colors. For instance, you might flag e-mails that require a follow-up action, or you might color all e-mails from a key client in red.

Note   Because unread e-mails appear in bold, marking them as unread makes them easier to see. You can mark e-mails as unread by right-clicking them in your Inbox, and then choosing Mark as Unread from the shortcut menu.

Flag E-mail

When you flag an e-mail message, a flag icon appears next to it. You can also choose a phrase that describes the type of flag it is, such as Follow up, For your information, or Review. You can use this to organize your e-mails by, for instance, flagging all e-mails that must be returned this week. When you open your Inbox, you can quickly spot all e-mails that require a quicker response. To flag an item or edit an existing flag, do the following.

1. Right-click the message you want to flag, and choose Follow Up from the shortcut menu.

2. In the Flag For Follow Up dialog box, choose the type of flag from the Flag To drop-down list, or type your own text if desired.

3. If you would like a pop-up reminder, enter a date and time in the Due By boxes.

4. Click OK to return to the main Outlook window.

Once you've set a flag, you will see the flag icon if the Flag Status field is included in the view you're using, or you will see the flag text if the Follow Up Flag field is displayed. If you use flags frequently, you may wish to use two alternate views for your e-mail folder.

- The By Follow Up Flag view shows your e-mail grouped by flag status.

- The Flagged For Next Seven Days view shows only those e-mails that are flagged for action with a due date within the next seven days.

After you've completed the follow-up action and want to clear the flag, you can right click the item and choose Clear Flag.

Display E-mail Subjects in Color

Alternatively, if you want a somewhat more sophisticated way to mark messages, you can display them in colors. This gives you the additional capability of specifying different colors for different types of messages. To color-code e-mails, do the following.

1. Choose Organize from the Tools menu.

2. In the Ways To Organize pane shown in Figure 7-3, click Using Colors. Choose whether you want to color messages from or to a specific person, type the person's name, and pick the color you want the messages to be.

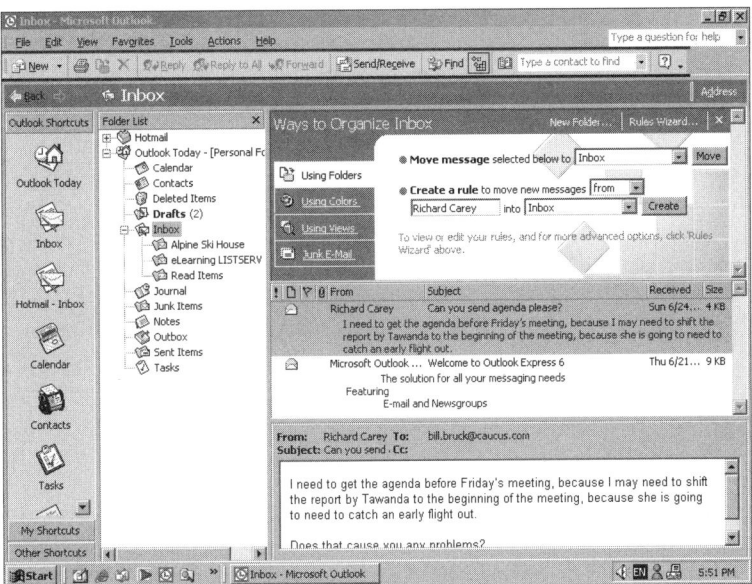

Figure 7-3 *You can use different colors to highlight messages from specific people.*

3. Click the Apply Color button.

4. If you want to color messages sent to only you (in other words, with no cc:), pick the color you want the messages to be and click the Turn On button.

The message color option is an example of an Outlook rule—albeit one that Outlook allows you to apply in a very simple way. For more information about rules, see "Creating Other E-mail Rules" on page 138.

Archiving Old E-mail

As you continue to save e-mails, your Outlook .pst file (the file that stores all your contacts, appointments, tasks, notes, and e-mails) continues to grow. It's not unusual to see .pst files that are 100 MB or larger—especially because e-mails can contain attachments that might be 1 MB or larger in size themselves. As the .pst file grows, your Outlook performance might get slower and you might find it harder to find old e-mails you are looking for in the morass of ancient storage.

For this reason, Outlook provides an automatic archive feature. Using AutoArchive, you can move items that are older than a specified date to a different .pst file—by default, called ARCHIVE.PST. You can also specify that Outlook should archive files that are older than a different specified number of days for each folder in Outlook. This can be handy, because you might want to keep a longer history of your calendar or tasks than your e-mails. How often you should archive your e-mail depends on how much e-mail you get, but the default setting of archiving items older than six months might be too long if you get scads of e-mail each day. Many knowledge workers set e-mail folders to be archived after two or three months, rather than six.

> **Tip**   If you want to archive your files before the regularly scheduled time, choose File, Archive. You can archive all folders according to the default Archive settings, or specify a folder and its subfolders to archive, specifying the date to archive items before.

In addition to setting the schedule for archiving your e-mail, you might want to reset the location of your archive file. If it's located on a server, it's probably being backed up regularly. If it's on your local drive, you may want to move it to youe My Documents folder. This way, every time you back up this folder, you're backing up your Outlook e-mail as well.

To change your default archive settings, follow these steps.

1. Choose Options from the Tools menu.

2. Click the Other tab, and then click the AutoArchive button.

3. In the AutoArchive dialog box, you can specify how often AutoArchive should run, how old items should be to be archived, and whether to move old items or delete them.

4. If necessary, specify a new folder for your archived items.

Tip After a year or two, your archive file might also become unwieldy. An easy way to avoid this is to periodically rename your archive file. For instance, if you did this every year, you might rename Archive to Archive 2001. When Outlook archives your data next, a new file named Archive will automatically be created.

Since you may want to archive different Outlook folders at different intervals, you can set preferences for an individual folder. If you set preferences for a folder that contains subfolders, the preferences are not automatically applied to the subfolders. You will need to set preferences independently for each Outlook folder or subfolder.

To set preferences for a folder, do the following.

1. In the folder list, right-click the folder and choose Properties.

2. On the AutoArchive tab of the Properties dialog box, specify that the folder should not be archived, specify that the folder be archived using default settings, or set different settings for how old the items must be or the destination for the archive.

Automating E-mail Organization

While the techniques described in the first part of this chapter are powerful, they can take valuable time each day. To enable you to organize your e-mail as easily and quickly as possible, Outlook provides *rules*—automated processes that act on e-mails that fit certain criteria in specific ways. If you get a lot of junk e-mail or if you're targeted by adult mailings, Outlook has built-in rules that handle these incoming e-mails automatically. If you consistently process certain types of e-mails in the same way, you can create your own Outlook rules to help out; for example, you can choose to sort incoming e-mail into different folders or forward it to others based on the sender or keywords in the subject line.

Banishing Junk and Adult Mail

Outlook provides automatic ways to banish those junk mails that can both clog your mail system and annoy the heck out of you every day. Outlook identifies junk or adult mail by comparing the subject, sender, and text of incoming e-mail to a list of junk and adult content senders. This list is initially provided by Outlook, but you can add names to it. You can set Outlook to automatically color-code, move, or delete junk and adult e-mail as it arrives. To set a junk or adult mail filter, do the following.

Note Since the rules aren't perfect, a valid e-mail may occasionally be classified as junk. For this reason, it's not a good idea to automatically delete junk mail. Coloring the messages or moving them to another folder gives you a change to scan through the headers before deleting them.

---

1. Open your Inbox, and click the Organize button on the Standard toolbar. Click the Junk E-mail link in the Ways To Organize pane that appears.

2. In the leftmost drop-down lists, choose Move to move junk and adult e-mail to a different location (rather than just change its color in your Inbox).

3. In the drop-down lists on the right, select the folder to which you want to move the junk and adult e-mail. Usually, you will want to retain the default Junk E-mail folder.

4. Click both Turn On buttons.

Caution   Do not choose to move your junk or adult e-mail to the Deleted Items folder because this causes them to be immediately deleted. Although this sounds like a good idea, in practice you will find that occasionally a non-junk e-mail slips through. You should open the Junk E-mails folder every few days and scan through the headers, to ensure that no valid mail slipped through.

You can improve the ability of Outlook to recognize such e-mails by adding additional senders to the junk or adult e-mail lists when ones slip through the default filters. To do so, right-click the junk e-mail message and choose Junk E-mail, Add To Junk (or Adult Content) Senders List.

Creating Other E-mail Rules

You can create additional rules that automate the procedures for organizing your e-mail. An Outlook rule specifies which messages to operate on (selecting messages by criteria including sender, subject, priority, or text), what to do with them (including sending them to a folder, deleting them, or forwarding them), and when to do it (when they arrive, after they're read, and so forth).

You can create rules to automate the following actions:

- Moving e-mail about a specific project to a subfolder after you've read it
- Forwarding e-mail about a specific subject to the right person as soon as the message arrives
- Flagging or coloring messages from a specific person as soon as the message arrives
- Notifying you when high priority messages arrive

To create a rule, you can use the Rules Wizard to guide you through the process as follows.

1. Choose Rules Wizard from the Tools menu.

2. In the Rules Wizard dialog box, click New.

3. The first Rules Wizard screen contains a number of predefined templates for common situations. If one of the templates applies to your situation, click the Start Creating A Rule From A Template option and select a template from the list.

   If none of these templates fit your situation, click the Start From A Blank Rule option and select Check Messages When They Arrive or Check Messages After Sending, depending on which type of rule you need.

4. In the Rule Description box at the bottom of the first wizard screen, click each underlined term to specify the appropriate values for your rule. For instance, if you select the Move New Messages From Someone template, the term People Or Distribution List is underlined in the Rule Description box. When you click this term, the Rule Address dialog box appears where you can select the people or distribution lists that the rule should apply to.

5. Click Next. In the second wizard screen, select check boxes in the Which Condition(s) Do You Want To Check area to add one or more conditions to your rule. If the condition you select includes an underlined term, you can click that term in the Rule Description box and specify the value for the condition.

6. Click Next. In the third wizard screen, select check boxes in the What Do You Want To Do With The Message area to add one or more actions you want to take with the message. Again, if the action includes an underlined term, click the term in the Rule Description box to specify the value for the condition.

7. Click Next. In the fourth wizard screen, select check boxes in the Add Any Exceptions area to add exceptions to the rule. For example, you might move all messages to the Read Items folder after you looked at them *except* ones from your manager.

8. Click Next, and give your rule a name. Click Finish to complete the rule and return to the Outlook main menu. Your completed rule will look like the one shown in Figure 7-4.

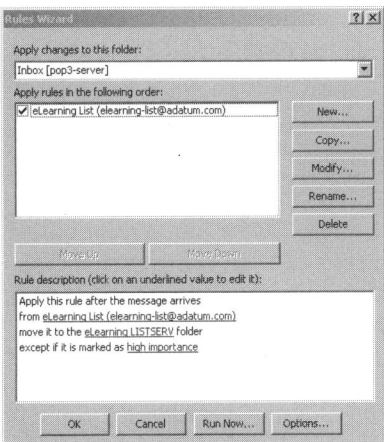

Figure 7-4 *You can set a complex series of conditions that specify actions to be taken on specific e-mails. This cuts down on the number of e-mails you have to process manually.*

Viewing E-mail in Different Ways

If you store your read e-mail messages in a Read Items folder, you might soon find that this folder holds hundreds of e-mails—even if you archive it every few months. Because this folder is the one you go to most often to review past correspondence, you might want to automatically organize it.

If you're like many people, when you look through your past e-mails you're looking for ones from a specific person. If that's the case, you can show items automatically grouped by author whenever you open the folder.

By default, your e-mail folders show a simple item list sorted by date. If you want to organize an e-mail folder so you see messages grouped by recipients, you can customize the default view as follows.

1. Open the e-mail folder.

2. Point to Current View on the View menu, and choose current View.

3. Click Group By in the View Summary dialog box.

4. Choose To in the Group Items By box in the Group By dialog box.

5. Click OK to return to the View Summary dialog box, and then click OK again to return to the main Outlook window. You see your e-mails grouped by recipient.

Finding Information in Saved E-mails

Because e-mail messages are a rich resource for knowledge workers, Outlook provides three ways to search your e-mails. The first is the File Search feature, accessed by choosing Search from the File menu in Microsoft Word, Excel, or PowerPoint and choosing Outlook in the Search In drop-down list in the Basic Search task pane. This is particularly useful if you're already working in one of these applications when you need to start a search, or if you want to search both Outlook and your files system for information at once.

More Info   For more information about searching in Word, Excel, or PowerPoint, see Chapter 5, "Organizing Your Files."

The other search methods are accessed from within Outlook. The Find feature allows you to search through an e-mail folder for specified text that can appear anywhere in an e-mail message. This is useful when you're already in Outlook and you merely want to find all messages that reference a specific person, e-mail address, keyword, or phrase.

To use the Find feature to conduct a simple search, do the following.

1. Open an e-mail folder, and click the Find button on the Standard toolbar.

2. In the Find pane, type the text you wish to search for in the Look In box, and specify the e-mail folders to be searched in the Search In box.

3. Click Find Now to conduct a simple search. The e-mails containing the target text appear in the item list.

The Advanced Find feature allows you to set multiple search criteria, including ones that cannot be set through Office's File Search function (such as finding messages where you are the only person in the To line). To use the Advanced Find feature, do the following.

1. Open an e-mail folder, and click the Find button on the Standard toolbar.

2. In the Find pane, click Advanced Find.

3. Select advanced options as needed in the Advanced Find dialog box. Be sure to look at options on all three tabs (Messages, More Choices, and Advanced) so that you can properly pinpoint your search.

Tip   You can even save these searches so that you can use them over again. To do so, while you are in the Advanced Find dialog box, choose Save Search from the File menu.

---

4. Click Find Now to conduct the search. Figure 7-5 shows an example of how the search results might appear.

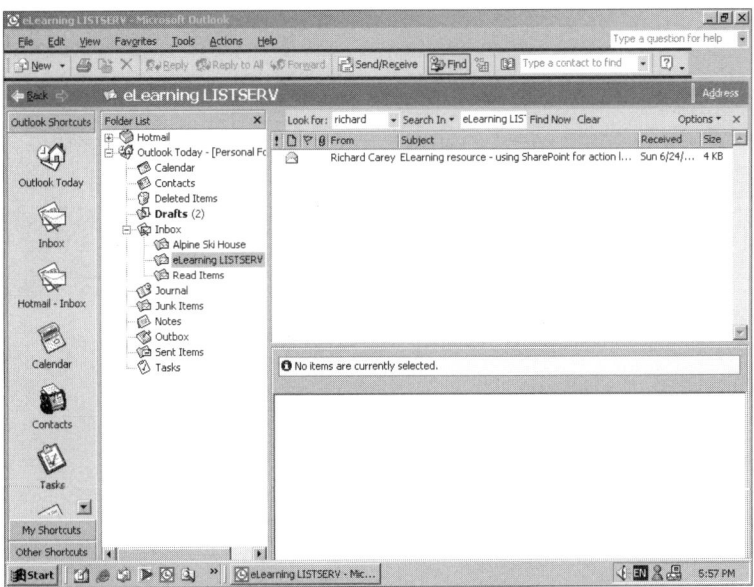

Figure 7-5   *You can refine your search with complex conditions that apply to specific fields within the e-mail items.*

Finding Related Messages

Occasionally, you do not need to search through the text of every e-mail message in your e-mail store; you merely need to see all the rest of the messages related to an e-mail you just received. You can quickly find messages related to the currently highlighted message in an item list by right-clicking the message, and then choosing Find All, Related Messages from the shortcut menu. You see the Advanced Find dialog box, and the related messages are displayed. This feature uses an automatically created field for e-mail messages—the Conversation field. This equals the subject line of the message, less any prefix such as RE: or FW: (for replies or forwarded messages).

Summary

As you've seen in this chapter, you don't need to be overwhelmed by your e-mail. You can take proactive steps to organize it; you can systematically process e-mail so that it doesn't interrupt your day; you can automate many of the ways that you handle incoming e-mail; and you can easily find old e-mails that you need.

Checklist for Organizing Your Data

The following topics will help you effectively organize your e-mail.

[ ] Identify groups or categories your e-mail falls into, and create folders for storing them.

[ ] Look through your saved e-mails and determine which e-mails you should keep and which you can delete.

[ ] Review the archive rules for each of your e-mail folders and, where needed, update them.

[ ] Create a set of guidelines to help you efficiently process e-mail as it arrives.

[ ] Assign views to different e-mail folders to help you quickly find old e-mails.

[ ] Turn on your junk and adult content e-mail filters, and create rules to automate the processing of your e-mail.

[ ] Search for e-mails containing important information with Office's File Search feature and Outlook's Find feature.

[ ] See e-mail sorted, filtered, and grouped in different ways by customizing views of your e-mail folders.

Organizing Your Mobile Tools

Cynthia Randall is an information data architect for a 100-person company that provides Web-based solutions for insurance companies. She determines what a client's information needs are, and then scopes a solution for her team to build. She splits her time evenly between working at the corporate offices, at home, and at client sites all over the country. On any given day, she might be working on her desktop computer at home, her notebook computer on the road, or any one of five desktop computers for remote workers at the office. When she's on the road, Cynthia uses her Microsoft Pocket PC to track appointments, tasks, and contacts; to get her e-mail through a wireless connection; and to take notes at client meetings. Many of Cynthia's deliverables build on previous work. The scoping documents and evaluation reports she writes, for instance, are often based on work she's done for other clients. So it's particularly important for her to have all that previous work available to her, no matter where she is.

Cynthia faces several challenges as she works from multiple locations. She must find effective ways to do the following.

- Keep her Microsoft Outlook data on a variety of computers: desktops, her notebook, and her Pocket PC

- Access her e-mail from home, office, or on the road

- Have the files she needs available to her wherever she is

- Ensure that she has the latest versions of her files, and that she doesn't work on two different versions from two different computers

- Maintain the same working environment on every computer—especially the Microsoft Word templates she uses as the starting point for the documents she writes

Cynthia's situation is shared by an increasing number of knowledge workers. Research by Gartner, Inc. indicates that soon, 80 percent of all enterprises will have at least 50 percent of their knowledge workers engaged in some form of telecommuting or other nomadic work. Microsoft has taken this trend into consideration. One of the design considerations of Microsoft Office XP was to optimize it for location independence, and what you find in this chapter are the techniques needed to organize your tools and files so you can easily switch between working at the office, the road, or at home. In this chapter, you learn how to do the following.

- Synchronize your Outlook data between computers or with a handheld device

- Handle your e-mail while you're on the road

- Create a mobile filing system that ensures you have up-to-date versions of all the files you need

- Replicate the same working environment and toolset throughout all the computers you use

- Use the Web as a repository for your critical data

Managing Your Personal Information

Often, the most important type of information for a knowledge worker to have on the road is an address book or calendar. This, along with a task list, is normally stored in a personal information manager such as Outlook.

If you are using a notebook computer while you're away from the office, you need to have your Outlook information available. Although Outlook has no built-in tool to synchronize two Outlook data files, there are several approaches to using Outlook on two different computers that you can utilize.

Increasingly, mobile workers are replacing their paper-based organizers with Pocket PCs or Personal Digital Assistants (PDAs). PDAs have become easier to synchronize with your desktop's Outlook data file, and with the addition of a modem, provide access to e-mail and the Web. In addition, Pocket PC users gain the ability to work on Word documents and Microsoft Excel workbooks.

After you decide to keep your personal information with you electronically when you're away from the office, you need to be able to do two things: synchronize your desktop and notebook versions of Outlook, and synchronize Outlook with your handheld device.

Using Outlook on a Desktop and Notebook

When you're away from the office using a notebook computer, it's extremely convenient to have Outlook with you. As a result, you need to ensure you have the same Outlook information available on your notebook as on your desktop.

Unless you're using Outlook with Microsoft Exchange Server, your Outlook data is stored in one file—an *Outlook data file* with the extension .pst—that includes not only your contacts, appointments, and tasks, but also all your e-mail. Thus, the Outlook data file can get quite large—well over 100 MB unless you take steps to periodically archive it.

There are three strategies you can use to synchronize your Outlook data. Each has advantages, and is best used in specific situations.

Share One Outlook Data File

The best way to ensure that the Outlook data on your desktop is the same as the data on your notebook is to use the same data file for both computers. You can use this solution if you can attach your notebook computer to a network that your desktop is on, and if you can access the local drive of your notebook computer from your desktop. Then you do not need to copy any files or folders from one computer to the other when you undock your notebook computer from the network. Because both computers use the same data file, there's no chance of losing important appointments or e-mails.

The disadvantage of this technique is that unless your notebook computer is attached to the network, you aren't able to access your Outlook data with your desktop. This solution is ideal for people who work on both types of computer, and who regularly attach their notebook computer to their network when they are working at their desktop.

After you connect both computers to the network, specify that your desktop computer should use the Outlook data file located on your notebook computer as follows.

1. Locate the Outlook data file on the notebook computer by clicking the Windows Start button, pointing to Search, and clicking For Files and Folders. Next type **outlook.pst** in the Search For Files Or Folders Named box, and note the location of the file when it is found. If you have specified another name for your Outlook data file, type that name in the box instead.

2. Open Outlook on your desktop computer, and choose E-mail Accounts from the Tools menu. In the E-mail Accounts Wizard, leave the default of View Or Change Existing E-mail Accounts and click Next.

3. In the next E-mail Accounts screen, click the New Outlook Data File button and then click OK in the New Outlook Data File dialog box.

4. In the Create Or Open Outlook Data File dialog box, navigate to the folder on the laptop computer containing the Outlook data file, select the Outlook data file, and then choose OK.

5. In the Personal Folders dialog box, rename the file (for example, Notebook File) so you don't confuse it with the default Personal Folders file and then click OK.

6. In the E-mail Accounts dialog box, choose your new file in the Deliver New E-mail To The Following Location box and click Finish. You see a warning message that you changed the default location for e-mail.

7. Close and restart Outlook. You are asked whether you want to recreate your shortcuts. Click Yes to update the shortcuts on the Outlook Bar.

8. Choose Folder List from the View menu to open the Folder List. You see two sets of folders—your original one (Personal Folders) and the new one (Notebook File). Close the original folder by right-clicking it, and choosing Close from the shortcut menu.

Now, you can access the same Outlook data from either your desktop or your notebook computer. Just be sure the notebook computer is attached to the network when you want to access Outlook from your desktop.

Copy the Outlook Data File

Another way to keep your data synchronized is to copy your entire Outlook data file back and forth from your desktop computer to your notebook (if you're on the same network), or to a removable storage medium (such as a Zip drive) that holds your entire data file.

This strategy ensures that you have all the data on both computers, and provides the additional benefit of creating a backup of your Outlook data file. It is especially appropriate if you need to use Outlook from your desktop computer when your notebook computer is not connected to the network, so you can't use the first strategy. However, if your data file is large, it might not fit on a removable storage medium and you might not enjoy waiting for the large Outlook data file to be copied every time you want to use Outlook on your notebook computer.

To copy the Outlook data file, use step 1 of the previous procedure to locate the data file on both computers and then use standard Windows file copying procedures to copy the latest version to the other computer.

Tip   If you decide to copy your .pst file to a removable storage medium, consider using Microsoft Briefcase. This way, you can synchronize your Outlook files at the same time you synchronize other files in your briefcase. Just create a briefcase on your Zip disk, and then copy the data file into it. You can then synchronize the Zip disk with the notebook or desktop machines when you move from one to the other. For more information about using briefcases, see "Carrying Files in a Briefcase" on page 162.

Copy Selected Outlook Folders

If sharing or copying the Outlook data file is not convenient or possible, there is another alternative. You can copy only contacts, appointments, and tasks—but not your e-mail. This makes the copying process easier and faster, because e-mail and its attachments usually account for most of the size of an Outlook data file. You might find that without the e-mail, the file you need to copy easily fits on a Zip disk and might in fact be small enough to fit on a floppy disk.

Of course, this implies that your e-mail will not be synchronized on both computers so don't use this strategy if that's one of your requirements.

To copy selected folders from one computer to another, you need to create a new Outlook data file and then move your contacts, appointments, and tasks into it. The new file will be the one you copy from one computer to the other. To do so, follow these steps.

1. Choose Folder List from the View menu to open the Folder List, if it is not already displayed.

2. In Outlook, point to New on the File menu and click Outlook Data File. Click OK in the New Outlook Data File dialog box.

3. In the Create Or Open Outlook Data File dialog box, navigate to the folder into which you want your new file to be saved, give the new file a name, and click OK.

4. In the Create Microsoft Personal Folders dialog box, specify the name that will be displayed in the Folder List (such as Transfer File) and click OK.

5. Select the new data file in the Folder List.

6. Create a new Appointments folder by pointing to New from the File menu, and clicking Folder.

7. In the Create New Folder dialog box, specify the name (Calendar) and type (Calendar Items) and click OK. Outlook displays a prompt asking if you would like to add a shortcut to this folder in the Outlook Bar. Click No to continue.

8. In the Folder List, select the Calendar folder that is a subfolder of your old Personal Folders Outlook data file.

9. Point to Current View on the View menu, and select a view such as Active Appointments, which displays all the appointments you want to move.

10. Select all the appointments, and then drag them to the new Calendars folder.

11. Repeat steps 7 through 10 for Tasks and Contacts. Your calendar, task, and contact information is now in the Transfer File, like the empty one shown in Figure 8-1.

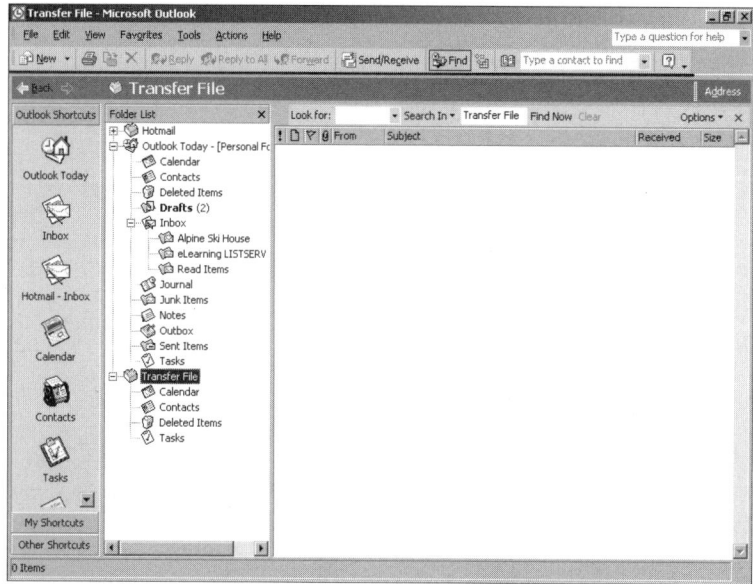

Figure 8-1   *You can use a second Outlook data file to keep your calendar, contacts, and tasks, so you can copy this information quickly from one computer to another.*

Of course, this leaves your e-mail unsynchronized but there's a partial workaround for that as well. You can use the Outlook option to leave a copy of e-mail you receive on your mail server. That way when you get your e-mail, you're getting only a copy of it and you can get the same e-mail again on your other computer. For instance, you can get your work e-mail from home without fear that you won't be able to access it again from your office computer the next day. Of course, e-mail you send to someone else is not available from the other computer but you are able to access e-mail that's sent to you. You can opt to leave messages on the server as follows.

1. Open Outlook, and choose E-mail Accounts from the Tools menu.

2. In the E-mail Accounts Wizard, select View Or Change Existing E-mail Accounts and click Next.

3. In the E-mail Accounts dialog box, select the account you want to modify and then click Change.

4. Click More Settings, and then select the Advanced tab.

5. Check Leave A Copy Of Messages On The Server, and then click OK.

6. Click Next to return to the E-mail Accounts dialog box.

7. Repeat steps 3 through 6 for other e-mail accounts as needed.

Tip   When you check Leave A Copy Of Messages On The Server, you may want to also check Remove From Server After, and specify a number of days, otherwise the server will become clogged with your stored e-mail. Select a number that will give you access to the majority of e-mails you might refer to while on the road—often between a week and a month's worth.

Using Microsoft Exchange

Microsoft Exchange is a server-based application that enables Outlook to serve as a powerful groupware tool in addition to being a personal information manager. Outlook users who are also using Exchange can easily see each others' calendars, coordinate task assignments, and share contact lists and other folders (for example, folders containing files and group calendars). Because many Outlook users do not use Exchange, later versions of Outlook have contained ways to coordinate work without requiring Exchange (such as sharing free-busy times on the Web). Some groupware functionality, however, still requires Exchange such as e-mail rules that operate on e-mail before it comes to your mailbox.

Exchange provides robust methods for synchronizing with your notebook or home computer. You can synchronize using a dial-up connection or when docked into your corporate network. Procedures for synchronizing are set up by Exchange administrators, so you need to contact them to get the specifics for your particular situation.

Synchronizing with a Pocket PC

Pocket PCs are handheld devices running the Microsoft Windows Pocket PC operating system. As of this writing, Casio, Compaq, and Hewlett-Packard all make Pocket PC models. All of them are handheld devices, and included is a version of Outlook, Word, Excel, and Microsoft Internet Explorer. This provides an immediate benefit of the Pocket PC versus other handheld devices such as the Palm or Handspring PDAs, because the operating system and applications are already familiar to most users. Pocket PCs also include

- Windows Media Player (so you can download MP3 files for those long plane trips)
- Microsoft Reader (for e-books)
- Pocket Access
- A picture viewer (a great high tech way to show those baby pictures that used to get crunched up in your wallet)
- Other downloadable applications, such as Microsoft Pocket Streets, that integrate with Microsoft MapPoint to provide street maps of selected cities

One of the beauties of the Pocket PC is the seamless integration it provides to your main desktop or notebook computer. The Pocket PC comes with Microsoft ActiveSync, which allows you to easily synchronize your Outlook data and copy files from your main computer to your Pocket PC and vice versa.

When ActiveSync is installed, you see it as an icon on your taskbar. You also see a new entry in Windows Explorer. In the list of disks within My Computer, you see the Mobile Device folder, shown in Figure 8-2. You can use this to browse the files on your Pocket PC, and drag files from your main computer to the handheld device and vice versa. Word documents, Excel workbooks, and Microsoft Access databases are converted automatically to the simpler format used in Pocket PC version of the applications. Other files, such as MP3 and picture files, can be copied as well to be accessed through the Pocket PC's media player or picture viewer.

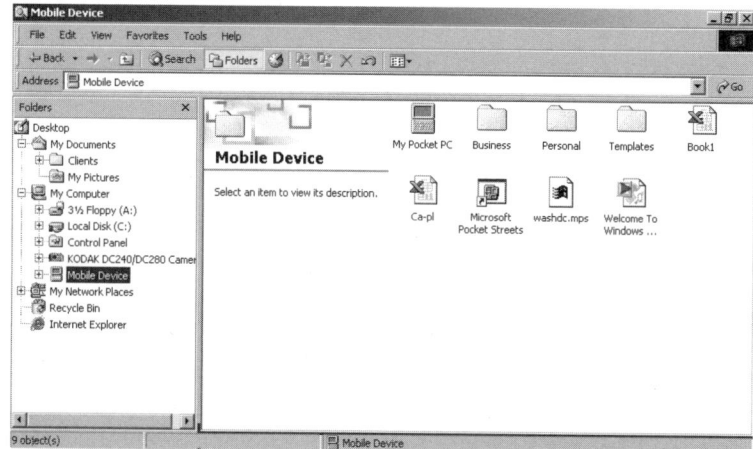

Figure 8-2 *Your Pocket PC becomes another folder on your system, so you can quickly copy files back and forth from it to your desktop.*

When you plug your Pocket PC into its cradle and attach it to a Universal Serial Bus (USB) port, the ActiveSync application automatically opens and starts checking your Outlook calendar, contacts, and tasks to see whether they are synchronized with those in your Pocket PC. If ActiveSync does not start automatically, right-click the Outlook taskbar icon and choose Open Microsoft ActiveSync.

You can synchronize your Pocket PC continuously when it is connected to your computer, synchronize it once when it is first connected, or manually when you click the Sync button. You can also choose which Outlook folders to synchronize. Consider synchronizing your Inbox if you want to read your e-mail offline, or if you have a wireless modem for your Pocket PC. You can also synchronize files, which creates a Synchronized Files folder. This is a handy way to keep the Word or Excel files that you always want to have on your Pocket PC up-to-date. Set your synchronization options by following these steps.

1. On the Taskbar, double-click the ActiveSync icon to open ActiveSync.

2. Choose Options from the Tools menu.

3. In the Sync Options tab, select each item you want to synchronize.

Note   To synchronize Office files, check Files. A Synchronized Files folder is created on the desktop computer. Using standard Windows move commands, you can move files you want to keep synchronized into that folder.

---

4. In the Sync Mode tab of the Options dialog box, choose when you want synchronizations to occur.

5. Click OK to return to ActiveSync.

You can also synchronize your Pocket PC with selected Web sites, so you have the latest version of important Web-based information available to you when you're on the road. On your desktop, browse to the page you want to synchronize in Internet Explorer and then choose Tools, Create Mobile Favorite. Ensure that Favorite is checked in the ActiveSync Options dialog box, and when you synchronize you have your favorite Web pages available to you.

There is also a link in the Pocket PC's Internet Explorer to AvantGo (*http://www.avantgo.com*). This site allows you to create a personalized list from more than 1,000 channels of information covering business news, travel information, and comparison shopping. Proprietary channels are also available, such as EventPro (*http://www.eventpro.com*) for professional speakers, who can download their calendars and itineraries from the Web into their Pocket PC. Whenever you synchronize to a desktop that's connected to the Internet or if you have a wireless modem attached to your Pocket PC, you can download the latest information.

Palm Pilots

Although the Palm Pilot family of PDAs held the greatest market share for knowledge workers before 2001, the Pocket PC is emerging as the new mobile standard. In fact, Gartner Dataquest suggested that in terms of revenue, Palm had lost its lead to Compaq's iPAQ family of Pocket PCs. The analysis went on to say that a growing portion of users want more functionality than is available in Palm Pilots.

If you have a Palm, however, all is not lost! You can still synchronize your Outlook Inbox, calendar, task list, and contact list (though the Palm organizer files do not provide as accurate a synchronization as with Pocket Outlook). You can even access AvantGo channels and use a wireless modem to get your e-mail. Functionality that is not present includes

- Word, Excel, and Access
- Media Player, Picture Viewer, and Reader
- The ability to drag Office files
- The native ability to synchronize Web pages

Synchronizing Your Office Settings

Recognizing that many knowledge workers today are mobile, Microsoft has built a Save My Settings feature into Office XP that allows you to save common Office settings on the Web and then apply them to another computer. Settings that can be saved in this way include many of the changes you make in Office applications under the Options command; arrangements and customizations of your toolbars; history files; and AutoCorrect and AutoText entries. To save your settings on the Web, you need a free Microsoft Passport account and if you don't have one, you can sign up for one as part of the process of saving your settings.

To synchronize your Office settings, do the following.

1. Close all Office applications.

2. Click the Windows Start button, point to Programs, Microsoft Office Tools, and click Save My Settings Wizard.

3. Choose whether to save or restore your settings, as appropriate.

4. Unless you're working in an organization where your system administrator specifies a network location, choose Save The Settings To The Web.

5. Sign in with your Passport sign-in name (your e-mail address) and password. If you don't have a Passport account, click Get One Here and follow the instructions to obtain an account.

6. If you want a notification before Microsoft deletes your saved settings (which happens three months after you save them), type an e-mail address for notification purposes.

7. Click Finish. Your Office settings are saved to the Web.

Whenever you want to duplicate the setup on another computer, you can use this same process except that you choose to restore the settings in step 3.

Tip   If you are working on someone else's machine for the day, you can save their settings to a file on the local disk rather than to the Web. Then restore your settings from the Web, and their machine will have your configuration. Reverse this process at the end of the day to restore their original configuration for them.

Handling E-mail on the Road

E-mail doesn't stop just because you're on the road. There's nothing more disconcerting than getting back from a week when you've been "unplugged," and finding 500+ e-mail messages in your Inbox. Fortunately, there are several techniques you can use that will enable you to take care of your e-mail while you're away from your desktop. Which one you use depends on how frequently you need to check your e-mail and what type of Internet access you'll have. Some of the most frequent scenarios for mobile knowledge workers are shown in Table 8-1. The table also shows the best technology solution for each scenario; all solutions are discussed in the sections that follow.

Table 8-1   Mobile E-mail Scenarios and Solutions

Scenario	Solution
• You're traveling, and need to check your e-mail frequently each day. • You'll be in a major metropolitan area in the U.S. • You can't connect to the Internet through a hard-wired connection (dial-up or a network connection).	• Wireless E-mail Access
• You're traveling, and need to check your e-mail frequently each day. • You can connect to the Internet from someone else's computer through a high-speed hard-wired connection (commonly from a client's office).	• Hotmail Account • Temporary E-mail Configurations
• You're traveling, and need to check your e-mail from your hotel, which offers dial-up access.	• Send/Receive Groups • Download Headers Only
• You're traveling and won't be checking your e-mail until you get back, but want to manage your e-mail while you're away.	• Away From Office Rules
• You work from two offices (for example, home and work), and need to synchronize your Outlook mail folders.	• Synchronized Inboxes

Choosing to Go Wireless

Some people require immediate access to e-mail throughout the day, so they don't miss potential sales opportunities or because they need to make and communicate critical decisions quickly. If this describes your job, you might want to consider wireless e-mail access. There are many alternatives for wireless e-mail, and each has its own advantages, as you can see in Table 8-2.

Table 8-2   Wireless Modem Alternatives *

Alternative	Pros and Cons
Wireless modem for Pocket PC	Pros • Integrates with Outlook Inbox • Small and unobtrusive Cons • No keyboard, hard to write long messages • Attachments are problematic • Potential security problems with sensitive data
Wireless modem for notebook	Pros • All e-mail is in one place • Keyboard allows easy e-mail composition • Large screen makes it easy to read e-mail • No problem with attachments Cons • Notebook computer is much larger than other solutions • Might not be convenient to use (for example, in meetings), easy to get to (for example, in luggage), or with you • Potential security problems with sensitive data
E-mail enabled cell phone	Pros • You only need one device • The cell phone might be with you more than other devices Cons • No keyboard • No data entry aids (as on Pocket PCs) • Small screen and little memory makes long e-mails problematic • No attachments
Text pager	Pros • Small • Always on Cons • Small keyboard • Small screen and little memory make long e-mails problematic • No attachments

*   If you choose to obtain wireless e-mail from your Pocket PC, you need to carefully review the currently available alternatives because they change almost monthly.

As of this writing, the best alternative is to obtain a wireless PC card modem and access service through vendors such as OmniSky (*http://www.omnisky.com*) or GoAmerica (*http://www.goamerica.com*). Unfortunately, this alternative is not inexpensive. You can expect to pay $300 for the modem, and between $30 and $60 per month for wireless access, depending on the brand of Pocket PC you have. (For some reason, service for Compaq iPAQs costs significantly more than for Hewlett-Packard Jornada Pocket PCs.) Some services provide modems that work with your laptop as well as your Pocket PC. Some provide coverage in hundreds of metropolitan areas but access speeds of only 19.2 Kbps, while others provide coverage in limited areas but offer speeds up to 128 Kbps.

Note By the time you read this book, some other alternatives might be available. These include digital phone cards that connect your Pocket PC to a wireless phone with a cable, Bluetooth devices that permit a wireless connection between your Pocket PC and your wireless phone, and wireless phones that have Pocket PCs built into them.

In general, you find the best information about currently available alternatives by going to the Microsoft Pocket PC Web site, *http://www.microsoft.com/mobile/pocketpc/ default.asp*. In general, it's wise to make a wireless investment only if you believe it will pay for itself in 6 to 12 months. Given the rate of technological change, your wireless Pocket PC will probably be out of date after that time.

Accessing E-mail from Others' Computers

Sometimes you can use someone else's computer to download your Outlook e-mail. You might be at a client's office who gives you this permission, or you might be connecting through a cyber café. To connect to your e-mail account, you need to know four things.

- Your UserID for that e-mail account
- Your password for that e-mail account
- The URL for your POP3 (Post Office Protocol 3)(incoming) mail server
- The URL for the SMTP (Simple Mail Transfer Protocol)(outgoing) mail server used at the site you're at (you might need to ask an administrator or user for this)

It's often easier to use Microsoft Outlook Express for your temporary e-mail configuration, because Outlook Express—being a part of Windows—is more likely to be on the computer you're using. Also, Outlook Express is less likely to be used by the computer's owner as his or her e-mail application—so you run less chance of confusing the owner's Inbox items with yours. Here's how to set up Outlook Express and check your mail remotely.

1. Open Outlook Express, choose Accounts from the Tools menu, click the Add button, and then click Mail.

2. Follow the steps of the Internet Connection Wizard to create your account. Type your name, e-mail address, POP3 and SMTP servers, account name, and password. After you complete all the steps in the wizard, you return to the Internet Accounts window where you see your new account in the account list.

3. To ensure that downloaded messages remain on the server, click the Properties button in the Internet Accounts window. In the Properties dialog box, click the Advanced tab, then click Leave A Copy Of The Messages On Server. Click OK twice to return to Outlook Express Main window.

4. Choose Send And Receive from the Tools menu, and then select the account you just created.

5. Outlook Express downloads your mail, then read your mail as you normally do.

6. When you are finished, delete the mail from the Inbox so the next user does not see it. You might also want to empty the Deleted Items folder by choosing Empty Deleted Items Folder from the Edit menu, if you want to be sure your e-mails are not retained on the system.

Getting E-mail Through a Hotmail Account

Another alternative for obtaining your e-mail on the road is to create a Hotmail account. Hotmail, operated by Microsoft, permits you to send and receive e-mail from your browser. This can often be more convenient than creating a temporary e-mail account at a computer you are at temporarily. Hotmail has some useful features that make it worth looking at, including the following.

- You can retrieve messages from up to four Internet (POP3) e-mail accounts through Hotmail.

- Conversely, you can retrieve your Hotmail accounts through Outlook.

- An Inbox Protector filters junk mail.

- You can be notified when e-mail arrives through your instant messaging, digital wireless phone, or digital pager.

- Your Hotmail Sign-In Name and password also serve as your Passport account.

To sign up for a Hotmail account, go to *http://www.hotmail.com*. Fill in the required information and your free Hotmail account is activated.

Note   Hotmail is used by a host of Internet marketers to send spam throughout the Internet. You will undoubtedly start receiving a lot of junk mail if you use your Hotmail account. Worse, if you're a small businessperson, you might be inadvertently sending a message to potential customers that you're not professional by using a Hotmail address or be filtered from their e-mail systems because so much spam comes from Hotmail.

Scanning E-mail on a Dial-up Connection

If you're connecting to the Internet through a slower, dial-up connection, you might want to download only the headers of your e-mail messages. The body of the message (including any attachments) is left on the server, so the download proceeds very quickly. You can then delete any junk mail messages you receive, and download just the ones you want to read from the server. This can be especially useful if you are on the road and connecting only sporadically, or if you're traveling globally and paying per minute for your dial-up connection.

Note You may not see the Work with Headers option if you are using Hotmail or certain other types of e-mail accounts.

Use e-mail headers with Outlook by following these steps.

1. Choose Send/Receive from the Tools menu, point to Work with Headers, and then point to Download Headers From.

2. In the submenu menu, choose All Accounts or one specific e-mail account. The headers for e-mail in the selected account are downloaded to your computer.

3. When you finish downloading the headers, you see a new Header Status icon in the Inbox item list as shown in Figure 8-3. Decide which e-mails to download by right-clicking each, and then choosing from the following options.

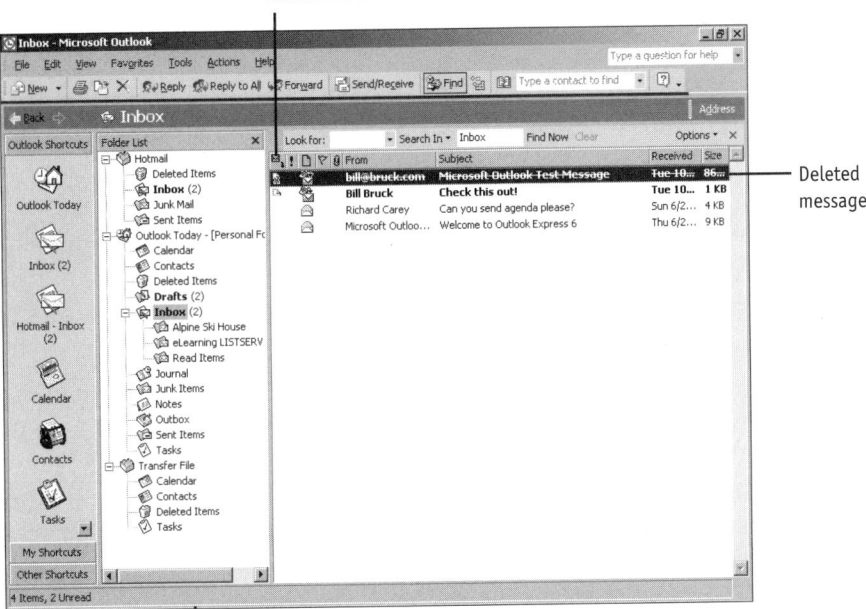

Figure 8-3 *When you download headers only, you can specify which e-mails should be downloaded and which ones deleted before you actually download them.*

- **Mark to Download Message(s).**   Download the message and remove it from the server when you process the headers.

- **Mark To Download Message Copy.**   Download the message and leave a copy of it on the server when you process the headers.

Caution   On some Web servers, the Download Message Copy removes the message from the server. Be sure to test this function with your Internet service provider (ISP) prior to relying on it.

- **Delete.**   Remove the message from the server when you process the headers.

- If you do not choose one of these options, the message remains on the server and you can retrieve it when you next process messages by choosing one of the options.

4. When you have marked all your headers, choose Send/Receive from the Tools menu, point to Work With Headers, and then point to Process Marked Headers From.

5. Choose the All Account or a specific e-mail account. A connection with the mail server is established, and the selected messages are downloaded or deleted.

Controlling Multiple E-mail Accounts

Increasingly, many knowledge workers have multiple e-mail accounts. As you travel or work from home, you might find that you want to download mail only from specific accounts rather than all of them. In addition to supporting multiple e-mail accounts, Outlook supports Send/Receive Groups. These groups let you specify a set of accounts you want to get your mail from. You can even specify that mail you get from a certain account group downloads only headers. This is a convenient way to automate the process of seeing only headers when you're using a slower, dial-up connection. To set up a send/receive group, do the following.

1. Open Outlook, and choose Options from the Tools menu. Click the Mail Setup tab, and click the Send/Receive button.

2. To create a new group, choose New in the Send/Receive dialog box, give the group a name in the Send/Receive Group Name dialog box, and click OK.

3. In the Send/Receive Settings dialog box shown in Figure 8-4, click an account to be included and then check Include Account In This Send/Receive Group. Choose properties including

- **Send Mail Items/Receive Mail Items.**   You might want to receive e-mail but not send it from a specific account—especially if you are on the road and the outgoing mail server for the account doesn't work from where you are.

- **Download Item Description Only.** This option has the same effect as choosing Download E-mail Headers, described in the last section.

Tip You can create a send/receive group called Dialup that includes all your e-mail accounts, but specifies to download only the item description. This can make getting e-mail from your hotel room much faster!

- If you choose Download Complete Item Including Attachments, you can still filter out large items by checking Download Only Item Description For Items Larger Than and specifying the size of the items to filter. Items that are too large have their header downloaded, so you can decide whether to download the entire item.

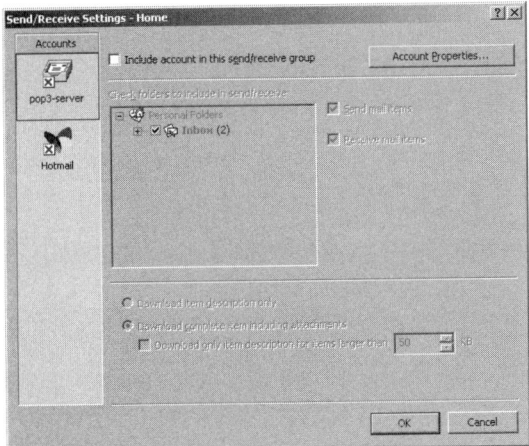

Figure 8-4 *All your e-mail accounts are shown in the Accounts bar at the left, and options for each are available on the right. By default, none of the accounts are included in the new send/receive group.*

4. When you click OK you return to the Send/Receive Groups dialog box, displaying a list of your groups. For each group, you can decide whether to include it in send/receive commands (the Send/Receive button on the Standard toolbar), and whether to include it in automatic send receives (at specified intervals or when exiting). You can use one group for your send/receives when you are online, and another group when you are not and must establish a dial-up connection.

Letting People Know You're Away

When you're on vacation or a professional retreat, you might not check your e-mail for a week or more. Before considering alternatives for handling your e-mail when you're away, it's important to understand one crucial fact about how e-mail works. E-mail comes from the sender to your e-mail server, where it stays until you retrieve it using Outlook or another e-mail client. The server is usually either a standard e-mail POP3 server, a Hotmail server, or Microsoft Exchange. To handle e-mail when you are away, either your computer must be on and checking e-mail regularly or it must be handled at the server. Given this, there are three alternatives for handling your e-mail when you're away.

- **From Microsoft Exchange.**   If you are connected to Microsoft Exchange, you can access the Out Of Office Assistant—a wizard that helps you create rules that are stored on the Exchange Server to handle your e-mail. Contact your Exchange administrator for details about what functionality has been enabled on your system.

- **From a POP3 server.**   If you have a POP3 account (as most Internet e-mail accounts are), there are three functions your ISP may provide. First, it might be possible to forward your e-mail to another address. In this case, a coworker might be able to respond to e-mail for you. Second, the ISP might provide a simple Away From Office utility that sends a message to the sender saying you are away and keeps the e-mail in your POP3 Inbox. Third, your ISP might provide autoresponders so you can automatically send a file back to the sender (containing your "I'm away" message). However, the autoresponder might not save the e-mail so use this with caution. Most major ISPs have a Web-based administration screen that allows e-mail users to configure these preferences by logging on with a user name and password—often your e-mail UserID and password. Check with your ISP for details.

Tip   Be careful about using an autoresponder if you belong to an e-mail list. It can be very annoying to list members to receive your out of office message for a week. You may want to temporarily stop your e-mail list subscriptions while you are gone. See "Participating in an E-mail List" on page 25 for more information.

- **From your computer.**   Leave your computer on, set Outlook to check for messages periodically, and create a rule that handles your e-mail. Generally your first rule should be one that filters junk mail. Common additional rules you might consider are ones that respond to all messages with a "I'm away" message, forward all e-mail to a colleague, or forward mail from selected senders or with selected subjects to a colleague.

See Also   For more information about creating rules, see "Automating E-mail Organization" on page 137.

Synchronizing Your Inboxes

If you are sending and receiving e-mail from two computers, you will encounter a problem in keeping your sent and received e-mail folders synchronized. Unfortunately, there's no perfect solution but there are a few tips you might find helpful.

- The only foolproof ways to keep your e-mail folders synchronized are to use a mapped drive, or copy your Outlook data file from one computer to another. Although this works for notebooks that are docked into networks and then taken away to be used, it does not help if you're accessing your e-mail from someone else's computer or trying to synchronize your home and office computers.

- Be sure to keep a copy of the messages on the server, as described earlier in this chapter. Although this keeps your Inboxes synchronized, it does not help your outgoing mail.

- Include yourself on the CC: or BCC: line of every outgoing e-mail. This way, the e-mail comes back into your Inbox and is stored on the server. (Unfortunately, you cannot sort items by recipient in the Sent Items folder because they appear in your Inbox as an e-mail to you, so even if you move them to your Sent Items folder they are listed under your name.)

Creating a Mobile File System

The goal of creating an effective mobile filing system is to ensure you have all the files you need with you when you're away from your office. Done right, keeping your mobile filing system up-to-date takes a few seconds when you leave the office. Done wrong, you can run into any of several common problems.

- You are missing important files you need, and there's no way to get them.

- You don't have the current version of files—or worse, don't know whether your version is current.

- You make changes to different versions of the same file on your notebook and desktop computer, making it very difficult to reconcile them.

The first decision you need to make in creating a mobile filing system is which files you must have with you. Unless you are severely short of disk space on your notebook computer or are transferring files between desktops at work and home using removable media such as Zip disks, it's usually a good idea to replicate your My Documents folder on both your desktop and notebook computer. This way, you're always sure you have the right files with you—because you have *all* your data files. You're also maintaining the same familiar working environment, whether you're in the office or on the road.

After you decide which files to transfer, you need to choose a method for synchronizing the files on your desktop with the ones you take with you. You can use two built-in methods for synchronizing your files that are built into Windows 2000: Briefcase and Offline Files. Each has its advantages but for a full synchronization of your file system, look at a synchronization utility.

Carrying Files in a Briefcase

The Windows Briefcase is an excellent way to "check out" specific files or folders onto a removable high capacity medium such as a Zip disk, or when you are creating a temporary connection between your desktop and notebook computers with a direct cable connection. The briefcase, as the name implies, is a portable "carrier" for folders and files. You can create many briefcases, and use them for different types of files. When you connect your notebook computer to the desktop or insert your removable media, you can then synchronize the files in the briefcase with the files on the desktop, and the latest copy of each file is automatically copied to both computers.

The briefcase is created on the computer or removable media you want to copy the files to—usually your notebook computer. To create and use a briefcase, take these steps.

1. Open Windows Explorer and navigate to the folder on your notebook or in your removable medium within which you want to create your briefcase.

2. Point to New on the File menu, and choose Briefcase.

3. If you intend to use multiple briefcases to store files of different types, rename your briefcase by right-clicking it in the Folder list and then choosing Rename.

4. Repeat steps 2 and 3 to create additional briefcases as needed.

5. Drag the files or folders you want to store to the briefcase. This makes a copy of them in the briefcase.

You can now undock your notebook or remove the media from the desktop computer, and then open, edit, and save the files in the briefcase as you do files in any other folder. When you redock your notebook or replace the media in the desktop, you can easily synchronize the files by taking these steps.

1. Open Windows Explorer.

2. In the Folders list, highlight your briefcase. You see a new Briefcase menu option.

3. Choose Briefcase, Update All. You see the Update Briefcase dialog box, showing the files in the briefcase and target folders and the actions that will be taken on update.

4. To change the action for any file, right-click it and choose the appropriate option, as shown in Figure 8-5.

5. Click Update to synchronize the briefcase and desktop.

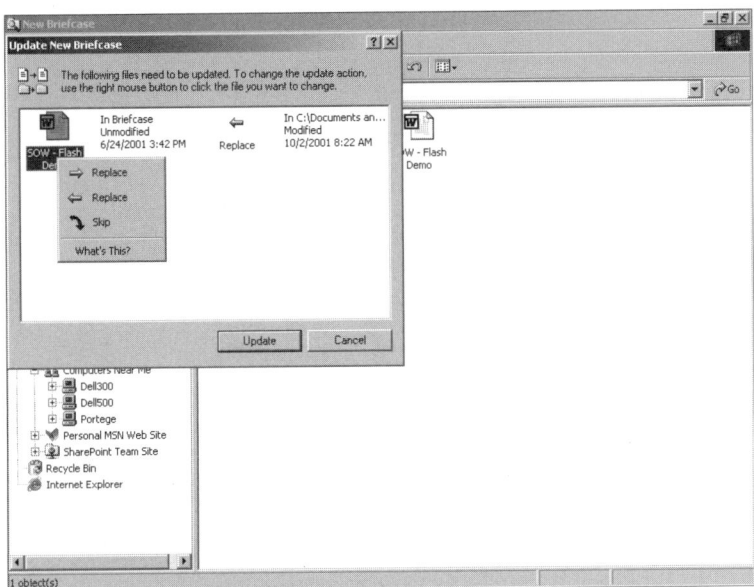

Figure 8-5 *You can synchronize files between your desktop and notebook or removable storage device with the Windows Briefcase.*

Using Offline Files to Synchronize Folders

The second way Windows 2000 provides to keep your files in synch is the Offline Files feature, which creates a duplicate of selected desktop folders on your notebook computer. Then, when you specify, the files in your offline folder are synchronized with those on the desktop so that the latest version of each is maintained.

Whenever you are not connected to the network, you still have your offline files and folders available. In My Computer, you can double-click a network drive containing offline files and you do not see an error message. Instead, as you browse through the folders of the network drive, you see only those folders and files you have made available offline as well as their parent folders. You can open, edit, and save files in these folders at will—just as if you were on the network. When you synchronize with the network, new files you created in synchronized folders are added to the network, files you delete are removed, and files you edit are updated.

Microsoft suggests that Offline Files is the preferred method if you are working with shared files on a network (rather than using a cable connection or removable media). This is because, with Offline Files, you can create synchronization schedules so that your folders automatically stay current and use the same network drives and folders as do you when you're connected to the network. To use Offline Files, you need to enable the Offline Files feature, specify which folders should be available offline, and set your synchronization options.

1. Open My Computer on your Notebook computer.

2. Choose Folder Options on the Tools menu.

3. In the Offline Files tab, check Enable Offline Files.

You now see the Make Available Offline option when you share a folder or file. To share a folder or file, do the following.

1. From your notebook computer, open Windows Explorer.

2. Navigate to the file or folder on the desktop that you want to share.

3. Right-click the folder, and choose Make Available Offline.

You can even specify when synchronization should occur: whenever you dock or undock from the network, whenever your computer is idle, or manually. To set synchronization options, do the following.

1. Open the synchronization manager by pointing to Programs in the Start menu, pointing to Accessories, and then choosing Synchronize.

2. In the Items to Synchronize dialog box, click Setup.

3. In the Synchronization Settings dialog box shown in Figure 8-6, specify when you want synchronizations to occur and then choose OK.

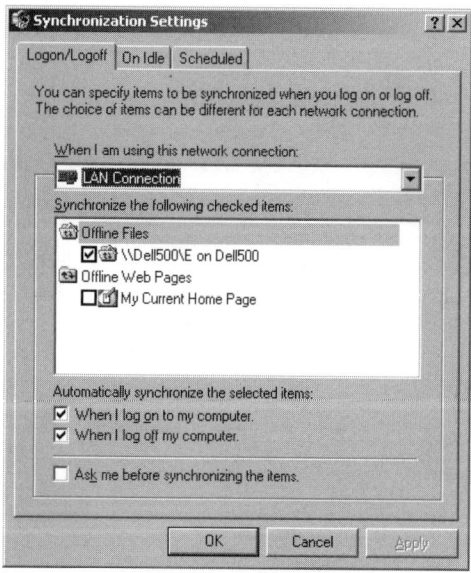

Figure 8-6 *You can synchronize your offline files at schedules you specify.*

4. To perform an immediate synchronization, click Synchronize in the Items to Synchronize dialog box.

Duplicating My Documents Folders

Sometimes, you might want to duplicate the My Documents folder on your notebook and desktop rather than taking selected files or folders with you when you undock from the network. If you want to have the same My Documents structure on both computers, neither Briefcase nor Offline Folders will do. What you need is a synchronization utility. There are several to choose from, including FolderMatch (*http://www.foldermatch.com*), File-N-Sync (*http://www.peersoftware.com*), or Directory Toolkit (*http://www. searchandreplace.com*).

With Directory Toolkit, for example, as shown in Figure 8-7, you can see both the source and the target files. You have a number of synchronization options. The most common option is to update each folder with the latest version of all the files. If you do this before you undock your laptop from your network, you can be sure it contains all the files in My Documents (or whatever folder you specify).

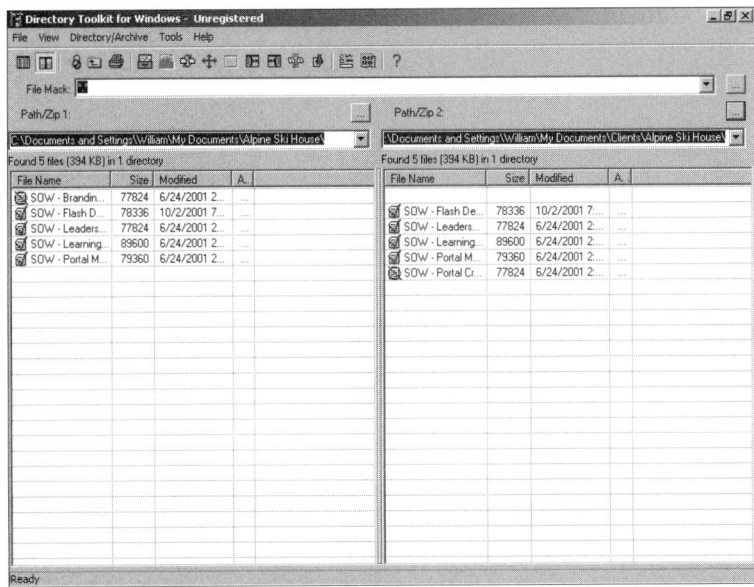

Figure 8-7 *Advanced road warriors will want all their files on their notebook computers, and might find it valuable to use a file synchronization utility such as Directory Toolkit from Funduc Software to synchronize with their desktop quickly and easily.*

The one slightly disconcerting fact about using a synchronization utility is that after you delete a file, it reappears when you perform your next synchronization because the utility detects that it is "missing" from one folder and replaces it with the other folder's version. To truly delete files, these utilities provide a second type of synchronization that exactly duplicates the files from one computer to another—thus deleting ones on the second computer that don't exist on the first.

Generally, synchronizating takes less than a minute over a network and ensures that you have everything you need when you go on the road.

Summary

This chapter has provided you with the essential tools and techniques to be able to work from the office and then take your essential tools with you on the road, to your home, or even to the beach. There are three elements you need to be an effective mobile worker.

- Have your personal information (contacts, appointments, and tasks) and desktop preferences with you
- Stay in touch through e-mail wherever you are
- Access your working files

You can use the following checklist to make sure you're prepared to go out on the road.

Checklist for Working Remotely

The following points will help you develop the tools and techniques you need to work effectively on the road.

[ ] Synchronize your desktop Outlook data file with the one on your notebook computer.

[ ] Synchronize personal information between your handheld device and your desktop or notebook computer.

[ ] Replicate your Office settings from your desktop computer to any other computer using the Web.

[ ] Get your e-mail when you're on the road—either by accessing the Web, creating temporary e-mail accounts on others' computers, or using a wireless device.

[ ] Get e-mail when you're on a slow dial-up connections by downloading headers only or using send/receive groups.

[ ] Respond to e-mail automatically when you're away from your computer for an extended time.

[ ] Synchronize your e-mail folders when you're using more than one computer for sending and receiving e-mail.

[ ] Use Briefcase, Offline Files, and Synchronization utilities to synchronize your files between your desktop and notebook computers.

Creating Knowledge

In the Parts I and II of this book, you learned about information—how to find it and how to organize it. Now, in Part III, you learn about knowledge. The field of knowledge management is alive with many models (and many debates) about what constitutes information versus knowledge. DIKW is one model that serves as a basis for many approaches to the practice of knowledge management in organizations.

Data -> Information -> Knowledge -> Wisdom

These terms are defined differently by various practitioners, but in general, the following definitions are true.

- **Data.** An objective fact about the world, data lacks context or meaningful relation to anything else. For instance, an acre consists of 5,128 square feet. This is an objective fact, but does it tell you how big an acre is?

- **Information.** Although information provides a context for data or the relationships between data elements, it does not provide information about why the data exists the way it does or how it might change over time. For instance, if I add that an acre is about the size of a football field without the end zones, you have a context that enables you to understand how big an acre is.

- **Knowledge.** When you understand the patterns of information and their implications for action, you have knowledge. In the acre example, you might put information about acres together with other information to conclude that with new tractors and high production corn seed, an emerging country can triple its food production.

- **Wisdom.** When you understand the foundational principles that underlie knowledge, you have wisdom. For instance, you might examine the immediate benefit of increased food production to see whether a country should take out low-cost loans on tractors, what the long-term environmental effects are of using high production corn seed, and what cultural impact this will have. Then, you might be better able to make a wise decision.

Although specifics of the model can be argued, it's clear knowledge workers add value to the data or information an organization has, to transform it into knowledge that can be acted on to meet organizational goals.

There are three types of information that are commonly transformed into knowledge: numeric data, text documents, and visual representations of trends and concepts. In addition, in today's increasingly collaborative workplace it's vital to understand how knowledge is created with other workers.

Part III shows you how to transform information into knowledge in these four central areas. Chapter 9, "Creating Knowledge Using Numbers," teaches you how to summarize your Microsoft Excel data by sorting, filtering, and subtotaling it. You learn how to analyze your data with formulas and advanced functions, and how to create PivotTables that summarize your information. You also learn how to solve what-if problems and project trends, so you have a sense of the implications of the information you have stored.

In Chapter 10, "Creating Knowledge Using Visuals," you learn how to illustrate patterns with charts and PivotCharts in Excel, and how to use charts to visually represent trends over time. You also learn how to illustrate concepts and processes in Microsoft PowerPoint by combining a variety of tools, including diagrams, clip art, and drawing tools, and to diagram complex illustrations with Microsoft Visio.

Chapter 11, "Creating Knowledge Using Documents," teaches you how to transform information into knowledge by organizing and supporting conclusions with Microsoft Word documents. You see how to organize your thoughts with outlines and mind maps, and build on previous work by recycling old documents, using templates, and creating a clause bank. You also learn how to support your points with data tables, integrated charts and diagrams, and references.

If you produce knowledge in collaboration with other people, Chapter 12, "Creating Knowledge with People," is for you. In it you see how to coordinate the work you do with others. You learn how to use the powerful review features of Word to quickly move through the review cycle. You also find out how to discuss your work online with Web discussions, instant messaging, and online meetings.

Creating Knowledge Using Numbers

Karen Khanna is a newly hired training manager for Contoso, Ltd., a midsized corporation with 2,500 employees. She has some ideas for improving the utilization of training resources, and evaluating the effectiveness of current training programs. She needs to find all the information she can about the current training offered by Contoso so she can provide a solid justification for any new initiatives she suggests. Fortunately, Karen's predecessor created a database that tracked students in every instructor-led and e-learning course offered by the training department, and which students were given funds by Contoso for pursuing additional degrees. Better yet, the database is linked to the employee database that provides information about employment status, career history, and performance evaluations.

With this raw data available, Karen has decided to do some research. Some of the initial questions she wants to answer include

- Where is Contoso spending its training dollars? How much is being spent on instructor-led training, e-learning, and academic programs? What are the spending trends in each of these areas?

- Which departments are often significantly under-budget? With this data, she intends to interview the department heads to assess what their training needs are and why present training is not utilized, and then present summary findings to management.

- How satisfied have employees been with instructor-led versus e-learning courses? Karen figures that if she can identify those employees who have taken three of each, she can send them a short survey that will answer this question and give her some "hard numbers" on training satisfaction.

Employees like Karen are adding value to their organization by looking at their corporate databases and asking questions like these. By so doing, they are taking the data that is maintained in their organization and transforming it into useful information and knowledge upon which decisions can be made. Properly analyzed, your organization's data might be able to help you see where inventory shortfalls might occur, price your goods and services, or see where your overhead expenses are out of line.

This chapter shows you how to analyze data using Microsoft Excel. It assumes that if the database is simple, you might have created it yourself in Excel or used a predefined template in Microsoft Access. If you are analyzing corporate data, however, this data is usually maintained in a Microsoft SQL Server, Oracle, or similar database system which you didn't design. Even if your database is maintained in Access, you will probably want to use Excel to analyze it because of the more extensive analysis tools and greater ease of use that it provides.

See Also   For more information about importing data from other database applications into Excel, see "Integrating Other Data into Excel" on page 116.

In this chapter, you learn the most important techniques for analyzing your data, including how to do the following.

- Sort and filter your database to examine subsets of your data that you are interested in

- Create PivotTables to see summary cross tabs that allow you to focus on totals and subtotals of database information

- Use functions and formulas that allow you to make statistical, financial, and other types of calculations, so you can quickly see trends as they emerge

- Conduct "what-if" analyses to create different scenarios, and manipulate different variables to find the best solution to a problem

Putting Your Data in Order

Often, the first step in analyzing a mass of data is to see it in some type of order. Sometimes that might be as simple as sorting the data on some criteria. For others, you have to create subsets of the information that allow you to focus your analysis on the data of interest. Excel provides three tools that help you summarize your database information, whether that database is maintained in Excel or whether you link to or import an external database:

- **Sort.**   Reorder your database by one or more fields, so you can see similar data together.

- **Filter.**   Create a subset of your data for examination or further analysis.

- **Subtotal.**   Show similar data grouped together, so you can see summary counts of categories of information.

Each of these tools is discussed in the sections that follow.

Sorting Your Excel Database

One of the simplest ways to put some order into your database is to sort it so you can see similar information together. The Excel Sort feature is extremely flexible, allowing you to sort by multiple fields (for example, Customer then Invoice Number) and non-numeric sequences such as days of the week or months of the year.

To sort your database, follow these steps.

1. Open the database you want to sort in Excel.

2. Choose Sort from the Data menu.

3. Specify the fields you want to sort by in the Sort dialog box, and whether the sorts should be ascending or descending.

4. To sort by non-numeric sequences, click Options, select the sequence in the First Key Sort Order drop-down list shown in Figure 9-1, and then click OK.

5. Click OK in the Sort dialog box to perform the sort.

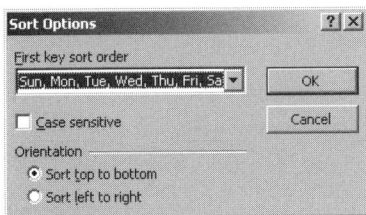

Figure 9-1   *Excel allows you to sort by days of the week and months of the year as well as numerically.*

Tip   If you need to sort your database by only one field, click in the column you want to sort by and then click the Sort Ascending or Sort Descending button on the Standard toolbar.

Filtering Your Excel Database

Often, when your database contains a large number of records—for instance, when you are linking to a corporate Human Resource database—you want to analyze a subset of the data. There are two ways to filter your Excel database—AutoFilter provides an easy way to create simple filters, while Advanced Filters enable you to filter your data on multiple criteria to see exactly the records you need.

Find Subsets of Data Using AutoFilter

If you merely need to see all the records that exactly match one or more values in your database, you can do so with the Excel AutoFilter command. The AutoFilter command displays a drop-down arrow to the right of each field name in your database as shown in Figure 9-2. This drop-down menu contains all the values this field has in your database, plus some additional options including the following.

Drop down menu shows all values in a field

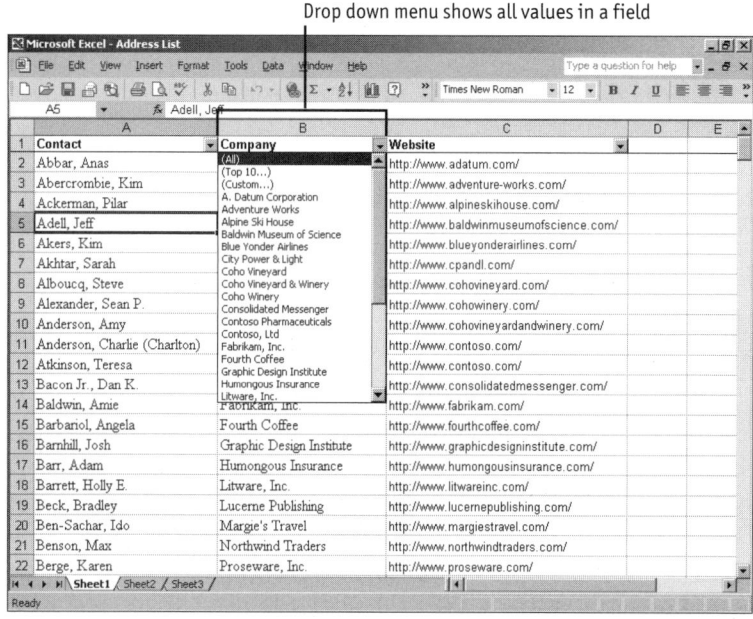

Figure 9-2   *AutoFilter allows you to quickly select records matching existing values in your database.*

- **Top 10.**   Available for numeric fields, this option allows you to filter on the topmost or bottommost values of your list. You can choose any number—not just 10, despite the name—or you can choose a percentage, such as the bottom 5 percent of values.

- **Custom.**   This option allows you to set comparison criteria, such as greater than (for numeric fields) or starts with (for text fields). You can even set two criteria for your field, such as greater than 10 and less than 20.

Using AutoFilter will probably suffice for 80 percent of your filtering needs, because it answers questions such as the following.

- Which records have no telephone number?

- Which contacts are from Indiana?

- Which 10 students got the top scores on the SATs?

To use AutoFilter, follow these steps.

1. Open the database you want to filter in Excel.

2. Click anywhere in the database.

3. Point to Filter in the Data menu, and then choose AutoFilter.

4. Click the drop-down arrow to the right of the field you want to filter on, and then select the field value to filter your database on or choose from additional options such as Top 10.

Tip   Because the drop-down list shows all the values the field has in your database, you can quickly spot different spellings for field entries, which provides an easy way to clean up your data.

---

5. Repeat step 4 as needed to filter your database on multiple criteria.

When you are finished filtering your data and want to remove the AutoFilter, choose Filter, AutoFilter from the Data menu a second time.

When you filter your list, the records that do not match your search criteria are hidden, not removed, as you can see in Figure 9-3. You can see where in the list items were hidden by looking for breaks in the row numbers in your database.

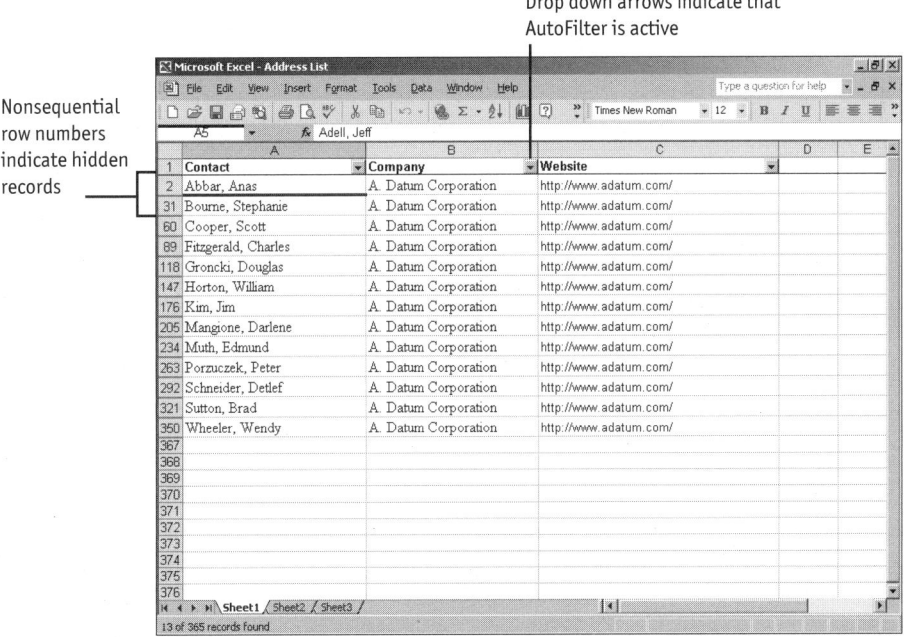

Figure 9-3   *AutoFilter drop-down arrows permit you to quickly filter your list with multiple criteria.*

Tip If you copy a filtered database to another location in your workbook, Excel copies only the filtered rows. This is a handy way of permanently purging your database of records you do not need to keep.

Use Multiple Criteria with Advanced Filters

Advanced Filter in Excel enables you to create filters on more than two criteria for a single field, and to create OR conditions as well as AND conditions for your filter. With Advanced Filter, you can get very specific about the data you're analyzing. For instance, you can filter a mailing list containing State, Income, and Employment Status fields to view only those people who live in Virginia or Maryland, and who either make more than $70,000 per year or are retired.

To use Advanced Filter, you create an area in your workbook that contains field names and, underneath them, the criteria by which the database should be sorted. Although in theory you can put the criteria range anywhere in the database and use only the field names you're going to filter on, it's strongly recommended that you create this area at the top of your database and copy all the field names into it. This ensures that you don't disturb the criterion area when you add or delete records from your database. Five rows should suffice for normal use—one row for field names, three rows for multiple criteria, and one blank row between the criteria area and the database.

Use Advanced Filter by following these steps.

1. Open the database you want to filter in Excel.

2. Choose Rows from the Insert menu to create five empty rows above your database.

3. Copy the row containing your field names from the top row of the database to row 1.

4. Type criteria in rows 2 through 4 following these guidelines (which are illustrated in Figure 9-4).

   - To filter on a text field, type the field value in the appropriate column of row 2. You can use the ? and * wildcards to represent one character or multiple characters.

   - To filter on a numeric field, type an operator and a value in the appropriate column of row 2. For instance, typing **<10** shows all records where the value of the field was less than 10.

   - To filter on two or more criteria where all the conditions must be met (for example, criterion 1 *and* criterion 2 must be true), put the criteria on the same row (for example, row 2).

- To create a filter where two conditions for the same field must *both* be met (for example, Income must be greater than $1,000 *and* it must be less than $5,000), type the field name in another column of Row 1 so it appears twice and then put each criteria in one of the two columns.

- To filter on two or more criteria where one of the conditions must be met (that is, an OR condition) put the criteria in different rows (for example, rows 2 and 3).

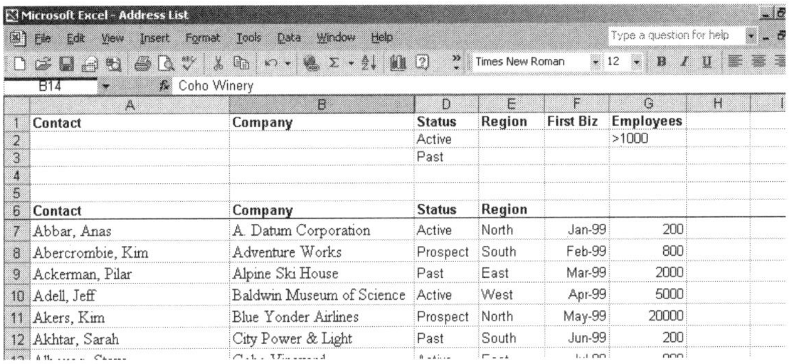

Figure 9-4 *Advanced filters are created by setting up an area in your worksheet to contain multiple AND and OR filter criteria.*

5. Point to Filter on the Data menu, and then choose Advanced Filter.

6. In the List Range box, put the range for your entire database, including the header row containing the field names.

7. In the Criteria Range box, put the range for the criteria (usually contained in rows 1 through 5). Be sure to enter only the range containing values and not the blank rows beneath.

8. Choose OK to display the filtered list.

Showing Groups and Subtotals

Occasionally, it's useful to see your data grouped or subtotaled by a specified field. For instance, if you have a database that's tracking course attendance, it might be useful to group your display of the data by course so you can quickly see how many people took each course and who those people were. By using the Excel Subtotal feature, you can group your data and display summary information, including the number of items in each group or the sum or average of numeric fields within them as shown in Figure 9-5. When you use the Subtotal feature, you also see Outline symbols that enable you to display the entire database or just summary information about each group.

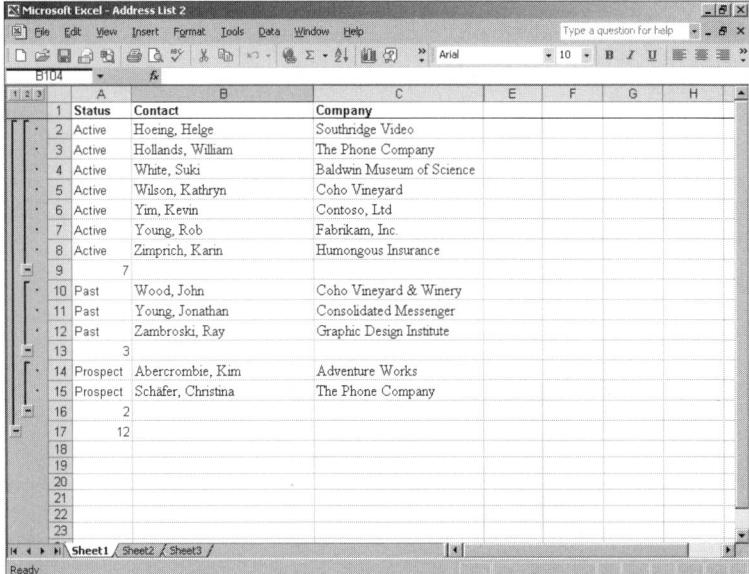

Figure 9-5 *The Subtotal command allows you to display your data in groups.*

For the Subtotal feature to work, you need to have fields (such as Status in Figure 9-5) that appear repeatedly in many records—these are the fields you subtotal on. To create subtotals for your database, follow these instructions.

1. Open your database in Excel.

2. Sort the database by the column you want to subtotal on by clicking in the column, and then clicking the Sort Ascending button on the Standard toolbar.

3. Choose Subtotals from the Data menu.

4. Choose the column you want to sort on in the At Each Change In drop-down list.

5. Choose the summary function (count, sum, or average) you want to use in the Use Function drop-down list, and the field or fields you want to have this function applied to in the Add Subtotal To box.

Tip If you are just counting the number of values in each category, you can choose any field.

---

6. Click OK to display your subtotaled database.

7. To display a summary report of your data, click one of the outline symbols shown in Figure 9-6. The 1, 2, and 3 symbols expand or collapse the entire database, while the + and – expand or collapse specific sections of the database.

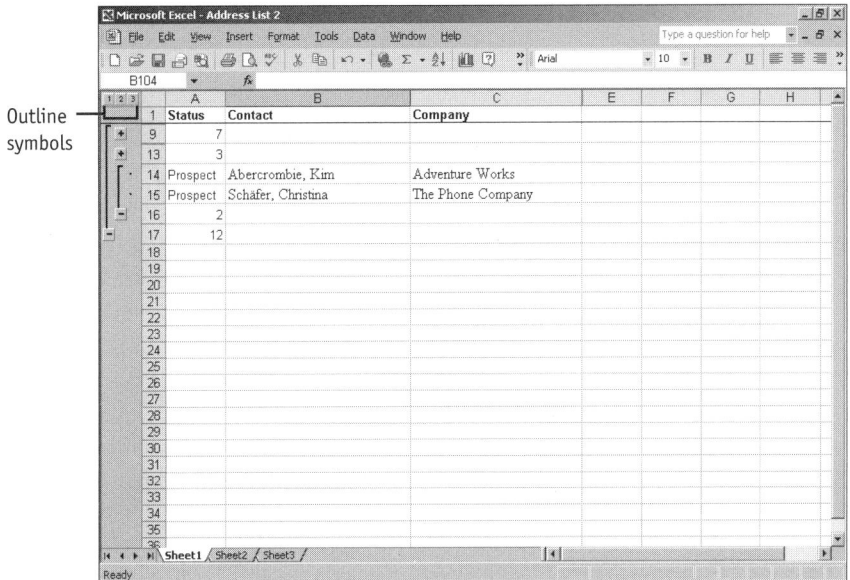

Figure 9-6 *You can expand or contract the display to show detailed or summary information.*

8. To remove the subtotals from your database, choose Subtotals from the Data menu and then click the Remove All button.

Analyzing Your Data

After you arrange your data and select the subset of it that pertains to the problem you need to solve, you often want to analyze your data. This section shows you how to use Excel to analyze your data, whether you created your database in Excel or are using it to link to an external database. Excel enables you to do everything from creating simple formulas that summarize your data, to using functions that provide an easy way to invoke complex formulas such as calculating the monthly payment on loan.

Creating Basic Formulas

Formulas are the key to making your database a true analytic resource. Formulas are equations that perform calculations on values in your database. Simple formulas can provide basic statistical information about your data (sums, averages, maximums, and minimums), while more advanced formulas can answer complex financial questions, calculate statistical significance, or project trends in your data.

A formula always starts with an = (equal sign), and then contains both *operators* that instruct the formula what calculation to perform and *operands* that specify the values to be calculated.

There are several types of *calculation operators* you may use in your formulas: Arithmetic operators include + (add elements); – (subtract elements); * (multiply elements); / (divide elements); % (percent); and ^ (exponentiation). *Comparison operators* compare two values and produce a True or False result. These operators include = (equals); > (greater than); < (less than); >= (greater than or equals); <= (less than or equals); and <> (not equal). The ampersand (&) is a *text concatenation* operator, and combines (concatenates) two text strings into one.

In addition to calculation operators, formulas can contain *logical operators* such as IF, AND, OR, NOT, TRUE, and FALSE that enable you to add conditional logic to your formulas.

There are three types of operands commonly found in formulas. *Constants* are values you type directly into a cell, and may consist of numbers, text, or dates. *References* are the addresses of cells (for example, A1), ranges of cells (for example, A1:A10), or named cells or ranges (for example, Markup_Percent). You might also find *functions*—built-in formulas that are predefined in Excel to do common calculations. For instance, the SUM() function totals all the numbers in a specified range.

Refer to Cells in Formulas

You start experiencing the power of formulas as you learn how to use cell references to enable you to copy formulas throughout your worksheet. After you create a formula that totals a column, for instance, you can copy that formula to an adjacent cell to total the adjacent column. This is because, by default, Excel addresses are *relative*—they are based on the relative position of the cell that contains the formula and the cell the reference refers to. Thus, after a formula is first created you can easily copy it to other cells.

For instance, if you have a monthly expenditure budget, with the last cell in the first (January) column containing the summary of that month's expenditures, you can copy that summary cell from the February to December columns. Each summary cell will reflect the total of the column above it, because the formulas, by default, use relative addresses.

Sometimes, the fact that default Excel addresses are relative can cause erroneous results. For instance, you might have a column containing the total expenditures per line item, contained in a column to the right of the December column, with a summary for the year at the bottom of this column. If you want to see the relative percent of expenditures for each month of the year, you might have a row below the January total row containing a formula that divides the total January expenditures by the cell containing the total expenses for the year. If, however, you copy this formula to the February column, both values (February total and Yearly total) shift to the right. This will give an erroneous result, and is a common problem with worksheets—you want certain values to be relative, but others to be *absolute* and unchanging.

To enter an absolute value in a formula, you can type it with a $ before each element of the cell reference that should not change. F6, for example, makes that cell reference absolute, while $F6 makes the column absolute but allows the row to change, and F$6 makes the row absolute and allows the column to change.

An easier way, however, is to create a *named range* for cells or ranges of cells that you want to hold constant when you copy formulas. To create a named range, highlight the cell or cells you want to name and then type the name in the Name box at the left of the Formula bar. After you name a cell or range of cells, you can use that name in your formulas which you can try by following these steps using the worksheet you just created.

1. Click in cell F6 and type **Total** in the name box.

2. Type **=B6/TOTAL** in cell B7.

3. Copy B7 to cells C7 through F7.

4. Click cell C7 and notice that the reference to cell B6 changed to C6, but the reference to F6 (TOTAL) remained constant.

Use Proper Calculation Order

To ensure you obtain the result you want from a formula, it's also important that you understand the order in which Excel performs calculations. For instance, if you have 50 apples and sell 20, you might want to know what percentage you have left. To calculate this, you take the initial number of apples, subtract the number sold, and get the remainder—30. You then divide 30 by the initial number of 50 apples, and see that you have .6 left, or 60 percent.

This seems simple, but try calculating this in Excel by typing = 50–20 / 50 The result is 49.6 rather than the .6 you expect. Excel firsts divide 20 by 50 to get .4, and then subtracts .4 from 50 to get 49.6, because of calculation order Excel uses.

When Excel calculates a formula, first it looks for operators and operands that are inside parentheses and calculates the result of these. If there are more than one set of parentheses next to each other, it calculates them from left to right. If there are more than one set of parentheses nested inside each other, it calculates the result of the innermost set first.

Next, Excel calculates arithmetic operators in the following order.

- Percent

- Exponentiation

- Multiplication and division

- Addition and subtraction

To obtain the result you want, you need to use parentheses to force Excel to do the subtraction first (50–20). The formula thus reads = (50–20) / 50.

Getting Advanced Answers Using Functions

As you start getting more comfortable with formulas, experiment with including functions in them. Initially, your functions might be simple arithmetic ones such as the SUM function. **=SUM(number 1, number 2, …)** returns the sum of up to 30 numbers, where each number can be a constant (for example, 23), a cell (for example, A1), or a range of cells (for example, A1:A10). Other similar functions you might use next include functions that return the minimum or maximum values in a range of numbers (**MIN, MAX**), or the average of those numbers (**AVERAGE**).

It's very difficult to insert functions manually unless you use that particular function very often because each function has different arguments, some of which are required and some not and they must be inserted in a specific order. For instance, the function =**PMT**(0.08/12,360,100000) calculates the payment on an 8%, 30 year, $100,000 mortgage. Who can possibly remember how to enter that?

Fortunately, Excel provides the Insert Function dialog box that guides you through the process of using a function. This dialog box allows you to choose functions by category and name, providing brief instructions on what each function does. It also allows you to type a natural language question, and suggests the appropriate function for the situation. For instance, if you type "How do I know what my monthly loan payment will be?" Excel suggests two functions, PMT and NPER. From the description of each, you might decide that the PMT function ("Calculates the payment for a loan based on constant payments and a constant interest rate") is more appropriate.

To create a formula that contains a function, do the following.

1. Click in the cell where you want the formula to be.

2. Click the Insert Function (looks like italicized letters fx) button to the left of the Formula bar to open the Insert Function dialog box shown in Figure 9-7.

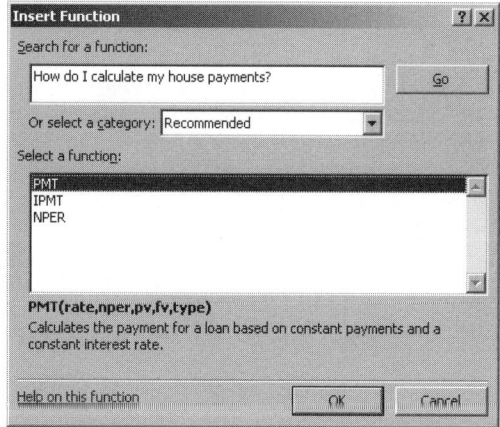

Figure 9-7   *The Insert Function dialog box guides you through the process of using a function.*

3. In the Search For A Function box, describe what you want the function to do and then click Go. Alternatively, you can select a category for your function in the Or Select A Category drop-down list.

4. Highlight the appropriate function in the Select A Function box, and then click OK.

5. In the Function Arguments box, type a constant for each argument or type a cell or range of cells. Alternatively, you can click in the appropriate box, click the Collapse Dialog box to collapse the Function Arguments dialog box, highlight a range of cells, and press Enter.

6. Click OK. You see the function in the Formula bar. Press Enter to finish entering the formula.

Creating Summaries of Your Data

One of the most powerful tools you have for analyzing data is the PivotTable report, a feature unique to Excel. PivotTable reports allow you to create a table that summarizes and compares information in your database. PivotTables allow you to display summary information about any field in your database, such as the total amount invoiced to each client during the past year. They also allow you to show summaries by more than one field, such as the amount invoiced by client by quarter. These two-way summaries are sometimes called *cross tabs*. PivotTables can even compare data from a third field, by creating *page fields* that display the subsets of the data from that field, as shown in Figure 9-8.

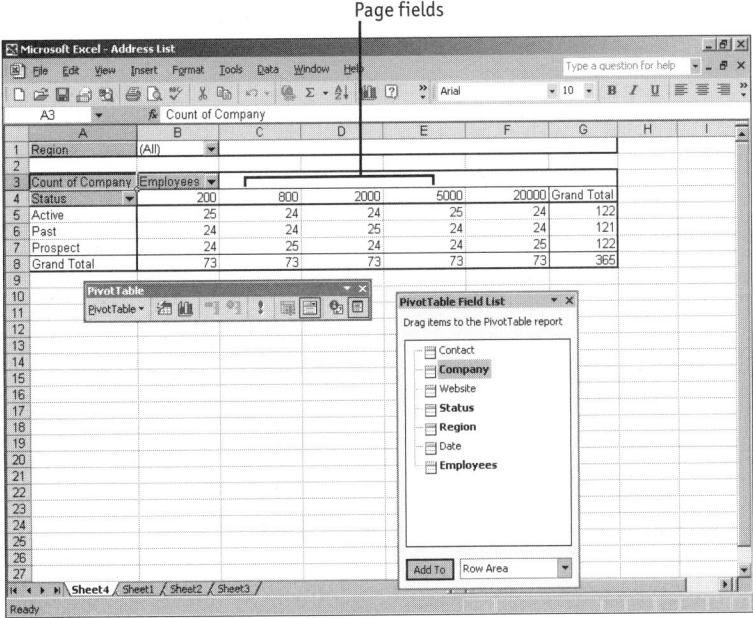

Figure 9-8 *PivotTable reports display cross-tabulated summary data from your database.*

Creating a PivotTable report is simple, yet the PivotTable Wizard provides options that allow you to accommodate very sophisticated requirements. To create a PivotTable, do the following.

1. Open the database you want to create a PivotTable report from in Excel.

2. Choose PivotTable And PivotChart Report from the Data menu.

3. Leave the default selections of Microsoft Excel List or Database and PivotTable, and then click Next.

4. Ensure that the correct data range is selected, and then choose Next.

5. Choose the location for your PivotTable—either on a new worksheet or in the existing one.

Tip   It's often better to place your PivotTable in a new worksheet for simplicity, so your data is in one worksheet and your analytic tools in another.

---

6. Click Finish.

7. Drag the first field you want to summarize from the PivotTable Field List dialog box to the Drop Row Fields Here area in the PivotTable as shown in Figure 9-9.

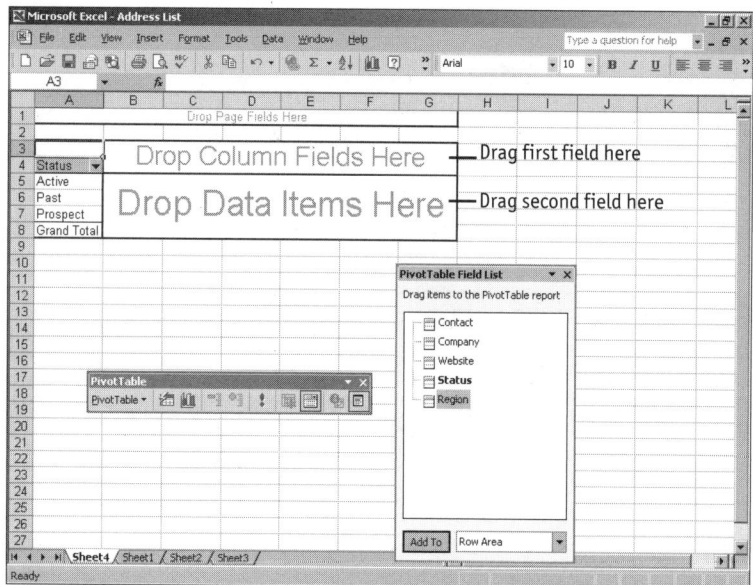

Figure 9-9   *When you drag fields from the field list to the PivotTable, you see summary results.*

8. Drag the second field you want to summarize from the field list to the Drop Column Fields Here area in the empty PivotTable.

Tip If you are creating a cross tab by dragging fields to both the rows and columns areas, drag the field that has fewer values to the columns area because columns take up more screen space than rows.

---

9. If there is a third field you want to subtotal by, drag it to the Drop Page Fields Here area.

10. Drag the field you want to summarize to the Drop Data Elements Here area.

11. To change the summary function used from the default Count, click the Field Settings button on the PivotTable toolbar, choose the desired function in the Summarize By box, and click OK.

12. To select or deselect field values for inclusion in the PivotTable report, click the drop-down arrow by the row or column. Check or uncheck the appropriate boxes, and then click OK.

13. To change the order of a field in your PivotTable, right-click the field name and then choose Order from the shortcut menu. You can then select Move Up, Move Down, Move To Beginning, or Move To End.

Solving What-If Problems

One of Excel's great features is that it allows you to solve "what-if" problems, situations in which you try to gauge future trends by changing variables such as operating assumptions or profit margins. Whether you need to look at best-case and worst-case scenarios or find the best solution given a specific set of circumstances, Excel has the tools to help you get the answer you need. Two of the "what-if" options you'll probably use the most are Excel Scenario and Goal Seek functions.

Creating Scenarios

Examining different scenarios is one type of what-if analysis you might often use in business settings. Perhaps you want to see what your gross profit would be under conditions of low, medium, and high sales volume, or forecast the effect that various levels of employee turnover might have on overall productivity given certain assumptions about resources required to replace staff. In cases like these, it is often helpful to create scenarios for the different possibilities and then present them in a summary table, like the one shown in Figure 9-10. You can create a set of scenarios by following these steps.

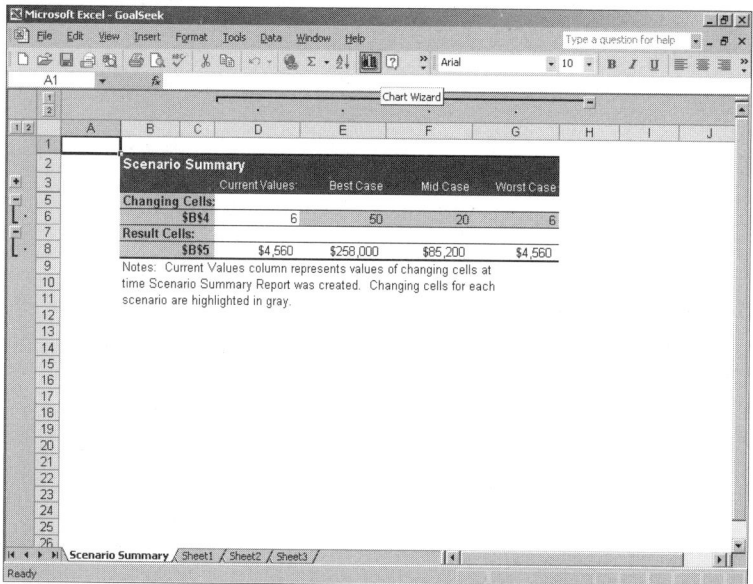

Figure 9-10   *Scenarios can be presented in a summary table that allows decision-makers to quickly see the effects of best-case and worst-case situations.*

1. Set up your worksheet so all the values are present to calculate the result, given one set of circumstances.

2. Choose Scenarios from the Tools menu.

3. In the Scenario Manager dialog box, choose Add.

4. Give your scenario a descriptive name (for example, Best Case), specify which cells may change in the scenario in the Changing Cells box, and click OK.

5. Repeat steps 3 and 4 for additional scenarios you want to create.

6. To see the results of a scenario, highlight it in the Scenarios box and click Show.

7. To see the results of all your scenarios, click Summary. In the Scenario Summary dialog box, choose Scenario Summary to see the results as shown in Figure 9-6 or choose Scenario PivotTable Report to see the results in a PivotTable.

Your scenarios are saved with your worksheet. If you need to edit them, choose Scenarios from the Tools menu again and you see the Scenario Manager dialog box with your saved scenarios. You can then add, delete, or edit scenarios as needed.

Using Goal Seek

Sometimes you don't want to see multiple scenarios—you merely need to adjust a variable until you come up with the right answer. For instance, you might want to know how many consulting days you need to sell on to net $100,000 given that your fee is $2,000 per day, your overhead is $30,000 per year, and your direct expenses per day average $500.

In this case, you can set up a worksheet with all these known values and add an artificial value in the "number of days" cell as shown in Figure 9-11. Use the Excel Goal Seek feature to find the "real" value (in this case, the number of consulting days you need to sell on). Follow these steps to use Goal Seek.

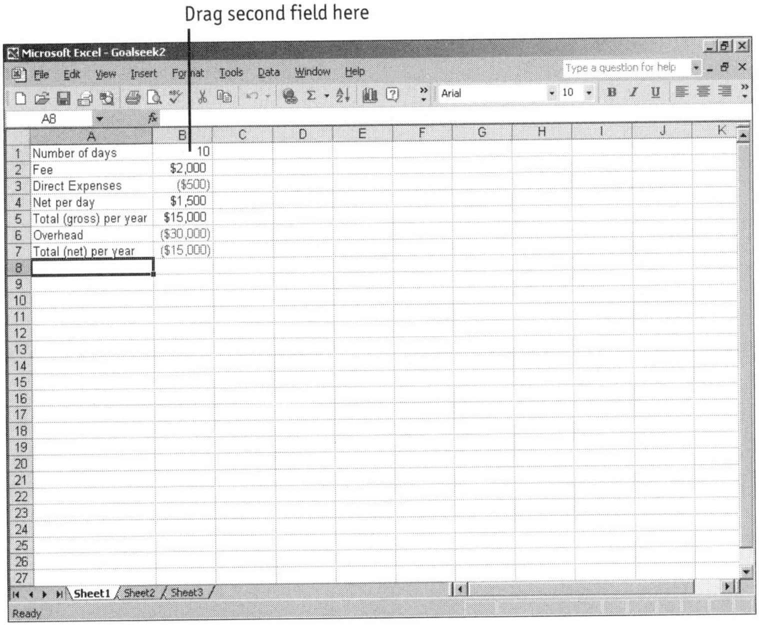

Figure 9-11 *Use Goal Seek when you need to vary one value to come up with the right solution to your problem.*

1. Choose Goal Seek from the Tools menu.

2. Choose the cell containing the value you want to obtain in the Set Cell box. (In this example, you select cell B7.)

3. Type the value you want to obtain in the To Value box—in this case, $100,000.

4. Choose the cell containing the value that will vary to obtain the result—in this case, A1.

5. Click OK. The Goal Seek Status dialog box shown in Figure 9-12 informs you whether a solution was found, and you see that solution in both the dialog box and in the worksheet.

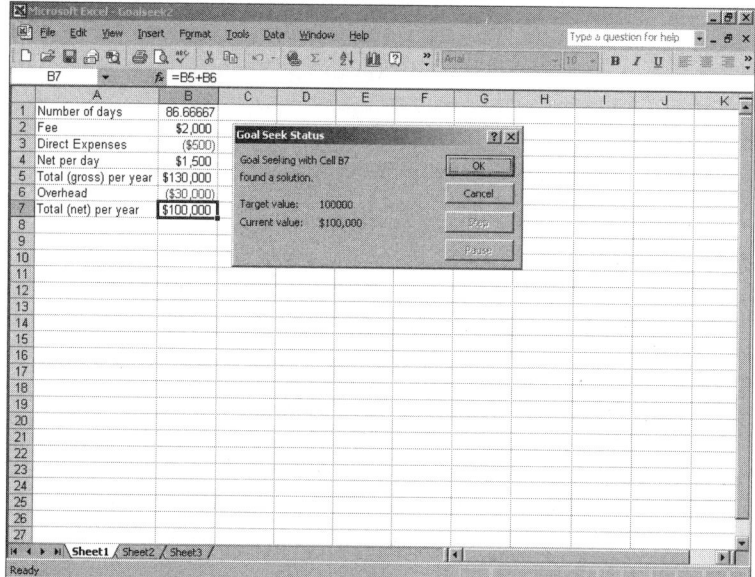

Figure 9-12   *The Goal Seek dialog box shows you whether a solution was found.*

Note   Excel also provides a Solver add-in for more complex business analysis problems that contain more than one variable that have constraints on their values. For instance, the Solver add-in can determine the best product mix to achieve maximum profits, given different costs of production and constraints on number sold. For more information, look up Solver in the Excel help system.

Projecting Trends

On occasion, you might have a range of data and need to make a projection. For instance, in creating a projected profit and loss for next year, you want to estimate revenue based on projected sales. In this case, you have to project the trend that your data is displaying using Excel.

You can create a linear trend that generates a "best fit" straight-line projection, or a growth trend which extends an exponential projection into the future. A simple way to create a trend is as follows.

1. Select the adjacent cells that contain the data on which the trend will be based.

2. Right-click the Fill Handle, and drag it through the number of cells you want to make projections into.

3. In the resulting shortcut menu, choose Linear Trend or Growth Trend. The existing data is unchanged, and the selected cells are filled with the appropriate type of projected data.

4. Alternatively, if you want to replace the existing data to fit the trend line, choose Series in the shortcut menu. Then, in the Series dialog box, check Trend, choose Linear or Growth, and click OK.

Caution   Before creating a series, copy your existing data to a nearby row or column so you do not lose it when you create the series.

This simple way of creating trends will meet most people's needs for a quick projection of future values. If you need more sophisticated trend lines, you can use the TREND, GROWTH, LINEST, and LOGEST functions that come with Excel or perform a regression analysis with the Analysis ToolPak add-in. See the Excel Help system for more details. Trends can be more accurately made with trend lines attached to charts, because you can choose from seven types of trends and see each one's R-squared value: a statistical measure that indicates how accurate the trend line is.

See Also   For more information about trend lines, see "Illustrating Patterns and Trends" on page 190.

Summary

Quantitative data is explicit, specific, and exact. To be able to turn that data into knowledge that leads to actionable decisions, however, you need to understand what that information means for your organization. To do that, you have to be able to select the right information, summarize it, and analyze it to get to the answers you need, usually using Excel. Excel is an extremely useful tool for the knowledge worker. You can easily create simple worksheets with minimal instruction, or perform sophisticated analyses in a wide variety of business situations.

Checklist for Creating Knowledge with Numbers

The following skills are ones that will help you use Excel to analyze data to produce meaningful knowledge.

[ ] Sort an Excel database by one or more fields.

[ ] Filter an Excel database to show the specific records you need.

[ ] Subtotal your database to display groups and counts of related records, and subtotals of numeric data.

[ ] Create formulas that refer to absolute and relative cell addresses, and use parentheses to specify the calculation order.

[ ] Use functions in fields appropriate to your work, such as financial or statistical functions.

[ ] Create cross tab and summary tables with PivotTable Reports.

[ ] Create scenarios and use Goal Seek to solve what-if problems.

[ ] Project trends for your data.

Creating Knowledge Using Visuals

When Kim Ralls became Chief Marketing Officer for Litware, Inc.—a startup company that manufactures decision support software—she realized there was a real problem with the positioning of her company. She looked over the materials on the Web site including Litware's proprietary decision process, the product positioning pieces, and the competitive analysis. She discovered that both the Web pages and the downloadable collateral were virtually 100 percent text. It was well written, it was well thought out, but it was *just too much*. Kim realized that to be persuasive, she needed to create knowledge with visuals. As a result, she enhanced the company's materials in a variety of ways. Using Microsoft Excel, Microsoft PowerPoint, and Microsoft Visio, she created

- A process map that not only illustrates the decision process, but also extends its definition from a simple five-step process to a cyclical process that incorporates external constraints and enablers. (Constraints and enablers are terms used in decision processes to refer to situational factors that inhibit or constrain a solution, and factors which promote or enable a solution.)

- A product positioning chart that allows potential customers to see how Litware's software is different from its competition

- Graphs that illustrate the return on investments that were realized by previous clients who used Litware's software

- A decision chart that potential customers can use to quickly see whether Litware's software is a good fit for their needs

Today, PowerPoint presentations are replacing Microsoft Word documents for a variety of business purposes, from corporate positioning briefings to research reports for clients. Charts and sophisticated process diagrams are illustrating more Word documents, Excel worksheets, and even e-mails. This reflects the increasing emphasis on knowledge that is created through visual means, which enhances (and sometimes replaces) knowledge created through text. Visuals engage the right as well as the left brain. They are uniquely optimized to show patterns, processes, and trends. Although text can analyze details, visuals can present a whole picture that shows the structure and meaning of the information.

In this chapter, you learn how to create knowledge with visuals. You discover how to do the following.

- Use Excel charts to illustrate patterns and trends
- Create simple diagrams with built-in Microsoft Office tools
- Use the Drawing toolbar to enhance your visuals
- Draw more complex illustrations with Visio

Illustrating Patterns and Trends

One of the primary ways to create knowledge with visuals is to illustrate patterns and trends in numeric data. The exponential growth curve of compound interest communicates the importance of savings in a way that a table containing the same data cannot.

Office provides many ways to chart numeric data. You can create charts within any Office application with Microsoft Graph; however, the most powerful way to create charts is with Excel. Because Excel wizards make charting extremely easy, you might want to consider it your first choice for charting requirements.

Tip   To open Microsoft Graph, choose Object from the Insert menu. In the Object dialog box, scroll down to Microsoft Graph Chart in the Object Type list on the Create New tab.

There are two ways to create charts with Excel. If your data is already summarized in a worksheet and you merely need to make a chart of it, use the Chart Wizard. If you have a database that needs to be summarized *and* the summary results charted, use the Excel PivotChart report. In either case, you first need to decide what type of chart to use. The following section shows you how.

Choosing the Right Chart

If you're a person who doesn't work with numbers and charts every day, you might not have ever thought much about when to use different types of charts. To use charts effectively, it's important to know what the purpose of each type is and what type of information it's designed to highlight. Table 10-1 shows you when to use the most common types of charts you can make with Excel. See the Gallery of Chart Examples in the Excel Help system for more information about the uses of various types of charts.

Table 10-1 Excel Chart Types

Chart Type	Use
Column	Shows how discontinuous data changes over time (i.e., yearly grade point average) or shows comparisons between groups.
Bar	A horizontal version of a column chart. The horizontal lines highlight the highest and lowest values, so it's especially useful for illustrating group differences. Do not use it to show changes over time.
Line	Shows continuous changes, most commonly, changes over time. Use line charts rather than column charts whenever the change is presumed to be continuous. For instance, population growth grows steadily, even if it is only counted once every 10 years.
Pie	Shows relative proportion of different elements in making up a whole. For instance, a pie chart quickly shows the areas where you're spending most of the money in your budget.
XY Scatter	Was originally used primarily in the scientific community to show clusterings of data points. In business, it is often used to illustrate product comparisons along two axes, such as Expense and Feature Richness. Items in the low expense and high richness quadrant are presumed to offer the most value.

Note In addition, Excel has other standard types of charts including Area, Bubble, Radar, Surface, Cone, Cylinder, Pyramid, Doughnut, Stock, and 20 custom types. These are also described in the Gallery of Chart Examples in the Excel Help system.

Using the Excel Chart Wizard

The Chart Wizard in Excel provides a powerful way to chart your data, offering you a number of options while making the process of creating a chart extremely easy. Before you create a chart, prepare by understanding what point you are trying to illustrate, choosing an appropriate chart type, and ensuring that your data is properly sorted. You also have to decide whether to display your chart on the same worksheet as your data or on a separate worksheet. This decision is guided primarily by how you intend to use it, and whether you want the viewers to see the data as well as the chart. To create a chart using the Chart Wizard, follow these steps.

1. Click inside the worksheet containing the data to be charted.

2. Click the Chart Wizard button on the Standard toolbar.

3. In the first step of the wizard, choose the appropriate chart type and sub-type. If needed, click the Custom Types tab to see additional choices, as shown in Figure 10-1.

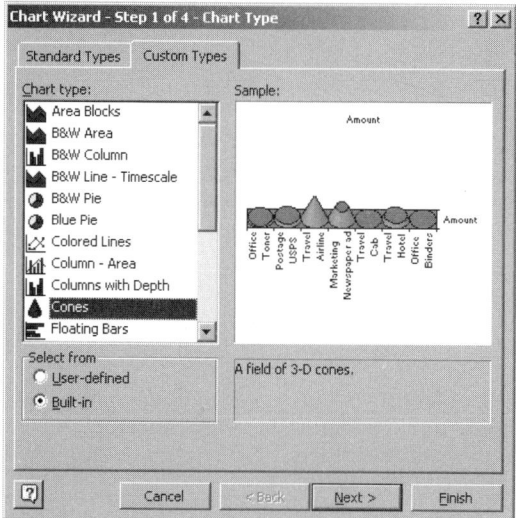

Figure 10-1 *For each type of chart, Excel provides sub-types that provide a variety of formatting options.*

Tip   With the Chart Wizard, you can preview what your chart will look like by selecting the appropriate chart type and subtype and then clicking and holding the Press And Hold To View Sample button.

---

4. In the second step of the wizard, verify that Excel has chosen the appropriate values for your data series. If not, type the appropriate range in the Data Range box. In the Series tab, ensure that the appropriate ranges are specified for each data series and for the Category (x-axis) labels.

5. The third step of the wizard permits you to specify options for your chart. Some of the most common that you might look at include the following.

   • **Titles tab** enables you to type titles for the chart, the x-axis, and the y-axis.

   • **Legend tab** allows you to choose whether to show a legend for your chart.

   • **Data Table tab** enables you to choose whether to display the data upon which the chart is built.

6. In the fourth step of the wizard, choose whether to display the chart in its own sheet or on the sheet the data is in.

After you create a chart, you can edit it by double-clicking any of the chart elements to display a format dialog box for that element. You can also restart the wizard by clicking the chart, and then clicking the Chart Wizard button on the Standard toolbar.

Creating PivotChart Reports

Sometimes, you want to both summarize and chart data in one operation. This can be especially useful when you have a database source, such as a list of expenditures for a project, and you want to show the relative amount spent by line item in a pie chart. In this case, you cannot use the Chart Wizard because you would get a chart that illustrates every single item instead of a chart that summarizes information by line item. The PivotChart Report creates a chart from a PivotTable that summarizes your data, and displays this summary information graphically with one easy-to-use wizard, as illustrated in Figure 10-2.

See Also   For more information about PivotTables, see Chapter 9, "Creating Knowledge Using Numbers."

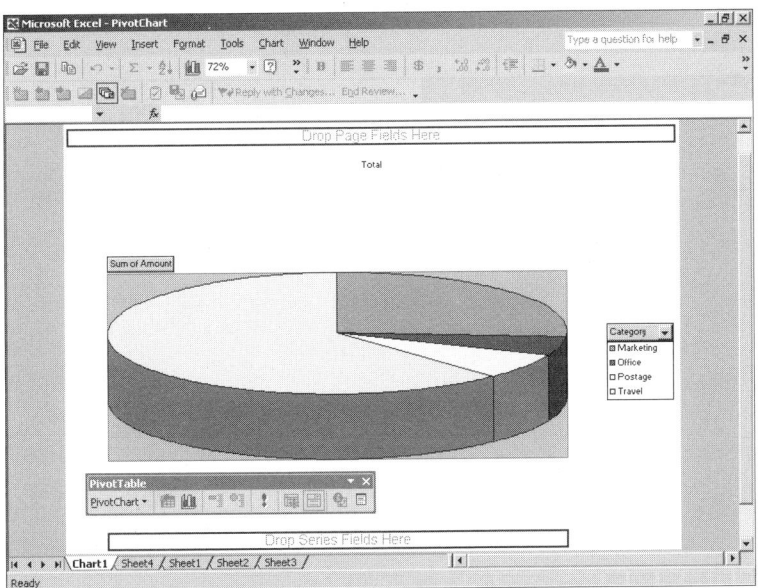

Figure 10-2   *PivotChart Reports illustrate summary information from your database visually.*

To create a PivotChart, do the following.

1. If your data source is an Excel database, open it and choose PivotTable and PivotChart Report from the Data menu.

2. Ensure that Microsoft Excel List Or Database is selected and that the type of report you want to create is a PivotChart Report (With PivotTable Report), and then click Next.

3. Ensure that the correct data range is selected, and then choose Next.

4. Choose the location for your PivotChart—either on a new worksheet or in the existing one. It's often better to choose a new worksheet for simplicity, so that your data is in one worksheet and your analytic tools in another.

5. Click Finish to display the empty PivotChart and the PivotTable Field List dialog box, as shown in Figure 10-3.

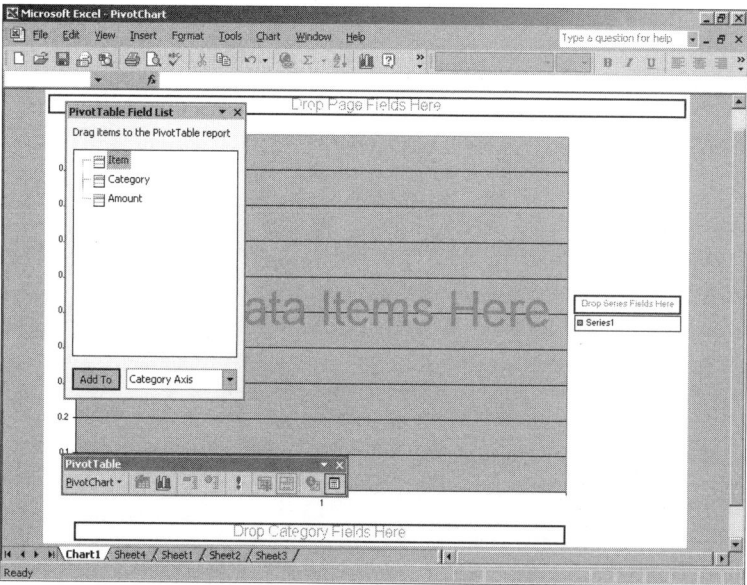

Figure 10-3   *Create your PivotChart by dragging fields from the PivotTable Field List to the appropriate area of your chart.*

6. Drag the appropriate fields to the Drop Category Fields Here and Drop Data Items Here areas of the empty PivotChart. If you want to create a multipage chart that displays individual charts for each value of a third field, drag that field to the Drop Page Fields Here area.

7. Drag the field you want to summarize to the Drop Data Elements Here area.

8. To change the summary function used from the default Count, click the Field Settings button on the PivotTable toolbar, choose the desired function in the Summarize By box, and click OK.

9. To select or deselect field values for inclusion in categories that are charted, click the drop-down arrow by the Category box. Check or uncheck the appropriate values, and then click OK.

10. To change the type of chart (for example, from the default column chart to a pie chart), click the Chart Wizard button on the PivotTable toolbar and then choose the appropriate Chart Type and Chart sub-type.

Displaying Trends

If you ever need to make projections of trends into the future, Excel trendlines provide a powerful, visual solution for you. Not only are the trends illustrated for your audience to see, but you can also choose from seven types of trends and see the R-squared value for each, which indicates how accurate the trend line is. By selecting each of the seven types of trends, you can choose the one that statistically is a "best fit" with your data.

See Also You can also make simple trends within your worksheet by right-dragging a series' fill handle. For more information about creating simple trends, see Chapter 9, "Creating Knowledge Using Numbers."

To create a trend line, follow these steps.

1. Select the cells that contain the series you want to project.

2. Click the Chart Wizard button on the standard toolbar, and create a chart as described in "Using the Excel Chart Wizard" earlier. A line chart is often a good type to choose when displaying trend lines.

3. With the chart created, choose Add Trendline from the Chart menu.

4. Choose the type of trend line in the Trend/Regression Type group.

5. To see the R-squared value, check Display R-Squared Value On Chart on the Options tab.

6. Choose the number of periods you want to forecast your trend into in the Forward and Backward boxes.

7. Click OK to see the trend line on your chart.

You can repeat steps 3 through 7 to add additional trend lines. The one with the R-squared value closest to 1 is the trend line that is statistically most significant.

Note You can find more detailed information about charts, crosstab reports, and trends in *Microsoft Office XP Inside Out* by Michael Halvorson and Michael J. Young (also from Microsoft Press).

Displaying Concepts and Processes

Creating knowledge visually isn't just about charts and graphs any more. Increasingly, process maps are being used to allow audiences to see the process as a whole: artwork is used to illustrate points and graphical elements are bringing text documents to life.

In this section you learn four techniques for showing concepts and processes.

- Incorporating clip art
- Drawing simple diagrams
- Using the built-in Office drawing tools
- Creating sophisticated diagrams with Visio

Incorporating Clip Art

One of the simplest ways you can add visual interest to your documents and presentations is to incorporate clip art. Clip art helps break up the monotony of text, and if you use clip art with a consistent theme, can bring the different parts of your work together in a coherent, visual whole. The tight integration of Microsoft Design Gallery Live with Office XP allows you to access thousands of pieces of clip art, and search for the right clip art by keyword or theme.

Choose the Right Clip Art

To find the right clip art, you can use keywords to search through clip art libraries that come with Office XP, libraries you maintain on your intranet, and the huge library Microsoft maintains on the Web—all with one simple search. To find the right clip art, do the following.

1. In Word, Excel, or PowerPoint, choose Picture, Clip Art from the Insert menu.

2. In the Insert Clip Art task pane, type the keywords you want to search for and click Search. You can modify the search keywords as follows.

   - Type two keywords to search for both of them; for example, **man cart** searches for pictures that have both "man" and "cart" as keywords.

   - Type two keywords with a comma between them to search for either of them; for example, **man, cart** searches for pictures that have either "man" or "cart" in them.

   - Use the * wildcard to represent zero or more characters in a keyword; for example, **man*** finds both the keywords "man" and "manual."

   - Use the ? wildcard to represent zero or one characters in a keyword; for example, **car?** finds "cart" and "carp" but not "car."

3. From the list of results, shown in Figure 10-4, drag the clip art you want to include from the task pane into your document, slide, or worksheet.

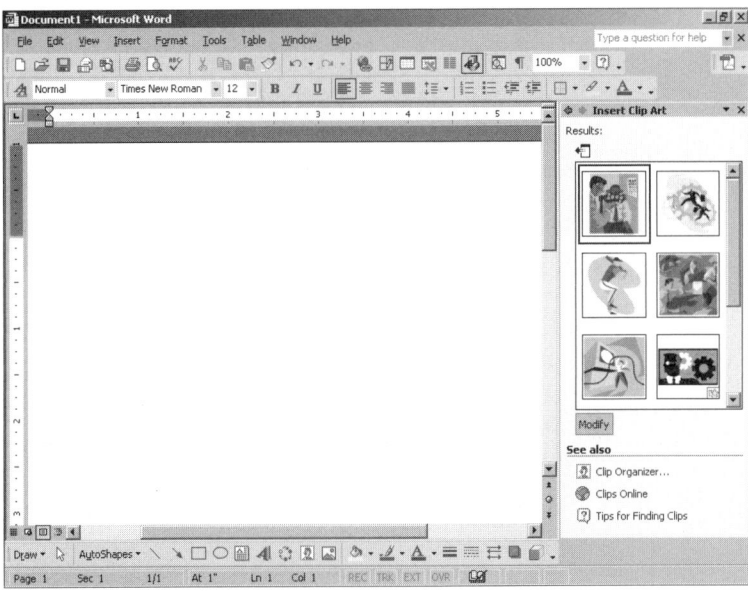

Figure 10-4   *You can see thumbnail representations of your selected clip art and then drag your selected clip art into your document.*

After you include a piece of clip art, you can modify its appearance and position as follows.

- To move clip art within your document or slide, drag it to its new position.
- To resize it, drag the sizing handles. To keep the same aspect ratio, use the corner handles.

By default, Office automatically searches through all your personal clip art collections, Office collections, and clip art on the Microsoft Design Gallery Live Web site (which you access by clicking the Clips Online link at the bottom of the Insert Clip Art task pane). You can limit the areas and the type of clip art that are searched as follows.

1. If Results are displayed in the Insert Clip Art task pane, click Modify to see the Other Search Options.

2. Click the drop-down Search In box to specify which clip art collections to search. You can click the plus sign (+) next to a heading to see the collections within it.

3. Place a check by the collections to search. To select an entire group of collections, check the box next to the heading if the group of collections is minimized and a + sign appears next to the heading. If the group of collections is maximized and a – sign appears next to the heading, click the check box next to the heading twice.

4. To restrict your search to a specific type of clip art, click the Results Should Be drop-down box and check or uncheck the different media types—clip art, photographs, movies, and sounds.

Many Microsoft clip art pieces have unique graphical styles, like the ones shown in Figure 10-5. When you're using multiple pieces of clip art in the same document or presentation, use clip art that all has the same style—providing a unified visual look and feel to your work. You can easily see other clip art that has the same style as the first piece you select by clicking the arrow to the right of the clip, and choosing Find Similar Style. You see all the clips that share the style with the selected one.

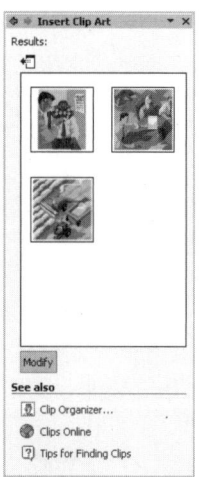

Figure 10-5   *Using clip art with the same style provides a unified visual look and feel to your documents and presentations.*

Customize Your Clip Art

After you select a piece of clip art, you can use the Picture toolbar to alter its appearance and positioning. If the toolbar is not visible, right-click the picture and select Show Picture Toolbar. You can then choose to do the following.

- **Change image colors.**   Click the Color button, and you can select Automatic, Grayscale Black & White, or Washout (to make a watermark of the image).

- **Adjust brightness and contrast.**   The More Contrast, Less Contrast, More Brightness, and Less Brightness buttons permit you to change the appearance of the image. These are especially good for creating a more subdued effect with your clip art.

- **Crop.** To crop the image, click the Crop button and drag the crop handles you see around the image. Click the Crop button a second time to complete the operation.

- **Rotate.** You can rotate clip art 90 degrees by repeatedly clicking the Rotate Left button.

- **Draw lines.** You can put a line around your image using a variety of styles with the Line Style button.

- **Recolor picture.** If the picture is a bitmap such as a GIF file, to recolor elements of the picture, click the Recolor Picture button. In the Recolor Picture dialog box, you can select the color(s) to be recolored and choose a new color for each.

- **Set transparent color.** If the picture is a bitmap such as a GIF file, you can set a transparent color by clicking the Set Transparent Color button and then clicking the area containing the color to be made transparent.

- **Compress picture.** You can reduce the resolution of the picture to the maximum resolution required for use on the Web or printer. This can dramatically decrease the file size—an especially important consideration for using pictures on the Web. Click the Compress Picture button and then in the Compress Picture dialog box, choose whether to compress all pictures in the document or the currently selected one, what resolution to compress it for, and whether to delete cropped areas of the picture.

Creating Simple Diagrams

Another way you can add visual interest to your documents and presentations is to add simple diagrams to them. In addition to their graphic appeal, diagrams can illustrate processes and structures in a way that adds value to the text information you present because they provide a picture that can be remembered more easily than a series of bullet points or paragraphs. In previous versions of Office, you could create Organization Charts—one type of diagram. In Office XP, six commonly used types of diagrams are supported in PowerPoint, Word, and Excel. These are described in Table 10-2.

Table 10-2 Office XP Diagram Types

Diagram Type	Use
Organization Chart	Shows roles and responsibilities within an organization
Cycle Diagram	Shows processes that have continuous cycles
Radial Diagram	Shows relationships with a core element
Pyramid Diagram	Shows foundation-based relationships
Venn Diagram	Shows overlap between elements
Target Diagram	Shows steps toward a goal

To insert a diagram into a PowerPoint slideshow, Excel worksheet, or Word document, do the following.

1. Choose Diagram from the Insert menu.

2. Select the type of diagram you want to insert, and then click OK.

3. Click AutoFormat on the Diagram toolbar, select your preferred diagram style in the Diagram Style Gallery dialog box, and then click Apply.

4. To insert an additional element into the diagram, click Insert Shape on the Diagram toolbar. For Organization Charts, you can choose whether to add a Subordinate, Coworker, or Assistant by clicking the down arrow next to the Insert Shape button and then making a selection. For other diagram types, when you click the Insert Shape button a new shape is added to the diagram and there are no additional choices.

5. To add text, click Click To Add Text in the diagram and then type the text to be added.

6. To move elements within your diagram, select the element. If the sizing handles are clear, move the element by dragging it to its new location. If the sizing handles are gray, AutoFormat is on and you must first turn it off. Do so by clicking the Layout button on the Diagram toolbar, and choosing AutoLayout.

Using Drawing Tools

Office XP provides a suite of tools you can use to create your own drawings in Word, Excel, and PowerPoint. Although you can use these to create complex diagrams, process maps, and your own artwork, most ordinary folks don't have that level of graphic skill. However, these tools are still extremely valuable because you can use them to call attention to elements in your documents, worksheets, and slides with simple graphic shapes, as well as use them to order, align, rotate, and position graphic elements.

The drawing tools are contained on the Drawing toolbar, shown in Figure 10-6. If it is not visible, you can display it by right-clicking any visible toolbar and choosing Drawing. Some of the more common uses of the tools on the Drawing toolbar allow you to do the following.

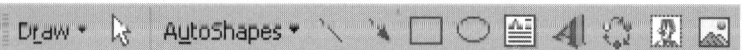

Figure 10-6 *The Drawing toolbar provides basic graphics capabilities throughout the Microsoft Office suite.*

- **Add a basic shape to your document.**   To add a line, arrow, rectangle, or oval to your document, click the appropriate button and then drag over the area you want the shape to appear in. Constrain the shape by holding down the Shift key while you drag: lines and arrows are limited to 15 degree angles from the starting points, while rectangles and ovals are limited to squares and circles.

- **Add other shapes to your document.**   You can also add more complex predefined shapes by choosing AutoShape from the Drawing toolbar, and then selecting the category of shape you want and clicking the specific shape. Drag to create the shape. You can create a variety of shapes with the AutoShape command; among them are additional basic shapes (beyond those discussed above), stars and banners, and a variety of block arrow types.

- **Add a text box to your document.**   A text box is a graphic element that contains text. It is especially useful for creating pull quotes or callouts in a Word document, or inserting explanatory text in a PowerPoint slide or Excel worksheet. To create a text box, click the Text Box button and then drag over the area for the text box and type the text you need.

- **Format your drawing object.**   You can change the color of the object's fill, line, or text by selecting the object, and then clicking the Fill Color, Line Color, or Text Color button. You can also change the thickness and dashes of the object's lines with the Line Style and Dash Style buttons, or change the type of arrows that lines have with the Arrow Style button. The Shadow Style and 3-D Style buttons allow you to add depth and perspective to your objects.

- **Order and position drawing objects.**   You can group multiple objects together so they can be moved and resized as one object by Shift-clicking the objects you want to include in the group, and then choosing Draw, Group from the Drawing toolbar, or control which object appears in front of another by choosing Draw, Order. You can then choose to move the selected object backward or forward by one object, or totally to the back or to the front. Other Draw commands allow you to align objects with each other, distribute them evenly, flip them, and rotate them around an axis.

Annotating Web Sites

Increasingly, presenters are displaying screen shots in their PowerPoint slideshows to draw attention to specific areas or features of a Web site. One way to display an annotated picture of a Web page is to copy it into PowerPoint, and add callouts to illustrate your points. To make this type of illustration, follow these steps.

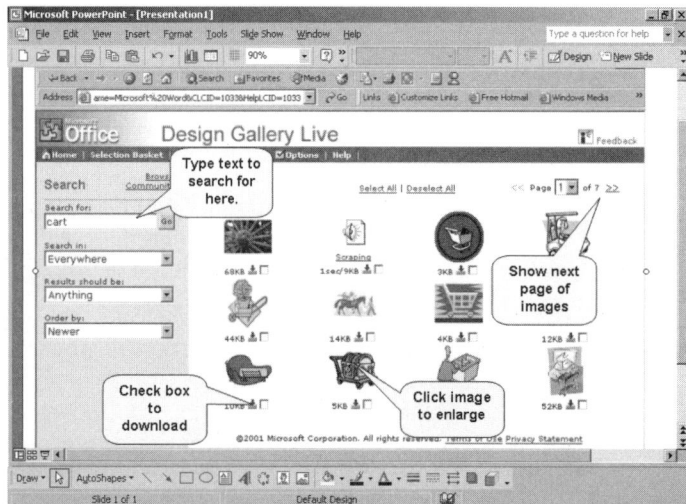

1. Navigate to the Web site in Internet Explorer, and then press Alt+Print Screen to capture the Internet Explorer window without capturing the rest of your desktop.

2. Open PowerPoint, and paste the screen shot into a new slide.

3. Choose Callouts from the AutoShapes button on the Drawing Toolbar, and select Rounded Rectangular Callout or another shape that you prefer.

4. Drag in the vicinity of the area you want the callout to cover.

5. With the callout selected, change the font as needed by selecting Font from the Format menu. An Arial 12 pt bold often works well.

6. Type the text of your callout.

7. Consider changing the fill color of the callout to a faint yellow by clicking the Fill Color drop-down arrow on the Drawing toolbar, clicking More Fill Colors, and then choosing the color from the Standard tab of the Colors dialog box.

8. Drag the sizing handles as needed to make the size of the callout appropriate for your text, and position the callout if needed by dragging its border.

9. Drag the yellow handle at the tip of the callout's arrow to position the arrow over the appropriate part of your Web page.

The easiest way to create additional callouts is to copy the first one, and then drag it to the new position and edit the text. This ensures a consistent look and feel to all the callouts.

Drawing Complex Illustrations

If you are interested in creating knowledge with visuals, you need to check out Microsoft Visio. The diagrams and tools of Visio are exponentially better than those of PowerPoint. Whether you are making a timeline, a map to your building, or a space diagram for your office, Visio provides all the basic shapes you need along with simple ways to connect them to quickly create a beautiful diagram, much like the floor plan shown in Figure 10-7.

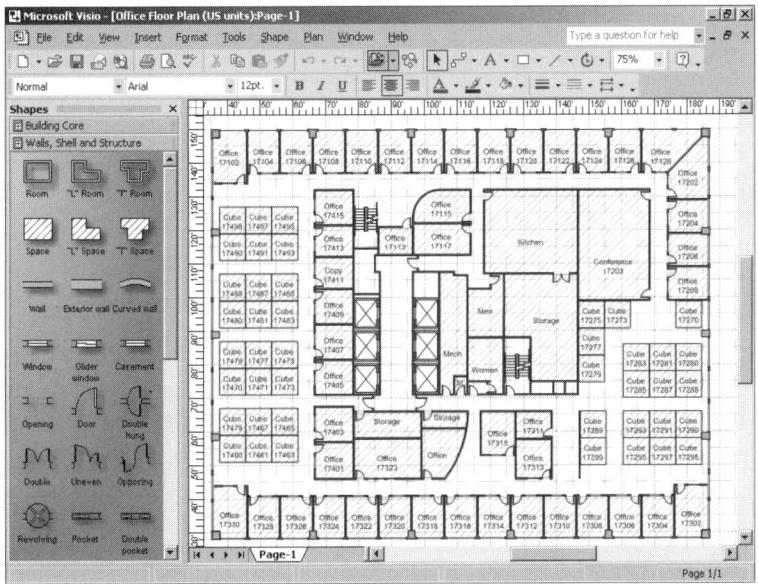

Figure 10-7 *Visio provides tools for creating many types of drawings, like the floor plan illustrated here.*

At the "top end," Visio provides drawing types for people in specific specialties like database developers, electrical engineers, mechanical engineers, network architects, piping system designers, software architects, and Web designers. You can even associate custom properties with objects that are stored in a back-end database so that as you assemble a diagram using visual tools, you are also collecting information on the total amount of time, materials, or costs associated with that project. If you are using Visio for such specialty applications, you can learn all you need from books such as *Microsoft Visio Version 2002 Inside Out* by Nanette Eaton (also from Microsoft Press).

Common Visio Diagram Types

Most people, however, use Visio when they need to create a great-looking diagram of a common process or object. You can quickly learn the skills you need by understanding some of the basic Visio components and procedures. Some of the more common types of diagrams you can quickly create with Visio are described in Table 10-3.

> **Tip**   You can see sample Visio drawings by pointing to New from the File menu, and then choosing Browse Sample Drawings

Table 10-3   Common Visio Diagrams

Diagram Type	Use to
Block Diagram	Construct a diagram out of basic shapes like squares, rectangles, and blocks, along with connecting lines. These may also include raised shapes and a 3-D perspective for a stronger visual appeal.
Building Plan	Construct floor plans, home plans, office layout plans, site plans, space plans, and many other plans that show you how to lay out elements of your buildings.
Flowchart	Document procedures, analyze processes, show workflow, show causes and effects, diagram business processes across cross-functional units, document TQM (total quality management) projects, create mind maps, and create many other types of flowcharts.
Map	Create a 2-D or 3-D map providing directions for visitors.
Organization Chart	Create stunning organizational charts with a variety of options with Visio if the built-in organizational chart used by Office is not visually appealing enough for you.
Project Schedule	Create a variety of diagrams to illustrate your project schedule, including calendars, Gantt charts, PERT charts, and timelines.

> **Tip**   You may also wish to use Microsoft Project if you're working with planning tasks that require calendars, Gantt charts, PERT charts, and timelines.

Create a Basic Visio Drawing

Visio drawings are based on *templates*, which (like Word templates) provide the basic tools you need for the type of drawing you are creating. There are several Visio templates for each category of drawing you might create; for instance, for the Project Schedule category, there are templates for calendars, Gantt charts, PERT charts, and timelines. Each template contains several *stencils*—an electronic version of the old plastic stencil that contained cutouts of several drawing shapes. A Visio stencil contains a collection of *masters*—shapes that can be dragged into your drawing and reused. For instance, the Timeline template contains stencils for backgrounds, borders and titles, and timeline shapes. In addition, each template contains a drawing page that you drag the shapes onto and styles for text, lines, and fills that are most appropriate for the type of drawing you are making. For instance, the Timeline template contains text styles for milestones and markers and line styles for rulers and intervals.

You can create a Visio drawing by following these steps.

1. When you open Visio, you see a Choose Drawing Type pane. If this pane is not visible, display it by choosing New, Choose Drawing Type from the File menu.

2. Choose the category for your drawing (such as Project Schedule), and then the specific template you want to use (such as Timeline). You see the blank drawing page, and the Shapes pane containing a number of stencils, as shown in Figure 10-8.

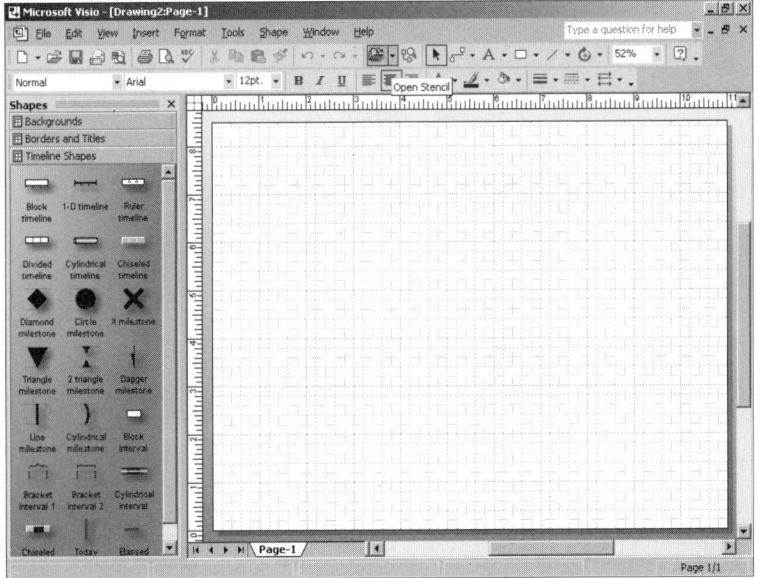

Figure 10-8   *Visio templates provide all the basic shapes for the specific type of drawing you are creating.*

3. Drag a shape onto the drawing page to insert it into the drawing. Depending on the shape you choose, you might see a Configure dialog box that provides information for the shape. For instance, if you drag the Cylindrical Timeline shape onto the page, you see the Configure Timeline dialog box that provides important information about the timeline as shown in Figure 10-9. The shape might also have text associated with it; for instance, a milestone shape has text for the milestone description. Click the text box to edit the text.

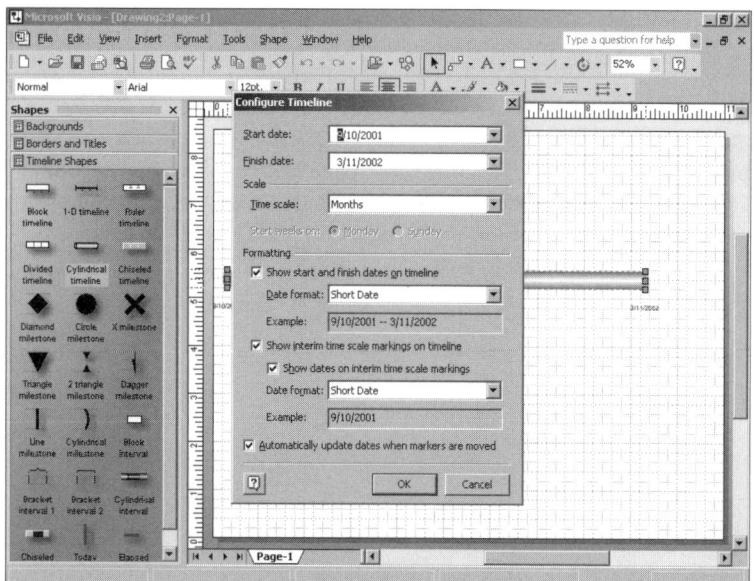

Figure 10-9   *The Configure Timeline dialog box allows you to determine attributes associated with the timeline shape and set formatting options.*

4. Drag other shapes onto the drawing page as needed to complete the diagram.

Tip   Add the borders and titles shapes before you add other shapes so you know how much space you have to work with, and add the background shape after you add all others because it will obscure the page grid that helps you align other shapes.

Some types of diagrams include *dynamic connectors*. These are lines that connect two other shapes. They are called dynamic because when you move either of the two shapes, the line moves as well so it continues to connect them. It even changes the path it follows to route itself around shapes that are between the two shapes it is connecting, and provides *line jumps* when two connectors intersect. Dynamic connectors are used extensively in electrical wiring diagrams, network diagrams, and other illustrations that need to clearly show multiple paths between objects. To use a dynamic connector, follow these steps

1. Create a Visio drawing that has two shapes you want to connect with a dynamic connector.

2. Drag the dynamic connector from the Shapes pane onto the drawing.

3. Drag the connector's *begin point* (the green box with an "x") to the parent shape (the one you're connecting *from*), and drag its *end point* (the green box with a "+") to the child shape (the shape you're connecting *to*). The green begin or end point turns red when it is glued to a shape.

Visio has a host of additional commands and functionality that allow you to create drawings and shapes from scratch, and fine-tune your drawing's appearance. You can also assign properties to shapes, and run reports on those properties that allow Visio to act like a "visual database." For instance, in an office layout diagram you can report on the number of chairs, desks, and trashcans, or in a process diagram you can quickly see how long the shortest path of a process would take. You can even link your Visio drawing to an external database, allowing you to keep an inventory both in the database and visually within the Visio drawing.

Summary

For many people, creating knowledge with visuals is not as easy as working with numbers or words. Fortunately, Office provides so many wizards, drawing tools, and templates that even people who can't draw a cow that has four legs can create complex charts, effective diagrams, and beautiful artwork.

In this chapter, you learned the basic techniques for creating knowledge visually. This type of knowledge appeals to audiences in very different ways than does text-based and number-based knowledge. It is literally perceived differently—by the right side of the brain—and evokes an emotional response that left-brain learning (that is, text and numbers) does not. Smart knowledge workers remember this fact, and always weave the two types of knowledge together to effectively communicate their points.

Checklist for Creating Knowledge Visually

The following skills are ones that will help you use Office tools to produce charts and diagrams to create knowledge and illustrate points.

[ ]   Use pre-defined Office diagrams to illustrate a variety of processes.

[ ]   Determine which type of chart you need to best present your data.

[ ]   Chart summary data with the Chart Wizard.

[ ]   Use PivotCharts to summarize *and* chart data in one operation.

[ ]   Create graphical trend lines to show growth.

[ ]   Illustrate points with clip art.

[ ]   Create simple diagrams such as organization charts and process maps.

[ ]   Use Microsoft drawing tools to add visual interest to your documents.

[ ]   Make complex illustrations with Visio templates.

Creating Knowledge Using Documents

Tad Orman is a senior consultant with Trey Research. His responsibilities include delivering research reports for clients, and supporting the sales staff by writing the technical statements of work (SOWs) for proposals for new clients. Tad has consistently been recognized by both his manager and colleagues for the number of SOWs and research reports he produces, *and* for their quality as measured by percentages of accepted proposals and number of client testimonials.

Tad's been asked to mentor some younger consultants, and to do so he's been trying to figure out the secrets of his success. By his calculations, he spends half of his work days with Microsoft Word open at his desktop—about the same as other consultants. But as he looked how he *uses* Word, he realized he has developed some "best practices" he could share.

- Tad systematically organizes his thoughts rather than just starting to write, using both the Outline feature of Word and a visual tool called mind mapping.

- Unlike several of his colleagues, Tad has several methods for ensuring that he builds on previous work. In fact, by his informal calculations, each new report or statement of work usually contains less than 30 percent new material!

- Tad methodically structures his documents so he clearly states the points he wants to get across to his audience, and then supports each one with logic, data, charts, and diagrams.

Today most knowledge workers share one important attribute with Tad—they produce most of their knowledge with documents. If this describes your work, this chapter's for you. In it, you'll find many techniques that are extremely simple—ones you probably learned in the past but forget to do in a systematic way. You might find others that are new to you, and require some initial work to master.

Investing energy at the front end, however, helps save you time by creating shortcuts that pay off month after month. Making shortcuts, however, requires a new way of thinking about using your PC to accomplish work. No longer can you think, "How quickly can I get this thing off my desk?" There's nothing wrong with trying to be efficient, but you need to expand your thinking to be efficient over the long term by constantly asking two questions.

- Have I done this before and will I do it again?

- Can I take a few extra seconds to automate this task, so it'll be easier the next time?

In this chapter, you learn how to create knowledge with documents, with techniques such as how to

- Break through writer's block to get your thoughts on paper.

- Organize your thoughts with outlines and mind maps.

- Build on your previous work by reusing old documents, creating templates, and creating AutoText entries.

- Support your points with tables, charts, and footnotes.

Overcoming Writer's Block

The first step in creating knowledge with documents is writing those thoughts down. If this is not a problem for you, skip this section. But if you're one of those people who occasionally suffers from writer's block, here are a couple of hints for getting past it.

Many people who have a hard time writing their thoughts find it much easier to express those thoughts orally. If, in your work, you speak to other people about the ideas you need to write about, the solution is easy. Bring in a small micro-recorder, and transcribe what you say. This can give you a good head start on your writing, because a 30-minute talk can be approximately 25 transcribed pages.

If you don't have an occasion to present your ideas to others, *make one*. (As a personal note, I've used this technique to write more than two dozen articles.) Ask a colleague to interview you on tape about the subject you need to write about. Give him or her a few questions to get started. What you will probably find is that as you start talking, your colleague will ask you for more details, an example, or to explain something that's confusing.

When you transcribe this tape, you will find a wealth of material. You might find that it's much easier to modify and reorganize this raw material than to write it from scratch.

Tip   If you're like most people, you probably never thought of using a transcriber—and certainly in many situations it's not appropriate. But you'll be surprised at how affordable and easy it is.

A search on the Web for "transcription service" turns up scores of them. They don't need to live near you. Just mail them the tape, and ask them to e-mail you back a document in the appropriate format. It's that easy.

Organizing Your Ideas

Whether you're writing a report, a review, an article, or even a book, in order to create knowledge that can be shared with others, you need to organize your thoughts in some logical order. If you are more of a linear thinker, the Outline feature of Word can become an indispensable tool. If you're more of a spatial type, you might want to try a less well-known tool—a mind map.

Creating an Outline

If you are creating a document from scratch, it can be useful to start by creating the outline using the Outline feature in Word. This technique has the advantage of helping you build the logical flow of the document first—its skeleton, so to speak. When you start with the outline, you can easily promote and demote headings until you create a solid structure for your document.

Outline view, shown in Figure 11-1, enables you to see the overall flow of your document, and building your documents with an organized outline as its base helps to ensure there is a clear, logical progression to your thoughts. For instance, if you are writing the text for a presentation, you might have three major points you want to make and you want to ensure that you support each of them with between two and four facts or observations. By creating a short outline, you can see whether everything you want to say fits into one of these two points and whether you in fact are making the right number of supporting points for each. With the Outline feature, you can do the following.

- Quickly switch to the Outline view of your document by clicking the Outline View button from anywhere in your document

- Create a document in Outline view that allows you to start with an outline that automatically turns into section and subsection headings

- Collapse and expand your outline to just show selected headings, or to display the text under one or more specific headings

- Move an outline family by dragging and dropping it

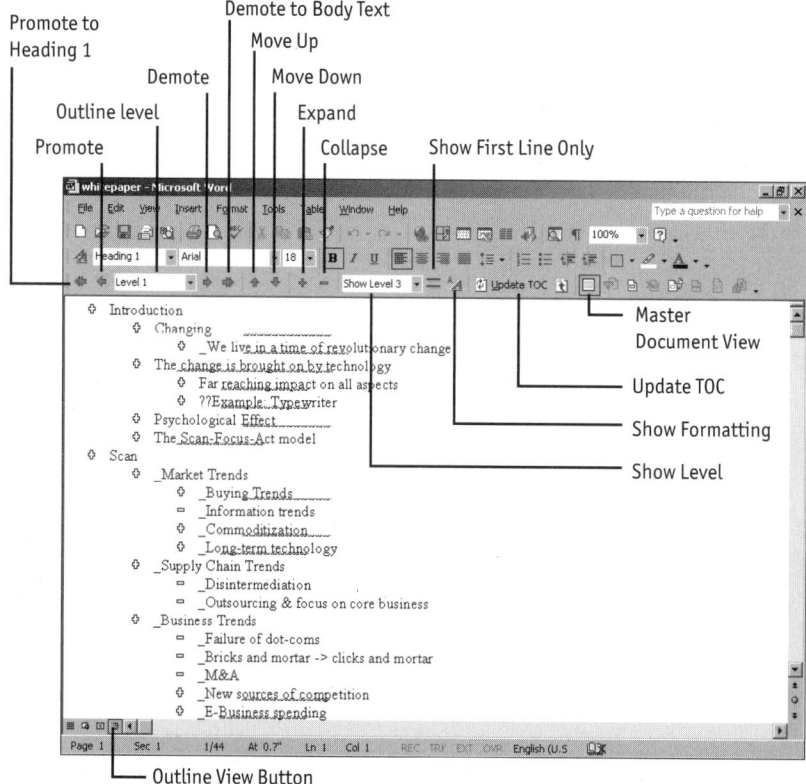

Figure 11-1   *The Outline view provides a way to organize your thoughts in a logical, hierarchical manner.*

Note   An outline family is a heading, its subheadings, and text.

Use the Heading Styles

An outline of your document is created automatically whenever you format your outline points with Heading styles, so you must use styles, rather than manual formatting, when you create the document you want to be able to view as an outline.

Tip   Using Heading styles also enables you to create tables of contents and use the Document Map. The Document Map feature of Word lets you open a pane on the left of your editing window that displays all the headings, by clicking the Document Map button on the Standard toolbar. You can quickly navigate to a desired section by clicking its heading.

See Also   For more information about tables of contents, see Chapter 13, "Sharing Knowledge Using Documents."

To apply a Heading style to a section heading, click anywhere in the heading and then choose a Heading style from the Style drop-down list, as shown in Figure 11-2. If you haven't added the heading yet, you can choose the Heading style from the style drop-down list first and then type the heading text.

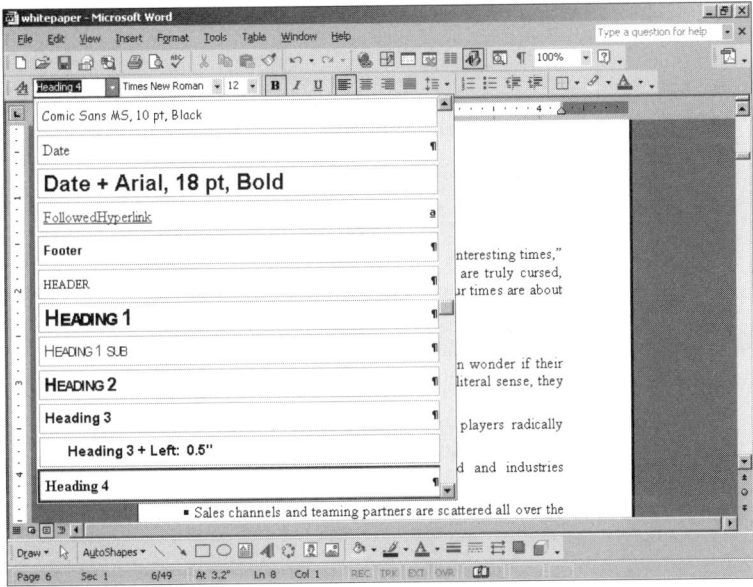

Figure 11-2   *The Style drop-down list allows you to quickly apply styles to your section headings.*

Tip   If you frequently create documents that contain headings, consider using the shortcut keys for Heading styles. By default, Alt+Ctrl+1 applies the Heading 1 style to the selected paragraph, Alt+Ctrl+2 is mapped to Heading 2, and so on.

View Your Document's Outline

As you write, it is sometimes helpful to see the larger context of the points you are making. For instance, you might be describing a situation and want to ensure that what you are writing is supporting the appropriate point. By switching to Outline view, you can immediately see the context of what you are writing. When you click the Outline View button (shown along with Outline Toolbar buttons in Figure 11-1), you see the Outline view of your document along with the Outline toolbar that provides options for viewing and manipulating the document outline. While you are in Outline view, you can view or edit your document in the following ways.

- Use the Show Level drop-down list to select which outline levels to display, and whether to display the document's text as well.

- To expand a section of the document, click the section heading and then click the Expand button (which looks like a plus sign). If the section was not already fully expanded, you see an additional heading level. Clicking the button repeatedly shows you further heading levels, and eventually the text of the section.

- To contract a section, click the section heading and then click the Contract button (which looks like a minus sign). If the section was fully expanded, you see the headings without the text; successive clicks show you fewer heading levels.

- If the headings display with formatting as is the default, click the Show Formatting button to show plain text (which can make your outline more readable).

- To promote or demote a heading, click in it and then click the Promote To Heading 1, Promote, Demote, or Demote to Body Text buttons, or choose a specific heading level with the Outline Level drop-down list.

Rearrange Your Outline

As you start filling in the pieces of your outline, you might realize it would read better if it were ordered differently. Although you can use Cut-and-Paste to move sections manually, the Outline view provides a simpler way to rearrange your document. After you are in Outline view, you can do the following.

- Click the plus sign to the left of a heading to select an *outline family*. The outline family includes the heading, and all subheadings and text underneath that heading.

- Click anywhere in a heading to select only that heading, and not its entire family. The heading is not highlighted, but you see the insertion point inside the selected heading.

- Click the Move Up or Move Down button to move the selected heading or outline family up or down one displayed line. If the outline is expanded so that text is displayed, the family moves up one line of text. If it is contracted so that only headings are displayed, the buttons move the selected family before or after the heading that is displayed above or below the selected family.

- Click Promote or Demote to promote or demote the selection. If a single heading is selected, it is promoted or demoted independently of its subheadings. If you select an entire heading family, the selected heading and all its subheadings are promoted or demoted.

Using a Mind Map

Mind mapping, a technique developed by Tony Buzan, is as a way of getting both halves of your brain to work together. It uses a graphic visualization of your thoughts (right brain) in a coherent, organized manner (left brain).

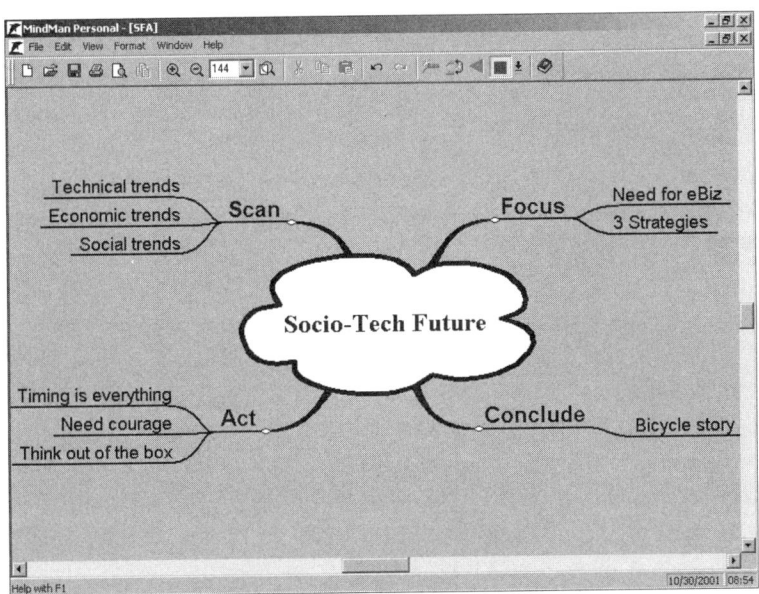

You can use mind maps for situations you normally use an outline for. However, unlike a linear outline, the mind map method allows you to instantly see how all the topics interrelate. (And *seeing* the interrelations in a spatial way is a right-brain activity.)

You might find that this technique can unleash enormous creativity. People use it to sketch out ideas for new articles or books, take notes at a meeting, and even create To Do lists. Mapping tasks rather than listing them shows you the "big picture," so you can see how everything you do fits into everything else.

You can sketch mind maps on paper, or purchase software to create mind maps such as MindManager 2002, available from Mindjet (*http://www.mindjet.com*). MindManager 2002 Business Edition allows you to create mind maps that can be exported to Word or Microsoft PowerPoint, and will synchronize with Microsoft Outlook and Microsoft Project.

Building on Previous Work

For most knowledge workers, true value comes when you can leverage your existing knowledge for the organization by producing high-quality deliverables in a short amount of time. This is the sign of true mastery, when workers do a task quickly and confidently because they have done it countless times before and instinctively know the best way to accomplish it. One of the best ways to save time while creating knowledge with documents is to build on your previous work, and reuse the concepts, explanations, and supporting points that have worked well in the past.

There are several ways you can do this, ranging from the very simple to the somewhat sophisticated. It's worth reviewing even the simple techniques, however, because it's often the case that although you know how to do them, in practice you sometimes forget. The three ways you can build on existing work are covered in the following sections.

Recycling Old Documents

Although this seems like a simple tactic, you'd be surprised how many people reinvent the wheel whenever they are asked to create a new statement of work, proposal, or analysis. Instead of sitting down, creating your outline, and filling it in from scratch, follow these simple steps.

1. Start by organizing your thoughts using an outline or mind map as described in previous sections.

2. Before you start to write, think about similar documents that might be stored in your electronic filing system. Consider whether there might be boilerplate text about your company that can be reused.

3. Open the relevant documents, skim through each, and copy any sections that might be relevant to your new file. Don't worry about duplication or whether it will "really fit." When in doubt, copy it into the right section of your new document.

4. Read through your new document, and eliminate duplicate or irrelevant material. Copy the remaining text into the appropriate section of your outline, and then modify it to your new purpose.

After doing this, it's quite possible you've completed 50 percent or more of your work already!

Saving Documents as Templates

If you know that a document you are creating might be valuable to others in the future, you can prepare it for reuse. For instance, say you're writing a proposal for a new service that can serve as a model for future proposals, or creating a monthly progress report that can serve as the basis for future reports. In this case, when you finish your work, you can create a *template* of it that can be used as the basis for future documents.

Create a Basic Template

A template can save not only the formatting of your document, but also the headings, front matter, and boilerplate text that doesn't change from one document to the next. Here's how to create one from a current document that even contains temporary text you can use as placeholders you can search for to personalize your document:

1. Save your original document.

2. Delete all text from the document that is unique to its current use, leaving all the boilerplate text that can be reused in future documents.

3. Replace all instances of text that you can search and replace with placeholders you can remember. For instance, you might replace all occurrences of a client's name with [client], so that when you use the template you can search for [client] and replace it with the new client's name.

4. Choose Save As from the File menu, and choose Document Template in the Save As box.

5. Give your template a name, and click Save.

Tip   If you are working with a distributed team and have a Web site that has Microsoft Office XP, Microsoft FrontPage, or Microsoft SharePoint extensions installed, you can also save your template to your Web site. Any team member with an Internet connection can then base a document on this template by choosing New from the File Menu, and then clicking Templates On My Web Sites in the New Document task pane.

To use a saved template, choose New from the File menu. In the New Document task pane, you see options for creating documents from previously saved templates including recently used templates, templates on your disk, templates on your personal Web sites, and templates on the Microsoft Web site.

Include Information with Document Properties

If you want to automate the process a little further, here's a way to make it easy for others to use your templates with just a little extra work on your part. What you can do is use the properties of the document template to save information such as the client name, document title, or header text, and then put codes in the document that automatically transfer the information from the document properties into the document itself. After you decide which elements in your document should be contained in the document properties, set up your document to use properties as follows.

1. Choose Properties from the File menu.

2. On the Summary tab, insert any appropriate elements in the predefined property fields such as Title, Subject, and Author.

3. On the Custom tab, select additional fields for the other elements you want to save or type the name of a field such as Header Text in the Name box that is not on the custom field list. You can type generic information such as [client] or [header text] in these fields.

4. Close the Properties dialog box.

5. Choose Options from the Tools menu, and then check Prompt For Document Properties on the Save tab. This ensures that users will remember to fill in the required information when they save the document that is based on your template.

6. Check Update Fields on the Print tab to ensure that the most current elements are used whenever the document is printed.

7. Click the location in the document where one of your saved elements should go.

8. Choose Field from the Insert menu, and then select Document Information in the Categories drop-down box. Select DocProperty in the Field Names box, and select the appropriate property where you saved the element to be inserted in the document, as shown in Figure 11-3.

9. Repeat step 8 until all the elements are inserted in your document, or in its header and footer.

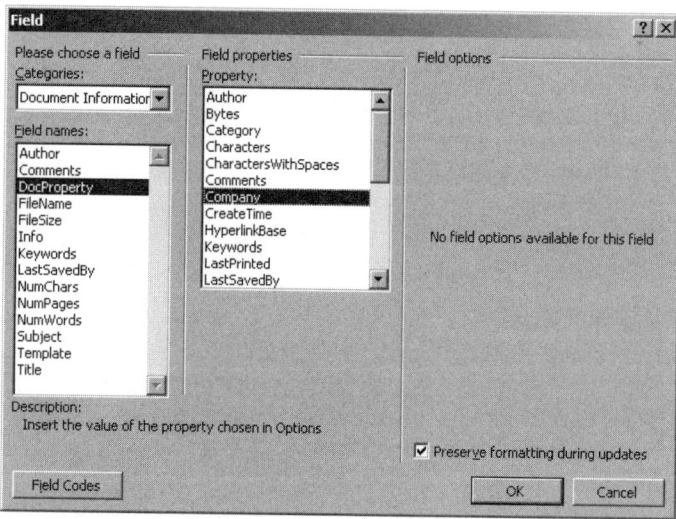

Figure 11-3   *You can use the custom fields of the Property dialog box to insert repeated text elements into your new documents.*

Tip   To make the template more user-friendly, you can insert a comment at the top of the document by choosing Comment from the Insert menu. The comment can let users know you are using fields for repeated elements, the names of the fields used, and that when they save the document they will be prompted to insert this information. You might also want to note that users can choose Select All from the Edit menu, and then press F9 to update the field information throughout the document.

Creating AutoText Entries

Another way to save time while building on previous work is to reuse those phrases, sentences, or paragraphs that you type over and over every day. It might be as simple as saving 15 seconds in not having to retype the long name of the company you work for, or saving 15 minutes in not having to re-create your two-page corporate capability statement.

Word can automatically save these bits of text for you, whether they are as short as a phrase or as long as several pages of boilerplate text for your documents. This allows you to build a "clause bank" of frequently used elements that you can turn into AutoText entries to create new documents with. You can even save pictures as well as text as Auto-Text entries. Possibilities for using AutoText entries include

- Corporate capabilities, corporate histories, or biographical statements for key personnel
- Standard paragraphs in business letters, standard closings, or address blocks you use frequently
- Your company logo or other graphics you use frequently
- Empty tables that are preformatted and have the column headings already filled in
- Contract clauses, terms and conditions, or payment policies

To create an AutoText entry, follow these steps.

1. Type the clause you want to save in Word, and format the text as it should appear in the final document including all styles, bullets, and numbering.

2. Select AutoText, New from the Insert menu. Click OK to accept the first few words of your entry as the default name in the Please Name Your AutoText Entry box, or create a unique abbreviation for your AutoText entry.

3. When you see the AutoText ScreenTip shown in Figure 11-4, press Enter and the abbreviation is replaced with the full AutoText entry.

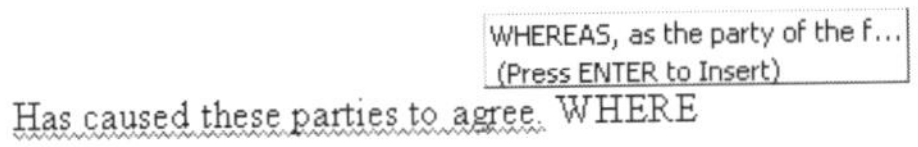

WHEREAS, as the party of the f...
(Press ENTER to Insert)
Has caused these parties to agree. WHERE

Figure 11-4   *As you type, you see the first words of your AutoText entries and a prompt to press Enter to insert them.*

If you want to replace or update an AutoText entry, do the following.

1. Type the abbreviation, and press Enter to insert the old entry into your document.

2. Edit the entry as needed.

3. Select the entire entry, and choose AutoText, New from the Insert menu.

4. Ensure that you are using the same abbreviation you used when you originally created the entry, and click OK to replace the old entry with the new one.

Tip   As you write your document, whenever you type an abbreviation for an AutoText entry, you see a Tool Tip appear with the first few words in the AutoText entry and the message (Press ENTER to insert). Press Enter and the abbreviation is replaced with the full AutoText entry.

Providing Evidence to Support Your Points

Writing good documents is not an esoteric art form. There are several simple guidelines that can ensure that your writing will be logically persuasive. These include organizing your document to have a clear introduction, body, and conclusion; organizing each paragraph of your document similarly; and supporting your arguments with evidence. The three types of evidence that are commonly used are data, logical argument, and references to trusted sources. As you create your documents in Word, that evidence may often take the form of worksheets, charts, and diagrams as well as footnotes that document sources.

Integrating Data Tables

Sometimes, the best way to illustrate your point is with a table showing supporting data. You can create a data table directly in your Word document, you can insert part of a Microsoft Excel worksheet, or you can link to an Excel worksheet. All three options are discussed in the following sections.

See Also   For more information about creating summary data tables in Excel, including PivotTable Reports, see Chapter 9, "Creating Knowledge Using Numbers."

Create a Word Table

If you merely want to display a data table that doesn't include calculations, it's often easiest to create a Word table directly in your document. You can quickly do so as follows.

1. Click the Insert Table button on the Standard toolbar, and drag over the number of columns and rows you need.

2. Type the headers and data into the table. To add additional rows, press the Tab key when your insertion point is in the last column of the last row.

3. Choose Table AutoFormat from the Table menu, and then choose an appropriate format for your table from the Table Styles list.

Tip Although you can enter formulas in tables by choosing Formula from the Table menu, it's often easier to enter them in an Excel worksheet because most people are more familiar with Excel formulas.

Insert an Excel Worksheet

Sometimes your supporting data includes calculations you want to be able to easily update. For instance, a price proposal might have a table showing the pricing formula, and you want to be able to easily update the price depending on the number of hours required.

To include an Excel spreadsheet that you can create inside your Word document, do the following.

1. Click the Insert Microsoft Excel Worksheet button on the Standard toolbar.

2. Type the column headers, data, and formulas in the Excel worksheet that opens inside your document. Note that the toolbars change to Excel toolbars while the worksheet is selected.

3. Choose AutoFormat from the Format menu to format your worksheet.

4. Click anywhere outside the selected worksheet to finish embedding the worksheet into your Word document and display the Word toolbars again.

Insert an Existing Excel Worksheet

Alternatively, you might have an existing summary table of data in Excel already, especially if you have created a PivotTable Report from your existing database of information. In this case, you'll want to either *embed* the worksheet in your Word document or create a *link* to it, depending on your requirement. When you embed the worksheet, you're copying the information into Word. Future changes in the worksheet will not be reflected in your Word document. Embedding is appropriate when your Word document provides a final record, such as a year-end report. Linking the worksheet merely creates a pointer in Word that refers to the worksheet itself. When you make changes in the worksheet, they are reflected in your Word document when you update the link. Linking a worksheet is most appropriate when your Word document should reflect the latest information available to you.

To embed or link an Excel worksheet into your Word document, follow these steps.

1. Open both your Excel worksheet and Word document.

2. Select the desired range of cells in the worksheet, and then click the Copy button.

3. Click the position in your Word document where you want the cells to go, and then click the Paste button.

4. Hover your mouse over the Paste Options smart tag that appears near the imported cells, and then click the arrow on the button.

5. Choose linking and embedding options as follows from the shortcut menu.

- To embed the worksheet, choose Keep Source Formatting or Match Destination Table Style, depending on whether you want to retain the formatting from the original Excel worksheet or format the data in Word. (You can also choose Keep Text Only to merely embed the text rather than the structure of the worksheet.)

- To link the worksheet, choose Keep Source Formatting And Link To Excel or Match Destination Table Style And Link To Excel, depending on which formatting option you prefer.

Caution   Make sure the workbook to which you link always stays in the same place and that its data stays up-to-date so your link remains valid.

Integrating Charts and Diagrams

To illustrate your points visually, you can insert a chart or diagram you make with Excel, PowerPoint, or Microsoft Visio into your Word document. Visuals that can be especially effective in supporting your points include

- Excel charts that illustrate facts and figures you are highlighting, such as graphs of sales trends or market share for a sales presentation

- Excel scatter charts that show your product placement in comparison to others

- A PowerPoint diagram that illustrates a work flow process

- A Visio timeline that makes your project plan come to life for your audience

- A Visio organization chart that reflects the recommendations you're making in your report

---

Tip   Simple process diagrams and organization charts can be made within Word by clicking the Insert Diagram Or Organization Chart button on the Drawing toolbar.

See Also   For more information about creating simple diagrams and organization charts, see Chapter 10, "Creating Knowledge Using Visuals."

To insert a chart or diagram, do the following.

1. Open Word and the other application—Excel, PowerPoint, or Visio.

2. Select the chart or diagram, and then click the Copy button.

3. Click the position in your Word document where you want the drawing object to go, and then

- Click the Paste button to embed the object.

- Alternatively, to create a link to it, choose Paste Special from the Edit menu and check Paste Link if the option is available.

Tip   To edit an embedded object, right-click it. Choose Edit Picture to edit an Excel chart; Chart Object, Edit to edit a PowerPoint object; or Visio Object, Edit to edit a Visio diagram.

Using Footnotes

Although traditionally more popular in academia than in business, footnotes can be a useful tool to support your points with additional facts and references or to provide sources for claims you are making. Unfortunately, they tend to break the flow for many readers who interrupt their sentence-to-sentence reading to take their eyes to the bottom of the page, and then back to the body text. For this reason, use footnotes sparingly and in accordance with any style guidelines in your profession or business. Times you might consider a footnote include

- When making a controversial claim in a bullet point, where you need a paragraph to fully justify the point but do not want to break the flow of one-sentence bullets

- When listing a series of otherwise dry facts that support your point, but are not very readable in the flow of your text

- When citing a reference for a specific fact, *if* such references are appropriate in your business and in the particular type of document you're writing

   To create a footnote in your document, follow these steps.

1. Click in your document where you want the footnote to appear.

2. Choose Reference, Footnote from the Insert menu.

3. In the Footnote And Endnote dialog box, change footnote options as desired, such as the numbering style, or whether the footnote should appear at the bottom of the page or below the text. You can also choose to use endnotes that appear at the end of the document or section rather than footnotes, if you prefer.

4. Click Insert, and then type the text of your footnote at the bottom of the page (if Word is in Print Layout view) or the Footnote pane at the bottom of the window (if Word is in Normal view).

Summary

True mastery of creating knowledge with documents comes when you can quickly create high quality documents that persuasively argue for points you need to make. To create high quality documents, they must be well organized, and points you make must be supported effectively. To create such documents quickly, you need to consistently reuse your previous work so that after you painstakingly wordsmithed phrases, paragraphs, and pages, you can leverage them through reuse.

Checklist for Creating Knowledge Using Documents

The following tools will help you as you create knowledge using documents.

[ ] Use the oral interview technique to get your thoughts on paper.

[ ] Use the Outline feature in Word to organize your thoughts in a linear way.

[ ] Use a mind map to organize your ideas visually.

[ ] Build on previous work by recycling old documents.

[ ] Create templates to get a head start on new documents.

[ ] Create AutoText entries to reuse complex terms, boilerplate paragraphs, and document sections.

[ ] Support your points by including data tables, charts, diagrams, and footnotes.

Creating Knowledge with People

Contoso Pharmaceuticals is in the process of redefining its mission statement. Their old one focused on their role in curing illness; their new one focuses on positive approaches to enhancing and maintaining health. This has created a culture change at Contoso, and Michael Emanuel has been tasked with leading a nationwide group of facilitators who are getting feedback from employees from all levels across the nation. His team met once, but probably won't be able to afford to see each other face to face again. They have several tasks, however, that they need to do together, including the following.

- Prepare a standard list of focus group questions to be used in all regions of the country.

- Conduct the focus groups with a representative sampling of employees.

- Collate results, and develop a survey to verify them.

- Distribute the survey to every employee.

- Based on the results, write a comprehensive summary and make recommendations to senior management on how to better communicate the new direction to the company.

Michael knows he will be hard pressed to get these tasks coordinated among his 30-person team, while ensuring that everyone's voice is heard in deliberations and creating deliverables that represent everyone's thoughts.

His situation parallels that of many knowledge workers in today's distributed organizations. Quick-forming, quick-dissolving teams are becoming more the norm than the exception, as are teams that are partially or completely not co-located. To be competitive, organizations are looking for ways that distributed teams can leverage their intellectual capital and collaborate on deliverables, even though they might never meet face to face. If you're a member or leader of such a distributed team, there are several skills you must acquire. These include

- Coordinating the work of a distributed team

- Creating an effective review cycle for draft deliverables when the reviewers are not co-located with the authors

- Holding conversations about the work being done in new ways—using online meetings, instant messaging, and Web-based discussions—to supplement the more familiar e-mail and conference calls

In this chapter, you learn about all three of these basic competencies that allow distributed teams to produce knowledge together and the technologies that make these possible, such as the reviewing and routing features of Microsoft Word, the Microsoft Discussion Server, MSN Messenger Service, and Microsoft NetMeeting.

Note   The procedures in this chapter focus on reviewing Word documents, because those are the ones most commonly worked on by teams. However, you can also send Microsoft Excel spreadsheets and Microsoft PowerPoint slideshows for review and for routing. Both of these applications provide limited ways to track changes as well.

Coordinating Work

Although many people use Microsoft Outlook for maintaining a personal task list, you can also use Outlook tasks for coordinating the work of a team. The secret is the Assign Task feature. When you assign a task, you send it to another Outlook user in a way that parallels sending a meeting request. You can then keep track of the task by seeing when the other person has completed it.

See Also   For more information about meeting requests, see "Scheduling Meetings with Others," on page 75.

When you assign a task to another person, that person becomes the owner of the task. If they reassign it in turn to a third party, that party becomes the task owner. Only the owner of a task can update the task by changing its start and end date, priority, status, or percent complete, or by marking it complete. When the task owner updates information about the task, that update is sent to all prior owners of the task—hence it becomes easy for you to track the activities of your team.

To assign a task to another person, follow these steps.

1. Click the arrow on the New button on the Standard toolbar, and choose Task Request.

2. Fill out the Task Request dialog box shown in Figure 12-1, including specifying an Outlook user to send the task to.

3. If you want to keep an updated copy of the assigned task on your own task list or receive a status report when the task is complete, select the appropriate check boxes.

4. Click Send to assign the task to the other person.

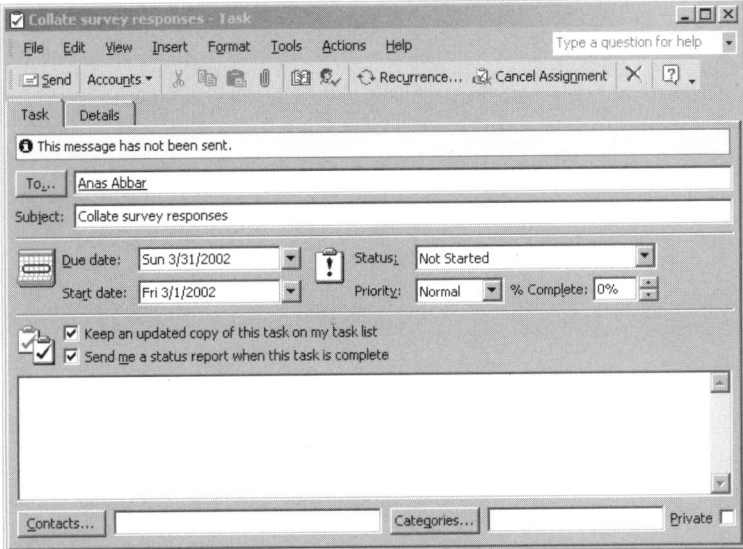

Figure 12-1   *You can coordinate the work of your team by sending a task request to another person.*

Note   If you assign a task to more than one person, you cannot track its progress. If you need to track several people's work on the same task, create multiple identical tasks and assign one to each person.

When someone sends you a task, it appears as an e-mail in your Inbox. When you open the e-mail, however, you see an item with options that allow you to accept, decline, or reassign the task by clicking the appropriate button. If you accept it, it is moved to your task list.

To view the tasks you assigned other people, choose Current View and then Assignment from the View menu while you're in the Tasks section of Outlook. You see a list of all the tasks you have assigned to others. Double-click a task to see its updated status.

Using Microsoft Project

Usually, all that's required to coordinate the work of a group is Outlook. Project plans, when created, usually contain fewer than 20 tasks and it's clear who is to do what. In these circumstances, you can track tasks adequately with Outlook. There are other circumstances, however, when you need more power for coordinating your team's work. In these cases, it's worth looking at Microsoft Project.

Project allows you to create formal project plans with tasks, subtasks, and milestones. You can assign these tasks to others, and Project automatically calculates how much of each person's available time is required. You can even track multiple tasks with overlapping groups of people—a common occurrence in today's workplace—and Project lets you know when you are overscheduling your resources. Gantt charts allow you to see a timeline with the tasks, milestones, and their dependencies, while PERT charts permit you to identify the critical path for task completion and calculate best-case and worst-case scenarios. You can even record billing rates for different resources, to calculate projected and actual project costs.

You can also set up Project so that tasks you create are automatically added to the Outlook task list of team members, your Project information is published to the Web, and your team is connected to Microsoft Project Central. A Web-based product, Project Central allows team members to view project information, share task assignments, and request and send status reports over the Web.

Consider using Project to coordinate the work of your team when you need to

- Track dependencies between tasks associated with a project.
- Estimate project costs and compare them against actuals.
- Allocate resources between projects, and see where potential resource shortages will occur.

A full discussion of Project is beyond the scope of this book. If you are serious about learning how to use Project, you might want to take a course from your local training center because using Project effectively is as much about learning project management as it is learning commands and procedures. If you want a simple introduction, get *Project 2000 Step by Step* by Carl Chatfield and Tim Johnson (also from Microsoft Press).

Creating Documents with Other People

One of the most common tasks that knowledge workers collaborate on is the preparation of documents. As your team starts using the collaboration features of Word, you'll find that you can easily send drafts back and forth; see the changes, comments, and questions that others have made; and quickly finish the review cycle by accepting or rejecting them. In addition, to manage the production of more complex documents, you may create a version control system by periodically saving versions of documents in production.

Reviewing Others' Documents

If you work on documents with others, it soon becomes vital to keep track of who has made what changes and understand why they are making the edits they do. The Track Changes and Comment features of Word, along with the Reviewing toolbar, can assist you in this process. Together with the ability of Word to save different versions of your document, you can create a smooth system for version control and the review process.

Track Changes Made to Documents

When you turn on Track Changes, Word keeps track of every deletion and insertion you make. Insertions are identified with colored, underlined text. In Print Layout View, you can see deletions in the right margin. In Normal View, you see deletions as struck-out text. When you hover your mouse over a change, you see who made the change and the date and time they made it.

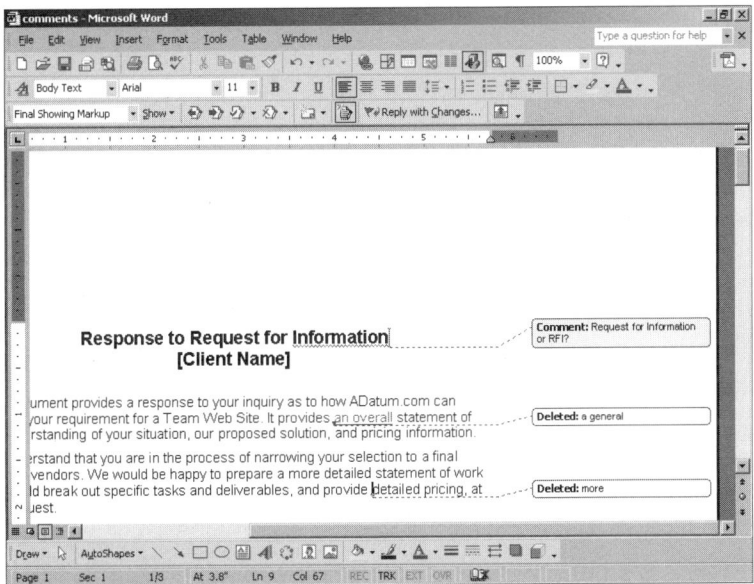

To turn Track Changes on or off, click the Track Changes button on the Reviewing toolbar.

Tip   You can also toggle Track Changes by double-clicking TRK on the Status bar. This also turns on the display of the Reviewing toolbar.

Insert Comments into Documents

When you want to explain a change you made or ask a question of the author, you can insert a comment into the document. Comments appear in the right margin in Page View, and as colored brackets or a colored Revision bar in Normal View. You can view all the comments in either view by clicking the Reviewing Pane button on the Reviewing toolbar.

To create a comment in the document, do the following.

1. Click where the comment should appear, or select the text to which it pertains.

2. Click New Comment on the Reviewing toolbar, and type the text of your comment.

3. Alternatively, to attach a voice comment to the document, click the arrow on the New Comment button and choose Voice Comment. You can then record your comment into a microphone attached to your computer.

4. Edit or delete a comment by selecting it, clicking the arrow on the New Comment button, and choosing Edit Comment or Delete Comment.

Tip   If you want to add text to the document, *don't use comments*. When you suggest additional text in a comment, the author must manually copy the text from the comment box into the document itself to accept your suggestion—an awkward and slow procedure. Instead, use comments for explanations of edits you make and questions to the author, and make proposed edits in the document (after turning Track Changes on).

Use the Reviewing Toolbar

The Reviewing toolbar shown in Figure 12-2 is a helpful tool for both reviewers and the original author. Reviewers can quickly toggle the Track Changes feature on or off, and add comments using toolbar buttons. For the original author, the Reviewing toolbar helps you finish the review process quickly and easily: It allows you to see the edits and comments others added to your document, accept or reject changes they made, and delete unneeded comments.

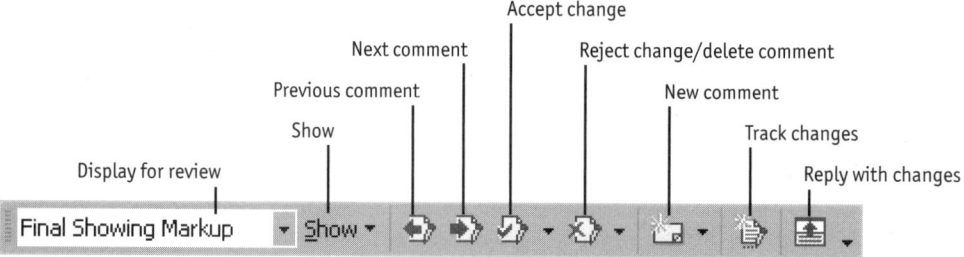

Figure 12-2   *The Reviewing toolbar allows you to easily view, accept, and reject edits that others made to your document.*

To see the edits and comments others made, use the following features of the Reviewing toolbar.

- To see your final document with the edits and comments others made, choose Final Showing Markup from the Display For Review drop-down list.

- To see your final document as it would appear if all edits are accepted and comments are deleted, choose Final from the Display For Review drop-down list.

- To see your original document with the edits and comments others made, choose Original Showing Markup from the Display For Review drop-down list.

- To see your original document before the review process, choose Original from the Display For Review drop-down list.

- To choose which changes to see, check or uncheck Comments, Insertions And Deletions, and Formatting from the Show drop-down list.

- To choose specific reviewers' comments and edits to display, point to Reviewers on the Show drop-down list and then check or uncheck specific reviewers' names or check All Reviewers.

- To see all comments and edits in one pane, toggle the display of the Reviewing pane by clicking the Reviewing Pane button.

To finish the review process, it's frequently a good idea to set the display to Final Showing Markup and ensure that comments, edits, and formatting from all reviewers are displayed. Then, starting at the top of the document, repeatedly click the Next button on the Reviewing toolbar and then click the Accept Change or Reject Change/Delete Comment button.

Save Multiple Versions of a Document

When you are working on documents with other people, you might find it valuable to save versions of your document as it progresses. The result is one Word document that contains all the versions you saved. If you choose Version from the File menu, you can save a new version of your document, view a list of saved versions and open any of them, or choose to automatically save a new version each time the document is saved.

There are two issues you must consider, however, when you use this feature.

- Using this option can result in extremely large documents and slow the save process.

- Be extremely careful to delete the intermediate versions before sending the final document to clients—unless you want them to see your thinking process as it's evolved!

To delete past versions, choose Versions from the File menu, highlight the versions, and click Delete.

Sending Drafts of Documents in E-mail

When you create a draft of a deliverable, you often want to send the document to others on your team to review. Although you can do this by attaching it to an e-mail, you can send the document for review using the Mail Recipient for Review feature which provides additional functionality you might find useful. You can also send it to routing recipients, if you have multiple reviewers.

Send a Document for Review

When you finish drafting your document, you can quickly send it to a reviewer by using the Mail Recipient (For Review) feature. When you use this feature, reviewers automatically see the Reviewing toolbar, and the Track Changes feature is on by default. They are also able to return the document to you by clicking one button when they are finished reviewing it. To send your document to a reviewer in this way, do the following.

1. Save the document to be reviewed.

2. On the File menu, point to Send To and click Mail Recipient (For Review) from the File menu. You see an Outlook e-mail window, with a Review bar above the To: box.

3. Enter the recipient(s), and then click Send. The e-mail is placed in your Outlook Outbox, and sent the next time you send e-mail.

When you get an e-mail containing a document for review, it appears with a flag in your Inbox. When you finish reviewing the document, click Reply With Changes on the Reviewing toolbar. A reply is sent to the document's author with your document attached, including the edits you made.

As the original author, when you receive the response and open the reviewed document you see a dialog box stating that the document was sent for review, and asking whether you want to merge changes in the reviewed document back into the original one. This can be especially useful if you send the document to multiple reviewers, because all the reviewers' changes will be merged into the original document. After the reviewed document is open, you can use the features of the Reviewing toolbar to accept or reject changes made by reviewer(s). End the reviewing process by clicking the End Review button on the Reviewing toolbar.

Tip   To send an Excel workbook for review, it must be shared. Sharing allows multiple people to work on an open workbook simultaneously. If it is not shared, you are prompted to save it for sharing when you send it for review.

Attach a Routing Slip to a Document

For small work teams, sending documents for review might be all you need. If you work in a larger organization or deal with legal or financial documents that must go through a specific approval chain, you can add a routing slip to your document when you send it for review. The routing slip allows you to send the document to multiple reviewers, either sequentially (for example, in an approval chain) or all at once when you want reviewers to review it simultaneously (for example, when reviewers each concentrate on a different section of the document). The routing process allows you to track when each sequential reviewer sends the document to the next person on the list, and permits you to have the document sent back to you at the end of its route. One especially useful feature of the routing slip is that you can protect the document so reviewers always see all changes, but cannot change others' comments and forms.

To attach a routing slip to your document, do the following.

1. Save the document to be reviewed.

2. On the File menu, point to Send To and click Routing Recipient.

3. In the Routing Slip dialog box shown in Figure 12-3, click Address and then add names of the recipients from the Address Book dialog box in the order you want them to receive the document.

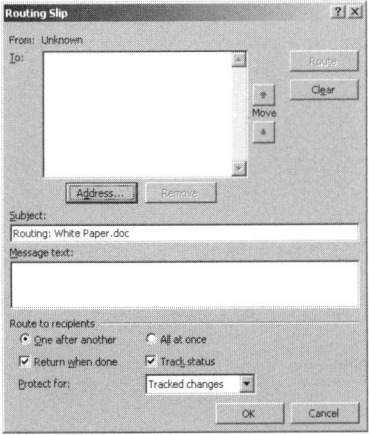

Figure 12-3 *The Routing Slip dialog box allows you to select who will review your document and the order in which the document will be routed to them.*

4. If needed, change the recipients' order by clicking the up and down arrows in the Routing Slip dialog box and then typing a subject and text for the e-mail they will receive.

5. Choose how you want to route the document (One After Another or All At Once), whether you want the document returned to you after the last person reviews it, whether you want to track the status of the document through the routing cycle, and whether to protect the document for tracked changes, comments, or forms.

6. Click Route to send the document immediately, or Add Slip (at the bottom of the dialog box) to create the routing slip and return to the document without sending it.

7. If you choose Add Slip, you can route the document at a later time by choosing Send To and then Routing Recipient from the File menu.

After you review a routed document you receive, choose Send To and then Next Routing Recipient from the File menu to send the document to the next reviewer or back to the originator.

As the original author, when you receive the routed document back, you can use the Reviewing toolbar to accept or reject the changes made by the various reviewers. Each change has the reviewers' initials, so you can differentiate them from each other. End the reviewing process by clicking the End Review button on the Reviewing toolbar.

Sharing the Work

If you are creating a long document such as a book, you might want to work on separate sections as individual documents and then combine them back into the original document for printing; checking cross references; and creating the index, table of contents, and lists of figures. The Master Document feature of Word allows you to do exactly this, and in addition, to assign subdocuments to different authors.

The Master Document view is accessed from the Outlining toolbar, and is visible when you are in the Outline view. It allows you to break your document into subdocuments at, for instance, each Level 1 heading. Each subdocument is saved separately, and is recombined when you open the Master document.

See "About Master Documents" in the Word Help system for details about how to use this feature.

Discussing Your Work

Collaboration is the process of creating knowledge together. Whether it's done face to face or over the Web, collaboration requires *content* and *conversation*. To effectively create a new tagline for a company, people need to talk about many subjects—the fundamental mission of the company, who the tagline is for, and more. We're so used to doing this in a face-to-face context that we don't even think about it. Online, however, it's somewhat harder to structure appropriate conversations that get the right people together at the right time to produce the right results.

What's required is a combination of *synchronous* (same-time) and *asynchronous* (any-time) conversations. Synchronous conversation tools are ones like the telephone, instant messaging, and chat. They are great for getting quick reactions and coming to decisions. Asynchronous conversation tools are ones like Web-based discussions and e-mail. They are better for obtaining thoughtful responses, sustaining conversations, engaging all players, and maintaining a record of your discussions. Sophisticated distributed teams are increasingly finding that instant messaging and online meetings are replacing the ubiquitous conference call, because it's easier to ensure that everyone can contribute. Similarly Web-based discussions are taking the place of e-mail because all the discussions are organized and attached to the document being discussed.

In working together with a distributed team, you must be able to use all the available communications tools with equal ease. The three that Microsoft Office provides can dramatically add to your team's effectiveness. They are MSN Messenger for quick synchronous discussions, NetMeeting for synchronous group meetings, and the Office XP Web Discussions feature for asynchronous discussions about documents.

See Also   For more information about distributed teams, see Chapter 16, "Sharing Knowledge with Remote Workers."

Attaching Web Discussions to Documents

After you start using the review features of Word, you'll find that you use the Comment feature extensively to provide feedback and ideas about points in draft documents you're preparing together. One problem you might encounter is that the Comment feature does not provide an easy way to engage in a back and forth discussion about a point. This shortcoming has been addressed very elegantly with the Web Discussions feature that was implemented beginning with Microsoft Office 2000.

Web discussions are newsgroup-like threaded postings that are linked to a specific document, but stored on a Microsoft Discussion Server. Discussion servers are part of Microsoft SharePoint Web sites as well as Web sites that have the Microsoft FrontPage 2002 extensions installed, and might also be available through your corporate intranet.

To attach a Web discussion to a document, do the following.

1. Ensure that your Word document is saved.

2. Choose Online Collaboration and then Web Discussions from the Tools menu.

3. To attach a discussion about a specific point in the document, click the appropriate point or select the appropriate text and then choose Insert Discussion In The Document from the Web Discussions toolbar. To attach a discussion about the document in general, choose Insert Discussion About The Document instead.

4. If the document has not been saved on a server that has the Discussion Server installed, you see a message telling you that you must specify a discussion server and asking if you want to specify one now. When you click Yes, you are prompted to select a discussion server and can select one from the drop-down list or click Add and type the discussion server address you can obtain from your network administrator.

5. Type the discussion subject and text in the Enter Discussion Text dialog box.

When you open a document that has an attached Web discussion, you might see the Web Discussion toolbar and a discussion window, as shown in Figure 12-4. If you do not, choose Online Collaboration and then Web Discussions from the Tools menu to display it. You can then add new discussion topics or respond to existing ones by using the Web Discussions toolbar:

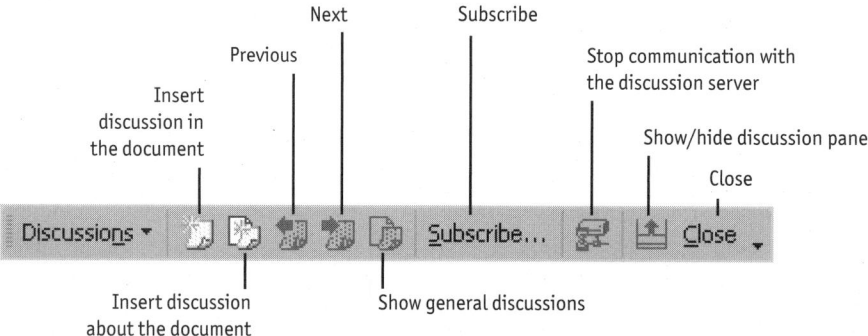

Figure 12-4   *Word allows you to attach threaded discussions to documents so your team cannot only comment on the document, but also hold extended conversations about important points.*

- Click the Show/Hide Discussion Pane to toggle the display of the discussions.
- Click the Previous/Next buttons to move from one discussion topic to another.
- To respond to a discussion topic or reply, click the icon to the right of it and choose Reply.
- To type a new discussion topic, use the Insert Discussion In The Document or Insert Discussion About The Document buttons.
- To close a discussion, click the icon to the right of it and choose Close.
- If you want to be notified when someone adds a comment to the document, click Subscribe and specify your e-mail address and notification options.

Using Instant Messaging

Instant messaging isn't just for teenagers anymore. It is starting to gain acceptance in corporate America, and some sources such as Gartner, Inc. suggest that it will become—if not quite as ubiquitous as e-mail—a common business tool within the next couple years. Instant messaging provides a number of benefits, including the following.

- You can immediately see which of your team members is online, creating a sense of co-presence for teams—even when you're not working in the same location.

- Although instant messages pop up and can be responded to immediately, they are not as obtrusive as a ringing phone—you can wait two minutes to finish your call or complete the thought you're writing before answering.

- Nonetheless, the sender receives a response within a couple minutes—much faster than the usual e-mail response and only marginally slower than a phone call.

- You can hold several instant messaging sessions simultaneously, or be on an instant messaging session while you're on a conference call with a client for back-channel communication.

- You can do a quick "social" check-in with remote team members that takes only a few minutes, but builds and maintains connections over time and distance.

- You can transmit files using your instant messaging program rather than attaching them to an e-mail, for a more real-time experience of file sharing.

- If you have a fast connection to the Internet, a microphone, and speakers, you can conduct a "voice chat" with other instant messenger users or (for a fee) call a telephone from your instant messaging program.

However, instant messaging can be distracting and disruptive if you don't take steps to use it appropriately. Some guidelines for effectively using instant messaging in a business setting include the following.

- **Limit your availability.**   Do not publish your name in public directories, and give out your logon ID only to coworkers.

- **Use filters.**   Each instant messaging program has a method for limiting who can send you an instant message. Learn the commands for the application you use.

- **Create norms.**   Have a discussion within your team about how instant messaging should be used compared to how e-mail and the telephone should be used. Address questions such as whether to use instant messaging for social interactions, and when people should be available to respond to messages.

- **Respect individual differences.**   People will differ with respect to their preferences and availability. Use instant messaging with others who find it valuable, and don't force it on everyone.

- **Be honest.**   If you find that instant messages from a particular individual are distracting or overwhelming, let them know politely and directly that the nature of your work is such that it's better for you to communicate with them by telephone or e-mail rather than instant message.

There are several vendors who provide instant messaging services; as of this writing, they are all free. They include MSN, AOL, Yahoo!, and a number of other vendors. Many of them are not compatible with each other so your contact list in MSN Messenger Service might not be compatible with your AOL Instant Messenger (AIM) Buddy List, and if you are using MSN's instant messaging program you cannot send or receive messages with AIM users. Each of these services has similar features, but you might want to look carefully at MSN Messenger because it integrates with several applications and services such as

- **Microsoft Passport.**   This provides you with a single point to log on for all services that support Passport.

- **Outlook.**   You can enter an MSN Messenger address for Outlook contacts. When you open a contact who has an open Messenger session, you see a Contact Is Online message and, by clicking it, can start an instant message session with the contact.

- **NetMeeting.**   You can start a NetMeeting session from an instant message session, to enable you to access the more powerful features of NetMeeting such as application sharing and video conferencing.

- **Hotmail.**   You see a notice of unopened Hotmail messages in your Messenger window.

- **Mobile devices.**   You can send instant messages to mobile devices such as wireless pages, cell phones, and Pocket PCs of MSN Messenger users.

Caution   Instant messaging programs, including MSN Messenger, might not work from behind corporate firewalls.

- **Microsoft Exchange Server.**   If your company uses Exchange Server, it might be configured as an MSN Messenger server providing additional security, availability behind your firewall, and freedom from ads.

If MSN Messenger is not installed on your computer, you can download it from *http:// messenger.msn.com/download/download.asp*. Once it's installed, to start using MSN Messenger, you must sign up including creating (if needed) a Passport account. You can do so as follows.

1. Open MSN Messenger from the Start menu.

2. Click Click Here To Sign In, and type your sign-in name if you have a Passport. If you don't, click Get One Here and follow the instructions to obtain a Passport.

Note   You already have a Passport, which is your e-mail address, if you have an account at *http://www.msn.com* or *http://www.hotmail.com*. Otherwise when you create a Passport, you can simultaneously set up a Hotmail account or create one using your regular e-mail account.

---

3. When you are finished, return to the Sign In To Passport dialog box and type your Passport ID (the e-mail address you registered with Passport) and Passport password. It's handy to check Remember My Name And Password On This Computer, if you're the only person who uses the computer.

For MSN Messenger to be most convenient, start an MSN Messenger session automatically when Windows starts. To ensure that it does, open the MSN Messenger software and choose Options from the Tools menu. Then make sure that Run This Program When Windows Starts and Allow This Program To Run In The Background are checked in the Preferences tab. You can also set options for providing a message for when you are away and displaying alerts in this dialog box.

After you start a Messenger session, you see a window like the one shown in Figure 12-5. You can add users to your contact list with the Add button. You can either type their Passport e-mail address (which is usually their regular e-mail address or a second, Hotmail address), or you can search by name and location in the Hotmail member directory or on the Address Book on your computer. When someone adds you to their contact list, you see a message asking whether you want to allow this and whether you want to add them to your contact list as well.

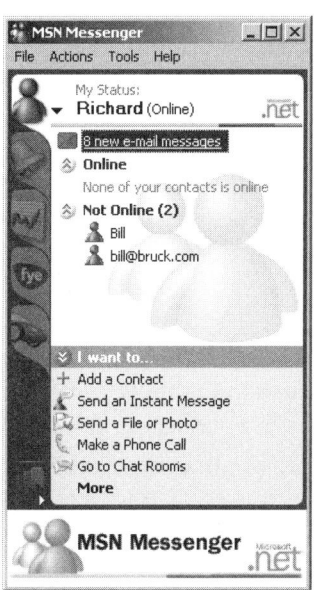

Figure 12-5 *If you keep Messenger open during your work sessions, you can easily see which of your teammates are online.*

You can also contact people in the following ways while Messenger is open.

- Click Send An Instant Message in the I Want To list at the bottom of the MSN Messenger window to start an instant message session, and send a quick message to someone on your contact list.

- Click Make A Phone Call in the I Want To list to call another person's phone number (there might be a charge for this), or to conduct a voice chat (if both of you have microphones and speakers or headsets).

- Choose Send a Message To A Mobile Device from the Actions menu to send a text message to the mobile device of someone on your contact list.

- Click More in the I Want To list, and then select Start NetMeeting to start a NetMeeting session.

- Choose Send A File Or Photo in the I Want To list to upload a file to your colleague.

Participating in an Online Meeting

Sometimes, you need more than a quick chat with a colleague. You need to get several people together online to discuss a topic, look at a workbook, hear a presentation, or decide on a course of action. To accomplish these goals, it's useful to have functionality that includes the ability to do the following.

- Create a chat room where several people can type comments in real time

- Connect by voice or video as well as by chat

- Share Microsoft Excel workbooks, Microsoft PowerPoint presentations, and Word documents

- Create a shared whiteboard where team members can sketch ideas

- Transfer files

- Have multiple users see a shared application for training purposes, and allow different users to "take control" of the application

There are several Web services that permit you to hold same-time online meetings including WebEx (*http://www.webex.com*), Placeware (*http://www.placeware.com*), and Latitude (*http://www.latitude.com*). They are all fairly expensive to use, but offer some specialized features that can be helpful for holding large-scale meetings (like a "raise your hand" feature that notifies the moderator that someone wants to make a point). If you are holding a meeting with a work team, however, NetMeeting might be all you need. It offers all the features noted in the previous bulleted list, and best of all, it's free!

NetMeeting is installed with Microsoft Internet Explorer by default. To start NetMeeting, click the Start button, then point to Programs, then to Accessories, then to Communications, then click NetMeeting. The first time you use it, you are prompted to enter some information about yourself and then you're all set. The only part of using NetMeeting that is at all tricky is finding the address of the people you want to connect with. You can do so by typing their IP address or by looking them up on the Microsoft Internet Directory, accessed by clicking the Find Someone In Directory button. The Microsoft Internet Directory shows you all the people in your MSN Messenger contact list and provides a More Information link to public directories to find other people. Unless your organization has its own directory server (which your system administrator will tell you), the best way to connect is often for one person to look up his or her IP address and then give it to the others by phone or e-mail.

Tip   To find your IP address, choose About Windows NetMeeting from the NetMeeting Help menu. Your IP address will be listed. Remember that your IP address might change from session to session, so look it up whenever you need to share it.

You can start a NetMeeting session by

- Opening NetMeeting from the Start menu, and clicking Place Call

- In an MSN Messenger session, clicking More in the I Want To list, and then Start NetMeeting

- In Word, Excel, or PowerPoint, choosing Online Collaboration and then Meet Now from the Tools menu

- In Word, Excel, or PowerPoint, choosing Online Collaboration and then Schedule Meeting from the Tools menu, and then scheduling the meeting using the Outlook meeting form that is displayed

- From Outlook, scheduling a meeting and ensuring that the This Is An Online Meeting Using box is checked, and Microsoft NetMeeting is specified as the method

When starting a NetMeeting session from Outlook, you can also specify an Office document to be opened and shared when the meeting starts by clicking the Attachment button in the Standard toolbar and selecting the appropriate document. When you start NetMeeting from Word, PowerPoint, or Excel, the file you want to collaborate about is automatically opened and shared so you can get right to work.

After you start a NetMeeting session, you can use the following features as shown in Figure 12-6.

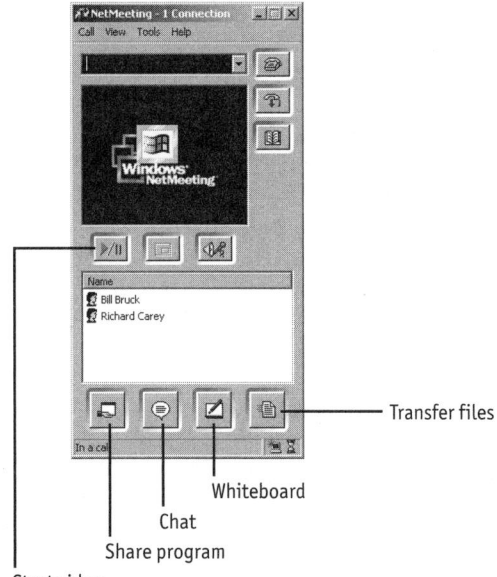

Transfer files

Whiteboard

Chat

Share program

Start video

Figure 12-6   *NetMeeting provides all the tools you need for a quick meeting with a group of colleagues.*

- Click the Start Video button to display your video to others in the meeting, if you have a Web camera connected to your computer.

- Click the Share Program button to share one or more active programs on your desktop with other meeting participants. You can also choose to give other participants control over these programs, if desired.

- Click the Chat button to start a text chat session with others in the meeting.

- Click the Whiteboard button to open a whiteboard that is shared with all participants. You can use the whiteboard to draw ideas, much like you do with a physical whiteboard.

- Click the Transfer Files button to upload a file to other participants.

Tip   You might find it easier to share PowerPoint than to use the Whiteboard feature, because PowerPoint provides more features for entering both text and graphics.

With practice, you'll find that NetMeeting can be a powerful adjunct to your other online tools, allowing distributed work groups to quickly convene, share documents, and come to quick decisions.

Conducting a Quick Poll

If your team is using Outlook, you can conduct a quick poll to help your work group come to closure on an issue. You can use the default responses of Outlook (approve/reject, yes/no, or yes/no/maybe), or you can enter any response that better meets your needs. As responses come in, they are automatically tallied and you can see the results whenever you like. To create a quick poll using Outlook, follow these steps.

1. Create an e-mail in Outlook and address it to your team. Be sure the body of the e-mail states the issue and the specific question you are asking.

2. Click the Options button on the Standard toolbar.

3. Check Use Voting Buttons.

4. Select one of the default response sets from the drop-down list adjacent to the Use Voting Buttons check box, or delete the default text in the drop-down list and enter your own response options separating them with semicolons.

5. Send the message.

When your coworkers receive the message, they see voting buttons above the message box as shown in Figure 12-7. They vote on the question by clicking the appropriate button. They can then choose to either send the message or edit it, if they want to include a comment with their vote.

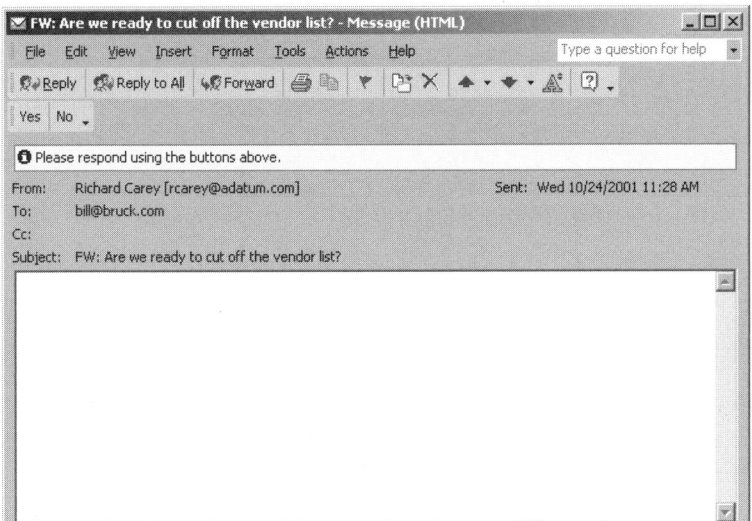

Figure 12-7 *Outlook options allow you to add a voting request to your e-mails, which are automatically tallied as the e-mails are returned.*

You can see the vote tally whenever you open one of the responses to your poll by clicking in the information box that says Click Here To View The Summary Of Responses. Alternatively, you can open the original poll in the Sent Items folder and click the Tracking tab to see the tally of responses.

Summary

Being able to create knowledge with other people—especially when they are not co-located with you—requires several new skills. You need to be able to leverage the tools that allow you to know what your teammates are working on, and work together effectively with them to produce the documents that reflect your best thinking. You also need to be able to supplement traditional ways of communicating like conference calls and e-mail with new methods—online meetings, instant messaging, and Web-based discussions—to keep as many channels of communication open as you can.

Checklist for Creating Knowledge with People

Check off the following points as you learn to use tools for creating knowledge with people.

[ ] Assign tasks to others with Outlook and track their status.

[ ] Know when using Outlook will suffice, and when Project is required for project coordination.

[ ] Track changes to documents, and make comments on others' drafts.

[ ] Use the Reviewing toolbar to consolidate reviewers' suggestions.

[ ] Save versions of your document to track changes over time.

[ ] Send documents for review, and add routing slips.

[ ] Attach an asynchronous threaded discussion to a document.

[ ] Use instant messaging for quick contacts with other team members.

[ ] Hold an online meeting with your team using NetMeeting.

Sharing Knowledge

As Jerry Useem writes in Business 2.0, "Increasingly, the value of a company is to be found not in its tangible assets, but in intangibles: people, ideas, and the strategic aggregation of key information-driven assets." One of the main strategic assets of corporations today is their intellectual property, and knowledge that is not shared is knowledge that does not add to that strategic asset.

There are four basic elements to effectively sharing knowledge with others.

- **Organization.** Your knowledge has to be organized in a way that others can follow your points, see why you made your conclusions, and get to the salient aspects of your document quickly.

- **Presentation.** The way your knowledge is presented needs to be a good fit for the medium it's presented in, and must be formatted in a way that enables rather than inhibits the audience from understanding what you're saying.

- **Distribution.** You have to be able to communicate your knowledge in a medium that is appropriate both to the subject matter and the audience, whether it be in printed Microsoft Word documents, projected Microsoft Power-Point slideshows, or on Web pages.

- **Interaction.** For today's audience, your knowledge must not be static. For your knowledge to be useful, members of your audience must be able to interact—with the information, with you, or with themselves—in order to continue the knowledge-building process.

Part IV addresses each of these elements, showing you how to effectively share knowledge with others. Chapter 13, "Sharing Knowledge Using Documents," teaches you how to format your documents so not only are readers able to follow your points, but also you are able to create a "personal brand" that identifies documents as yours. In addition, you learn how to organize your documents using tables of contents, hyperlinks, and cross-references, to allow readers to quickly find points of interest.

In Chapter 14, "Sharing Knowledge Using Slideshows," you learn how to create a professional look and feel for your PowerPoint slideshows using templates that you can then customize for your organization. You find out how to organize your thoughts in a slideshow and how to put slides together in a variety of ways to meet various audience needs. You also find out how to create self-running slideshows for use in kiosks.

Chapter 15, "Sharing Knowledge Using the Web," teaches you how to create Web sites with Microsoft FrontPage and how to maintain Web pages if you are a content manager for specific areas of your Web site. You learn how to repurpose documents for the Web, how Web documents differ from their paper counterparts, and how to publish content to the Web using Word. You also see how to share numeric data on Web pages with interactive worksheets and Microsoft Access databases and learn how to publish PowerPoint slideshows and insert video clips into your Web site.

If you're working as part of a virtual team, are a telecommuter, or work on the road, Chapter 16, "Sharing Knowledge with Remote Workers" is focused on your needs. In it you learn all about the Electronic Office—what it is, how it changes work practices, and the factors you need to examine when choosing a platform to support online work. You also find out about the small team offering from Microsoft—SharePoint Team Services. You learn how to create a SharePoint team Web site, how to work within it, and how to manage and customize it.

Sharing Knowledge Using Documents

Suanne Nagata is the Director of Institutional Research at the Graphic Design Institute. Her primary responsibility is to annually document institutional effectiveness for the national accrediting body that does site visits once every five years. To do this, she prepares yearly reports for each academic department documenting what the academic outcomes of their program are, what skills and knowledge they believe graduates should leave with, and how well, overall, they are meeting these goals. These reports, bound and presented together, total more than 1,000 pages each year. In addition, Suanne is asked to prepare frequent special reports, such as demographic studies assessing the viability of proposed new programs.

In studying the reports of other exemplar schools who consistently received their accreditation, Suanne realized the form was as important as the substance. These schools' reports consistently were professionally presented, possessed excellent design, and had a coherent look and feel. Other schools' reports looked like someone had stuck 10 different documents together in the same three-ring binder.

Suanne has several challenges in accomplishing her tasks.

- Although data and supporting text come from many sources, they need to be presented in a consistent format for the accrediting body.

- The volume of information requires that Suanne create a clear organizational system whereby readers can quickly find the information they deem important.

Suanne dealt with these challenges in the following ways. First, she developed a unique style guide that she applies religiously to every research report emanating from her office. It uses a slightly different font, a 2.5" left margin, and thick lines under headers and section headings. Every document starts with a one-page executive overview, continues with a table of contents and a list of figures, and ends with a glossary and an index.

Suanne created styles for all these formatting elements that could be easily applied using shortcut keys, and saved these styles (along with the boilerplate front text, the table of contents, list of figures, and index) in an InstResearch template that she distributed to every department. Not only did this provide the coherent look and feel and create a sense of organization for her documents that the accrediting body loved, but it also had a more subtle effect. She noticed that, over time, when people held up a page showing some data or other from one of her documents at a faculty meeting, they instantly knew it had been produced by Institutional Research. She had effectively *branded* her work, and started receiving appropriate credit for it.

In this chapter, you learn to use the same tools in Microsoft Word that Suanne used to organize and present your work. You find out how to create a unique look and feel using design principles, along with formatting functions such as headers, footers, fonts, and margins. You see how to organize your documents with tables of contents, cross-references, and hyperlinks. More importantly, you'll start to think about publishing your documents differently—incorporating elements of style at the same time you create your content—a process that's called *page processing*.

Creating a Distinctive Style

A good document layout does two things: It makes the material easily accessible to the reader, and it "makes your mark" by branding documents as ones you created. Although most people think about the former, they often forget the latter, and making your mark can be important.

Making your mark is creating a distinctive style for your documents. When people in your organization read a report prepared in your office, they consciously or unconsciously associate that document with you. This starts to "brand" your work. And make no mistake about it; branding is important, both internally and externally. Branding ensures that you get credit for your work and your ideas.

The style you create should be tasteful, and similar to the standard style used by others. However, within corporate guidelines, you will often be able to enhance that standard style by varying margins, fonts, headings, table formats, chart types, title pages, and more. For example, the report shown in Print Preview mode in Figure 13-1 allows you to see several elements of a distinctive style. These elements include the following.

- **Margins.**   Margins do not have to be symmetrical—in fact, nonsymmetrical margins can be a distinctive design feature.

- **Fonts.**   Try using a variation of standard fonts. People often use Arial when they want a sans serif font—one without the small line at the end of the main stroke of a letter—and they use Times New Roman when they want a serifed font. Instead of using Arial, try Verdana. It is similar to the sans serif Arial, but the width of the strokes is variable rather than uniform. Book Antiqua, Bookman Old Style, Century Schoolbook, and Garamond are fonts that you can use in place of Times New Roman. Each gives a slightly different flair that subtly sets your documents apart.

- **Bullets.** Consider using a different type of character for bullet lists. When you choose Bullets and Numbering from the Format menu and click Customize, you're able to choose from an almost infinite variety of bullets. Be sure to print them on others' computers, however, to ensure that the symbols on your machine are shared by others.

- **Headers and footers.** You can insert stylistic elements in your headers and footers, such as an especially thick or thin line under the header and above the footer, that set your documents apart visually.

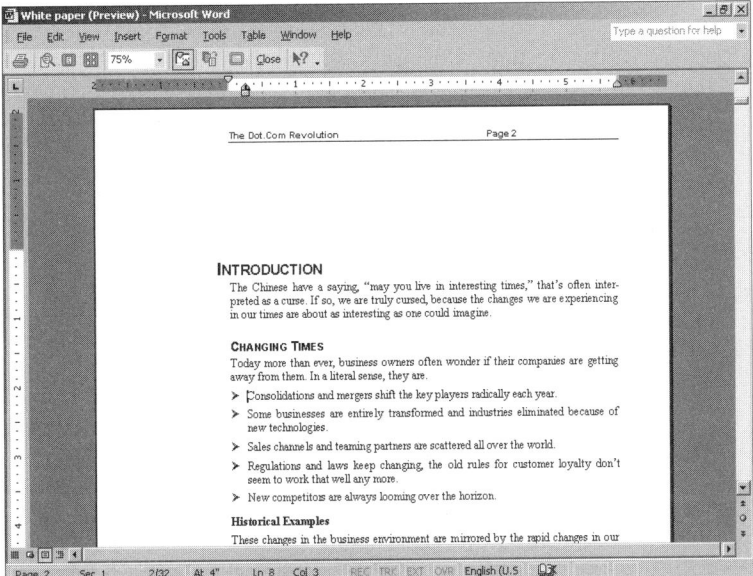

Figure 13-1 *Well-formed documents aren't locked into 1" margins anymore.*

Tip Choose a font that is likely to be on the computer of your recipient, or be sure to embed fonts with documents you send. Although embedding fonts increases your document size, it allows you to use fonts that aren't on the recipient's computer. To embed fonts, choose Options from the Tools menu and then check Embed TrueType Fonts on the Save tab. You'll probably want to use two (and no more than two) fonts in your documents—one for your body text and another for your headings. Even if you don't use a different font for the body text, using Verdana for headings rather than the default Arial can make a visual difference.

Setting Margins

Word allows you to set margins for each *section* of your document. If you have only one section, as documents do by default, the margins you set are for the entire document.

Tip   Try experimenting with a large top and left margin (1.5" to 2.5"), and a smaller right margin (.5" to .75"), by selecting Page Settings from the File menu. You can even place text boxes in the left margin to call attention to points you make.

Document Sections

Word allows you to break your document into *sections*. Page setup options such as footers can vary from section to section of your document, so you can have different footers for different parts of your document. Page setup options that can vary between sections include the following.

- Margins

- Paper size, orientation, source, and vertical alignment

- Headers, footers, and page numbering

- Columns

- Line numbering, footnotes, and endnotes

- Page borders

One common use for sections is to divide your front material from the body of your document. That way, you can use Roman numerals (or no numbers) for the front material and start your Arabic page numbering at the first page of the body text, or use different margins for the front material from the body. Another is to change your header text at each chapter or division, so that your headers reflect the name of the division. You can also create a new section if part of your document is multicolumn, or if you need to insert a landscape spreadsheet in a document whose orientation is portrait.

To insert a section, position your cursor where the section should start and then choose Break from the Insert menu. You can choose four ways to start your new section.

- **Next Page.**   Puts in a page break and a section break, so your new section starts on a new page. Use this for starting a new major division of your document.

- **Continuous.**   Starts the new section immediately, for example, if you want to have two columns in the middle of your page.

- **Even Page / Odd Page.**   Puts in a one-page or two-page break, as needed, so your new section starts on a new odd or even page. This is usually used for books, where a new chapter starts on a right-facing (odd) page.

To set your margins, do the following.

1. Click in the appropriate section of your document, if you want the margins to apply only to that section. (Otherwise, it doesn't matter where you are in the document.)

2. Choose Page Setup from the File menu, and click the Margins tab.

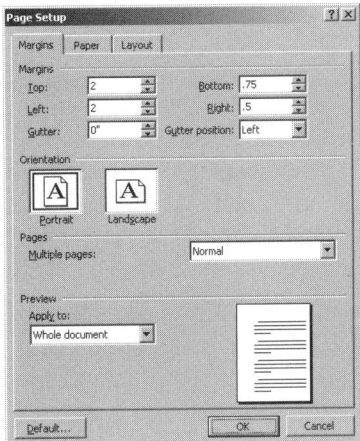

3. Set the top, bottom, left, and right margins.

4. Choose the appropriate area of the document to apply the new margins to.

   - Whole Document applies new margins to the entire document.

   - This Point Forward creates a new section at the insertion point, and applies the margins to that new section.

   - This Section appears only when there are multiple sections in the document, and applies the margin to the current section.

You might on occasion want to print text inside the margins. For instance, say you have a wide left margin and want your first-level headings to be inside the left margin. You can do this by changing the left indentation of the style to a negative number. Alternatively, if you want to put a comment or a pull quote in the margin, choose Text Box from the Insert menu and then drag the resulting box to the appropriate position in the document.

Creating Space in Your Document

The beauty of Japanese *sumi*—ink paintings of bamboo and other natural objects—is in its simplicity and use of white space. This same sense of the value of white space can be a good guideline for creating Word documents. It isn't a contest to see who can get the most ink on the page; it's a question of balance, of proportion, and of making it easy for the eye to quickly locate items of importance and read accompanying text.

One important way to create space in your documents is by judicious use of margins, as discussed earlier in this chapter. Another is by coordinating the formatting of your paragraphs with your text size and weight. Using small-sized text with multiple-line spacing, for instance, can give an open, airy look to your document.

Elements that you might want to consider as you develop your style for documents include

- **Open look.**   An open look gives your document an uncluttered appearance. Consider using line spacings between 1.25 and 1.5 lines within paragraphs, with a slightly smaller font size (10 or 11 point) and a font face that looks smaller (Garamond rather than Times New Roman, for instance). Use the same spacing between paragraphs, or possibly .25 lines greater. Indent the first line of paragraphs by .25" to .5". Use the same spacing within and between bullet points as you do within paragraphs.

- **Formal look.**   A formal look provides a tighter, more dense appearance to your documents, while still creating enough white space for good design. Use a line spacing of 1 line, and a regular Arial or Times New Roman font at 12 points. Double-space between paragraphs to create white space, but do not indent the first line of each paragraph. Use 1.5 to 2 lines before the first bullet point and 2 lines after the last one, but single space between and within the bullet points themselves.

Note   You can set the line spacing, indents, and spacing before and after paragraphs with styles, as discussed next, or by selecting text and choosing Paragraph from the Format menu.

Inserting Headers and Footers

The header of a document is the space above the body text in the top margin, while the footer is the space in the bottom margin. The header and footer allow you to insert a variety of information that is useful to your reader and to your organization such as page numbers, date of last revision, name of document, company name, and so forth. Many of these are AutoText elements that you can insert automatically by clicking the AutoText button on the Header and Footer toolbar.

You can also include stylistic elements that set your documents apart, such as an alternate font for the header/footer or a border line separating the header or footer from the rest of the page.

To insert a header or footer in your document, do the following.

1. Click in the section in which your header or footer should appear, if your document has multiple sections.

Tip   If you want to have a different header or footer for the first page than the remaining pages, be sure your document has at least two pages for each section in which you want to create different headers and footers or else you won't have a second page of the section to insert a header or footer in.

2. Choose Header And Footer from the View menu. You're switched to Print Layout view, if you are not already in it.

3. Change common header and footer options by clicking the Page Setup button on the Header and Footer toolbar and clicking the Layout tab.

   - Check Different Odd And Even to create different headers for odd pages and even pages.

   - Check Different First Page to create a different header (or no header) on the first page of a section.

   - Set From Edge to specify how far from the edge of the paper the header and footer should appear.

Tip It's best to change these options before you type the text, because otherwise you might be putting text into the wrong header or footer.

4. Type the text of your header or footer, noting the following.

   - By default, you are in the Header style for headers and the Footer style for footers, and there are three tab stops: A left tab at the left margin; a center tab in the center, and a right tab at the right margin. Thus, it's easy to position text at the common points for headers and footers.

   - You can easily insert common variables with the Insert Page Number, Insert Number Of Pages, Insert Date, and Insert Time buttons on the Header And Footer toolbar.

   - You can format text in the header and footer by selecting it and using standard formatting commands, or by modifying the Header or Footer style.

   - You can make a section header the same as the previous section by clicking the Same As Previous button. This creates a link between the text of the header or footer and that of the previous section, so that when you change one section's header or footer the remainder changes as well.

Tip If you have set document properties such as the title or author by choosing Properties from the File menu, you can automatically insert these properties into your header or footer. To do so, choose Field from the Insert menu. Properties such as title and author are in the Document Information category.

5. Enter other headers and footers by navigating as follows.

   - Click the Show Next and Show Previous buttons on the Header and Footer toolbar to switch to the next and previous section's header or footer.

- Toggle between a section's header and footer with the Switch Between Header And Footer button.

Note   If you merely want to number the pages of your document, you don't need to use the header/footer feature. You can choose Page Numbers from the Insert menu, and specify whether they will be in the top or bottom of the document, their alignment, and their formatting. Most business documents, however, take advantage of the header/footer to insert additional information, as mentioned earlier, so this feature is not used as often as it was in the past.

To edit your headers and footers, double-click in the gray header or footer if you're working in Print Layout view; otherwise, choose Headers And Footers from the View menu as you did when you first created them.

Processing Pages, Not Words

After you have learned to use the basic formatting features of Word, page processing is the next step. *Page processing* is the technique of using styles and other formatting commands to display your document in its final style while you are still creating the content. As you start using this new style of writing, you'll find that you are thinking about the look and feel of the document as you compose its content and that content and style will start to interact. You'll also find that you are creating documents that are more persuasive and powerful, because they appeal to the readers' visceral senses as well as their logical minds.

Here are some guidelines for page processing.

- Identify the amount of space you want the document to take up. For longer documents, identify the amount of space that sections such as introductions should take, or other spacing rules such as "Don't let a section end with fewer than five lines on the last page."

- Use the Print Layout view while composing your document by choosing Print Layout from the View menu to see the final format of the page.

- Use the Zoom drop-down list to see as much of the page as you can on your monitor while still easily reading the text.

- Use styles for your text elements rather than manually formatting your text, as described in the next section.

- Outline your document, or the section you're working on, so you can see how many points need to fit into the space available. As you fill in the outline with your text, you start to see after just a few sections whether your document is likely to be too short or too long.

- If a section is slightly too long, look for paragraphs that have one or two words on the last line and remove a couple words somewhere in the paragraph to save that line, or combine two bullet points into one if that saves a line.

- If a section is slightly too short, you can use additional examples to reinforce your points, add a few words to a paragraph if it takes it up another line, or divide bullet points to create extra lines.

Formatting Documents with Style(s)

After you decide on the look and feel you want your documents to have, it's important to be able to apply that look and feel consistently; and doubly important if more than one person will be working on your documents. The first tool to use to do this—and use religiously—is styles. Styles not only allow you to create consistency and save time, but also enable you to take advantage of other Word features such as tables of contents and outlining.

A *style* is a set of formatting commands that is attached to a document or template. There are two types of styles—the more common paragraph styles that apply formatting to the entire paragraph and the less-often-used character styles that override paragraph styles and apply formatting to selected characters.

A style can contain the following information.

- Character formatting (font face, size, style, color, underline style, effects)
- Paragraph formatting (alignment, line spacing, paragraph spacing, indentation)
- Tabs, borders, bullets and numbering

Styles are a great timesaver—when you modify a style, every bit of text in the document that has that style applied is immediately changed! You can quickly change your document from draft style to a final style by merely changing the attributes of the styles you used to create your document. Similarly, you can center all your level 1 headings or change the spacing in your bullet lists—all by merely changing the appropriate style. Styles can also *cascade*: a "child" style can be based on a "parent" style, so that changes to the parent style are reflected in the child style. Styles can also automate your document production in several ways.

- You can specify a style for the following paragraph, so by pressing the Enter key you move from one style to another. For instance, in creating a title page, you might have the Title style invoke the Subtitle style for the next paragraph, which invokes the Author style for the next, which calls the Company style for the next. Each of these styles can format its text entirely differently, and a user can quickly create a title page by selecting the Title style and then pressing the Enter key so each successive line is entered in the appropriate format.

- You can assign shortcut keys to styles, enabling you to quickly format your document without your hands leaving the keyboard.

- You can apply paragraph formatting that ensures that a section heading is never separated from the following text by a page break, and that paragraphs never have widowed or orphaned first or last lines separated by a page break. To do so, apply the proper option from the Line And Page Breaks tab of the Paragraph dialog box you see when you modify the Paragraph format of a style, as described in the next table.

Table 13-1 contains several styles you might find valuable to use consistently in all your documents.

Table 13-1   Commonly Used Styles

Style	Use For
Normal	All document text that is not in another style.
Heading 1, 2, 3	Section headings within your document. Text in these styles will be included by default in tables of contents, and will be the headings used in the Outline view.
Title, Subtitle, Contents	Headings of front material you do not want included in your table of contents.
Body Text	The regular text for your document, containing formatting specific to the type of document you're creating (for example, double-spaced or indented).
Bullet, Last Bullet	For bullet lists. If you want different spacing for the last bullet (for example, additional space between the list and the following text), use a Last Bullet style as well.
Numbered, Last Numbered	For numbered lists. If you want different spacing for the last numbered point (for example, additional space between the list and the following text), use a Last Numbered style as well.
Quote, [Other special elements]	Might be indented on both sides, single-spaced, and italic (or however you want long quotes to be noted). Use a style for quotes or any other special text element that is contained in your document.

Usually, you will find a style that already is provided in Word and you can use it and, if needed, modify it to meet your needs. To apply a style, select the text to which it should be applied and then select the style from the Style drop-down list on the Formatting toolbar. If you need to modify it or create a new one, do the following.

1. Click the Styles and Formatting button on the Formatting toolbar.

2. To create a new style, click the New Style button in the Styles and Formatting task pane; to modify an existing one, right-click the style from the Pick Formatting To Apply list and choose Modify. The resulting Modify Style dialog box has the same functionality as the Modify Style dialog box shown in Figure 13-2.

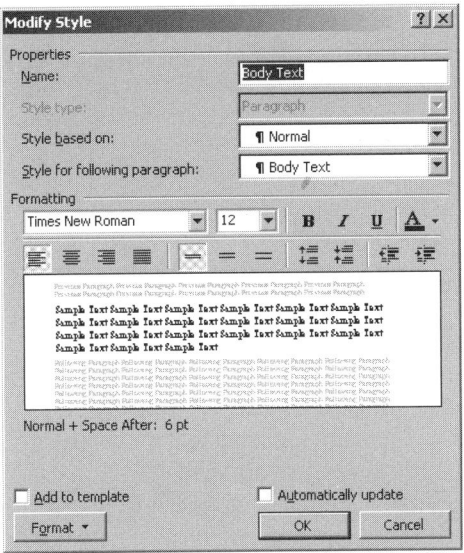

Figure 13-2   *You can quickly modify a style with the formatting toolbar in the Modify Style dialog box, or more extensively change formatting with the Format button.*

3. If it's a new style, enter the style name and type.

4. Choose the parent style that the current style should be based on, and the style for the following paragraph.

5. Select basic formatting options for your style from the Formatting toolbar.

6. Select advanced formatting options by clicking Format, and then opening the appropriate formatting dialog box by choosing Font, Paragraph, Tabs, Border, Language, Frame, or Numbering.

7. Assign the style to a shortcut key by clicking Format, and then choosing Shortcut Key and entering the keystroke sequence in the Customize Keyboard dialog box.

8. Add the style to the template on which the document is based by checking Add To Template.

9. You can check Automatically Update to update the style every time the formatting of any text that uses the style changes, but this can create very unpredictable results unless you're an expert user and very careful.

Styles and Templates

Every Word document you create is based on a *template*—a master document that contains a number of elements such as formatting commands that govern default attributes of documents based on them. In addition to formatting information, templates contain

- A list of styles
- Boilerplate text
- AutoCorrect entries that automatically correct your spelling as you type
- AutoText entries that replace key words or phrases with boilerplate text
- Macros that automate document production

Templates and styles work together. Because each template can have its own unique set of styles, you can give different types of documents a different look and feel by basing them on different templates. You might want to create templates for your common documents such as memos, reports, and proposals.

Organizing Your Knowledge Documents

In today's information economy, the most valuable resource is time. In publishing your work for other readers, it's essential to help them get right to the information they need without wading through your entire document word for word. Using three tools will help you organize your work for others: putting a table of contents at the front of your documents, using cross-references liberally, and (if the document is distributed electronically) creating hyperlinks to take people directly to the appropriate section.

Creating Tables of Contents

A table of contents can be one of the best organizing principles for the casual reader. Although it's hard for some authors to accept, many readers do not read their documents through from front to back, hanging on each word! Many want to get right to the section that interests them, or be able to tell from your contents what the flow of your logic is.

The tables of contents in Word are especially useful, because you can create them automatically using hyperlinks so readers of electronic versions of the document can click to the section of interest. When you create your contents using the Table Of Contents feature, you can update the table whenever you print the document so the page numbers and section names are always up to date.

To create your table of contents, format your section headings using the Heading styles (Heading 1, Heading 2, and so on). Word automatically recognizes these styles as ones that should be included in a table of contents, and uses them for the section headings by default. Word can use styles other than the Heading styles for the contents, but you need to take extra steps to specify which styles you want to include in the table of contents.

Tip Keep your table of contents short. For most documents that are fewer than 30 pages, the table of contents should fit on a page; if it's fewer than 100 pages, it should fit on 2. If you do need to create a detailed table of contents, consider creating a second one called executive overview that shows the first-level headings, or the first two heading levels. Remember, this is an aid to give readers an overview; it isn't an index that shows them where every element of the book is to be found.

To create your table of contents, follow these steps.

1. Position your insertion point where you want the table of contents to appear.

2. Choose Reference and then Index And Tables from the Insert menu, and click the Table Of Contents tab.

3. Select options for your table of contents.

   - Choose whether to show page numbers or right-align them, and specify the tab leader, if desired.

   - Choose whether you want the table to display as text, or as hyperlinks to the appropriate sections of your document.

   - Choose the format for your table of contents, and how many levels of headings you want to include in it. If you choose From Template as your format, you can click the Modify button to modify the formatting for the TOC styles (TOC1, TOC2, TOC3, and so forth).

Tip You can specify the format you want your table of contents to have. By default, the format is taken from the TOC1, TOC2, TOC3 styles in the document template. Other pre-defined formats are available such as fancy, distinctive, and classic.

   - Click the Options button, if you need to select styles other than Heading 1, Heading 2, Heading 3, and so on to be included in your table of contents.

4. Choose OK to create your table of contents.

After you create your table of contents, it exists as a field in your Word document. It is not automatically regenerated each time you make a change to your document, but can be regenerated in three ways.

- You can regenerate the table of contents field by clicking anywhere inside the table of contents, and pressing F9.

- Regenerate all fields in the document wherever your insertion point is by choosing Select All from the Edit menu, and then pressing F9.

- You can set Word to automatically regenerate all fields (including the table of contents) whenever the document is printed. To do so, click Options from the Tools menu, select the Print tab, and check the Update Fields check box.

Tip   If you included hyperlinks in your table of contents, press Ctrl and click any line of the contents to go to the appropriate section.

You can edit an existing table of contents or create a new one (perhaps to show an executive overview before the detailed table of contents), by following the same procedure you did when you created the original contents. After you press OK to complete the creation of the table, you see a dialog box that says Do You Want To Replace The Selected Table Of Contents? Responding No creates a new table of contents, while responding Yes replaces the old one.

Note   You can create indexes, lists of figures, and tables of authorities in a similar manner to creating a table of contents—by choosing Reference, Index and Tables from the Insert dialog box. See Index, Table Of Figures, And Table Of Authorities in the Contents, Long Documents section of the Word Help system for details.

Using Hyperlinks

Once the unique domain of Web pages, people are increasingly incorporating hyperlinks into their Word documents. Because many documents are now available electronically on the corporate intranet or on public Web sites, the inclusion of hyperlinks makes these documents more and more usable.

Hyperlinks can link your Word document to a variety of places—to an existing file on a shared drive, to a Web page on the Internet or intranet, to an e-mail address (that will open a Microsoft Outlook e-mail form to the linked person), to a heading in the current document, or to a place you marked in the current document with a bookmark.

Note   A *bookmark* is an invisible code that marks a spot in your document or a section of your document you select. After you bookmark your document, you can create hyperlinks to that bookmark or cross-references to it. To insert a bookmark at a selected place in your document, choose Bookmark from the Insert menu and give your bookmark a name.

To create a hyperlink in your Word document, follow these steps.

1. Click in your document where you want the hyperlink to appear, or select the text or graphic element you want to display as a hyperlink.

2. Choose Hyperlink from the Insert menu.

3. If you did not select anything in your document, type the link text in the Text To Display box.

4. Type the destination for your link.

   - If the link is to another document, ensure that Existing File Or Web Page is selected in the Link To bar. Navigate to the appropriate folder, and select the file that should be linked to. If a bookmark has already been created in that file, click Bookmark to select the bookmark that the link should take you to.

   - If you want to create a link to another place in the current document, click Place In This Document in the Link To bar. Select the heading or bookmark you want to link to.

   - If you want to create a link to someone's e-mail address, click E-Mail Address in the Link To bar and specify his or her address.

Tip   You can also choose to create a new document to link your hyperlink to, but generally this gets a little confusing because you then need to come back to the original document and reconsider where you were and what you were doing. It's better to create all needed documents before creating links between them.

Creating Cross-References

Cross-references allow the reader to quickly go to the sources for points you are making, find out more information about terms you're using, and—if you distribute your document electronically and make the cross-references hyperlinks—go immediately to the referenced spot in the document.

You can insert several types of references, to provide the maximum flexibility depending on the type of document you are working on. Some of the more commonly used are

- **Heading.**   Inserts a reference to a heading in your document that you specify. The reference can contain the text of the heading, the page number it appears on, and the heading number, among other options.

- **Footnote/Endnote.**   Inserts a reference to a specified footnote or endnote. Options include having the reference contain the footnote/endnote number or page it appears on.

- **Figure/Table.**   Inserts a reference to a particular figure or table in your document. The reference can include the caption (including number), caption text, or page number.

To create a cross-reference, follow these steps.

1. Click in your document where you want the reference to appear.

2. Choose Reference and then Cross-Reference from the Insert menu.

3. Choose the reference type (for example, heading, footnote).

4. Depending on which type you choose, you see different options in the Insert Reference To box (for example, heading text, footnote number). Choose the option that specifies what you want the reference to display.

5. Check or clear Insert As Hyperlink, depending on whether you want the reference to be clickable.

6. Depending on which type you choose, you see different options in the For Which box. For example, if you choose Heading, you see all the headings in your document. Select the appropriate option, and then click Insert.

Summary

This chapter has taught you several techniques for creating effective Word documents that are well formed and well organized. Margins, line spacing, headers, and footers can be changed to create a distinct look and feel and can be automated with Styles. Tables of contents, hyperlinks, and cross-references can provide the reader with easy ways to find the information they need within your documents. Many of you already know most or all of these techniques—at least in theory. The challenge now is to remember to use them consistently until they become automatic.

Checklist for Sharing Knowledge Using Documents

Use the following tools to help you share knowledge using documents.

[ ] Use the page processing technique as you compose the content for your documents.

[ ] Create white space in your document for both open and formal looks.

[ ] Use headers, footers, margins, and fonts to create your unique look and feel.

[ ] Capture your look and feel with styles for headings, body text, bullet lists, and numbered lists.

[ ] Save styles in templates for reuse.

[ ] Organize your documents with tables of contents.

[ ] Help readers quickly go to points of interest with cross-references and hyperlinks.

Sharing Knowledge Using Slideshows

When Jeffrey Piira first took the job as Special Assistant to the President of Blue Yonder Airlines, he wondered why the company focused on his graphic design and Microsoft PowerPoint skills. Now he knows. The president, Katie McAskill-White, is constantly on the road talking to different groups of people. In any given month, she might make presentations to Blue Yonder's Board of Directors, citizens' groups, a stockholders' meeting, senior management, a professional conference, or employees in a specific region.

Katie illustrates her talks with PowerPoint slideshows, and these slideshows must be professional. Although they can't take the focus away from Katie, they need to be concise and on target with impeccable style and a little flair.

In this chapter, you learn to create slideshows that can accompany *your* presentations and have these same qualities. In the coming sections, you learn how to do the following.

- Apply professional designs to your presentations
- Modify designs to give them your personal look and feel
- Use your design as the default for all your PowerPoint presentations
- Add zip to your presentations with transitions, animations, and multimedia
- Create shows that include subshows for different audiences, along with menus to help you navigate
- Create shows designed for unattended kiosk use

Creating a Consistent Look for Your Presentations

Although it's true looks aren't everything, a sense of style can certainly help in getting your message across. PowerPoint gives you the opportunity to truly express your style—whether bold and brash or understated and elegant; whether in bright bold colors or subtle muted grays. You can reinforce your message with the look and feel you give it. You also have the opportunity to create a *consistent* look and feel that you can include in everything you produce. This will tend to subtly identify your authorship and credit you with the ideas, thus creating a sense of personal brand.

There are three strategies you can use to design your personal look and feel.

- Use the professionally designed templates provided with PowerPoint.

- Tweak an existing template (or start one of your own), by adding your corporate logo, including graphic design features, and customizing your footer.

- Save your slide as a template—possibly containing boilerplate slides that will be used repeatedly—so you can reuse your slideshow over and over.

Building Your Slideshow with Predesigned Templates

PowerPoint comes with more than 40 predesigned templates that incorporate professionally designed graphic backgrounds with coordinating fonts and color palettes, allowing you to create a great-looking presentation even if you are completely "graphic-impaired." You can use these templates like the ones in Figure 14-1 as they are, modify them, or use some of their ideas to create your own.

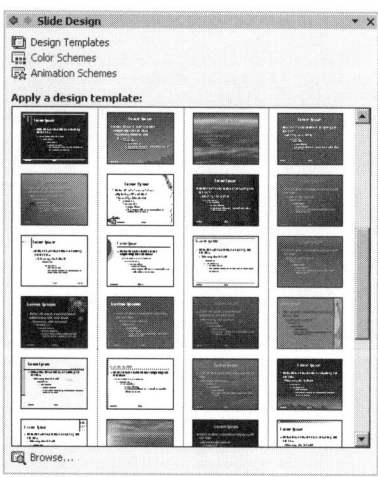

Figure 14-1   *PowerPoint includes templates that allow you to create professionally designed slideshows in minutes.*

To create a PowerPoint presentation based on a design template, follow these steps.

1. Choose New from the File menu.

2. In the Slide Design task pane, choose From Design Template.

3. Click the template you want to apply to the current presentation, or click the arrow on the template and choose Apply To Selected Slides.

Modifying the Design

You can personalize the look and feel of your design template, whether it's a predesigned template or one you create from a blank slide. At a minimum, you will probably want to incorporate a footer that appears on each page; if you feel more ambitious, you might want to add a logo or change graphic design elements, default fonts, or the color scheme used in each slide.

Tip Think of well-designed Web pages as you make changes in your PowerPoint design template. Increasingly, PowerPoint slides are beginning to resemble Web pages and you can include the elements you like from your favorite Web sites in your PowerPoint slides. Alternatively, consider giving your PowerPoint slides a similar look and feel to your corporate Web site.

Incorporate Footers

PowerPoint allows you to quickly create footers that have the date on the left, the slide number on the right, and your optional text in the middle. If you want to hide the display of the footer on your title slide, you can do that easily as well. To create a footer, do the following.

1. Choose Headers and Footers from the View menu.

2. In the Slide tab of the Header And Footer dialog box, choose options as necessary.

Note Typical footer text might include copyright information, a confidential or proprietary information notice, or the name of the presenter.

Change Color Schemes

The color schemes in PowerPoint consist of eight colors that govern the default colors for the slide's background, fills, lines, text, titles, hyperlinks, and a number of other elements. To choose and modify a color scheme for your slideshow, follow these steps.

1. Click the Design button on the Formatting toolbar, and choose Color Schemes in the Slide Design task bar to display the available color schemes.

2. Click a color scheme to apply it to your entire slideshow, or click the arrow on the scheme and choose Apply To Selected Slides.

3. To edit the colors, click Edit Color Schemes at the bottom of the Slide Design task bar, click the Custom tab of the Edit Color Scheme dialog box, and click any of the eight elements to modify.

4. Click Change Color, choose a color in the Standard or Custom tab in the Color Picker dialog box, and click OK. Repeat for other elements as desired.

5. If you want to add your customized color scheme as a standard choice, click Add As Standard Scheme. Click Apply to return to your slideshow.

Modify Your Slide Master

Whether you are starting from a predesigned template or a blank slide, you might want to modify the default look and feel that each of your slides has. This default information is contained in the *slide master*—a special slide that appears by default in the background behind every other slide you make. The changes you make to your slide master might include

- The areas in which your titles, text, and graphic objects appear by default
- The fonts, sizes, and colors for your titles, footers, and text
- Graphic elements that appear on each slide

Tip   While by default the slide master appears behind every slide, you can turn it off for individual slides by choosing Background from the Format menu, checking Omit Background Graphics From Master, and changing the background color if needed in the Background dialog box.

Change AutoLayout Areas

An *AutoLayout area* is the area of your slide where the title, text, and objects appear by default. One way to customize your design is to offset your title and text areas. For instance, say you want to have your title left aligned across the top of the page but have the text only on the right half of the page, leaving the left for clip art or graphics. To change your AutoLayout areas, do the following.

1. On the View menu, point to Master and click Slide Master.

2. Click either the Title area or the Object area, and drag the edges of the object to move it on the slide or use the sizing handles to resize it.

3. Click Close Master View on the Slide Master View toolbar.

Change Default Fonts

You might also want to change the default font face, size, or color of the text on your slide master. To change your default fonts, do the following.

Tip Consider using the same font face you use on your Web site or in your reports and letters, if you have a corporate style. However, balance consistency against readability—it is often the case that typefaces that are readable on paper are less so on slides.

---

1. On the View menu, point to Master and click Slide Master.
2. Click the text to be changed, and make simple changes to the font, size, color, alignment, bullets, or line spacing using tools on the Format menu or Formatting toolbar.

Note Changes you make to this text are reflected in the appropriate text in the slides, unless you applied specific formatting to that text that overrides the default formatting.

---

3. Click Close Master View on the Slide Master View toolbar when you are done.

Add Graphic Elements

You can add any graphic element to your slide master that you can to an individual slide, so it appears in the background of every slide in your slideshow.

Tip Nonprofessional designers should consider a few guidelines before adding graphic elements to slides. First, don't add graphic elements to a standard design template that is already visually complex and incorporates a number of graphics. Complex designs are best left to the pros. Look to your Web site for overall designs or specific graphics you might want to use. Also, consider using the eight colors in your color schemes for any graphic elements you add; these colors have been designed to work well together visually.

After you look over other sources and have some ideas in your mind for enhancing the graphical look and feel of your slides, do so as follows.

1. On the View menu, point to Master and click Slide Master.
2. Insert objects in the following ways.
   - To insert a picture, choose Picture, From File from the Insert menu, navigate to the picture, and double-click it.
   - To insert a graphic or logo from your Web site, right-click it, choose Copy, and then paste it into your design master.

- To insert a drawing object such as a line, rectangle, oval, or AutoShape, click the appropriate tool in the Drawing menu and then drag over the area the object should cover in the slide.

Note   Graphics copied from a Web page are usually low resolution, but you might be able to get a better resolution copy by asking your Web site administrator.

---

3. Modify drawing objects by selecting them, and then clicking the Text Color, Line Color, Font Color, Line Style or other button from the Drawing menu.

4. Click Close Master View on the Slide Master View toolbar.

Saving Your Default Design Template

You can also make your customized slideshow into a template you can use over and over again. If you save it as a .pot (template) file, it appears on the list of available templates when you create new slideshows. If you save it as a template named Blank.pot in your default file area, it is the design template loaded by default when you create a new slide-show. To save your work as a reusable template (and optionally make it the default template), do the following.

1. Open the slide master you want to save as a template

2. Choose Save As from the File menu. Click Design Template in the Save As Type drop-down list.

3. Give your template a name. If you want it to be the default template, name it Blank. Click Save.

Tip   If you are saving a slideshow for reuse as a template, it can contain more than an empty slide with the design specifications. Consider including all the slides containing your boilerplate text in the slideshow before you save it. These might include a title, corporate capabilities, contact information, or conclusion slide. You also might want to replace the specific title or reference to clients with placeholders like [Title] and [Client] to remind you to replace these elements when you make a new show.

Creating Unattended Slideshows

Sometimes you want to publish information to the public using PowerPoint. It might be in a kiosk in the waiting area of the lobby of your corporate headquarters, or a computer at the front of your tradeshow booth that's designed to encourage people to come in for more information. In either case, the information needs to be presented in a way that requires no further information or operations from you. It needs to be self-explanatory and self running.

To create a slideshow for use in a kiosk, do three things.

- Create slide timings so the slides advance automatically.

- Create navigation buttons or menus if you want users to be able to control how the slideshow progresses.

- Set your slideshow options for kiosk operation.

Before you set up your slideshow for a kiosk, take a few minutes to review it for appropriateness. There are slightly different guidelines for the content of kiosk-based slideshows than for slideshows that support your presentations.

- **Be clear about your purpose.** Is there a call for action (come in to our booth and get more information) or is the kiosk informational? If the latter, is it more marketing-driven (see the great things our company has done), educational (many people didn't know these trends), or persuasive (here's 10 reasons to get prenatal care)?

- **Include all the information on the slide.** This is a fundamentally different approach from creating slideshows to support a speech or briefing. In the latter situations, the main points come from the voice and the slideshow is there to add visual interest, provide supporting points, or present an outline of the speaker's top-level argument. In a kiosk, there are no speakers' notes and there's no speaker (unless you record narration with the slides)—all information must be on the slide to provide this extra information.

- **Good design principles still apply.** Just because you need to include all the information on the slide, you aren't allowed to put a 300-word page of information on it! You are still bound by the rules of good "slide style" discussed earlier. If you put too much information, passersby will not read it and you might as well not have gone to the expense. The challenge is thus being able to wordsmith your points until they are extremely concise yet persuasive; and use graphics creatively to make and support points visually.

After you create your slideshow with these points in mind, you can do a few things to get it ready for use in kiosk mode.

Creating Slide Timings

PowerPoint allows you to advance slides manually or to have them advance automatically after a specified number of seconds. Many times, in a kiosk situation, users prefer to have the slideshow automatically advance so casual passersby see several slides that might include transitions, animations, and multimedia, which will create enough interest for them to stop for more information.

To set slide timings, do the following.

1. Click the Slide Sorter View button. This makes it easy to see all your slide timings in one place and set multiple slide timings at once.

2. Select all the slides by choosing Select All from the Edit menu, so you can set a default slide timing.

3. Click the Transition button on the Slide Sorter toolbar.

4. Check Automatically After in the Advance Slide section of the Slide Transition task pane, and then specify the number of seconds and click Apply To All Slides. You see the transition information underneath the slide. If you want participants to be able to use the keyboard or mouse to manually advance slides in addition to the automatic slide timings, ensure that On Mouse Click is checked.

Tip   This is also a great time to apply a transition effect to your slides by choosing the default transition from the Apply To Selected Slides list.

---

5. Select one or more slides that require a different timing, and then specify that timing in the Automatically After box.

Tip   If you have a microphone attached to your computer, you can also record a narration that will play as the slideshow advances by choosing Record Narration from the Slideshow menu. See "Record Narration" in the PowerPoint Help system for details.

Using Navigation Buttons

If you have a kiosk where people will be interacting with the slideshow as opposed to just walking by it, you might want to put more detailed information on each slide and have users manually advance the slides. You should not rely on users to know the mouse and keyboard commands for navigating through a slideshow, so you can either use a menu (as discussed earlier) or put navigation buttons on each slide. Four buttons are commonly used: Back, Forward, Beginning, and End; however, other buttons (such as Return, Play Sound, and Help) are available.

To insert navigation buttons, do the following.

1. Ensure that there is an area free of text and graphics on each slide where the navigation buttons will go.

2. Create a navigation button by clicking Autoshapes on the Drawing toolbar, and then choosing Action Buttons and clicking the action button you want to insert.

3. Drag in the area of the slide where you want the action button to appear.

4. In the resulting Action Settings dialog box, you see the default action for that button. For instance, the default action for the Back button is Hyperlink to Previous Slide. Change this action if required, and click OK.

5. Because action buttons are relatively small and you want them to be exactly the same height, it might be hard to resize them accurately with the mouse. With the action button still selected, right-click it and choose Format Autoshape.

6. In the Size tab, ensure that Lock Aspect Ratio is checked and then set the height for your action button and click OK.

7. Repeat steps 2 through 6 for your other action buttons.

8. Select all the action buttons, and copy them to all slides they should appear on.

9. You might consider removing the Beginning button from the first slide and the End button from the last slide.

Setting Display Options

Before finishing your kiosk slideshow, set a few options to ensure that the show uses the slide timings you create (if appropriate) and repeats after it gets to the last slide. To do so, take these steps.

1. Choose Set Up Show from the Slideshow menu.

2. Choose Browsed At Kiosk in the Set Up Show dialog box, and then click OK if you do *not* want users to be able to override automatic timings or use menus or action buttons; otherwise, leave the default of Presented By A Speaker.

3. Choose Loop Continuously Until 'Esc' to ensure that your slideshow repeats over and over.

4. Leave the default of Use Timings, If Present so the automatic slide timings you set take effect.

5. Click OK and save your work.

You are now ready to run your slideshow from a kiosk, by moving to Slide 1 and clicking the Slideshow button.

Supporting Presentations with Slideshows

Whether it's corporate executives speaking to the company, vendors making a pitch, staffers briefing management, or professional speakers keynoting a conference, business professionals have come to expect presentations to be supported with PowerPoint slideshows. Although sometimes that expectation is a positive one, often it is not because many speakers do not do themselves a favor when they create their slideshows.

Fortunately, it's fairly easy to make a good supporting slideshow. The first step is to think about the relation between the spoken word and the projected image. In most cases, you want the central message to be *spoken* and have it *supported* by slides. Your slides can support spoken points in several ways. They can

- Provide additional information (think of TV news programs that offer visual factoids that are peripheral to the central story).

- Make the same point visually (for example, a graph trending downward, a chart showing the number of competitors rising).

- Illustrate the point with a photograph.

- Be blank. It's a great idea to insert blank slides in your slideshow for when you want the audience's attention totally on you.

- Provide a context. If your talk has four major points, you can show these points when first outlining your talk and then show the same slide again with the relevant point highlighted as you reach each section to help your audience understand the flow of your presentation.

Tip   Outline your points; don't detail them. Slides should have no more than six bullet points, according to many designers, and each should be one line long. This means you cannot make a point and provide supporting evidence for it—nor do you need to. The audience hears the point verbally, and uses a slide to understand the gist of all the points put together.

With these guidelines in mind, you can use several features PowerPoint provides to transform your presentation from a "yawner" to a "keeper." These include using wizards to organize your thoughts, adding visual interest to your slides with transitions and animations, adding rich media to provide additional support to your points, and creating sophisticated navigation systems that allow you to go to the right slide to make the point you need.

Organizing Your Thoughts

If you give presentations every week, you probably already know your general presentation outline by heart—the introduction, where the stories go, and where unique examples are. If you're like the rest of us, however, speaking in front of groups might make you a little nervous and you might not have your thoughts completely organized.

Fortunately, Microsoft PowerPoint provides a tool for organizing several types of common presentations—the AutoContent Wizard. To use it, follow these steps.

1. Choose New from the File menu.

2. Choose From AutoContent Wizard in the New Presentation task pane, and click Next to pass the introductory screen.

3. In the second step of the wizard, choose the general type of presentation you're going to make, choose the specific topic you're going to talk about, and then click Next. For instance, you might choose Corporate as the general type and Business Plan as the specific topic.

4. In the next steps of the wizard, choose the type of output you'll use for the presentation, then click Next and give it a title, and specify items for the slide footers if desired.

5. Click Finish to complete the wizard.

6. Ensure the Outline tab in the Normal view is selected to see the outline of your presentation. If needed, expand the pane by dragging its right border to see the outline more clearly.

You can now see a suggested organization for your type of presentation. It not only shows you the topics you need to address through the slide titles (such as Mission Statement, The Team, and Market Summary), but it also suggests points you need to make within each topic with the bullet points in each slide. Although you certainly should not be bound by the outline provided, it can give you a great first start on organizing your presentation and also suggest topics and points you might have forgotten.

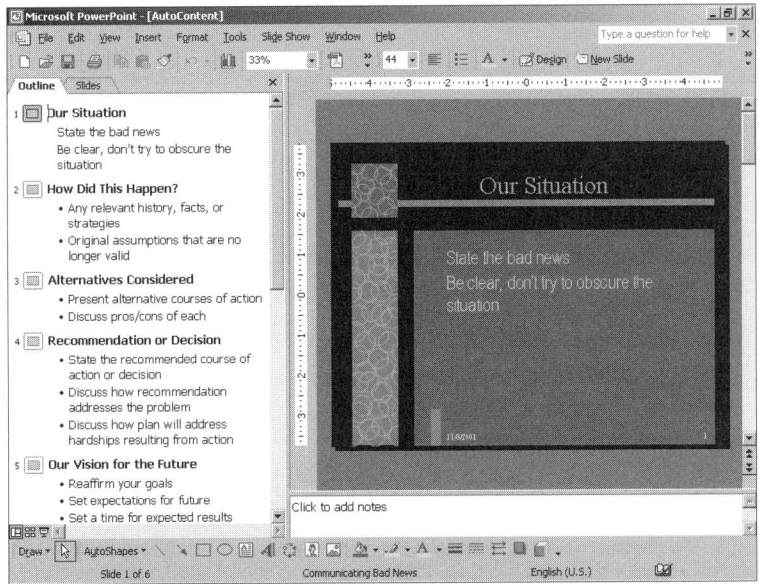

Organizing Presentations: Tips from the Master

Patricia Fripp (*http://www.fripp.com*) is truly a master professional speaker, being a Past President of the National Speakers Association and having won every award and earned every designation offered by NSA. In her coaching and workshops, Fripp teaches business executives to organize their material using the following simple diagram. What she suggests, in short, is that your opening and closing, while short, must be very powerful and should be memorized and practiced. The body of your remarks should be broken down into three major "points of wisdom." Each of these can be supported by up to three facts, stories, or illustrations. Add a transition between each of these stages, and your presentation is organized!

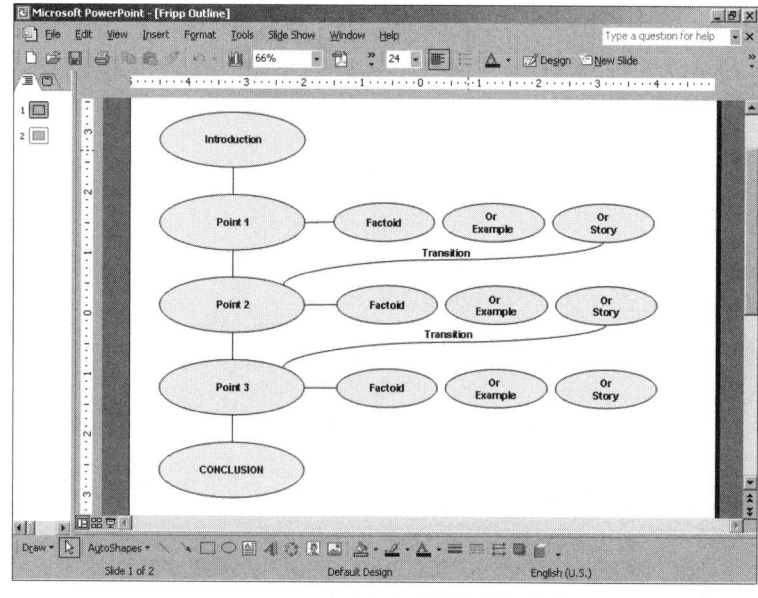

Adding Movement to Your Slideshows

Although you usually do not want your slides to be so visually stimulating that they distract from your presentation, it's also true static slides have become somewhat passé. Slide transitions and animations, used tastefully, can add the same type of interest to your presentations that judicious use of Flash animation adds to Web sites. Increasingly, presenters are also inserting audio and video files into their slides that add a new dimension to their presentation materials.

Create Transitions Between Your Slides

Transitions allow you to create a visual effect when you go from one slide to another. Rather than just having a new slide appear in place of the old, you can create fades, wipes, rolls and many other effects. The availability of effects, however, offers many possibilities for misuse. Although professional graphic artists can weave a variety of transitions into slideshows, for regular folks, a few guidelines are in order.

- Use one primary transition between all slides in your slideshow. Different transitions between every slide are extremely distracting. That said, if you want to use a second transition, use it for a purpose such as to mark the end of a section or between the title slide and the rest of your slides.

- If you have graphics on your master slides such as a logo, using the Fade transition can be particularly effective because the graphics remain visible and the only thing that apparently changes is the illustration and text on the particular slide. In any case, be sure the transition you pick allows the graphics to visually stay in place between slides.

To insert a slide transition, do the following.

1. In Slide Sorter view, select one or more slides to which the transition should apply.

Tip   The Slide Sorter view displays miniatures of each slide in your slideshow. You can drag slides to rearrange them in this view, or select multiple slides to apply effects such as transitions and slide timings.

---

2. Right-click a selected slide, and choose Slide Transition from the shortcut menu.

3. In the Slide Transition task pane, select the desired transition in the Apply To Selected Slides list and then choose the Speed of the transition.

Tip   Be wary of adding sounds like horns or clapping to slides, because this can be both distracting and hokey.

Animate Objects Within Slides

You can also animate individual slide objects, which can be a powerful and tasteful way to add visual interest to your slides and to hide points on the slide until you're ready to make them. For instance, using animations, you can

- Create a question/answer slide, where the answer is hidden until you click the mouse.

- Create a bullet slide, where each bullet point is displayed when you click the mouse.

- Create an arrow that flies in to point out an important statement on a graph.

The possibilities are almost limitless with object animation because you can animate every slide object individually, specify a type of animation for it, and create complex timings and dependencies for the animations. Although PowerPoint supports extremely complex animations, you can easily create basic ones and then build on them as your skills and interest grow. To animate a slide object, do the following.

1. Select the object or objects on your slide you want to animate. If you want to animate certain objects together, select them all and then Click Draw on the Drawing toolbar and choose Group.

2. Right-click the object you want to animate, and choose Custom Animation.

3. In the Custom Animation task pane, choose Add Effect and then choose options within the following categories.

   - Entrance, to specify how the object enters the slide

   - Exit, to specify how the object exits the slide

   - Emphasis, to change font size, spin the object, and so forth

   - Motion Paths, to choose the direction along which the object will move

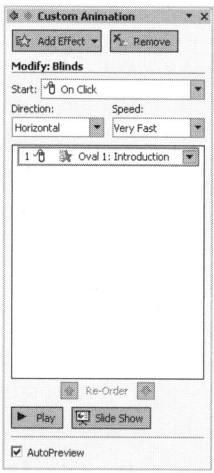

4. Repeat steps 2 and 3 to specify additional animation actions for the same object or other slide objects.

5. To preview how the slide animations will look, click the Play button in the task pane. To modify an animation, select it in the Custom Animation task pane, modify any options, click Remove to delete them, or click the Up or Down arrows to reorder them.

Note   You can also add a variety of predesigned animations to your slides by clicking the Design button on the Formatting toolbar, and then selecting Animation Schemes in the Design task pane.

Incorporate Audio and Video into Your Slideshow

Another way to add interest and information to your slides is to add audio and video files. An especially effective use of this can be to add a 30-second to 60-second interview with a trusted expert who reinforces the point you're making in your presentation. Adding sound effects like applause can be a little hokey, but appropriate in some venues.

To insert a sound or video file into your slide, do the following.

1. Choose Movies and Sounds from the Insert menu, and then choose one of the following.

   - To insert a video or audio from your Clip Organizer, choose Movie From Clip Organizer or Sound From Clip Organizer. Double-click the movie or sound from the Clip Organizer task pane, or see further options by clicking Clip Organizer in the task pane.

   - If you have a video or audio file on your disk but it hasn't been categorized into the Clip Organizer, choose Movie From File or Sound From File. Navigate to the desired file, and choose it from the Insert Movie or Insert Sound dialog box. Choose whether you want the movie or sound to play automatically when the sound starts, or whether to play them when you click them.

2. You see the icon for your sound file, or a placeholder rectangle for your movie file in your slide. When you play your slideshow, the movie or sound either plays automatically when the slide opens or you can play them by clicking them, depending on the options you choose.

Note There are two other rich media possibilities you might want to explore. If you have a microphone attached to your computer, you can record your own sound file by choosing Movies and Sound, Record Sound from the Insert menu. You can also play a specified track from an audio CD-ROM attached to your system by choosing Movies and Sound, Play CD Audio Track from the Insert menu.

Creating Nonlinear Slideshows

When you are giving a slide presentation, you might be lucky enough to be able to go through the slides one by one from beginning to end, pausing only occasionally to go back to the last slide. If this is the case, you can easily navigate back and forth using the commands in Table 14-1.

Table 14-1 Simple Slideshow Navigation

Next Slide	Previous Slide
Press the Enter key or N.	Press P.
Click the mouse.	Right-click, and choose Previous from the shortcut menu.

Many times, however, your navigation needs are somewhat more complex, such as in the following cases.

- If people have objections or want more detail on a specific point, you might need to branch to one or more slides that respond to their questions.

- If you are giving the same presentation to multiple audiences, there might be a sequence of slides that is unique to each.

- You might not have a predefined order of points, but want to have a series of slides available to answer specific questions.

In these cases, you have to be able to show your presentation in a different order. There are three features in PowerPoint you can use for this: Custom Shows, Hyperlinks, and Menus.

Use Custom Shows

A custom show is a subset of the slides in your entire slideshow that can be shown as a unit. For instance, if you have a 20-slide slideshow, you might define slides 15-20 as Subshow 1. To specify a custom show, follow these steps.

1. Choose Custom Shows from the Slideshow menu.

2. In the Custom Shows dialog box, choose New.

3. In the Define Custom Show dialog box, give your custom show a name in the Slide Show Name box.

4. Highlight the slides to be included in the custom show, and click the Add button.

5. To reorder a slide, highlight it in the Slides In Custom Show box and click the Up or Down arrow.

6. Click OK to save your custom show.

Note   From the Define Custom Show dialog box, you can select additional custom shows, edit existing ones, remove them, or copy them.

After you specify a custom show, you can use it in a variety of ways to enhance your presentations and customize them to your audience needs.

- You can specify that your custom show is shown by default when you click the Slide Show button, by choosing Set Up Show from the Slideshow menu, choosing Custom Show, and specifying the custom show to use.

- You can create a hyperlink to a custom show from any slide, as described in the following section. This is very helpful when you want to branch off to a series of slides if needed to answer objections, or to provide additional information to a unique audience such as a regional group. You can specify that the slideshow ends after the display of the custom show, or that the slideshow should return to the starting point so you can continue with your main presentation.

- You can create a menu as described next that makes all slides or just certain slides appear, or that takes you to either a specific slide in the presentation or to a custom show that will return you to the menu.

Create Hyperlinks

You can create a hyperlink to a custom show from any text or graphic object in your slideshow. This can be convenient when you don't need your audience to see this hyperlink, but merely want it available for use as needed. To create a hyperlink to a custom show, you need to ensure that the custom show has already been created and then you can do the following.

1. Select the text or graphic object that will be hyperlinked to the custom show.

2. Right-click the text or object, and choose Hyperlink.

3. In the Link To bar of the Insert Hyperlink dialog box, click Place In This Document.

4. Highlight the desired custom show in the Select A Place In This Document box.

5. If you want the custom show to be displayed and then have the show return to the slide containing the hyperlink, check Show And Return. If you want the slideshow to end after the custom show displays, leave this box unchecked.

6. Click OK to finish creating your hyperlink.

Using this same procedure, you can also create hyperlinks to a variety of other destinations, including

- **Existing files.** This can be useful if you want to refer to a Microsoft Excel workbook or Word document during your presentation.

Tip Open the other file in another window prior to the presentation, so your audience doesn't need to wait for Word or Excel to open, plus the time to open the file.

- **Web pages.** If you're connected to the Internet during your presentation, you might want to navigate to selected Web sites during the show. These open in a separate browser window.

- **Another slide.** Even if you don't create custom shows, you can create a hyperlink to any slide in your slideshow. The slideshow proceeds forward from the slideshow you linked to.

- **New document.** You can create a new document while you are in the Insert Hyperlink dialog box. This can be helpful if you want to be able to link to an empty Word document during your presentation to capture audience thoughts.

Create Menus

You can use hyperlinks to create menus that allow you to navigate quickly to any section of your presentation, by creating a slide that contains menu items that are links. The menu items can link to custom shows that consist of a section of your slideshow. Each custom show ends by returning to the menu slide.

To create a menu slide, do the following.

1. Decide which slide will be the menu slide, and decide your slideshow's sections: which slides each menu link will start and end at, and whether the users should return to the menu at the end of the section or move to the next section.

2. Create custom shows for each section as described in the previous section.

3. In the Slide Sorter pane of the Normal view, click where you want the menu slide to go.

4. Choose New Slide from the Formatting toolbar.

5. Create the text of your menu. Create a hyperlink from each menu item to the appropriate custom show. For each, check Show And Return if you want to return to the menu when the section has been displayed.

If you want the menu to appear on multiple slides, you need to do one more simple procedure.

1. Edit the slide master by choosing Master, Slide Master from the View menu.

2. Resize the Object Area For AutoLayouts using the sizing handles so there is enough space for the menu to appear. For instance, you might make the left margin of the area larger if you want the menu on the left.

3. Click Close Master View on the Slide Master View toolbar.

4. Navigate to your Contents slide, and copy the links containing the menu.

5. Paste this text box into all the other slides where you want a menu to appear.

Note You cannot put a text box containing hyperlinks into the Slide Master (an obvious solution)—the links will not be active on the slide master text because it is in the background behind the slide objects.

Rehearsing Your Presentation

Good speakers rehearse their presentations until they master the content and are comfortable making their points and coordinating them with their PowerPoint slideshow. As you rehearse, there are several things speaking coaches suggest you do.

- Have a strong beginning and a strong ending. These are so important you might want to memorize them almost word for word.

- Know what personal stories and anecdotes you can use to bring the points you make to life, and create a rapport with your audience.

- Make sure you know what is on each slide, so you are not constantly turning your back to your audience or looking down at your notebook to see what the next point on your slide says.

- Know how long your presentation takes, and ensure that it fits into the time allocated.

- Know which major points or supporting stories you will cut out, if you unexpectedly are given less time than you originally were told.

The Rehearse Timings feature in PowerPoint can help you with the timing of your presentation. You can use it to see how much time you spend talking about each slide, and this can tell you not only how long the entire presentation will take but also about the timing effect of skipping certain material. To rehearse your timings using PowerPoint, do the following.

1. Open the PowerPoint slideshow that you will be using for your presentation.

2. Choose Rehearse Timings from the Slideshow menu.

3. As you see the first slide of your slideshow, start to give your presentation as you would in front of an audience.

4. At each point where you intend to move to the next slide, click anywhere in the presentation.

5. After you finish with the last slide, click anywhere in the presentation again.

6. In the resulting dialog box, note the total time for your presentation.

7. If you want to apply these timings to each slide, choose Yes; otherwise, choose No.

If you chose to apply timings to each slide, you can easily see how much time different sections of the slideshow take by looking at the timing of each slide in Slide Sorter view. However, you will probably want to clear these timings before you use the slideshow in your presentation because otherwise the slides will automatically advance while you're speaking. Clear all the slide timings as follows.

1. In the Slide Sorter view, select all the slides.

2. Click Transition in the Slide Sorter toolbar to display the Slide Transition task pane, if it is not already visible.

3. In the Advance Slide area of the Slide Transition task pane, clear the Automatically After check box.

Taking Your Show on the Road

Sometimes, you might find yourself presenting your PowerPoint slideshow on someone else's computer, for instance, when you are using a conference room at another company that already has a PC hooked to their projection system. Often, it's best to e-mail your presentation to them ahead of time so they can do a preliminary test before your arrival. Whether you send it in advance, it's a smart idea to have your own copy with you on a disk just in case it's needed. You can transfer your slideshow to a disk with the Pack and Go Wizard. This wizard allows you to save a compressed version of your slideshow, along with any files linked to it and any fonts it uses. This can be especially helpful if you are using decorative fonts for titles or logos.

If you think the destination computer might not have PowerPoint, you can also include the PowerPoint viewer so the slideshow can be completely run from the files you bring with you on your disk. If the viewer is not installed on your computer, you're prompted to download it from the Microsoft Web site while running the wizard if you choose to include it with your slideshow.

To use the Pack and Go Wizard, follow these steps.

1. Open the PowerPoint slideshow you want to save on a disk.

2. From the File menu, choose Pack and Go.

3. Go through the steps of the wizard, specifying the destination for the compressed slideshow and whether you want to include linked files, fonts, and the PowerPoint viewer.

When you're ready to unpack (that is, uncompress) and view your presentation, you do so by running a program that was stored with the presentation when it was compressed: pngsetup.exe. Do so by following these steps.

1. Insert the disk in the computer you want to run the presentation on.

2. In Windows Explorer, navigate to the disk and double-click pngsetup.exe.

3. In the Pack And Go Setup dialog box, navigate to the folder to which you want to copy the presentation and then click OK.

4. Choose whether to run the presentation now or later.

   - If you choose to run it now, you see the presentation immediately.

   - If you choose to run it later, you can run it at any time by navigating to the saved presentation in Windows Explorer and then right-clicking it and choosing Show.

Summary

Powerful PowerPoint slideshows can add an entirely new dimension to your business presentations. They can add visceral appeal to your words, support your points with charts and pictures, and even make secondary points you don't say out loud. PowerPoint has become as sophisticated a tool for publishing your knowledge as Word, and is more commonly used in business every day.

In this chapter, you learned a variety of techniques that enable you to create sophisticated PowerPoint presentations that are well organized, well designed, and well presented.

Checklist for Sharing Knowledge Using Slideshows

The following points will help you creating knowledge using slideshows.

[ ]   Use design masters to apply professional designs to your presentations.

[ ]   Modify design masters by modifying footers, color schemes, AutoLayout areas, default fonts, and graphic elements.

[ ]   Save your design master as the default for all your PowerPoint presentations.

[ ]   Add transitions, animations, audio files, and videos to your slides.

[ ]   Use custom shows to create subshows for different audiences.

[ ]   Create hyperlinks and menus to quickly go to the slides you need.

[ ]   Create shows designed for unattended kiosk use.

[ ]   Make your slideshow portable by putting it on a disk.

Sharing Knowledge Using the Web

Michael Graff's job has evolved along with his company. A few years ago, he wrote copy for various types of public relations materials the Contoso, Ltd. produced, and all their materials were paper-based—their Web site consisted of only five linked pages. Now each division within Contoso has an extensive Web site, and Mike has been tasked with managing the Web content for the Outplacement Services division—even though he's not an IT professional. The Outplacement Services site has already been built according to corporate specifications, but its content is static and a little old. Mike has been given several requirements for upgrading the content.

- The home page must be updated weekly with news about Contoso, client testimonials, and the like.

- Senior staff must be positioned as thought leaders in the field. This means that in-depth articles need to be linked to the site and easily browsable.

- Assessment tools must be made into interactive Web-based forms.

- One of the marketing self-running presentations used at trade shows must be added.

- Several 90-second clips showing senior Contoso staff talking about their philosophy of outplacement must be added.

Although Mike's tasks might seem somewhat daunting, they are becoming more and more common throughout organizations. The days when Web sites were created and maintained by IT departments are rapidly leaving. There's too much content and need for new material, and this is driving Web site maintenance back to the departmental level. The amount of control that non-IT staff have of the Web sites (both internal and external) varies widely by type of organization. In many organizations, professional Web developers are used to create the basic Web site but the average knowledge worker who will be publishing material to the Web is well served by having the skills to

- Maintain Web sites using products like Microsoft FrontPage that do not require you to be a Web developer.

- Repurpose Microsoft Word documents for the Web, and publish them as Web documents.

- Make interactive forms for Web pages using Microsoft Excel.

- Create forms that query Web-based databases using Microsoft Access.

- Publish Microsoft PowerPoint presentations as Web pages.

- Insert digitized video files into Web pages.

See Also　The term "publishing" in this context refers to saving Microsoft Office files as Web pages. Saving files to Web sites in their native format, that is, saving a Word document to a Web site, is discussed in "Choosing Where to Save Your Data" on page 82.

Working with Web Sites

If you are tasked with maintaining a Web site or if you need to create a new one, consider using FrontPage. For the novice Web creator or content manager, FrontPage provides several benefits. There's a WYSIWYG (what you see is what you get) interface, so you don't have to learn hypertext markup language (HTML). And the fact that it's a member of the Microsoft Office family means you get the familiar Office interface, styles, and templates.

By default, FrontPage creates sites that use FrontPage Server Extensions if they are installed on the server. These are utilities that allow you to incorporate many features into your site like counters, search buttons, and tables of contents without extensive scripting and coding—all from drop-down menus.

FrontPage does have two drawbacks, however, that you must consider. First, FrontPage sites must be modified only with FrontPage or Office applications, not by using other HTML editors, then uploading files using the File Transfer Protocol (FTP) or other ways. Second, FrontPage inserts a lot of extra HTML codes into its Web pages, to support integration with Office and its own extra features. Both of these are not problems if you use only FrontPage, but can be concerns if you work with Web designers or programs who do not.

Introducing FrontPage

Although most knowledge workers have a working knowledge of Word, Excel, and Power-Point (if used in their jobs), many people are only now starting to build or maintain Web sites and accordingly have never used FrontPage. If this describes you, this section gives you the basics you need to get started.

Note   This section touches only on the basics of creating a Web site in FrontPage, which should be enough to get you started if you haven't used it before. FrontPage offers many other features for formatting and customizing a Web page to fit specific needs of a business, but they're beyond the scope of this book. If you want more advanced information about working with FrontPage, check out *Microsoft FrontPage Version 2002 Inside Out* by Jim Buyens (also from Microsoft Press).

When you open FrontPage, you see a number of tools that make it easy to create and modify individual Web pages or entire Web sites. (See Figure 15-1.) You can select from several views of your Web site using the buttons in the Views bar, and while looking at an individual Web page in the Page view, you can choose from three panes that provide different views of the Web page: Normal, HTML, or Preview.

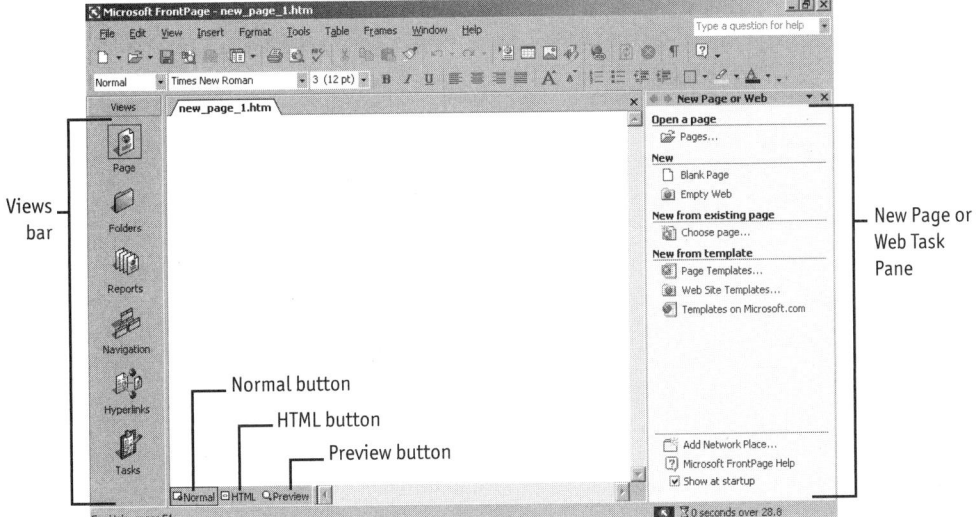

Figure 15-1   *FrontPage allows you to modify individual Web pages or manage your entire Web site.*

Highlights of the FrontPage screen include the following.

- The New Page Or Web task pane works just as its counterparts do in other Office applications, and enables you to open existing Web pages or create new ones from a variety of templates.

- Page view allows you to edit individual Web pages. Multiple pages can be open simultaneously and can be accessed through the Window menu, but only one is displayed.

- Folders view shows you a Microsoft Explorer–like listing of all the files in your FrontPage Web site, if one is open. You can double-click any HTML file in your Web site to open it in the Page view.

- Navigation view allows you to create links between your Web pages, and display them in an organization chart–like view.

- Normal view allows you to edit your Web page using a WYSIWYG interface.

- HTML view permits you to edit the source code for the page.

- Preview view shows you the page as it will be displayed in a Web browser.

Caution   How pages display can vary greatly between different browsers, and even different versions of the same browser. Checking a page in the Preview view does not replace testing the pages in several browsers.

Creating a Web Site

Creating an entire Web site in FrontPage is similar to creating a Word document or PowerPoint presentation. It's possible to create an entire multipage Web site within a few minutes, complete with navigation aids and a professional design, and then it's just a matter of putting in your text, graphics, and links to other Web sites.

The four tools that make the process so easy are described here.

- **Link bars.**   A set of hyperlinks that can be displayed as text or images. They provide links to various pages for your site, based on the navigation structure hierarchy you define in the Navigation view, or to pages that are external to your site. Also called Navigation bars, they are often used to create menus.

- **Shared borders.**   Areas at the edge of every Web page on your site that can contain information that you want displayed on every page. Conceptually, they are similar to headers and footer areas in Word. By creating a link bar in a shared border, you can create a Navigation bar that appears on every page.

- **Themes.**   Files that contain design elements such as default formats, styles, color schemes, shared borders, and link bars that are applied to any or all pages in your Web site. If desired, the chosen theme is applied by default to all new pages, thus making it easy to add to your Web site and retain a professional design.

- **Web site templates.** Contains a collection of pages that are appropriate to a specific type of site, such as a corporate presence Web site or a customer support Web site. Some templates contain wizards that help you do specific tasks, like create a database interface.

Note FrontPage also provides Page Templates that create pages with predefined formats, such as a one-column body with contents and a sidebar. Some page templates contain wizards for specialized tasks, such as creating data entry forms.

To use these tools as you create your Web sites, follow these steps.

1. In FrontPage, choose New from the File menu.

2. In the New Page Or Web task pane, choose Web Site Templates.

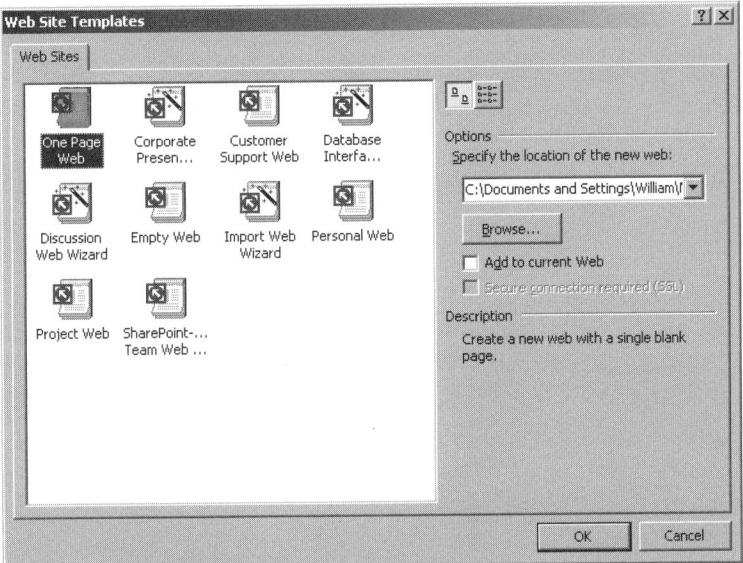

3. Specify the location for your new Web site. It can be on your local drive, or you can create it directly on an Internet site.

See Also Saving files to the Web is discussed further in "Choosing Where to Save Your Data" on page 82.

---

4. Double-click the type of Web site you want to create.

5. Go through the steps of the wizard, if you chose a template containing one. Otherwise, your new Web site is created immediately.

To see the pages in your new Web site and their navigation structure, click the Navigation button on the Views bar. To see them in a list, click the Folders button instead. In either case, you can open any page (that is, display it in Page view) by double-clicking it.

You might want to take a tour of your new Web site to see what it includes. To do so, open the home page (index.htm) and then click the Preview button. Navigate through the site using the menu that's provided. After you examine the site, you need to enter your own text and graphics. You might also want to make some global changes to the site, such as changing the theme, the text in the shared borders, or the way link bars display navigation links.

To make changes, open any page of your Web site in Normal view and then follow the steps in Table 15-1, depending on what you want to do.

Table 15-1   Making Global Changes to Your Web Site

Change	Procedure
Change your site's theme.	1. Choose Theme from the Format menu.
	2. In the Themes dialog box, choose All Pages.
	3. Click each theme to preview it as shown in Figure 15-2, and then click OK when you select the one you want.
Display shared borders and navigation bars.	1. Choose Shared Borders from the Format menu, and then select each shared border and navigation bar you want to display.
	2. Click in a shared border to add or edit text, graphic elements, or links.
Specify which pages a Navigation bar links to and how it is displayed.	1. Double-click the Navigation bar.
	2. In the Link Bar Properties dialog box, check the appropriate options.

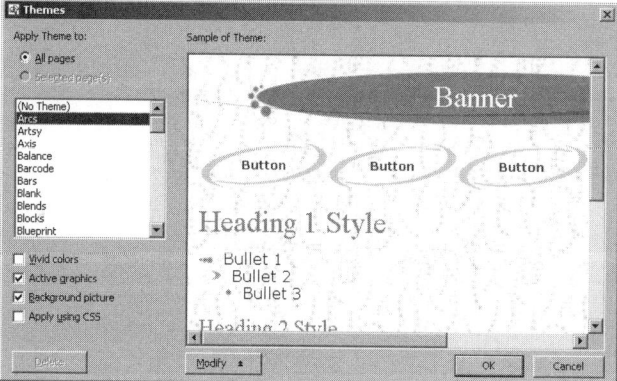

Figure 15-2   *FrontPage offers more than 50 themes that provide a professional look and feel to your site.*

You can add empty pages to an existing Web site by clicking the New button on the Standard toolbar. To add pages based on a page template and add them to your navigation structure, follow these steps.

1. Point to New on the File menu, and then choose Page or Web.

2. In the New Page Or Web task pane, click Page Templates.

3. In the Page Templates dialog box, double-click the desired template.

4. Choose Save from the File menu, provide a name for your new page, and click Save.

5. Click the Navigation button on the Views bar.

6. Drag the new page from the folder list to its parent page in the navigation structure.

Maintaining Web Pages

If you're not a professional Web designer, you might need to maintain existing Web pages more frequently than build new Web sites. Whether or not the site was created using FrontPage, you can often use FrontPage to edit its pages. As long as you have the appropriate UserID and password, you'll be able to get the page from the site and save it, even if it isn't a FrontPage site. FrontPage recognizes when it needs to save a page to a non-FrontPage Web site, and uses FTP to save the page there.

Most of the changes you will commonly make include adding and editing text, graphics, or links to keep your page's content current. On occasion, you might need to look directly at the HTML source for a page as well. Before getting started, however, determine whether it's appropriate to use FrontPage. You will probably want to talk with the person who designed the Web site, or is in charge of administering it, to make a final determination. Here are some points to consider when deciding whether to use FrontPage.

- If the site was created with FrontPage, FrontPage is the editor of choice for its Web pages.

- FrontPage tends to put a lot of its own HTML codes that only it can use into Web pages. If the page will also be maintained by others who use other HTML editors or Web page design products, they might object to your using FrontPage.

- Some site design tools like DreamWeaver can produce sites that display numerous overlapping tables, and editing them with a different product like FrontPage can be difficult or impossible.

- If the Web page was created in Word or PowerPoint, you might find it easier to edit in the product that created it. In fact, the page may open in the original product when you try to edit it.

After you determine you will be editing your page in FrontPage, you'll find that it's almost identical to editing a Word document, as you can see in the following steps.

1. From the Normal pane of the Page view, make editing changes as described after this procedure.

2. If you need to view or edit the HTML source code of the page and you're familiar with writing HTML, click the HTML button to switch to the HTML pane. (See Figure 15-3.)

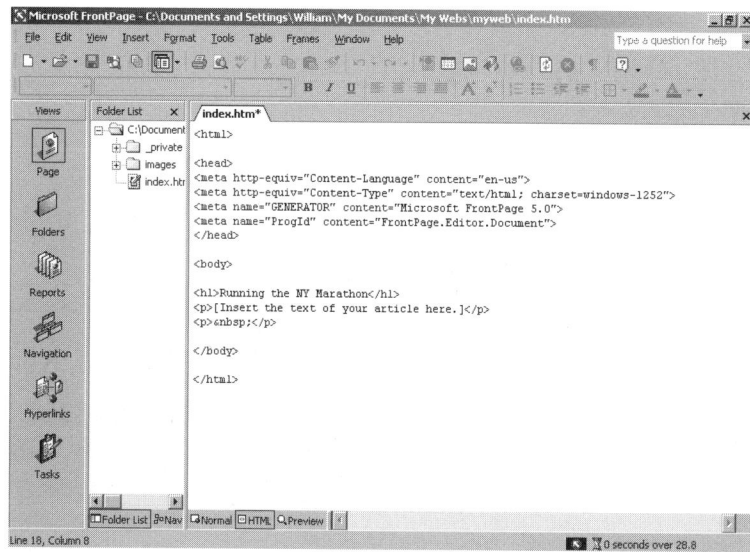

Figure 15-3 *You can edit HTML directly in FrontPage.*

3. Save your page when you are finished editing it.

Some of the more common editing tasks include

- Inserting, deleting, copying, and moving text just as you do in Word
- Formatting text
- Applying styles to paragraphs
- Inserting a graphic using the Insert Picture From File button on the Standard toolbar
- Drawing in your Web page using the commands on the Drawing toolbar

Note   As browsers have evolved, they have supported more sophisticated formatting commands. For instance, style sheets were not supported in early versions of browsers but are now. In addition, Netscape and Microsoft Internet Explorer support different advanced features, and implement certain formatting features in different ways. As you work with Web pages, you will discover that certain formatting techniques work better with one browser than another, or better with newer browsers than older. Consider testing your Web pages on the oldest version of each browser you intend to support before publishing them.

- Inserting a hyperlink by selecting the text or graphic, and then right-clicking and choosing Hyperlink
- Inserting a table by clicking the Table button on the Standard toolbar, and dragging to specify its size

Tip   Because HTML files do not support some of the alignment and positioning commands in Word, many Web sites position text and graphics by putting them in tables, which gives more control over where the object appears on the page. Experiment by editing existing pages that contain tables. Right-click the table, and choose Cell Properties or Table Properties to see the options that enable you to position things in different ways.

Publishing Documents on the Web

Many Web sites today are not just marketing vehicles; they are knowledge repositories that are available to everyone in the organization, to selected partners and clients, or to the world at large. Publishing content on the Web has become an important task for an entirely new category of workers—sometimes called Web content managers. For most organizations, the majority of that content consists of Word documents.

There are two primary ways to upload Word documents to the Web. You can either upload them in their original format so they appear as a link and can be opened in Word or saved to your local drive, or you *publish* it—that is, convert it to a Web page.

See Also   Saving files to Web sites in their native format is discussed in "Choosing Where to Save Your Data" on page 82.

To publish content to the Web, you need to understand some critical factors in transforming a document designed for print to one that does its job effectively on the Web. This is called *repurposing* documents for the Web. You also must understand the basic techniques of converting and editing your Web document in Word.

Repurposing for the Web

The medium of the Web is different from that of paper, and effective Web documents leverage this fact. It's harder for most people to read long documents on the Web than it is on paper. You can't hold a highlighter or pen in your hand while you read and mark up the document, and most people are used to being able to thumb through a paper document to see headings or review a past point.

Moreover, people read Web documents differently. They scan rather than read word-for-word. They do not expect to spend as much time reflecting and considering, because essentially the Web is a quick, mobile experience.

As you think about how to repurpose your Word documents for the Web, consider these factors and use guidelines like those in the sections that follow.

Decide to Repurpose

Repurposing might take some effort, as you recast information in a different format. Before doing so, ask yourself the following questions to decide whether it's worthwhile. If the answers to these questions are all yes, repurposing is probably worthwhile. Otherwise, it might be better to upload the file in its original format, and provide a link to it.

- Will readers be satisfied with reading this content online, or will they want to print it and read it more thoroughly anyway?

- Will the content be current for long enough to obtain a return on the time it took to repurpose it?

- Will I add value to the content with the additional features (such as hyperlinks to external sites) I add when repurposing it?

- Does this material integrate into my site's purpose and its existing structure?

Repurposing Guidelines

After you decide to repurpose your Word document, you have to save it as a Web page as discussed in "Working with Word Web Documents" on page 296. You then need to edit it to make it more readable on the Web, using guidelines such as the ones in this list.

- Sentences and paragraphs must be short and to the point. Convoluted sentence structures and long paragraph are even harder to read on the screen than they are in print.

- Use more headings and other text elements that stand out, like bold sentences for key points. Readers tend to scan Web documents more, rather than read them in depth.

- Recognize that readers see one screenful of information at a time, so where possible, design for the screen. For instance, you might want to make one point on each screen in a multiscreen document, or put an "up to top" link at the top of every screen.

- Use hyperlinks liberally. Consider using links for technical words that might appear in a glossary, or using links to other Web sites that provide more information about people, companies, or concepts you mention. If you think your reader will take a short detour and want to come back to the document consider having links open in a new window as described in "Working with Word Web Documents" on page 296.

- Enrich the graphics that appear in your original Word document. For example, a picture can be an embedded video (as discussed in "Incorporating Media Files" on page 306); or a graphic might link to a PowerPoint slideshow (as discussed in "Including PowerPoint Slideshows" on page 303).

- Make the experience interactive. Check lists and data tables may be made into interactive forms that allow users to make choices and display results (see "Creating Forms and PivotTables" on page 298), or create a link to the authors' e-mail addresses so people can contact them for more information.

- Consider the "bite, snack, and meal" approach developed by Marilynne Rudick and Leslie O'Flahavan (*http://www.ewriteonline.com/newsletter/issue8R.html*): On your home page, put a "bite" about your content—a headline with a message, for example, "Interest rates to plummet next month." Interested readers can click this to get a "snack"—a paragraph that summarizes the content in one or two sentences. This might be contained on a page with summaries of several other documents. The "meal," of course, is the entire document itself that is linked to the "snack."

- Include a link to the original Word file, so people can download it if desired.

- Create a custom property called Expiration, and put the date after which the file should be removed from the Web. You can then use the Search feature in Office to regularly purge your outdated content.

See Also   Creating custom properties and searching for documents containing them are discussed further in "Accessing Your Information" on page 92.

Working with Word Web Documents

Because HTML is now a native Word document type (along with Rich Text Format [.rtf] and the original document format [.doc] in Word), working with Web pages in Word is now very simple and very similar to working with other Word documents. The only details you need to know are which type of Web page will work best in your situation, and differences there are between editing Web pages and other Word documents.

Choose a Web Page Type

Word can actually save a file as a Web page in three ways. They are each used for a somewhat different purpose, and you have to determine which one to use before you save your file.

- **Web Page.** This option saves your file as an HTML document. Special codes are included in the document that support *round trips*—the ability for the HTML document to be converted back into a Word .doc file while losing hardly any formatting in the process. Even formatting that is not supported in the HTML file is saved so that if it is ever converted back into a .doc file, the formatting can be restored. The file size is somewhat larger, however, because of the extra codes, and these codes can be confusing if you are using another Web page editor or editing the HTML code directly. Use this option when you require round-trip support.

- **Web Page, Filtered.** This option also saves your document in HTML. However, it is a "clean" HTML; that is, it does not contain the Office codes needed to support round-trips. However, it is much easier to understand and edit the HTML source code of the document. Use this option when you do not require round-trip support, and will be publishing the document only as a Web page, not as a print document.

- **Web Archive.** Although both the preceding files save embedded graphics and certain other objects as separate files, saving a file as a Web archive saves the document as one file with any graphics embedded in it. This option is frequently used to save sites from the Web so they can be stored on your local drive or e-mailed to others, because you have only one file to deal with.

Edit Word Web Documents

After you decide which format you want to use, you can create, edit, and save your document using the same commands you use with other Word documents. To save an *existing* document as a Web page, choose Save As Web Page from the File menu and then choose the appropriate file type (Web Page, Web Page, Filtered, or Web Archive). To create a *new* document as a Web page, do the following.

1. Choose New from the File menu.

2. If you want to create an empty Web page, choose Blank Web Page in the New Document task pane.

3. Otherwise, if you want to create a Web page from a template, choose General Templates.

Tip Additional Web templates may be available by choosing Templates On Microsoft.com rather than General Templates.

---

4. In the Templates dialog box, select the Web Pages tab and then double-click the desired template or wizard.

You see your document in the Web Layout view (Figure 15-4). This shows your document as it appears in a Web browser—without page breaks, headers, or footers, and with text wrapping to fit the window and backgrounds displayed.

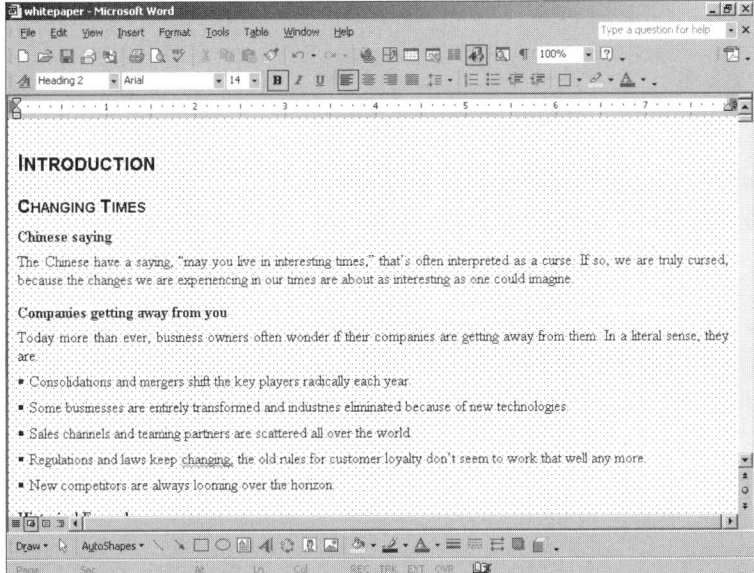

Figure 15-4 *The Web Layout view in Word shows how your document will look in a browser when you publish it as a Web page.*

You enter, edit, and delete text just as you do in Word, and you can include styles, graphics, hyperlinks, and tables as well. Menus are the same with a few exceptions, for example, New Blank Document becomes New Web Page. Certain formatting features may not be supported, and they appear dimmed. You can insert text effects such as a blinking background or shimmering text by choosing Font from the Format menu, and then clicking the Text Effects tab.

Also consider which browsers your readers might use, because different browsers support different features. The formatting choices available when you edit your Web pages in Word depend on the browsers you specify you want to support in displaying your Web page. Specify your browser support as follows.

1. Choose Options from the Tools menu.

2. On the General tab of the Options dialog box, click Web Options.

3. In the Browsers tab of the Web Options dialog box, choose the appropriate browsers to support.

Tip   If you are creating content for a FrontPage Web site that uses themes, you might want your Word Web file to share the same formatting. You can apply a theme to a Word document by choosing Theme from the Format menu.

Including Data on Your Web Pages

As Web sites become more than just electronic brochures on the Internet, knowledge workers are starting to publish more data on the Web. Sometimes the data is fixed, and they want to publish ways to access it or make calculations from it; sometimes it's important to publish databases that can be edited, added to, and searched.

In the past, publishing databases and interactive forms required Web developers, custom coding, and complex file permissions. Today, you can easily publish them with Microsoft FrontPage 2002. Of course, creating a complex PivotTable or database system for the Web still takes a more advanced understanding of Excel or Access, but you can now publish your work to the Web with relative ease. This section shows you the basics of how to publish data on the Web; for more detailed information refer to *Microsoft Office XP Inside Out* by Michael Halvorson and Michael J. Young, also published by Microsoft Press.

Creating Forms and PivotTables

One way to keep visitors on your site longer and provide extra value is to make your site interactive. You can do this by creating forms, assessments, and the like that allow people to answer questions and then see the results, according to some formula you have created. For instance, Figure 15-5 shows a simple form that calculates the return on investment from training.

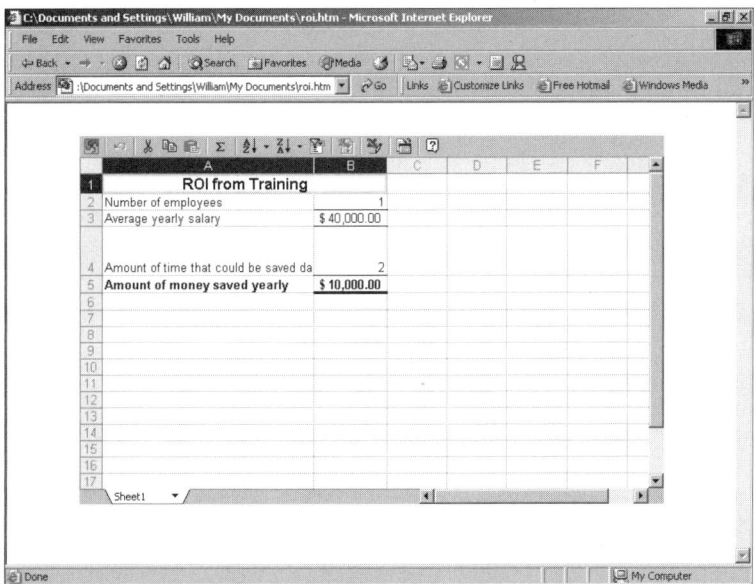

Figure 15-5   *Interactive Excel worksheets can be used to create forms that add value to your site.*

Alternatively, you might have a PivotTable that provides summary information about an Excel database that you want to share on your Web site. In either case, if you can create the appropriate workbook in Excel, you can upload it to your Web site so visitors can enter data and see results, given two simple caveats.

See Also   Creating PivotTables is discussed further in "Creating Summaries of Your Data" on page 181.

- The visitor must be using Internet Explorer 4 or later.
- The results are not saved; each time visitors open the page, they see the workbook in its original form.

To create an interactive workbook and upload it to a Web site, follow these steps.

1. Open the Excel workbook you want to publish to the Web.

2. Choose Save As Web Page from the File menu.

3. In the Save As dialog box, navigate to the folder where you want to save your workbook.

4. Select Add Interactivity, and then click the Publish button.

5. In the Publish As Web Page dialog box, choose the sheet, range, or item you want to publish.

6. In the Add Interactivity With box, choose Spreadsheet Functionality or PivotTable Functionality.

Tip   If your data changes frequently, you might want to choose AutoRepublish Every Time This Workbook Is Saved from the Publish As Web Page dialog box.

---

7. Click Publish.

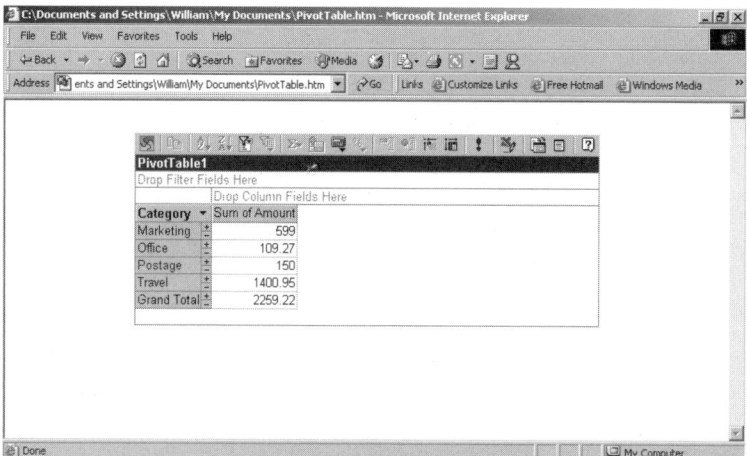

A Web page is created that contains the workbook, worksheet, range of cells, or Pivot-Table. You can edit any of the unlocked cells if it is a worksheet. If it is a PivotTable, you can perform such PivotTable functions as adding fields, selecting values, and changing calculation operators.

Including Databases

In a number of situations, you might want to include a database on your Web site. If you have an Internet site, your customers might want to be able to see your product list or price sheets. In an intranet, you might want to include one of your corporate databases. In either case, you can easily create a database that's linked to your Web site using FrontPage. This section introduces you to two ways to do this—by creating a new Access database on your Web site in FrontPage, or by uploading an existing Access database and creating *Access Data Pages* (Web forms created by Access that link to your database) to access it.

Note Your Web site must have FrontPage Server Extensions 2002 enabled for these techniques to work. If you're unsure about whether you do, ask your Web site administrator or Internet service provider (ISP).

When you create a new database or Access Data Pages, work with your site on the Web rather than working with it on your local drive and uploading it to the Web later. If you use the latter strategy, some of the database links might not work properly.

Create a New Web Database

Using FrontPage, you can create a simple, single-table Access database on your Web site and create forms for data entry, viewing data, and editing data. These forms can be pasted into other pages on your Web site, or you can apply themes to them and include them in your navigation structure to integrate them into your Web site, as discussed in "Maintaining Web Pages" on page 291. This can be a great way to include a simple signup list on your Web site, or publish an employee phone directory that can be easily updated. To create a database using FrontPage, use the following procedure.

1. Open your Web site that has FrontPage Server Extensions installed.

2. Point to New on the File menu, and then choose Page or Web.

3. On the New Page Or Web task pane, choose Web Site Templates.

4. In the Web Site Templates dialog box, check Add To Current Web.

5. Double-click the Database Interface Wizard.

6. Choose Create A New Access Database Within Your Web, and click Next.

7. In the next step of the wizard, accept the default name for the connection and then click Next.

8. Add or modify any fields you want to include in your database table, and then click Next.

9. Wait while the database is created in the fpdb folder, and then click Next.

10. Check all three types of Database Interface Pages to provide full functionality for your database, including the ability to delete and update records, and then click Next.

11. Provide a username and password, and then click Next. Click Finish to create your database.

You can test your new database by previewing it in your browser, and adding, deleting, and editing records in it. You can also edit the Web pages that were created to add explanatory text above or below the form, or right-click the tables containing database links and choose Table Properties or Cell Properties to change the way they are displayed.

Tip   To insert database results in an existing Web page, point to Database on the Insert menu and choose Results. You see the Database Results Wizard, which guides you through the required steps.

Upload an Access Database to Your Web Site

You might want to upload an existing Access database to your Web site, rather than creating a new one in FrontPage. Not only can you import existing data this way, but you can also upload a relational Access database that contains linked tables and drop-down lists for data entry, and then convert the existing forms, which provide a more professional user interface.

See Also   For a more detailed discussion of Access databases, including relational databases, linked tables, and forms, see "Organizing Data Using Access" on page 121.

To upload an Access database and convert existing forms to Data Access Pages, you need to do three sequential procedures. The first uploads your Access database to your FrontPage Web site, and can be done as follows.

1. Open your Web site in FrontPage.

2. Choose Import from the File menu, and click the Add File button.

3. In the Add File To Import List dialog box, click Add File, then navigate to the folder containing your Access database and then double-click it to add it to your import list.

4. In the Import dialog box, click OK to import the file to your Web site.

5. In the Add Database Connection dialog box, click Yes to accept the default name for your database connection.

6. In the information dialog box, respond Yes when you are asked whether the database can be stored in the fpdb folder.

Next, you need to convert your forms to Data Access Pages. To do so, take the following steps.

1. In FrontPage, click the Folders button.

2. In the Folders pane, navigate to the fpdb folder and then double-click your Access database to open it in Access.

3. In Access, choose 1 from the Window menu to open the main window for your database.

4. In the Objects bar, choose Forms.

5. Right-click the form you want to convert, and choose Save As.

6. In the Save As dialog box, choose a name for your form and then choose Data Access Page in the As box and click OK.

7. In the New Access Data Page dialog box, navigate to your Web site, which may be in My Network Places.

8. Navigate to the folder within your Web site that you want to save your file in, and then choose OK.

9. Repeat steps 4 through 8 for additional forms you want to convert.

10. Close Access.

After you convert your forms, you see them in the FrontPage Folder view of your Web site. You can then use the techniques discussed in "Maintaining Web Pages" on page 291 to add themes, shared borders, navigation bars, and other formatting to the Data Access Pages. You can also use the Navigation view to add them to your navigation structure, as discussed in the same section.

Users are able to navigate to your form and, if they have the appropriate permissions for the Web folder, make and save changes to the database using the Data Access Page.

Note   You can also display results from other types of databases by creating database links to them. See your Web and database administrators for details about how to create these links.

Enhancing Web Pages with Media Files

As the Web becomes a major source for public as well as internal corporate information, media files are increasingly being stored on the Web. This is especially true because disk storage prices have continued to tumble over the past few years, the availability of broadband access has increased, and the quality of streaming media at lower bandwidth has increased. In addition, as corporate audiences become more used to receiving knowledge from PowerPoint slideshows versus Word documents, it is becoming increasingly important to be able to publish slideshows on the Web as well. In this section you learn to publish your PowerPoint slideshows, audio files, and digitized video files to the Web.

Including PowerPoint Slideshows

When you publish a PowerPoint slideshow to the Web, it can be easily viewed by your audience as a series of Web pages, as shown in Figure 15-6. By default, they appear inside a framed environment that contains a number of controls that make it easy to navigate through the slideshow. Features you can include when you save your slideshow as a Web page include the following.

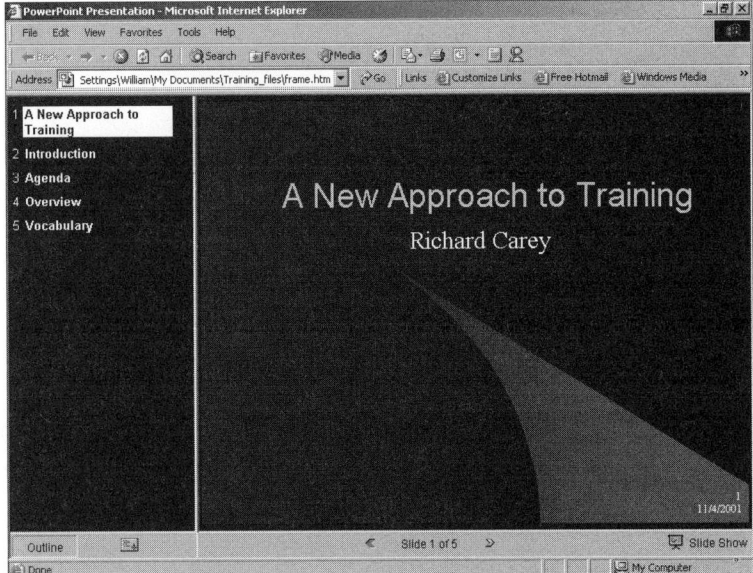

Figure 15-6   *Web-based slideshows are a convenient way to communicate visual data to your audience.*

- You can select the browser type (for example, Internet Explorer, Netscape) and version that are required to view your presentation, or make larger presentation files that support more than one type of browser. Your presentation will use additional features that are supported by later browser versions; for instance, if you restrict supported browsers to Internet Explorer 6 and above, your slideshow will use the new, higher quality Portable Network Graphics (PNG) format for saving pictures.

Note   The page people first reach when they view your slideshow on the Web detects which browser they are using, and automatically sends them to the slideshow Web pages that are appropriate for that browser.

- You can choose to watch the animations you have included in your PowerPoint slideshow.

Caution   This option isn't selected by default so if you use animations, you need to select it manually as described in the next procedure, or else your slides might have superimposed graphics or other effects you do not intend.

- You can add slide navigation controls, which will display your presentation as shown in Figure 15-6, or not have navigation controls, which will display each slide in the full browser window.

- You can choose whether to include speaker notes, and can automatically resize the graphics for the browser window.

- You can compress all the Web pages that are created, along with supporting graphics files and even a PowerPoint viewer, to take with you on disk or send by e-mail.

When you use the Save As Web Page feature, PowerPoint actually creates an entire set of files—HTML, graphics, and media files—that are called from one central Web page. You can organize these files in a subfolder, which is recommended because otherwise you might have 100 files related to the slideshow in your main folder, and it's hard to tell which ones they are.

To save your PowerPoint slideshow as a Web page, do the following.

1. Create and save your slideshow as you normally do in PowerPoint.

2. Choose Save As Web Page from the File menu.

3. In the Save As dialog box, browse to the folder you want to save your slideshow to. You can save it on your local drive, or directly to your Web site if you defined it as a Network Place.

See Also   For more information about saving files to Network Places, see "Choosing Where to Save Your Data" on page 82.

---

4. Click Publish to specify options for your Web slideshow.

5. In the Publish As Web Page dialog box, make the following choices.

   - Select the slides you want to publish, and whether you want to publish speaker notes.

   - Specify the filename for your central slideshow Web page, and, if desired, click Change to change the name that appears on the title bar.

6. Click the Web Options button. Some of the common options you'll probably want to specify include the following.

   - In the Browsers tab, select the browsers you expect your audience to use in the Target Browsers. You see the options related to the chosen browsers in the Options area, and can customize them if you want.

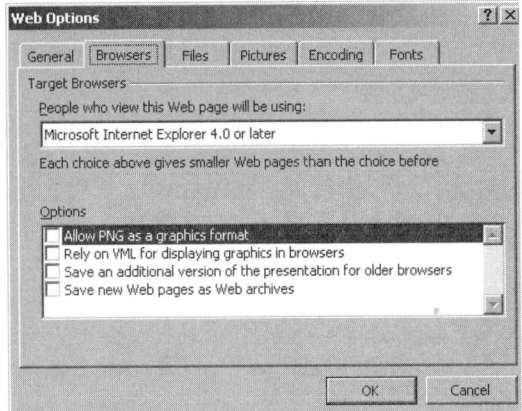

- In the General tab, select whether to add navigation controls, and whether to publish your slide notes as well as your slides.

- In the Files tab, select whether to organize the supporting files in a subfolder.

7. Choose OK to return to the Publish As Web Page dialog box, and then choose Publish to save your slideshow.

Note PowerPoint provides a Pack And Go Wizard that can compress your slideshow into one file, and include a PowerPoint viewer in that file. Today, most PCs have PowerPoint and it's easier for most people to upload their presentation directly to their laptop from a network or e-mail it to the recipient. If you want to put a slideshow on a disk or CD-ROM, however, the wizard can be useful. Choose Pack And Go from the File menu and follow the steps of the wizard.

Incorporating Media Files

One way to add value to your Web site is to add multimedia files, such as short video clips, to it. It's important to consider the medium of the Web when using video, however. People watch video in real time—a 60-second video takes 60 seconds to watch. As a result, it's a very "slow" experience for users. Thus, it's always important to ask the question, "Can this message be gotten across without perceptible loss in richness in any other way?" For many messages, the answer is yes. Having your CEO introduce a new product doesn't provide much additional information—especially if what you see is a "talking head." If, however, there's a video of the sleek new sports car in action while the product manager introduces it, that's a different story. Times you might want to include short videos on your site include

- When the video is of a product or has inherent production quality, and is not the face of the person talking

- When you are making a point for which the visual image is important, such as a video on presentation skills on your intranet

- When you need people to see body language, such as a demonstration of the right versus the wrong way to confront a troubled employee in an e-learning module

Using Windows Media Player to publish rich media is extremely easy. If your users are using Internet Explorer, you can embed it into your Web page. First, you need to convert the file to a Windows Media file, if it's in another digital format (such as an .avi file).

Note If your audience might be using Netscape or another browser, you can still embed the file. The procedures, however, are somewhat complex and require HTML coding that provides dual-browser support, and are better left to professional Web developers.

You can create Windows Media files by using the free Windows Media Encoder, which can be downloaded from Microsoft (*http://www.microsoft.com/windows/windowsmedia/default.asp*). After you install Encoder, you can create your Windows Media files as follows.

Note Windows Media Player and Encoder go through version changes fairly often. These instructions are for version 7.1, and should be used for general guidelines if you are using a different version.

---

1. Start Windows Media Encoder, and choose Broadcast, Capture, Or Convert A File Using The New Session Wizard and then choose Next.

2. From the New Session Wizard window, choose Convert An Audio Or Video File Into A Windows Media File and then click Next.

3. Enter the name of the file you want to convert in the File to Convert box or click Browse to locate the file. After you select a file, the output file name appears in the File to Create box with a .wmv extension. Leave the default or type a new name or path for the file , and then click Next.

4. Unless your Web administrator tells you you have a Windows Media Server, choose File Will Stream From A Web Server Or Play Directly On A Computer, and then click Next.

5. Choose a profile that fits with the type and speed of Internet access you expect your users to have, as well as the type of video source you have, and then click Next.

Tip   To insert a video that's doesn't involve a lot of fast motion so it can be viewed from a high speed dial-up connection (a good lowest common denominator), choose Video For Web Servers (56k).

---

6. Fill out the display information, click Next, and then click Finish. The program converts your file and displays the results in the Encoding Results dialog box.

Note   This same wizard can be used to convert files from a Web cam or a camcorder, if a compatible video capture card has been installed in your computer.

Your file will be saved as a .wmv file in the location you specified. You can insert it into your FrontPage Web page as follows.

1. In FrontPage, choose Page Options from the Tools menu.

2. In the Compatibility tab of the Page Options dialog box, choose Microsoft Internet Explorer Only from the Browsers drop-down list and then click OK.

3. Open the destination Web page in Page view, and click where you want the video to appear.

4. Point to Picture on the Insert menu, and then choose Video.

Note   If the video option is dimmed, either your Web site is hosted on a server that does not support this functionality or you have not limited your browser support to Internet Explorer.

---

5. In the Video dialog box, navigate to the appropriate folder, and then double-click the video file.

6. To see the video as it will appear to viewers, click the Preview in Browser button.

Summary

As you add your documents, data, slideshows, and media to your Web site, it transforms from a simple online brochure for your services to a repository that allows you to share accumulated knowledge with visitors from both within and external to your organization. By publishing your knowledge on the Web, you are sharing it in a format that can be read by people with any operating system, any desktop suite, and any type of hardware.

As you have found out, sharing content is not merely a matter of dumping a document onto the Web. By repurposing your documents for the Web, you optimize your content for this new medium. When you add interactive spreadsheets and PivotTables, the ability to display summary information from your databases, selected slideshows, and media files, you have a knowledge repository that can truly leverage your intellectual capital.

Checklist for Sharing Knowledge on the Web

The following skills are ones that will help you share various types of knowledge on your Web site.

[ ] Create a variety of Web sites using FrontPage templates.

[ ] Change the look and feel of your Web site using themes.

[ ] Edit individual Web pages using FrontPage.

[ ] Utilize systematic criteria for deciding whether it's cost effective to repurpose your Word documents for the Web.

[ ] Edit your Word document to optimize it for Web readers.

[ ] Know when to save a Word document as any of three types of Web pages.

[ ] Create interactive forms and PivotTables on Web pages using Excel.

[ ] Upload your Access database to your Web site, and create Data Access Pages to link to it.

[ ] Convert your PowerPoint slideshow into a Web page.

[ ] Embed a video file in your Web page.

Sharing Knowledge with Remote Workers

Patricia Esack has taken on a special assignment to try and solve a key problem for Humongous Insurance—a major property and casualty insurer with offices throughout the United States and Europe. As the company has branched out, folks in Claims and Underwriting no longer talk to each other every day informally because they are no longer located near each other. To develop new lines of business, however, underwriting needs to come up with creative ideas that are tempered with the experience of senior claims adjusters.

Patricia has researched best practices in knowledge sharing, and wants to implement three initiatives to jump-start knowledge flow. First, she wants to bring together 100 of the key staff in Claims and Underwriting for a summit. Following that, she wants to create a volunteer group of approximately 30 people who will stay in touch regularly and share ideas. Simultaneously, she intends to create a group that will build on the work of the summit and to recommend at least three new insurance products to senior management. Because key players are scattered in offices throughout the country and a few of them work from home, she wants to utilize some of the new Web-based technologies that allow meetings, communities, and teams to be supported online.

Challenges like the one faced by Patricia are becoming more common as organizations are increasingly distributed, travel budgets limited, and collaboration required. In fact, research by Gartner, Inc. suggests that in the near future, more than 80 percent of all enterprises will have at least 50 percent of their knowledge workers engaged in some form of telecommuting or other nomadic work.

In this chapter, you learn about technologies your organization can use for online collaboration, as well as some of the organizational factors you need to consider in implementing them. You also find out how to create online environments using a new technology provided by Microsoft: SharePoint Team Services.

Creating the Electronic Workplace

An *electronic workplace* can be defined as a Web-based environment that contains all the tools and processes required for workers to collaborate effectively, even if they are not co-located and are working in different time zones. It has several characteristics, including the following.

- It is person-specific and job-specific, providing just the tools that each individual needs to do his or her job.

- It provides a sense of *place* for groups of people, where the experience is of "coming to an office or conference room," not "using an application."

- It supports the four principal activities of knowledge workers: finding information, organizing that information, creating knowledge, and sharing it with others.

- It reaches beyond the enterprise to include partners and key customers as needed.

Although employees who primarily work alone and report results to management can use an electronic office, it is increasingly used by groups who need to collaborate online to produce knowledge products with other workers where the primary interaction is through the Web. Examples of this type of interaction include the following.

- An *online meeting* where four people work on a financial projection through a conference call, while they use an application-sharing program to view a worksheet that's on one of their computers

- A *Web-based offsite* where 200 senior managers identify restraints and enablers to the new corporate strategy using a variety of tools, located in one central "virtual conference center" over a two-week period, that include asynchronous (anytime) discussion forums, Webcasts, and periodic synchronous online meetings

- A *virtual project team* where 15 people produce a Request For Proposal, review responses, and choose a vendor in a "virtual team center" that contains tools for document storage and review, instant messaging and chat, discussion forums, and polling tools

- A *community of practice* where 30 people can meet over weeks or months using discussion forums, and informally share knowledge about topics of interest

Global organizations are doing all of this and more, as they begin to leverage the power of the Internet to connect people to people, not just allow people to access information. To see what's needed for online collaboration, it's important to understand the nature of online work (what's different about it and how to manage the change process) and identify the critical factors in creating an environment to support the type of work you're engaged in.

Understanding Critical Success Factors

Remote workers—especially those who spend most or all of their time working from home or on the road—face unique challenges that arise from the fact that they are often not co-located with their peers and managers. They lack the richness of face-to-face communication, can experience more isolation, and might have more problems getting visibility for accomplishments or participating in professional development opportunities. Their organizations face parallel challenges. It's harder to incorporate their viewpoints into decisions, they might be less readily available for quick conversations, and it's more difficult to monitor their performance.

There are three critical success factors required to effectively incorporate remote workers into the organization.

- Work practices that integrate the remote worker with the organization

- Organizational processes that effectively include and manage remote workers

- Technology tools that support the nature of the work to be done

---

Note   In my experience with supporting organizations bringing their work online, these factors are like a three-legged stool. If one is ignored, the solution doesn't work. In particular, it's vital that organizations not see working online as a "technology problem," but as a change process that integrates people, processes, and technology.

Adopt New Work Practices

To be effective from a distance, remote workers often need to change aspects of the way they engage in their work day to day. The dynamics of not being co-located imply, for example, that you need to make an active effort at informal networking when you're working from home because you don't run into colleagues at the copier or the lunch line. For online collaboration to succeed, you need to do the following.

- Learn to use instant messaging, e-mail, and Web-based discussions to network socially with your team as well as about tasks. This can help you handle feelings of isolation and replace the informal grapevine that keeps co-located workers abreast of what's going on.

See Also   For further information, see "Discussing Your Work" on page 234.

- Be a self-starter and discipline yourself to getting work done in the absence of external structure. That can be tough for some people, and refreshing yourself on basic techniques can help. Consider taking a training course on working as part of a virtual team, or one on time management if needed.

- Learn to communicate effectively using electronic tools. Your e-mails, instant messages, and Web-based discussions should communicate your ideas clearly, your opinions persuasively, and your emotions professionally.

See Also   For further information, see "Being Nice on the Internet" on page 37, or look up "writing for the Web" in your search engine for articles about how this differs from writing paper-based documents.

- Be visible about accomplishments. Communicate regularly with your manager, and ensure that he or she knows what you're working on and the contributions you're making.

- Make sure you're included. Talk with your manager about how you'll be included in regular meetings, and be proactive in asking people for advance copies of materials. When you learn about the inevitable informal meeting that was held, let people know you want to be sure you're included in future ones.

Develop New Organizational Processes

Just as individual workers must develop new work styles, so too must the organization that supports them develop new policies, procedures, and informal practices.

Some of these are the organizational counterparts of changes required in *individual* work practices, while others involve new procedures and processes that *workgroups* use. In addition, the *organization as a whole* needs to change to adapt to the needs of its new workforce. Some of the more common organizational changes that enable you to leverage remote workers include the following.

- Managers need to recognize and publicize the work done by remote workers, just as remote workers need to make themselves visible to management.

- Managers have to ensure that remote workers are given equal access to professional development opportunities.

- Leaders of remote teams need to build a shared sense of purpose, clear understanding of roles and responsibilities, and consensus around norms for communication in their virtual teams.

- Project managers must develop processes that leverage the anytime nature of the online environment, such as brainstorming alternatives over a week in a team Web site rather than in an hour-long meeting.

- Supervisors need to develop and publicize performance-based procedures for monitoring work and evaluating performance. Performance, rather than activity, must be well defined in terms of quality, quantity, and deadlines.

- Human Resources departments must develop new policies for insurance options, reimbursable expenses, and benefits, while Information Technology staff need to supply the required technology, training, and support to varied locations.

Leverage Technology

Technology supports remote workers in fundamental ways, by providing access to corporate information and facilitating interaction with colleagues. Access to corporate information can be provided in a fairly straightforward way, using tools including

- Web-based document filing systems that can be accessed through the Internet, such as shared Web folders in My Network Places

- Document reviewing and routing through e-mail, like that provided by Microsoft Office

- Access to others' calendars, tasks, and shared contact lists, as incorporated into Microsoft Exchange

The second part of the equation is facilitating interaction: social interaction for team and trust building, ongoing interaction for knowledge sharing and professional development, and focused interaction for project work and managing deliverables. Tools that support the collaboration process include

- Instant Messaging, such as MSN Messenger, for quick questions and answers

- Chat and application sharing for same-time meetings, such as Microsoft NetMeeting

---

See Also MSN Messenger and NetMeeting are discussed further in "Discussing Your Work" on page 234.

- Web forums and decision support (polling, survey, brainstorming) tools to support work processes over time

- Webcasting for larger same-time meetings

- Specialized tools designed to support e-learning, project management, time and billing, or other specific tasks

Applications like these provide the basic tools that a remote worker needs; however, tools alone aren't enough. It's like having a filing cabinet, desk, and stapler, but no place to put them. To be an electronic office, these tools need to be available in an integrated environment designed with the tools and processes that support the work to be done. The movement from tools to an electronic office is characteristic of high performance distributed organizations.

Stages of Working Online

As organizations become more technologically sophisticated and utilize more remote workers, there is a four-stage progression in the way they support working online in the electronic office.

- **Stage I: Legacy Applications.**   The organization uses older, pre-Web technologies for communication, such as voice mail and e-mail. Parts or all of the organization may use Microsoft Outlook or similar programs for group calendaring.

- **Stage II: Same-Time Meeting Support.**   The organization incorporates its first online collaboration technologies. Usually, these support real-time meetings for a distributed group of people. The technology may be video conferencing, or it may be online applications such as NetMeeting, WebEx (*http://www.webex.com*), or Latitude (*http://www. latitude.com*). Although one or two online technologies are used, the dominant metaphor is the face-to-face collaboration that happens in real-time meetings.

- **Stage III: New Tools Introduced.**   In the third stage, other collaboration applications start being used by early adopters in pilot projects and sometimes become pervasive in specific workgroups or throughout the enterprise. These can include additional tools for synchronous communications (such as instant messaging or chat), asynchronous communications (such as Web forums), or decision support (such as GroupMind Express— *http://www.groupmindexpress.com*).

- **Stage IV: The Electronic Office.**   It is at the end of Stage III, when large numbers of collaboration tools are being used, that the organization is ripe to adopt the electronic office. At this point, the high performance organization looks for platforms that integrate its collaboration toolset, enable work processes that occur over time, and support multiple teams and projects.

Choosing a Collaboration Platform

You build your electronic office by deciding on a platform for your online environment, and then customizing with the tools, user interface, and workflow processes to match the work you need to support.

Choosing the right online environment is an important decision. You're creating new work styles for individuals and work teams, and the platform you choose impacts how successful you will be at getting people to change how they work. In addition, the wrong decision is hard to fix—it's extremely hard to get a group to adopt a second platform when they had bad experiences with the first. To exacerbate the difficulty, most platforms have no way to exchange data with others except manually, so much of your information (such as your online discussions) might be lost if you need to change platforms.

To make the right platform decision, you need to follow several steps.

1. Scope the project by identifying your needs and resources, including

   - The work to be supported

   - The present workflow processes

   - Legacy collaboration tools you want retain

   - Resources available

   - Corporate culture factors that restrain or enable online work

2. Develop functional requirements for your online environment. These should include

   - Interactions people will engage in

   - Data people need to access

   - The tools to be used

   - The workflow(s) to be supported

   - User interface and usability requirements

3. Select a platform that contains or can incorporate all the right tools and processes.

Unfortunately, the platform you select will most likely be somewhat of a compromise. Most organizations find that the ideal platform doesn't exist at present, and all choices have benefits and limitations. The user interface of some platforms cannot be customized, while other platforms do not allow you to integrate legacy tools or don't work with all browsers. Some have wonderful online project management, but require that you work within their workflow process. A number of vendors for platforms that support online collaboration are listed in Table 16-1. Most of them allow you to either buy a license for the software, or provide arrangements to host it externally and you can purchase a monthly seat license. However, online collaboration is still in its technological infancy. There are likely to be many changes in the short term in terms of available players and the look and feel of each platform.

Table 16-1 Online Collaboration Platforms

Platform	Points to Consider
SharePoint (*http://www.microsoft.com/sharepoint*)	• Work team focus • Enterprise support • Very customizable
Caucus (*http://www.caucuscare.com*)	• Work team and community focus • Strong conversation tools • Very customizable
eRoom (*http://www.eroom.com*)	• Work team focus • Work flow support • Strong integration of discussions and content
iCohere (*http://www.icohere.com*)	• Community of practice focus • Many discussion and co-presence tools • Integrated look and feel
K-station & Discovery Server (*http://www.lotus.com*)	• Knowledge management focus • Enterprise support • Large collaboration tool set
SiteScape (*http://www.sitescape.com*)	• Work team and community focus • Large collaboration tool set • Very customizable
Spoke (*http://www.spoke.net*)	• Work team and community focus • Strong content management tools • Very customizable
Team Center (*http://www.inovie.com*)	• Work team focus • Strong project management tools • Very customizable
Web Crossing (*http://www.webcrossing.com*)	• Community and work team focus • Strong conversation tools • Very customizable

Collaborating Using Microsoft SharePoint

Microsoft has created SharePoint as an entry into the online collaboration services market, with two offerings. SharePoint Team Services provides basic functionality for small work teams including document sharing, discussion forums, polls, customizable lists, and e-mail notification. SharePoint Portal Server provides a highly customizable collaboration environment suited for the large workgroup or enterprise, and is usually implemented by the IT department or an external solutions provider.

Table 16-2 outlines the differences in functionality between SharePoint Team Services and SharePoint Portal Server. Since SharePoint Portal Server is usually customized by professional developers, it is not discussed further in this book. However, if it appears to be a good solution for your company, you can get further information from Microsoft Corporation at *http://www.microsoft.com/sharepoint/portalserver.asp*.

Table 16-2   Differences Between SharePoint Team Services and SharePoint Portal Server

SharePoint Team Services	SharePoint Portal Server
Easily created and configured by end users	Created and customized by developers
Moderate degree of customizability	Extensively customizable using Web Parts
Document publishing	Document publishing, routing, check in/out, and version control
Search for data in files stored in your SharePoint Team Web site	Search for data in files across multiple servers and platforms
Per-user licensing from Internet service providers (ISPs) for small groups	Requires SharePoint Portal Server plus per-user license

Note   Web Parts are customizable components that can integrate customized views of data, interfaces into enterprise systems, and Web applications into your SharePoint portal. For instance, you can create views to your SAP or PeopleSoft Enterprise Resource Management system, present your Outlook Inbox, or create a link to MSN Instant Messenger that shows you who is currently online.

Understanding SharePoint Team Services

SharePoint Team Services is a set of program extensions that can be added to a Web server that provides the ability to create a SharePoint team Web site. The team Web site (shown in Figure 16-1) contains tools to help your team work together online—all available from your browser. Some of the basic features of SharePoint team Web sites include the following.

- **Document libraries.**   You can publish files to your team Web site directly from any Microsoft Office XP application, as well as Windows Explorer. This provides seamless integration between your local and Web-based filing system. You can even assign a Microsoft Word template to each library, and any new documents created for this library can use that template to ensure consistency.

- **Discussion boards.**   Team Web sites provide the capability to create any number of simple, threaded discussion boards for asynchronous discussions between team members.

- **Surveys.**   You can quickly create a one-question poll or a multiquestion survey in your Web site; if you provide appropriate permissions, users see results immediately.

- **Lists.**   In SharePoint team Web sites, *lists* are used to create everything from event calendars, announcements, task lists, contact lists, and lists of links. A list is basically a database table saved in SharePoint, where you can customize the columns (that is, database fields) and specify views of the list that sort and group the list and incorporate filters. The lists identified previously are predefined; you can use them "as is," modify them, or create new lists as needed.

- **Notification.**   SharePoint team Web sites allow you to subscribe to libraries, discussions, or lists so you are notified through e-mail when new material appears. In addition, you can send an e-mail invitation to new members that allows them to register immediately on the site.

- **User maintenance.**   You can assign users to a variety of roles and limit their participation, all from your team Web site.

- **Ease of creation.**   You can create your SharePoint team Web site directly from Microsoft FrontPage 2002 using its built-in templates, if your Web is located on a server that supports SharePoint Team Services.

- **Access.**   You can access the site with both Microsoft Internet Explorer 4.01 and Netscape 4.75, and do not need Microsoft Office to use your team Web site. However, if you have Office XP, you're able to view document libraries graphically and more easily share information between your Office applications and your team Web site.

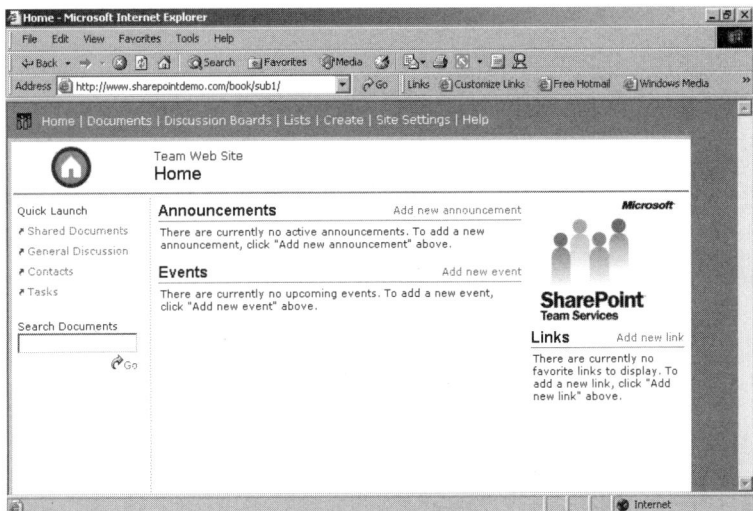

Figure 16-1   *SharePoint team Web sites can be quickly set up by non-IT staff and provide basic functionality for your remote team.*

Creating a SharePoint Team Web Site

You can create a SharePoint team Web site within minutes using FrontPage 2002. You merely need to be sure the Web site provider supports Microsoft FrontPage Server Extensions 2002 or SharePoint Team Services, and get the appropriate URL, UserID, and password from your Web site administrator. To create a SharePoint team Web site, do the following.

1. In FrontPage, point to New on the File menu and then choose Page Or Web.

2. In the New Page Or Web task pane, click Web Site Templates.

3. In the Specify The Location Of The New Web box, type the URL you were given by your Web administrator.

4. Double-click the SharePoint-based Team Web Site icon.

5. Click the Folders icon in the Folder List bar.

6. In the Contents pane, right-click default.htm and choose Preview In Browser to go to your new site.

You see a default team Web site that has the most common tools and options, which you can modify as needed. One of the first things you'll probably want to do is create UserIDs, and invite the rest of your team to your site and assign them roles. You can do so by following these steps, after you navigate to the site in your browser.

1. From the top link bar choose Site Settings.

2. In the Web Administration section of the Site Settings page shown in Figure 16-2, choose Send An Invitation.

3. Fill out the required information in each step of the Send An Invitation Wizard, including the e-mail address, name, text of invitation, and role.

You're ready to start working together in your site—or you can customize it as described in the next section.

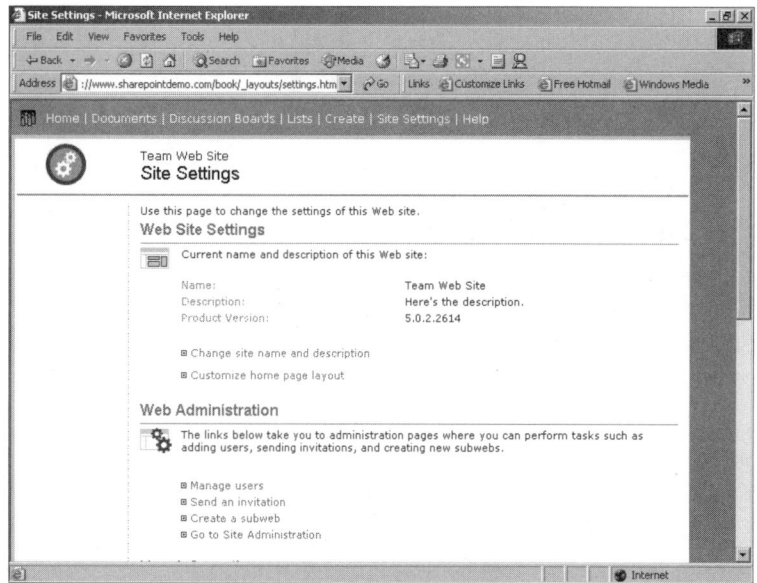

Figure 16-2   *You can easily administer your SharePoint team Web site from the Web site itself.*

Tip   By default, there are five roles you can assign users: Administrator, Advanced Author, Author, Contributor, and Browser. You can add and delete roles, as well as change their rights, by clicking Site Settings from the top link bar, clicking Go To Site Administration, and then clicking Manage Roles.

Managing Your SharePoint Team Web Site

Managing your SharePoint team Web site center is designed to be as easy as possible. Although you can make certain formatting changes to site pages using FrontPage, virtually all management functions are available through menus in the Web site itself if you are assigned an Administrator role, as the site creator is by default. Three things you must know how to do are create new libraries, discussions, and lists; customize their behavior; and choose which ones appear on your home page.

Create Document Libraries, Discussion Boards, Surveys, or Lists

By default, your SharePoint team Web site contains one discussion board for general discussions, a document library for shared documents, and five lists: for contacts, tasks, announcements, events, and links.

You need to create new discussion boards, lists, surveys, or file libraries to support multiple activities that your team is engaged in. For instance, say you want to have a separate discussion board, file library and task list for each project your team is working on. To create a new document library, discussion board, survey, or list, do the following.

1. From anywhere in your SharePoint team Web site, choose Create from the top link bar.

2. On the Create Page screen, click Document Library, Discussion Board, Survey, or the type of list you want to create.

Tip From the Create Page screen, you can also import a list from a spreadsheet.

---

3. In the New screen, fill in options including

   - The name that appears in all references to the Document Library, Discussion Board, Survey, or List

   - An optional description field that is displayed under the top of the Document Library, Discussion Board, Survey, or List screen

   - Whether to put the Document Library, Discussion Board, Survey, or List on the Quick Launch bar

   - Other options that are specific to Document Libraries, Discussion Boards, Surveys, and Lists

4. Finish the process by clicking Create.

5. Customize your document library, discussion board, survey, or list, if desired, as described in the next section.

Customize Document Libraries, Discussion Boards, Surveys, or Lists

Each document library, discussion board, survey, or list can be modified to display views, and to specify its descriptive information, access rights, and columns (that is, fields) it contains. This enables you to extensively modify how the document libraries, discussion boards, surveys, or lists function for your team. For instance, you can

- Create a discussion board that includes an evaluation process by adding a required "Approval" column, so that in addition to stating an opinion, the user must choose Approve or Disapprove

- Add a column to a task list that specifies the project that the task is related to

- Add a view that shows only the "approved" responses, and another that shows the "disapproved" ones

- Display only the latest three announcements or the events coming up in the next seven days

   To customize your document library, discussion board, survey, or list, do the following.

1. Navigate to the document library, discussion board, survey, or list you want to modify.

2. In the document Library, Discussion Board, Survey, or List page, click Modify Settings And Columns.

3. In the Customize screen, choose options including the following.

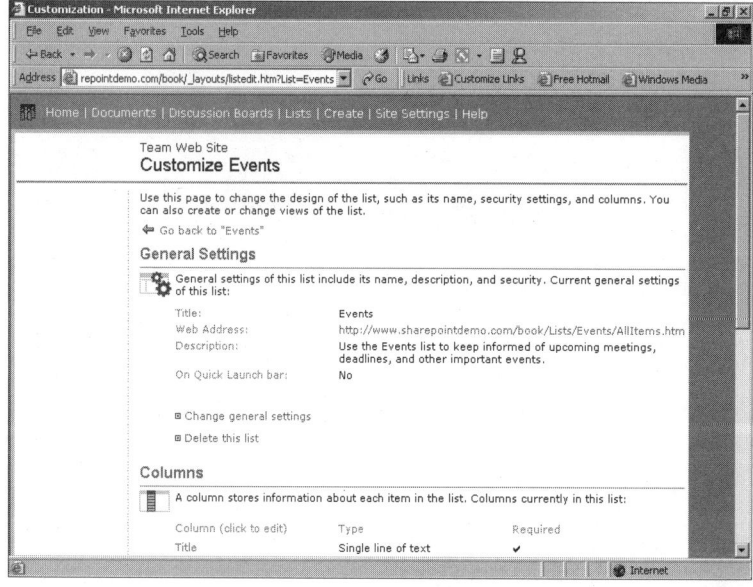

- In the General Settings area, click Change General Settings to change the component's name, description, visibility on the Quick Launch bar, and permissions, and then click OK.

- In the Columns area, edit a column by clicking its name. You can then edit the column's name, and modify additional settings that depend on the type of column.

Note   Optional settings that depend on column type include the display format for the column, whether it's required, choices for drop-down lists, and default values. After you create a column, you cannot change its type (for example, from text to numeric) and some column options (for example, the data source if the column's data comes from a lookup).

- In the Columns area, add a new column by clicking its name. You can then specify all the settings for your column, including the column type.
- In the Views area, edit a view by clicking its name. You can then edit the view's name, displayed columns, sort order, and filter options to display a subset of your data.

Tip   You can also choose whether a view is the default view in the Views area. If a component is displayed on the home page, the default view is displayed. You can show the newest three announcements, for instance, by creating a new view of the Announcements components, setting the appropriate options, and making it the default view.

- In the Views area, create a new view by clicking Create A New View and then setting the view options.

Change Your SharePoint Team Home Page

Your SharePoint team home page is the page team members see when they first access the team Web site. It contains the information they see first, and the navigation controls that take them to other parts of the site. Thus, to make the Web site most useable, it is important to put the information everyone should see first on the home page (such as important announcements or events), and to create links that make navigating the site easy and intuitive.

You can determine the content that appears in the main area of your team Web site by dragging page elements—for example, Document Libraries, Discussion Boards, Surveys, or Lists—into the two columns in the main area.

To edit the page elements that appear on your home page, do the following.

1. Navigate to your SharePoint team Web site.
2. In the top link bar, choose Site Settings.
3. In the Web Site Settings area of the Site Settings page, click Customize Home Page Layout.

4. In the Home Page Layout screen (Figure 16-3), drag the page element you want to display to the appropriate column and then click Save.

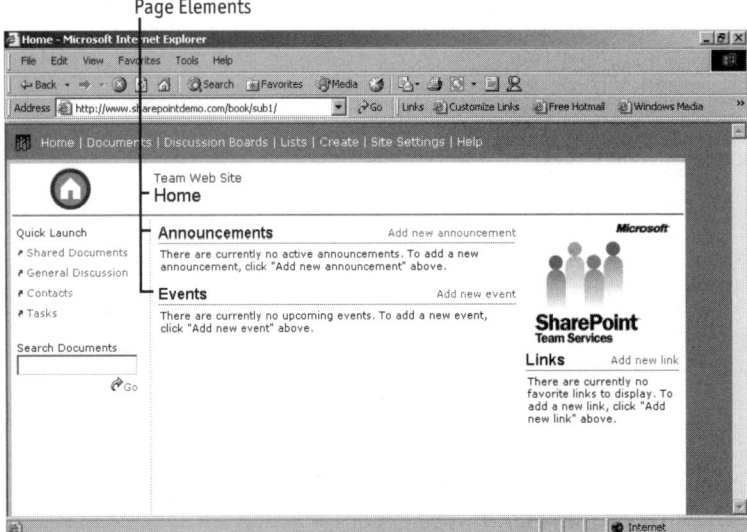

Figure 16-3   *You can determine which page elements are presented in the main area of your home page so your team can see just the information pertinent to them.*

As your team Web site becomes more robust, you can have multiple discussion boards, document libraries, surveys, or lists. Some of them might be of general interest, while others are specific to a few people. To make it easier for team members to quickly navigate to the most commonly used document libraries, discussion boards, surveys, or lists, put a link to them on the Quick Launch bar—the menu that appears on the left side of the home page. To specify what appears on the Quick Launch bar, do the following.

1. Navigate to the document library, discussion board, survey, or list you want to add or remove from the Quick Launch bar.

2. On the component screen, click Modify Settings And Columns.

3. In the General Settings area of the Customize screen, click Change General Settings.

4. In the Navigation area of the Settings screen, click Yes to display the item in the Quick Launch bar. Click No to remove it. When you are finished, click OK.

Tip   To further customize your SharePoint team Web site, open it in FrontPage 2002. From there, you can change certain formatting and add Web components. Note that certain items such as the top link bar cannot be modified, and others (such as the look and feel of the home page) cannot be changed without changing all other sites on that server. Thus, if you are using an ISP to provide your SharePoint Team Services, you might not be able to change the look and feel of your team Web site.

Working in a SharePoint Team Web Site

Usually, you join a SharePoint team Web site by receiving an e-mail sent by the site administrator. This e-mail contains a link that allows you to enter the site and change your password. When you click the link, you're asked to supply the name and password contained in the e-mail, and then you're taken directly to a Web page where you can change your password (if you want to). After you change your password, you see the home page of your SharePoint team Web site.

From here, you can easily share documents, post information, and participate in conversations and polls with teammates. To get started, you must understand how everything's put together and how to find what you need.

The default SharePoint team Web site is displayed earlier in Figure 16-1. The top link bar remains the same no matter where you are on the Web site. It provides access to the major types of tools: document libraries, discussion boards, surveys, and lists (for example, task lists, events, announcements).

The Quick Launch bar appears on the site's home page, and shows links to some of the most important or often-used tools on the site. You go to a specific document library, discussion board, survey, or list by clicking its link if it appears on the Quick Launch bar, or otherwise by clicking the appropriate page in the top link bar, which shows all the document libraries, discussions, surveys, or lists on the site. The working area of the home page is customized by the site administrator, and typically contains information of interest to the entire team, such as announcements or events.

Note   You see links for all options on the site—even ones you don't have rights to. For instance, even if you aren't an administrator you still see the Site Settings link, and if you have only view rights you still see Add New links. However, when you click such a link you are asked for a password and are not able to access the linked page.

When you go to a specific document library, discussion board, survey, or list, you see a screen like the one shown in Figure 16-4. The top link bar remains the same, but you usually see a View bar in the left pane depending on how the site has been configured. These commands can be very handy. They allow you to quickly switch between types of calendars, a list versus folder view of documents, a variety of filters for your task list, or a summary versus expanded view of your discussion.

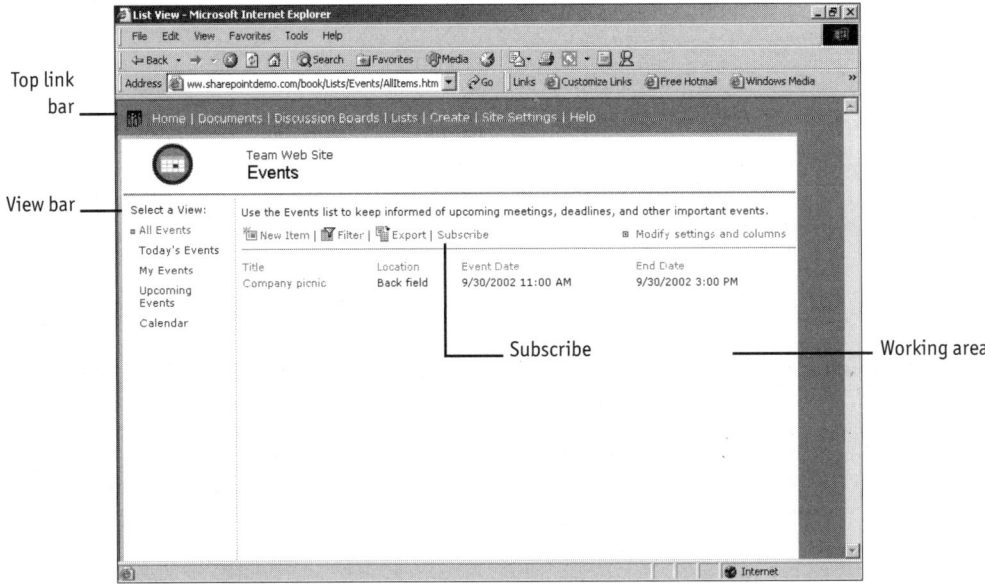

Figure 16-4   *The View bar allows you to see information in a variety of formats.*

From this screen, depending on your access rights, you can view and participate in discussions, download files, or add, edit and delete list items depending on the type of tool you're using.

Tip   Items that have been created within the last day are marked with a new icon so you can quickly identify them.

One of the most helpful attributes about working in a team Web site is that you don't need to check the site every day to find out if there's anything new. Instead, you can subscribe to discussions, document libraries, surveys, or lists and you are notified via e-mail when something new is posted. All you need to do is select Subscribe when viewing any document library, discussion, survey, or list, and you see a New Subscription page that allows you to specify your e-mail address and when you want to receive notifications.

Because SharePoint team Web sites are so intuitive, within a very short time you'll be collaborating about documents, participating in discussions, and sharing team information such as contacts and important links—thus enabling you to work together effectively even when you are not co-located.

Summary

The dot-com revolution has ended, but the realities of global organizations in the new, digital economy remain. The challenge is clear. To succeed, companies must leverage the intellectual capital of an increasingly distributed workforce. The challenge is that this is a boundary-crossing problem: it has both organizational and technological aspects, and solving it takes an integration of OD and IT—organization development and information technology.

Although the solution is not as simple as deploying a new application onto every desktop, the potential is great: the ability to work anytime, from any place, to create the high performance distributed organization. In this chapter, you learned about the basic concepts of working virtually, as well as critical factors to consider when choosing a platform for your electronic office. In addition, you saw how to use one such platform—Microsoft SharePoint Team Services—to quickly create a working environment for your distributed team.

Checklist for Working with Remote Workers

The following skills are ones that will help you work with remote workers and distributed teams.

[ ] Identify new work practices for individuals working remotely.

[ ] Identify new processes and procedures that organizations can use to support remote workers.

[ ] Choose a collaboration platform that will support the type of work you do.

[ ] Differentiate SharePoint Team Services and the SharePoint Portal Server.

[ ] Create a SharePoint team Web site.

[ ] Use a SharePoint team Web site to see team events, share documents, and hold asynchronous discussions.

[ ] Customize your SharePoint team Web site by adding and modifying components, and changing its look and feel.

Index

Symbols

A

F

G

H

N

Bill Bruck   Dr. Bruck is a highly respected consultant, author, and speaker in the rapidly emerging arena of online technology to enable virtual interaction. Because Bill integrates technical experience honed over two decades with his understanding of organizational systems and the people who make them work, his expertise is widely sought after by organizations deploying online work environments, e-learning, and virtual events.

With an A.B. from Brown University, an M.A. from Duquesne University, and a Ph.D. in Counseling Psychology from the University of Florida, Bill has been a licensed psychologist, tenured full professor of psychology, and Director of Institutional Research at Marymount University. A prolific author, Bill has written ten books for other publishers on human behavior and the effective use of technology, including books on Microsoft Office, WordPerfect Suite, PerfectOffice, and GroupWise.

Dr. Bruck was the Chief Knowledge Officer at Caucus Systems, Inc. prior to joining Collaboration Architects *(www.collaborationarchitects.com)*, where he designs electronic workspaces that support the work of distributed teams and consults in the adoption of new styles of work.

In Japanese, sensei means teacher, and as the *Technology Sensei (www.bruck.com)*, Bill gives keynote presentations throughout North America on how to manage technological change using principles derived from the martial arts. You can reach Dr. Bruck at *bill@bruck.com*.

The manuscript for this book was prepared and galleyed using Microsoft Word Version 2002. Pages were composed by Microsoft Press using Adobe FrameMaker+SGML version 6.0 for Windows, with text set in Sabon and display type in Officina Sans. Composed pages were delivered to the printer as electronic pre-press files.

Cover Illustration:	Todd Daman Design	Interior Graphic Artist:	Patty Fagan
Interior Graphic Designer:	Joel Panchot	Principal Proofreaders:	Darla Bruno, Seth Morrison
Principal Compositor:	Patty Fagan	Indexer:	Jack Lewis

Using the CD-ROM

The companion CD contains a fully searchable electronic version of this book, and additional applications that you might find useful. Follow these instructions to use this companion CD.

1. Insert the companion CD into your CD-ROM drive.

2. If a menu screen does not launch automatically, double-click StartCD.exe in the root folder of the CD-ROM to display the starting menu screen.

3. The menu provides you with links to all the resources available on the CD.

Choose the Explore Software link on the menu to open a Software Demos and Trials Web page that offers access to software products, add-ins, demos, and trials.

Choose the eBook link to set up the eBook. Microsoft Internet Explorer 5.01 or later and the proper HTML Help components are required to view the eBook. If your computer does not have Microsoft Internet Explorer 5.01 or later, the setup program will offer to install Internet Explorer 5.5 for you. The setup program has been configured to install the minimum files necessary to view the eBook, and it will not change your current settings or associations.

Choose the Internet Explorer link to install a U.S. English version of Microsoft Internet Explorer 6.0, which has been included on this CD.

System Requirements

If your computer runs on Microsoft Windows NT 4.0, or Microsoft Windows 2000, or Microsoft Windows XP you will need administrative privileges to install the eBook. For more information about the eBook installation, refer to the readme.txt file in the \eBook folder. For more information about what is included on the CD-ROM and how to access this information, see the readme.txt file in the root folder of the CD-ROM.

To install and run an eBook, your system must meet the following minimum requirements:

- 166-MHz or higher Pentium-compatible CPU

- Microsoft Windows 95 or later operating system (including Windows 98, Windows Millennium Edition, Windows NT 4.0 with Service Pack 3 or higher, Windows 2000, or Windows XP)

- 8X CD-ROM drive or faster

- 20–31 MB of free hard disk space to install the eBook to the hard drive

- 121 MB to install Internet Explorer 5.01 and the eBook

- Microsoft Internet Explorer 5.01 or later

The additional applications Web site lists the system requirements for the Software Demos and Trials.

Technical Support for the CD-ROM

Every effort has been made to ensure the accuracy of this book and the contents of the companion CD. Microsoft Press provides corrections for books through the World Wide Web at:

http://www.microsoft.com/mspress/support/

If you have comments, questions, or ideas regarding this book or the companion CD, please mail them to Microsoft Press at the following addresses:

Postal Mail

Microsoft Press
Attn.: *Tsunami* Editor
One Microsoft Way
Redmond, WA 98052-6399

E-Mail

mspinput@microsoft.com

Please note that product support is not offered through the above mail addresses.

Work anywhere, anytime
with the Microsoft guide to
mobile technology

U.S.A. **$29.99**
Canada $43.99
ISBN: 0-7356-1502-0

Okay. You're at the airport but your flight has been delayed. For four hours. No worries—you've got your laptop so you're ready to work. Or are you? Can you connect to the Internet? What about reliable battery power? Here's the answer: MOBILIZE YOURSELF! THE MICROSOFT GUIDE TO MOBILE TECHNOLOGY. This comprehensive guide explains how to maximize the mobility of the technology you have today. And it provides smart answers about the mobile technologies and services you might be considering. From PDAs to the wireless Web, this book packs the insights and solutions that keep you—and your technology—up and running when you're out and about.

microsoft.com/mspress

Work smarter—
conquer your
software *from the*
inside out!

Hey, you know your way around a desktop. Now dig into Office XP applications and the Windows XP operating system and *really* put your PC to work! These supremely organized software reference titles pack hundreds of timesaving solutions, troubleshooting tips and tricks, and handy workarounds in a concise, fast-answer format. They're all muscle and no fluff. All this comprehensive information goes deep into the nooks and crannies of each Office application and Windows XP feature. And every *Inside Out* includes a CD-ROM full of handy tools and utilities, sample files, links to related sites, and other help. Discover the best and fastest ways to perform everyday tasks, and challenge yourself to new levels of software mastery!

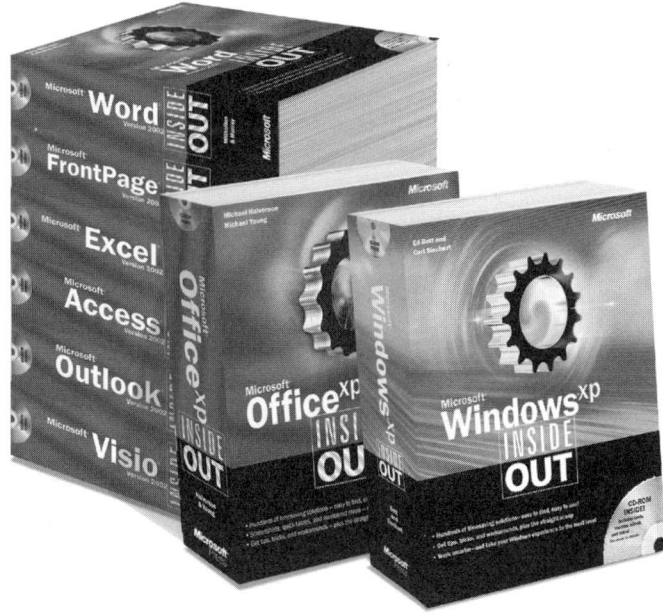

MICROSOFT WINDOWS® XP INSIDE OUT
ISBN 0-7356-1382-6

MICROSOFT® OFFICE XP INSIDE OUT
ISBN 0-7356-1277-3

MICROSOFT WORD VERSION 2002 INSIDE OUT
ISBN 0-7356-1278-1

MICROSOFT EXCEL VERSION 2002 INSIDE OUT
ISBN 0-7356-1281-1

MICROSOFT OUTLOOK® VERSION 2002 INSIDE OUT
ISBN 0-7356-1282-X

MICROSOFT ACCESS VERSION 2002 INSIDE OUT
ISBN 0-7356-1283-8

MICROSOFT FRONTPAGE® VERSION 2002 INSIDE OUT
ISBN 0-7356-1284-6

MICROSOFT VISIO® VERSION 2002 INSIDE OUT
ISBN 0-7356-1285-4

Microsoft
microsoft.com/mspress

Self-paced
training that works
as hard as you do!

Information-packed STEP BY STEP courses are the most effective way to teach yourself how to complete tasks with the Microsoft® Windows® XP operating system and Microsoft® Office XP applications. Numbered steps and scenario-based lessons with practice files on CD-ROM make it easy to find your way while learning tasks and procedures. Work through every lesson or choose your own starting point—with STEP BY STEP'S modular design and straightforward writing style, *you* drive the instruction. And the books are constructed with lay-flat binding so you can follow the text with both hands at the keyboard. Select STEP BY STEP titles also provide complete, cost-effective preparation for the Microsoft Office User Specialist (MOUS) credential. It's an excellent way for you or your organization to take a giant step toward workplace productivity.

- **Microsoft Windows XP Step by Step**
  ISBN 0-7356-1383-4

- **Microsoft Office XP Step by Step**
  ISBN 0-7356-1294-3

- **Microsoft Word Version 2002 Step by Step**
  ISBN 0-7356-1295-1

- **Microsoft Excel Version 2002 Step by Step**
  ISBN 0-7356-1296-X

- **Microsoft PowerPoint® Version 2002 Step by Step**
  ISBN 0-7356-1297-8

- **Microsoft Outlook® Version 2002 Step by Step**
  ISBN 0-7356-1298-6

- **Microsoft FrontPage® Version 2002 Step by Step**
  ISBN 0-7356-1300-1

- **Microsoft Access Version 2002 Step by Step**
  ISBN 0-7356-1299-4

- **Microsoft Visio® Version 2002 Step by Step**
  ISBN 0-7356-1302-8

Microsoft Press® products are available worldwide wherever quality computer books are sold. For more information, contact your book or computer retailer, software reseller, or local Microsoft Sales Office, or visit our Web site at microsoft.com/mspress. To locate your nearest source for Microsoft Press products, or to order directly, call 1-800-MSPRESS in the United States. (in Canada, call 1-800-268-2222).

Prices and availability dates are subject to change.

microsoft.com/mspress

Target your problem and
fix it yourself—
fast!

When you're stuck with a computer problem, you need answers right now. *Troubleshooting* books can help. They'll guide you to the source of the problem and show you how to solve it right away. Get ready solutions with clear, step-by-step instructions. Go to quick-access charts with *Top 20 Problems* and *Preventive Medicine*. Find even more solutions with handy *Tips* and *Quick Fixes.* Walk through the remedy with plenty of screen shots. Find what you need with the extensive, easy-reference index. Get the answers you need to get back to business fast with *Troubleshooting* books.

Get a **Free**
e-mail newsletter, updates,
special offers, links to related books,
and more when you

register on line!

Register your Microsoft Press® title on our Web site and you'll get a FREE subscription to our e-mail newsletter, *Microsoft Press Book Connections.* You'll find out about newly released and upcoming books and learning tools, online events, software downloads, special offers and coupons for Microsoft Press customers, and information about major Microsoft® product releases. You can also read useful additional information about all the titles we publish, such as detailed book descriptions, tables of contents and indexes, sample chapters, links to related books and book series, author biographies, and reviews by other customers.

Registration is easy. Just visit this Web page and fill in your information:

http://www.microsoft.com/mspress/register

Microsoft®

MICROSOFT LICENSE AGREEMENT
Book Companion CD

IMPORTANT—READ CAREFULLY: This Microsoft End-User License Agreement ("EULA") is a legal agreement between you (either an individual or an entity) and Microsoft Corporation for the Microsoft product identified above, which includes computer software and may include associated media, printed materials, and "online" or electronic documentation ("SOFTWARE PRODUCT"). Any component included within the SOFTWARE PRODUCT that is accompanied by a separate End-User License Agreement shall be governed by such agreement and not the terms set forth below. By installing, copying, or otherwise using the SOFTWARE PRODUCT, you agree to be bound by the terms of this EULA. If you do not agree to the terms of this EULA, you are not authorized to install, copy, or otherwise use the SOFTWARE PRODUCT; you may, however, return the SOFTWARE PRODUCT, along with all printed materials and other items that form a part of the Microsoft product that includes the SOFTWARE PRODUCT, to the place you obtained them for a full refund.

SOFTWARE PRODUCT LICENSE

The SOFTWARE PRODUCT is protected by United States copyright laws and international copyright treaties, as well as other intellectual property laws and treaties. The SOFTWARE PRODUCT is licensed, not sold.

1. **GRANT OF LICENSE.** This EULA grants you the following rights:

    a. **Software Product.** You may install and use one copy of the SOFTWARE PRODUCT on a single computer. The primary user of the computer on which the SOFTWARE PRODUCT is installed may make a second copy for his or her exclusive use on a portable computer.

    b. **Storage/Network Use.** You may also store or install a copy of the SOFTWARE PRODUCT on a storage device, such as a network server, used only to install or run the SOFTWARE PRODUCT on your other computers over an internal network; however, you must acquire and dedicate a license for each separate computer on which the SOFTWARE PRODUCT is installed or run from the storage device. A license for the SOFTWARE PRODUCT may not be shared or used concurrently on different computers.

    c. **License Pak.** If you have acquired this EULA in a Microsoft License Pak, you may make the number of additional copies of the computer software portion of the SOFTWARE PRODUCT authorized on the printed copy of this EULA, and you may use each copy in the manner specified above. You are also entitled to make a corresponding number of secondary copies for portable computer use as specified above.

    d. **Sample Code.** Solely with respect to portions, if any, of the SOFTWARE PRODUCT that are identified within the SOFTWARE PRODUCT as sample code (the "SAMPLE CODE"):

       i. **Use and Modification.** Microsoft grants you the right to use and modify the source code version of the SAMPLE CODE, *provided* you comply with subsection (d)(iii) below. You may not distribute the SAMPLE CODE, or any modified version of the SAMPLE CODE, in source code form.

       ii. **Redistributable Files.** Provided you comply with subsection (d)(iii) below, Microsoft grants you a nonexclusive, royalty-free right to reproduce and distribute the object code version of the SAMPLE CODE and of any modified SAMPLE CODE, other than SAMPLE CODE, or any modified version thereof, designated as not redistributable in the Readme file that forms a part of the SOFTWARE PRODUCT (the "Non-Redistributable Sample Code"). All SAMPLE CODE other than the Non-Redistributable Sample Code is collectively referred to as the "REDISTRIBUTABLES."

       iii. **Redistribution Requirements.** If you redistribute the REDISTRIBUTABLES, you agree to: (i) distribute the REDISTRIBUTABLES in object code form only in conjunction with and as a part of your software application product; (ii) not use Microsoft's name, logo, or trademarks to market your software application product; (iii) include a valid copyright notice on your software application product; (iv) indemnify, hold harmless, and defend Microsoft from and against any claims or lawsuits, including attorney's fees, that arise or result from the use or distribution of your software application product; and (v) not permit further distribution of the REDISTRIBUTABLES by your end user. Contact Microsoft for the applicable royalties due and other licensing terms for all other uses and/or distribution of the REDISTRIBUTABLES.

2. **DESCRIPTION OF OTHER RIGHTS AND LIMITATIONS.**

    - **Limitations on Reverse Engineering, Decompilation, and Disassembly.** You may not reverse engineer, decompile, or disassemble the SOFTWARE PRODUCT, except and only to the extent that such activity is expressly permitted by applicable law notwithstanding this limitation.

    - **Separation of Components.** The SOFTWARE PRODUCT is licensed as a single product. Its component parts may not be separated for use on more than one computer.

    - **Rental.** You may not rent, lease, or lend the SOFTWARE PRODUCT.

    - **Support Services.** Microsoft may, but is not obligated to, provide you with support services related to the SOFTWARE PRODUCT ("Support Services"). Use of Support Services is governed by the Microsoft policies and programs described in the user manual, in "online" documentation, and/or in other Microsoft-provided materials. Any supplemental software code provided to you as part of the Support Services shall be considered part of the SOFTWARE PRODUCT and subject to the terms and conditions of this EULA. With respect to technical information you provide to Microsoft as part of the Support Services, Microsoft may use such information for its business purposes, including for product support and development. Microsoft will not utilize such technical information in a form that personally identifies you.

- **Software Transfer.** You may permanently transfer all of your rights under this EULA, provided you retain no copies, you transfer all of the SOFTWARE PRODUCT (including all component parts, the media and printed materials, any upgrades, this EULA, and, if applicable, the Certificate of Authenticity), **and** the recipient agrees to the terms of this EULA.

- **Termination.** Without prejudice to any other rights, Microsoft may terminate this EULA if you fail to comply with the terms and conditions of this EULA. In such event, you must destroy all copies of the SOFTWARE PRODUCT and all of its component parts.

3. **COPYRIGHT.** All title and copyrights in and to the SOFTWARE PRODUCT (including but not limited to any images, photographs, animations, video, audio, music, text, SAMPLE CODE, REDISTRIBUTABLES, and "applets" incorporated into the SOFTWARE PRODUCT) and any copies of the SOFTWARE PRODUCT are owned by Microsoft or its suppliers. The SOFTWARE PRODUCT is protected by copyright laws and international treaty provisions. Therefore, you must treat the SOFTWARE PRODUCT like any other copyrighted material **except** that you may install the SOFTWARE PRODUCT on a single computer provided you keep the original solely for backup or archival purposes. You may not copy the printed materials accompanying the SOFTWARE PRODUCT.

4. **U.S. GOVERNMENT RESTRICTED RIGHTS.** The SOFTWARE PRODUCT and documentation are provided with RESTRICTED RIGHTS. Use, duplication, or disclosure by the Government is subject to restrictions as set forth in subparagraph (c)(1)(ii) of the Rights in Technical Data and Computer Software clause at DFARS 252.227-7013 or subparagraphs (c)(1) and (2) of the Commercial Computer Software—Restricted Rights at 48 CFR 52.227-19, as applicable. Manufacturer is Microsoft Corporation/One Microsoft Way/Redmond, WA 98052-6399.

5. **EXPORT RESTRICTIONS.** You agree that you will not export or re-export the SOFTWARE PRODUCT, any part thereof, or any process or service that is the direct product of the SOFTWARE PRODUCT (the foregoing collectively referred to as the "Restricted Components"), to any country, person, entity, or end user subject to U.S. export restrictions. You specifically agree not to export or re-export any of the Restricted Components (i) to any country to which the U.S. has embargoed or restricted the export of goods or services, which currently include, but are not necessarily limited to, Cuba, Iran, Iraq, Libya, North Korea, Sudan, and Syria, or to any national of any such country, wherever located, who intends to transmit or transport the Restricted Components back to such country; (ii) to any end user who you know or have reason to know will utilize the Restricted Components in the design, development, or production of nuclear, chemical, or biological weapons; or (iii) to any end user who has been prohibited from participating in U.S. export transactions by any federal agency of the U.S. government. You warrant and represent that neither the BXA nor any other U.S. federal agency has suspended, revoked, or denied your export privileges.

DISCLAIMER OF WARRANTY

NO WARRANTIES OR CONDITIONS. MICROSOFT EXPRESSLY DISCLAIMS ANY WARRANTY OR CONDITION FOR THE SOFTWARE PRODUCT. THE SOFTWARE PRODUCT AND ANY RELATED DOCUMENTATION ARE PROVIDED "AS IS" WITHOUT WARRANTY OR CONDITION OF ANY KIND, EITHER EXPRESS OR IMPLIED, INCLUDING, WITHOUT LIMITATION, THE IMPLIED WARRANTIES OF MERCHANTABILITY, FITNESS FOR A PARTICULAR PURPOSE, OR NONINFRINGEMENT. THE ENTIRE RISK ARISING OUT OF USE OR PERFORMANCE OF THE SOFTWARE PRODUCT REMAINS WITH YOU.

LIMITATION OF LIABILITY. TO THE MAXIMUM EXTENT PERMITTED BY APPLICABLE LAW, IN NO EVENT SHALL MICROSOFT OR ITS SUPPLIERS BE LIABLE FOR ANY SPECIAL, INCIDENTAL, INDIRECT, OR CONSEQUENTIAL DAMAGES WHATSOEVER (INCLUDING, WITHOUT LIMITATION, DAMAGES FOR LOSS OF BUSINESS PROFITS, BUSINESS INTERRUPTION, LOSS OF BUSINESS INFORMATION, OR ANY OTHER PECUNIARY LOSS) ARISING OUT OF THE USE OF OR INABILITY TO USE THE SOFTWARE PRODUCT OR THE PROVISION OF OR FAILURE TO PROVIDE SUPPORT SERVICES, EVEN IF MICROSOFT HAS BEEN ADVISED OF THE POSSIBILITY OF SUCH DAMAGES. IN ANY CASE, MICROSOFT'S ENTIRE LIABILITY UNDER ANY PROVISION OF THIS EULA SHALL BE LIMITED TO THE GREATER OF THE AMOUNT ACTUALLY PAID BY YOU FOR THE SOFTWARE PRODUCT OR US$5.00; PROVIDED, HOWEVER, IF YOU HAVE ENTERED INTO A MICROSOFT SUPPORT SERVICES AGREEMENT, MICROSOFT'S ENTIRE LIABILITY REGARDING SUPPORT SERVICES SHALL BE GOVERNED BY THE TERMS OF THAT AGREEMENT. BECAUSE SOME STATES AND JURISDICTIONS DO NOT ALLOW THE EXCLUSION OR LIMITATION OF LIABILITY, THE ABOVE LIMITATION MAY NOT APPLY TO YOU.

MISCELLANEOUS

This EULA is governed by the laws of the State of Washington USA, except and only to the extent that applicable law mandates governing law of a different jurisdiction.

Should you have any questions concerning this EULA, or if you desire to contact Microsoft for any reason, please contact the Microsoft subsidiary serving your country, or write: Microsoft Sales Information Center/One Microsoft Way/Redmond, WA 98052-6399.